To my parents
David and Barbara Boies

Contents

1

Spring Training

IT WAS SHORTLY AFTER NOON ON MAY 14, 1997, WHEN I stepped out of 825 Eighth Avenue in midtown Manhattan on my way to meet my wife, Mary, for lunch. It was a sunny spring day, so I decided to walk the half dozen blocks to La Caravelle restaurant, where she was waiting. A few hours later, a *New York Times* photographer would try (unsuccessfully) to get me to pose in front of the fifty-five-story office tower with the name Cravath, Swaine & Moore chiseled in marble over the entrance; but at the moment I was alone with my thoughts on the crowded street.

As I walked, I thought back to the May thirty-one years earlier when I had taken a train from New Haven, Connecticut, to New York City. I had completed my last exam at the Yale Law School, and while graduation ceremonies were still three weeks away, I was scheduled to begin as a young associate at Cravath on Monday. For as long as I could remember, I had wanted to be a teacher like my father or a lawyer like Perry Mason. As I relaxed on the train (school finished, and work not yet begun), I lazily wondered whether I had made the right choice. I also reflected, as I had before and would many times again, on how lucky I was to have the choices I had.

Cravath was widely regarded as the best law firm in the country, and I was the object of much envy among my classmates. I was not, however, a typical Cravath associate and I did not know quite what was in store for me. One fact had been clear from my first interview at their offices, in those days on the fifty-fifth floor at One Chase Manhattan Plaza in lower Manhattan—Cravath, its people, and its practice were a long way removed from the life I had known until then.

Born nine months before Pearl Harbor in the northern Illinois farming community of Sycamore, I grew up there and in nearby Marengo, where my father taught U.S. history and journalism and coached football at the high school after he returned from the war. The June after I turned thirteen, my parents sold their house, put their furniture in storage, loaded our family and seven suitcases (two for my mother and one for each of the rest of us) into their 1950 Plymouth and set off for Southern California following old Route 66.

We took two weeks to make the trip, and for my brothers, sister, and myself it was a great adventure. We had been to Wisconsin, and even to Minnesota, but never nearly so far from home. When we saw our first cowboy on a horse Barbara (eight) and Richard (almost four) couldn't contain their excitement. Stephen (eleven) and I tried to act more nonchalant, but we were equally amazed. The Grand Canyon was interesting too, but it was the real cowboys and real Indians about which I wrote to the friends I'd left in Marengo. My father had neither a house nor a job waiting for him in California, but during the war he had been through Los Angeles and San Diego on his way to the Pacific and had talked about going back ever since.

California was growing, schools were expanding, and my father was soon hired to teach American history in Lynwood, California. Just before school opened that September, we moved into 1612 Tucker Street in nearby Compton. Some things were different (there were about as many students in my new school as in the whole town of Marengo), but much was the same. The Tower Theater in Compton was larger, and louder, than the Colonial Theater in Marengo, but the movies were identical. My paper route covered eastern Watts rather than western Marengo, but a morning paper route is a morning paper route, as any former newspaper boy will tell you.

I went to eighth and ninth grades in Compton. Years later I would be diagnosed as dyslexic. All I knew then was that reading was a lot harder for me than it was for my classmates. (I had not read until third grade, and while by the eighth grade I could get by, reading was never easy.) However, I also found that I could think and reason as well as anyone, including my teachers, and that no one (except me) seemed to care very much about my reading disability.

In the spring of my second year, a knife fight in school led my parents to move to Fullerton in Orange County. The housing development we moved into had orange groves on three sides, and if not bucolic, the environment was closer to what we had left in Marengo than what we had found in Compton. I missed the pace and excitement of Compton, and a couple of times frightened my parents as only a teenager can by disappearing without permission to hitchhike back to visit old friends.

Soon, however, I had new friends and new interests—including participation in the high school debate team. My dyslexia made it difficult to speak from notes or a prepared text, so I learned to speak without them—an ability that would be useful later. Except for history and related subjects like government and civics, I did not enjoy schoolwork. Debate, cards, and drag racing occupied more of my time. Not surprisingly, my grades were mixed.

In my junior year Caryl Elwell moved with her parents from Downey to Fullerton and joined the debate team. Five foot two with blue eyes and a mischievous smile, she had the looks and energy of a cheerleader (which she was not) and the intelligence and confidence to be a champion debater (which she soon became). It took me a day to fall in love with her, a week to convince her to become my debate partner, and a month to make her fall in love with me.

It was a great time to be young and in love in Southern California, and I made enough money playing cards to pay for gas and other necessities. I was having much too much fun outside school (and too little fun in school) to think seriously about going to college. At the end of my senior year Caryl and I married, and shortly before I turned eighteen I got a regular job, first on a construction crew, and later as a bookkeeper in a local bank.

Construction work was hard and bookkeeping was boring, but we were on our own, answering to no one but ourselves, and making enough money to party well. I had no sense that our lives would, or should, change.

I have tried to recall when it became clear to me that I was going to go back to school. When Caryl and I first talked about starting a family we agreed completely that becoming parents would not mean we had to change our life. However, a couple of months before our first child was born Caryl began to ask casually whether I had given any thought to going to college. The answer was that I had, and I wasn't—at least, not anything more than a class or two in the evening at Fullerton State.

It was not merely that I liked the life I had, it was that I knew going back to school would be hard to manage financially and I would have to compete academically with students who were better readers, and better prepared, than I was, and who had a lot more discipline than I had ever shown. I cannot remember whether I regretted giving up the idea of being a lawyer, but I had discovered that with two years of college credits (which I figured I could pick up from occasional classes at Fullerton State) I could get a certificate that would allow me to teach in many California public schools.

In 1960, shortly after our son, David, was born, Caryl stopped asking my views. It was time for me to go back to school, she explained. She had an answer to every question. We could pay for college with a combination of student loans and what she could earn. I could probably even get a scholarship. (My SAT scores had been high enough to prompt rumors that my father, being a teacher, must have somehow gotten me the answers, since my grades did not seem consistent with top test scores.) If it turned out that I couldn't handle college, she assured me, there would be bookkeeping jobs and card games waiting for me when I quit; but I owed it to myself, and to David, to try.

She was right, of course. She almost always was about important matters. I realized later two things that Caryl had known all along. First, I really did want to give college a try. Second, I would not worry how hard it might be on her if she was the one insisting that I go.

I got admitted to the University of Redlands in nearby San Bernardino County, a school with a good academic reputation and one of the country's premier debate programs. By the time Caryl, David, and I moved into married student housing that September, she and I were as excited about returning to school as we had been about leaving it a couple of years earlier.

For the first time, grades were important. The university had given me a scholarship, and I knew that if I were going to keep it I would have to do much better than I had in high school. Although I spent time traveling to debate tournaments, became features editor of the school paper, and took a part-time job teaching a class in journalism at Patton State Hospital for psychiatric patients (the class, under my supervision, put out a weekly newspaper), I devoted more time to studying than at any time before or since. Particularly my first year, when I was not sure how hard I had to work to get an A, I erred on the side of overdoing it.

The debate team traveled to tournaments throughout the western United States, mostly by car. In two years at Redlands we drove more than twenty thousand miles, and I learned a lot about our country and its people. Most of it was good; some was not.

On the way back from a debate tournament in New Mexico, we turned into the parking lot of a roadside café in a small community in Arizona. In the window of the café stood a red, white, and blue poster depicting the Spirit of '76 and urging all Americans to defend their heritage against the threat of international communism. Over the door of the café hung another sign, older, simpler, but still forceful, that declared, "No colored trade solicited."

The sign was a shock. It was probably a testimony to the cocoon of adolescence that I could have gone so long ignoring the reality of racial discrimination. It was not that I was unaware of racial tensions. While I had many black friends in Compton, it was like having friends in a different tribe. When, as happened from time to time, there were confrontations between black and white students, we tended to divide ourselves by color. But none of us, of either color, thought the other was inferior or should be restricted because of their race. If living together taught us anything, it was that each of us was as smart and dumb, as weak and strong, as kind and mean, as the other.

I had read about *Brown v. Board of Education*, which in 1954 outlawed segregation in public schools, but in a way the unanimity of the opinion masked the pervasiveness of the problem it confronted. As a young Republican* I watched with pride President Eisenhower's efforts to desegregate the southern schools, but I associated the accompanying violence and harassment with an unfamiliar culture far away. Certainly, I thought, no one I knew would act like that.

After that trip, I wrote an editorial for the school paper on discrimination. I did not, however, rush off to become a Freedom Rider or to do anything that was dangerous, unpopular, or even inconvenient. It would be nearly four years before I traveled to Jackson, Mississippi as a volunteer with the Lawyers' Committee for Civil Rights Under Law to try actually to do something.

By the middle of my first semester it was clear I could easily increase my academic load. We discovered that I could enter law school after completing three years of college, and we calculated that if I went to summer school and increased my course load by 50 percent my second year I could finish three years of work in two. My professors also pointed out that if after law school I wanted to teach history instead of practicing law, I could do so. In the spring of my freshman year I took the Law School Admission

---

*I became president of the University of Redlands Young Republican Club at the beginning of my second year.

test and applied to Stanford and Northwestern law schools (both of which at the time admitted students without an undergraduate degree).

Although Caryl wanted me to go to Stanford, I ultimately chose Northwestern. The more generous financial aid package was a factor, as was the pride I knew my family from Illinois would have in my being at Northwestern; and in a way I felt that I was going home. Over the years Caryl and I have occasionally talked about whether, and how, things might have been different had I taken her advice.

As it was, in late August 1962 we loaded our two children (our daughter, named Caryl after her mother, had been born five months earlier) and all our possessions worth keeping into our 1959 Fiat and returned by the route my parents had taken less than a decade earlier. We drove straight through without stopping. It had taken me until the last minute on Thursday to finish the college credits I needed, and I had to be at Northwestern Law School the following Monday. Also, we didn't really have the money for a motel.

When we arrived at the Old Town Gardens Chicago apartment complex, where Northwestern had arranged for us to rent an apartment, Caryl stayed in the car while I went in to sign the lease. The rental agent asked me where my wife was.

"She's outside in the car with the children. Does she need to sign the lease too?"

"No. But is there any reason she didn't come in with you?"

"One of us had to stay with the children. And we've been in a car for more than forty hours. She's more sensitive about her appearance than I am."

The rental agent seemed unusually solicitous about Caryl. She asked how long we had been married, how we had met, what Caryl planned to do while I was in school. Could she take my wife some water? Were there any questions she wanted answered? Would I like her to go out to the car and meet Caryl so that my wife would know someone to call?

I explained that we were fine, that I just needed to sign the lease and get my family out of the car and into our new apartment. Finally the rental agent got to the point I was far too dense to have seen.

"I'm sorry to have to ask," she said, "but is your wife colored?"

I should have been outraged. Later I would be. At that moment I was simply dumbfounded, and probably would have been even had I not been up for two days.

After a slight pause I said, "No. Does it matter?"

Perhaps my voice had more of an edge than I thought, or maybe the woman had some sense of shame.

"I personally don't care," she assured me. "But you have to understand that many of our tenants do, and a number of mixed race couples have tried to rent here by having only the white husband or wife come in."

As I walked back to the car with a copy of the signed lease and keys to our new apartment, I thought of all the reasons why it was right for me to have gone ahead and taken the apartment. I had a wife and two babies in the car. We had to have a place to live. School started in two days. We would not begin to know where to look for another apartment. And probably other buildings would have the same rules.

I also thought: This is not the way it is supposed to be. Maybe in the "backward," "bigoted" South. But not in the Midwest, not in Illinois, the "Land of Lincoln."—And if everyone just accepts it, as I'm doing now, how will it ever change? As I reached the car and saw Caryl smile, I also thought: What would I have done if she were "colored"? Perhaps it was natural that such thoughts were quickly shelved in favor of the self-absorbed concerns of a young husband and father of two about to start a new adventure.

The following morning we bought a mattress and box spring and two cribs. And on Monday I walked the mile and a half to the Northwestern Chicago campus where the law school was located. The moment I was inside, surrounded by old wood and stone and decades of history, I was struck again by how lucky I was. It was hard to imagine that two years earlier I had been getting ready to leave my job as a bookkeeper at the Fullerton branch of United California Bank.

When courses started later in the week, I found law school both easy and fun. Class was a daily Socratic discussion of interesting and challenging issues. I undoubtedly liked it in part because I was good at it, but as with singing (at which I am not particularly good), I think I would have enjoyed it anyway.

I had a scholarship that paid my tuition with enough left over to cover my books and rent. The first week of school, based on my status as a law student and experience as a bank bookkeeper, I got a job as the night auditor at the Sands Motel (then a large, modern inn on the north side of Chicago) from midnight until eight in the morning. My dual job was to balance the books for the day and to check in any guests who arrived after midnight.

Since the bookkeeping usually took only a few hours, and since virtually no one arrived after one-thirty a.m., I had more than enough time to study. It was the perfect job for a student (or, at least, one who needed to work), and I made more money than I had at the bank. I also discovered that I could borrow several thousand dollars from the government at no interest, which I did. Caryl and I opened our first savings account, and we put half the money there and half in the stock market.

Everything, it seemed, was going well. Under the surface, however, my relationship with Caryl was under increasing strain. She never liked the congestion and pace of Chicago, and as winter arrived she liked the cold even less. She tried to be a good sport, but the unhappiness showed. To make matters worse, she was cooped up in our apartment caring for two small children. With work and school I slept most of the time I was home, and when not sleeping I played with the children. Until our daughter had been born, Caryl had had a job and we had divided caring for David. Now she bore almost the entire burden at home, with neither the release nor the satisfaction of an outside job. Living on campus at Redlands, I would come home between classes; now I spent the entire day at the law school. She had more work to do; I was giving her less help; she was largely confined to the apartment; when she did go out, she did not like the weather or the city.

Even more troubling to her was the fact that I was changing. I was increasingly occupied with new ideas and interests. Even when we found time to get a babysitter and go out, or when we would have friends over to our apartment, I was focused on what was happening at school. For the first time in her life, Caryl felt uncomfortable. She felt that she could not keep up, and that my classmates looked down on her. The initial premise was true—I was changing; most of the rest was not.

My classmates envied Caryl's looks and wit, and she was smart enough to keep up with anyone—as she repeatedly proved, including when she eventually went back to school and earned her own law degree with honors. However, illusions can be as stubborn as facts, and her discomfort and resulting withdrawal contributed to her unhappiness, and ultimately to mine.

After my last exam in June of my first year, approximately ten months after we arrived in Chicago, Caryl returned to the West Coast, taking both children with her. I later learned that she had decided to leave six weeks earlier but did not tell me until my exams were over because she did not want me distracted. We talked, briefly, about my leaving school and returning with her to California, but we both knew that would be a mistake. Thanks to her I was doing what I wanted to do, what I was good at doing, maybe even what I was meant to do.

On the strength of my grades and professors' recommendations, I replaced my night auditor work with a job doing legal research at a law firm. I missed Caryl and the children a lot; and it did not help when she told me that she had started seeing someone. Nevertheless, work and school were an exciting challenge, and in most ways I was having the time of my life. I found it difficult to find people willing to play bridge for money, but there were frequent poker and hearts games with classmates who had more cash than experience. My toughest opponent was a savvy classmate from South Orange, New Jersey, named James Miller.

At the end of the first year the top 5 to 10 percent of the class were selected for the Northwestern *Law Review*, and in the second semester of my second year I was chosen as the *Review's* editor in chief. The person chosen for the *Review's* second highest position, that of managing editor, was my classmate Judith Daynard.

Judy was the smartest and most attractive woman in our class, and earlier in the year she and I had started dating. Both we and our friends thought it was a perfect match, except for one problem. She was married to my evidence professor. Eventually, of course, reality intruded, and over the summer the dean offered to help us transfer to any law school we wanted if we would agree to leave. Judy, a native of New York City who had never fully appreciated Chicago, chose Columbia. I chose Yale, an hour's train ride away.

Judy gave me many gifts over the years. However, except for our two sons, none was more appreciated than the unintended opportunity she provided for me to attend Yale. With a large and brilliant faculty and a student body of about five hundred, Yale Law School was as intellectually exciting a place to be as I can imagine. For two years I divided my time between it and the Yale Graduate School across the street, where I studied economics.* Judy graduated after one year at Columbia, and we were married in March of my last year.

Early in my second year I was convinced that I wanted to teach law. However, it seemed desirable actually to practice law before teaching it, and I interviewed with several firms that came to campus to recruit. When Cravath offered me a job, it was an easy choice both because of its reputation and because it was in New York City, where Judy was keen on staying.

After my graduation we moved into an apartment in Green-

---

*I had concluded during my first two years of law school that many legal questions were primarily issues of economics. One of my fellow students at the graduate school was William Baxter, already a highly regarded professor of law at Stanford, who had reached the same conclusion and was spending the year at Yale. Baxter, who headed the Department of Justice's Antitrust Division under President Reagan, went on to become one of the leading scholars applying economics to legal issues.

wich Village, midway between my office on Wall Street and hers at Paul Weiss in midtown. I accepted an adjunct faculty position at New York University Law School, a few blocks from our home, and for the next decade taught a course most semesters. Twin sons, Christopher and Jonathan, were born in March 1968.

In my early years at Cravath I had the opportunity to work with two exceptional lawyers. The first was Allen Maulsby, an elegant and courtly attorney who epitomized grace under pressure; no matter how late we worked or how hectic the pace, he never seemed harried or raised his voice. A polished and compelling writer and speaker, he set a high standard for a young and impressionable associate. He also taught by word and example two lessons that stayed with me throughout my career—the importance of integrity and credibility, and the ability to be tough, even aggressive, without being mean or unpleasant.

Associates at Cravath are normally rotated from partner to partner every twelve to eighteen months. Following a year with Allen Maulsby I was assigned to work with Thomas Barr. I was still assigned to him five years later when I became a partner. When I went to work for him in 1967, Tom was the youngest litigation partner in the firm, but he was already recognized as a leader. Within a decade he was the acknowledged head of the Cravath litigation department. One of the great trial lawyers of his generation, he taught me about practicing law, about people, and about life.

I was still a young associate, and Tom Barr a young partner, when the United States sued IBM for monopolizing the market for general-purpose computers. The suit was filed in January 1969 on the last business day of the Johnson administration.* A number

---

*During the eighteen-month investigation that preceded the lawsuit, Lyndon Johnson's attorney general, Ramsey Clark, had repeatedly promised us that if he concluded a complaint was warranted, he would give us an opportunity to review his concerns and attempt to convince him otherwise. However, he called in January to say he was not going to be able to keep his commitment. He said that he was not certain that suing was the right thing to do and

of private cases followed the government's complaint, and in 1973, Tom and I tried one brought by the Telex Corporation in Tulsa, Oklahoma. We lost the case in spectacular fashion, with the court awarding Telex $350 million—at the time the largest private civil judgment in history. Eventually the judgment was reversed on appeal, and Telex was ordered to pay IBM $20 million. However, the trial result was a character-building experience for a young lawyer participating in his first major trial as a new partner.

By 1975, when the government case finally went to trial, the two senior Cravath partners originally in charge (the legendary Bruce Bromley and Albert Connolly) had retired. Tom, then forty-three, was the oldest partner representing IBM; at thirty-three I was the youngest, although I had already been a partner for two years (which at that time seemed like a lot of experience). When the trial began, Tom, our partner Paul Dodyk, and I shared both the opening statements and the initial cross-examination of the government's witnesses.

The case against IBM was one of the four or five most important government monopolization trials since 1890. It was also the longest. In January 1976, with the case still dragging on, the trial of a major private antitrust case against IBM brought by the Calcomp Corporation was scheduled for October in California. The next month I was in northern Japan touring with my son David when Tom and IBM's general counsel Nick Katzenbach decided that Tom should stay in New York at the government trial and that I should go to California to try the Calcomp case.

The *U.S. v. IBM* litigation was proceeding at a snail's pace, and when I did not have witnesses to examine, I worked on other matters. As Caryl and I had agreed when we separated, David had come to live with me in 1974 after eighth grade, and we were as

---

that he wished he had more time to consider the issue, but that he was sure that the Nixon Administration would not bring the suit if he left it to his successor. "If I have made a mistake," he tried to reassure us, "the case can be dismissed. However, if I fail to act and should have, my grandchildren will never forgive me."

inseparable as my work and his school allowed. In early 1976 I had a week-long international arbitration in Bombay, India, during his spring vacation, so I took him with me. After the arbitration I kept him out of school an additional two weeks to visit Thailand and Japan. Judy and I had been divorced in 1972, so David and I were without adult supervision.

The first day I was back Barr offered me the case, and I immediately accepted. As a number of people noted then and later, I was not the obvious choice for an assignment for which IBM could have selected almost any trial lawyer in the country. I had participated in the Telex trial (which had not yet been reversed) with Tom, and I was participating in the government case with Tom and Paul Dodyk; but the Calcomp case would be the first major commercial jury trial in which I was the lead lawyer. I had learned much from Tom Barr, Allen Maulsby, and others, but I knew that this trial would be unlike anything I had done before.

The judge was Ray McNichols, who ran a fair courtroom but let the lawyers try their case without micromanaging them. My opponent was Max Blecher, one of the country's preeminent plaintiffs' antitrust lawyers and a master at presenting complicated issues to juries. It was clear that this was going to be as much a test of competing morality plays as it was a battle of economic and political theories.

I relied on **five** principles that worked for me then and, with some refinements, since.

First, explain what makes your client good and successful and, if possible, show how what the other side complains about should be applauded, not criticized. IBM's strength was that it was constantly improving its products and lowering its prices. Calcomp's claim that IBM was driving it out of business was, I came to argue, simply a reflection of the better products and lower prices that IBM offered consumers.

Second, whether you are plaintiff or defendant, go on the attack. Find your opponent's weak points and pursue them. Calcomp's vulnerability was that its business was copying IBM designs, sometimes legally and sometimes, as we were to discover, illegally.

Third, a trial, like a battle, is a zero-sum game. What advantages one side disadvantages the other—and vice versa. Something that advantages both sides, but one more than the other, is a dagger directed at the side advantaged less. If you have the will and resources to out-work your opponent, never seek and always oppose delay. Until I took over the Calcomp case, Blecher had been pressing for a trial and IBM's lawyer had been seeking delay. The judge, not surprisingly, was becoming impatient—and interpreted IBM's desire for delay as lack of confidence in its position. In April at my first hearing I told Judge McNichols, "We are prepared to try this case as soon as Your Honor can set it for trial. There is much work to get done, but we will do it in whatever time remains. All we ask is that Mr. Blecher not complain about our taking too many depositions or serving too many interrogatories in too short a time." The judge set the trial for October. We got all our work done. Max didn't.

Fourth, it is important to be able to improvise but critical not to depend on improvisation. There is no substitute for preparation, and more cases are won and lost by preparation, or the lack of it, than for any other reason. Researching and analyzing relevant facts and data; reviewing and selecting documents; finding, recruiting, preparing witnesses; taking depositions and separating the important testimony for use at trial; creating charts and visual aids—these tasks are not as dramatic as the trial itself, but they are crucial to a trial's success.

Fifth, don't rely on drama alone, but be prepared to dramatize the key points of your case so that they come alive for the jury. Shortly before trial I was shopping in Los Angeles for nightlights for the room my sons Jonathan and Christopher would use when they visited. I discovered that some of the products I was looking at were made by a division of Calcomp, and I purchased as large a selection as I could. The day I opened to the jury half my counsel table was covered with Disney-figure nightlights, novelty lamps, and similar Calcomp products. On the other half of the table was an IBM product about which Calcomp complained—with the covers off to reveal the complicated circuitry and wiring inside. This, I told the jury, was the difference between the two companies. IBM concentrated all its energies and resources on making better computer products. Calcomp diverted its resources to making nightlights and other novelties, content to wait and copy what IBM invented. It should be no surprise that IBM wanted to make its products hard to replicate, or that Calcomp would eventually discover that copying complicated computer products was more difficult than making plastic copies of Disney characters.

The trial began in early October 1976 and finished in mid-February 1977. We won, and that judgment was ultimately affirmed on appeal by a panel of judges that included Justice Anthony Kennedy, then a young judge on the federal court of appeals. I essentially took the three and a half months from February until David got out of school as an extended vacation. In the summer of 1976, David and I had moved to California and rented a house on Amalfi Drive in Pacific Palisades. (His sister Caryl did not come to live with me until the following year, and Jonathan and Christopher were still with Judy.) David spent his junior year at Palisades High. When my trial was over I did not want to interrupt his school year in the middle, so I took the opportunity to enjoy time with him without the pressure of work. Raising children is difficult under any circumstances. It is particularly difficult for a parent with a job that can be as demanding as mine. As a result, over the years I have taken advantage of breaks in the action to take extended periods off, a practice that met with mixed reactions at Cravath.

In June 1977 I returned to New York and to the *U.S. v. IBM* trial to cross-examine the government's chief economic expert (Dr. Alan McAdams of Cornell). It says much about the pace of the government case that it seemed as if I had not missed anything. In the middle of Dr. McAdams's examination, the government took a three-day recess during which it tried to revise and reframe its case to address problems with its original theory that my questioning of McAdams had revealed. Eight years after a case has been filed, and more than three years after the trial has begun, radical surgery on a plaintiff's case is rarely successful, and it was not here. The government continued to put on witnesses for four more years, but damage had been done from which it never fully recovered.

In the fall of 1977, I took a leave from Cravath and went to Washington to serve as chief counsel and staff director of the Senate Antitrust Subcommittee, at the time chaired by Senator Ted Kennedy. When, a year later, Ted became chairman of the Senate Judiciary Committee, I became its chief counsel and staff director.

Shortly after my Senate appointment was announced, I was invited to have lunch with Carter administration officials to discuss airline and trucking deregulation. The issue was high on the agendas for both Carter and Ted Kennedy.* The lunch, held at the White House in June, had been set up by Don Flexner and Simon Lazarus. Don, an old friend, headed the Justice Department's task force on regulatory reform. Lazarus was on the White House domestic policy staff. Also joining us for lunch was an attractive young woman who was introduced as Mary McInnis Schuman, the assistant director of the domestic policy staff responsible for airline and trucking deregulation. Mary was twenty-six years old and looked younger. During the meal she was playful, even flirtatious, until we turned to business—at which point she became deadly serious. She was obviously smart and had thought the issues through. She had previously worked on regulatory reform as counsel to the Senate Commerce Committee, and she was armed with a raft of facts and statistics to support and emphasize her points. When the discussion drifted back to sports, politics, or my

---

*I had written a law review article in 1968 and a book (with Paul Verkuil) published in 1977, arguing that while government regulation had been intended to protect consumers from the market power of companies in industries where competition was limited, in many industries the regulators had become so influenced by the industries they regulated that they ended up reducing, not increasing, competition. I discussed the trucking and airline industries as two prime examples.

Cravath cases her playfulness reemerged. I was intrigued, but I could see she could be dangerous.

It was five months before I returned to Washington to begin my work on Capitol Hill, but one of the first things I did was to take Mary to dinner—ostensibly to discuss our respective legislative agendas. We soon abandoned any pretense of needing a business purpose to see each other, and while we continued to work on deregulation issues and other legislation, we limited those discussions to daylight hours. When Mary and I began seeing each other, another marriage was far from my mind. Between my work and four children another serious relationship seemed unrealistic. However, as Mary and I spent more and more time together it became clear to me that when I went back to New York I wanted her to come with me.

I returned to Cravath in late 1979. Mary, who had moved from the White House staff to become general counsel of the Civil Aeronautics Board, continued to work in Washington but spent weekends and a night or two during the week in New York. In January 1981 Ronald Reagan was inaugurated, and Mary moved to New York full-time. She soon joined CBS, where she impressed Bill Paley and Tom Wyman as much as she had impressed President Carter and Stu Eizenstat; she was named a vice president the following year. We were married in August 1982. The reception was held at a country home in Armonk, New York, that we had bought the year before.

In September 1982 General William Westmoreland sued CBS for libel. Westmoreland, the American commander in Vietnam, had been accused in a CBS documentary of knowingly understating the strength of the enemy in order to reassure an increasingly skeptical home front that there was "light at the end of the tunnel." The program had been produced by George Crile and narrated by Mike Wallace. Because of Wallace's stature and the explosive nature of the broadcast—in which army officers and CIA officials admitted on camera their role in the deception—the documentary had been the subject of front-page news articles and editorial-page praise.

The problem was that Westmoreland quickly assembled a virtual who's who of the Vietnam era (from secretaries of state and defense and CIA directors to presidential advisers and senior intelligence officers) to swear that he personally had always been truthful. He and his allies also convinced several officials quoted in the broadcast to say that their statements had been misrepresented and taken out of context.

To make matters worse, the program's film editor, Ira Klein, told reporters that the broadcast had been manipulated—and based in significant part on Klein's statements, a CBS internal investigation had harshly criticized its own program.

Westmoreland had sued in his home state of South Carolina, in the town of Greenville. In a state partial to Westmoreland and not enthusiastic about the "liberal media," Greenville was viewed as particularly so. CBS's concern with the venue was increased when it learned that Westmoreland was the grand marshall for Greenville's Veterans Day parade that year.

CBS was determined to defend the case. Although the CBS internal report had criticized the fairness of the program, many within the network believed that the report itself was unfair, and even those critical of the broadcast agreed that the documentary's central thesis was true. The network's decision was reinforced when Westmoreland's lawyers made clear that to settle they wanted a minimum of $100 million and substantial free airtime. Since Westmoreland's case was being supported by the conservative Accuracy in Media, and bankrolled by the even more conservative Capital Legal Foundation, CBS knew it was in for a fight.

I had never handled a defamation case before, and my previous work for CBS had been mainly antitrust and corporate litigation. However, the previous year I had succeeded in obtaining an order preventing President Reagan from excluding television cameras from the White House news pool, and the company believed I would be better at trying a case to a South Carolina jury than the nationally prominent libel lawyers upon whom the network usually relied. Still, when it was announced that I would be representing

CBS in what was clearly a bet-your-reputation if not bet-your-company case, some at the company were worried. Spotting Mary in the elevator, a high-ranking news executive told her that he was concerned that I was not a First Amendment expert.

"Don't worry," she reassured him. "It's a short amendment."

Contradicting the conventional wisdom that a defamation plaintiff has a right to sue in his home state, we succeeded in moving the case to New York for trial. This gave us a more favorable forum, but we still had to prove our case. Most defamation suits were, and are, defended on the ground of absence of malice. (In the United States, unlike the rest of the world, a plaintiff who is a public figure must prove both that the libel was false and that it was "malicious" in the sense that the defendant knew or should have known it was untrue.)

Absence of malice is usually a much easier defense than truth, but it posed two problems here. First, CBS, which continued to believe that the broadcast was true and was concerned with its reputation, did not want to imply that it was false. Second, if we failed to prove truth, I was concerned that a jury would not be sympathetic to an absence of malice defense given the critical internal report.

Convinced that truth was our best defense, and armed with the power of subpoena, we demanded documents and testimony from military and civilian officials and agencies both in the United States and abroad. We deposed Robert McNamara (who for the first time admitted that he had known the war was lost even while he had been insisting publicly it was being won), Dean Rusk, several CIA Directors and presidential advisers, numerous generals and intelligence officers, two members of Congress, and of course Westmoreland himself. We obtained documents from each branch of the armed services, every intelligence agency, and even the White House.

By the time trial commenced in October 1984 we had much of the evidence we needed. However, I knew I would need to do four things:

- convince the jury that Mike Wallace and CBS producer George Crile had a basis for the broadcast,
- bring key officers interviewed on the broadcast
  to court to testify that their views were fairly represented,
- discredit Ira Klein, the disgruntled CBS film editor,
  and
- attack Westmoreland's personal credibility without
  offending the jury.

The first task was the easiest. No one matches Mike Wallace's five-decade record of integrity and credibility. He would be a powerful witness. Some were worried whether George Crile could do as well. However, throughout his several days on the witness stand, his total mastery of the subject and his obvious belief in the truth of his program were compelling.

The second task fell to my case manager Ellen Brockman and to Catherine Flickinger, a former Cravath lawyer who was then associate general counsel of CBS. Together with Cravath lawyers Bob Baron and Bill Duker they worked with key military officers to convince them to say in court what they had said in the interviews. Two witnesses were particularly devastating—General Joseph McChristian, a two-star general who had been Westmoreland's chief intelligence officer both in Vietnam and later in Washington; and Colonel Gains Hawkins, the intelligence officer directly responsible for enemy troop estimates. Convincing these men and others to come forward to confront their former commander in court was a remarkable accomplishment.

The third task required detective work by Cravath lawyer Randy Mastro and a little stage-managing by me. Klein initially asserted that he bore no personal animus toward Crile and was simply coming forward with his criticisms out of a sense of fairness to Westmoreland. He might have said, "Sure, I despised George but that's irrelevant to my testimony," but he didn't.

As I pressed Klein the question of his feelings about Crile be-

came a central issue—a litmus test of his credibility. At that point I
handed the witness a transcript of a telephone interview that he
had had with a reporter. Klein had not known that the reporter
was recording the call, and I had deliberately not marked the transcript as an exhibit until my cross of Klein began.* Using the transcript I forced the now stricken-looking witness to admit he had
called Crile "a social pervert," said "I couldn't stand to look at
him," described Crile as "devious and slimy," and told the reporter
that Klein was "just too good and that bothered Mr. Crile."

Whatever remaining credibility, if any, Klein had disappeared
when I confronted him about a conversation he claimed to have
had with Crile during the preparation of the broadcast. The alleged substance of the conversation, which related to a General
Davidson, was critical to Westmoreland's claim, and it had been a
central point of Klein's direct testimony. This time I placed an audio tape recorder on the railing surrounding the jury box. Pushing
the play button, I let Klein and the jury hear the witness deny not
once, but three times, to his reporter friend that such a conversation had even taken place.

The last task was the most difficult. General Westmoreland, six-
foot-two with a full head of gray hair, looked every inch the career
military officer. Ramrod straight whether sitting or standing, he
answered questions directly and with sincerity. He had devoted his
entire life to serving his country, and whatever one might think of
the Vietnam war, it was hard not to be grateful for his service. My
job was to show the jury that this patriot was, in at least one important matter, not telling the truth.

I had begun to prepare the jury for my cross in my opening
statement. I acknowledged Westmoreland's patriotism and told
the jury that it was that very patriotism, coupled with the belief
that it had been critical to America that we stay in Vietnam to

---

*Ordinarily, exhibits to be used in direct examination must be marked and exchanged
before trial. However, documents to be used on cross-examination for impeachment need
not be pre-marked.

fight and defeat communism, that had led him to misrepresent how the war was going. Only in this way, I explained, did he believe he could preserve public and political support at home long enough to let him finish his job.

The first day of my cross was respectful, even gentle. Point by point I drew the general's attention to something he had said during his direct, then showed him where he had stated the contrary in a document or at his deposition. My approach, with all the patience I could muster, was: I am sure there is an explanation, but I am having difficulty reconciling what you are saying now with what you said then. Can you help me?

The second day I began to pick up the pace, letting just a hint of impatience, a suggestion that the statements *were* inconsistent and Westmoreland had to know it, creep into my voice. At one point Mrs. Westmoreland, who was sitting in the audience, was overheard by a reporter to whisper to a friend, "Those damn depositions."

The turning point of the cross came when I suggested directly to the witness that he had been trying to persuade the home front that there was "light at the end of the tunnel." Westmoreland denied it, asserting with conviction that while he had heard the phrase used, he would never have said it himself because he did not believe it was accurate. What he had forgotten, and what his lawyers had failed to prepare him on, was that he had made that precise statement in a previously classified cable that we had obtained in response to a subpoena.

Faced with the testimony of McChristian and Hawkins, the convincing testimony of Crile, the threat of Mike Wallace to come, and his own performance on the witness stand, four months after the trial started and with only two weeks to go, General Westmoreland dismissed his case. He received no money, no apology, and of course no airtime. We did agree not to seek repayment of our costs.

The *Westmoreland* case, like *IBM*, was a milestone. The chance to try a major case at a young age is largely a matter of being in the right place at the right time. If a lawyer does so and succeeds, he or she will be on a short list for the next high-profile matter. Under different circumstances, the opportunity to try a case like *US v. IBM*, *Calcomp*, or *Westmoreland* might have come decades later, if at all.

The next ten years were a whirlwind of exciting and interesting cases. I joined the team defending Mike Wallace and CBS in a libel suit by Colonel Anthony Herbert. In the *Westmoreland* case Wallace and CBS were charged with being biased against the military effort in Vietnam; in *Herbert* they were charged with being biased in its favor when they debunked some of Herbert's more extreme allegations of war crimes (following extensive discovery, the case was dismissed by the court before trial). I represented Continental Airlines in successfully recovering $100 million from American Airlines and $95 million from United Airlines for antitrust violations. I represented CBS in fending off a takeover attempt by Ted Turner, and Texaco in defeating a takeover bid by Carl Icahn and in appealing and resolving a $15 billion judgment Pennzoil won against it in Texas.

In 1986 I represented the Democratic National Committee in obtaining a court order permanently barring the Republican National Committee from conducting programs designed to reduce voting by minorities. In my early years at Cravath, I had been able to devote a significant amount of time to civil rights work in the South. Most of this work was in Mississippi, including during the summer of 1967 when Judy and I spent two months doing voter registration work and representing civil rights activists who had been arrested. In the 1970s I worked with other partners at Cravath representing the students who were injured and the families of the students who were killed at Jackson State College when Mississippi Highway Patrol and Jackson police officers fired continuously for more than forty seconds at a student dormitory building to extinguish a nonviolent demonstration.

By 1986 the threats of violence that had been an everyday fact of life in the civil rights movement two decades earlier had largely subsided. However, there were many subtle and not so subtle efforts to prevent African Americans from enjoying full citizenship. A few weeks before that year's general election I was asked by the Democratic National Committee to investigate reports of Republican efforts to interfere with the right of African Americans to vote in key districts. After a whirlwind of interviews and research, we brought an action in federal court in New Jersey.

The Republicans argued that their efforts were race-neutral attempts to prevent people who were not qualified to vote from getting a ballot, and that it was merely a "coincidence" that statistics showed their efforts to be focused on districts with a large percentage of African Americans. Our case was made when we obtained discovery of the word processors used by RNC staff assigned to the project. We printed out from the processors' hard drives copies of memos sent by persons working on the project, and found several that no longer existed in the RNC's files. One of them expressly stated that the Republicans' efforts were intended to "hold down the black vote." It was an explosive revelation that provided political ammunition in the closing days of the election, as well as a legal basis for eventually obtaining a permanent injunction against the Republican National Committee.

In the 1990s Tom Barr and I represented the Federal Deposit Insurance Corporation in claims against Michael Milken and his investment banking firm for losses suffered by failed savings and loan associations as the result of their purchases of junk bonds. (We collected over $1 billion for the FDIC.) I tried a predatory pricing case in Galveston, Texas against American Airlines, my second antitrust case against the company in less than a decade. (Even with the legendary Texas trial lawyer Joe Jamail as my co-counsel, this time we lost.) I represented Westinghouse in an international arbitration and subsequent jury trial in which the Republic of the Philippines sued to recover the $2.5 billion it had paid for a nuclear power plant on the ground that Westinghouse had procured the contract to build the plant by bribing President Ferdinand Marcos. (We won both the international arbitration and the jury trial.)

I had a law practice that I enjoyed, I earned a multimillion-dollar a year income, and I had the help and support of a seemingly endless supply of the best and the brightest recent law school graduates. Depending on your perspective, Cravath might or might not be a great place to be an associate; it was unquestionably a great place to be a partner.

The last week of every December our family and the family of our friends Jim and Barbara Miller retreat to some Caribbean resort. It is a chance to relax in the sun and reflect on our life and plans. We began these annual adventures in the 1980s and they are now a well-established family tradition. In December 1996 we were in the Dominican Republic, and on New Year's Eve Mary and I watched the children set off fireworks on the beach and toasted what we hoped the next few years would bring.

Much of what we hoped would happen came true. Our family stayed healthy; Caryl, Christopher, and Jonathan followed my son David's example and married wonderful people; three healthy new grandchildren were born to join the three that were with us that vacation; and I managed to teach Mary Regency and Alexander to drive without them killing me or me them. My professional life, however, was to take an unexpected turn. This book is about that turn and some of the cases that followed over the next four years.

2

The Firm that Ruth Built

THE SECOND THURSDAY IN MAY, 1997, I FLEW TO LAS Vegas for a long weekend with my son David and my friend Jim Miller. As I relaxed on the plane, I had no hint that before the weekend was over the professional life I had enjoyed for more than thirty years would explode in my face.

The fuse had been lit in early 1996 when I received a call from David Sussman, the general counsel of the New York Yankees, asking whether I would consider representing the team in connection with a dispute with Major League Baseball. I cautioned him that I was not an expert in sports law in general or baseball law in particular. He said they were not looking for a baseball expert; they had plenty of those. What they wanted was my antitrust expertise and my reputation for taking on difficult cases. Intrigued, I agreed to meet with him as soon as I had consulted my partners. I found that the firm, like myself, was enthusiastic. The Yankees were a highly visible client with the kind of important legal issues that Cravath considered its province. Moreover, as a number of my partners noted to me, as their lawyers we should be able to improve our seats at Yankee Stadium.

In my initial conversation with David Sussman he explained that the dispute concerned what was referred to as "revenue-sharing." For several years there had been an effort to induce baseball's financially more successful teams to subsidize those less successful. The assumption was that a team's success depended on how much money it had to spend, and that the only way to achieve "competitive balance" was to ensure that each team had about the same amount.

There are several reasons to question this assumption. Historically, teams that have spent the most money have often lost to rivals who have spent much less, as the Marlins' World Series victories in 1997 and 2003 illustrate. Other teams, like Baltimore, have spent much more with dismal results. Moreover, revenue-sharing has the same effect of dampening competitive incentives that causes suspicion of socialism and leads free market economies to adopt antitrust laws to ensure that firms are forced to compete. Why, for example, should a team invest and risk capital if the return on a successful investment will have to be shared with competitors?

Nevertheless, the Yankees' success made the club an attractive target. No other team has so dominated a sport for so many years— and few have invested as much to achieve that success. Looked at in a certain way, the Yankees are the team that Ruth built. After acquiring Babe Ruth from the ill-fated Boston Red Sox in 1920, the Yankees went on to win the American League Pennant in 1921, 1922, and 1923; in 1923, the year Yankee Stadium opened, they won their first World Series.* In the eighty-two years from 1920 through 2003 the Yankees won thirty-nine American League Pennants and twenty-six World Series. (The Red Sox, who had won five World Series in the first two decades of the twentieth century, never won another.)

Ruth's popularity, the winning to which he contributed, and the club's location in America's largest city made the Yankees MLB's

---

*The significance of the investment in Ruth is best understood by remembering that the Yankees paid Boston $125,000—and loaned Boston $325,000 more—to purchase Ruth's contract less than five years after Colonels Ruppert and Huston acquired the Yankees lock, stock, barrel, and players for $460,000.

most profitable team. But for the winning, popularity, and profitability to continue, profits had to be reinvested in the teams of the
future. The Yankees might be the team Ruth built originally, but
they were constantly rebuilt by the team's owners over the following
eight decades.

Since the Yankees are a separate, privately owned company one
might think that there was no way to take their money without
their consent. However, if Major League Baseball made a decision
to implement revenue-sharing and any team refused to accept it,
MLB could impose a variety of sanctions, including expulsion from
the league.

Soon after my representation was approved by Cravath, I met
with Sussman and George Steinbrenner at Yankee Stadium. Steinbrenner is an imposing figure who seems in person even larger than
his physical size. He loves baseball, and he loves the Yankees; and he
believed that revenue-sharing was bad for his team and, in the long
run, for the sport itself. He recognized, however, that the perenni-
ally higher revenues of the Yankees and a handful of other clubs
made an attractive target for the "share the wealth" arguments of less
financially successful clubs.

I also noted that the League's acting commissioner, Bud Selig,
had a personal interest in revenue-sharing since he was the owner of
the financially strapped Milwaukee Brewers. George, who a few
years earlier had led the effort to replace Fay Vincent as commissioner with Bud, considered Selig a personal friend and trusted him
to treat the Yankees fairly. I was not so sure. The arguments for and
against revenue-sharing were not all one way; reasonable people
might well differ as to what made the most sense for baseball as a
whole. In such a situation a person's self-interest could, I warned,
influence even a man of integrity.

Steinbrenner wanted me initially to advise him on what rights
he had to resist revenue-sharing. He also wanted me to represent
him in any negotiations or litigation that might be necessary to enforce his rights.

There were a number of issues relating to the authority of Major League Baseball to require revenue-sharing, but antitrust issues were the most important. Ordinarily, an agreement among competitors to share revenues would violate the Sherman Antitrust Act. The 1890 statute has been described by the Supreme Court as a charter of economic freedom and has been enforced for more than a century by Democratic and Republican administrations alike. However, as every antitrust lawyer knows, the applicability of the antitrust laws to cases involving baseball is complicated by the so-called "antitrust exemption" granted the sport more than eighty years ago.

In 1922 the Supreme Court held that the antitrust laws did not apply to baseball because it was not a "business" and because it was local or intra-state, not interstate, commerce.* The decision is now uniformly regarded as a mistake. Baseball was already a business in 1922; it is silly to pretend it is not one now. It was interstate in 1922; with its television contracts, Internet activities, and travel schedules, it is indisputably interstate commerce today.

The Supreme Court itself has recognized its error, calling the ruling an "aberration" and refusing to apply it to football, hockey, basketball, and other leagues that have developed since 1922. Nevertheless, in 1972, by a five to three vote, the Court held that even though its 1922 decision was wrong and other sports leagues would not have an antitrust exemption, they would not overrule it as it applied to baseball.

"How," Steinbrenner asked at a later meeting at Yankee Stadium, "can there be one rule for baseball and another for other sports?" I had no good answer. One of the basic elements of the rule of law is that the result in a particular case should not depend on the identity of the parties involved, on whether the price-fixing is done by baseball teams or basketball teams. The court-created

---

*The federal antitrust laws are enacted by Congress pursuant to its power to regulate interstate commerce; they do not apply to activities that are entirely intra-state (*i.e.*, conducted within a single state).

antitrust exemption for baseball was bad law made worse by its inconsistency with the rules applied to other sports.*

Whenever I take on an important new matter it is my practice to read all significant prior decisions relating to the key issues in the case. Reading those opinions helps me understand the courts' reasoning and identify points that I can use later in briefs and arguments. Many lawyers leave legal research and analysis to young associates; this saves time, but most junior lawyers will know only part of the case well, and may miss an important point or relationship. And by personally reading the relevant cases, I am better prepared to respond to unexpected questions and issues when they arise in court.

I had a second set of cases sent to Robert Silver, one of the two smartest lawyers I know. I first met Bob when he was a twenty-four-year-old summer associate at Cravath soon to graduate from Yale with four degrees. After several years at Cravath, he returned to Yale as a fellow. With his intellect, objectivity, and ability to solve complicated problems, he could have been a great teacher and scholar. However, Robert missed the challenge and excitement of practicing law. By 1996 he had set up his own small firm, where he specialized in providing advice on difficult corporate and litigation issues. I often called him to get a second opinion on important legal matters.

We could argue that the baseball exemption was inconsistent with the plain language of the antitrust laws and should now be overruled; that would bar Major League Baseball from imposing revenue-sharing on the Yankees without their consent. But it is always difficult to be confident that the Court will overturn a prior decision, however wrong, particularly where it has refused to do so previously. Accordingly, it was important to see whether there was a way to support an antitrust challenge based on existing decisions.

---

*A great Supreme Court justice, Felix Frankfurter, wrote in 1955: "It would baffle the subtlest ingenuity to find a single differentiating factor between other sporting exhibitions . . . and baseball."

Robert and I found a few cases (including one before the Florida Supreme Court) that permitted antitrust claims against baseball owners for agreeing to impose limits on cities to which a club could be moved. One way of reconciling such cases with the existence of an exemption was to view the exemption as extending only to activities necessary to the operation of a baseball league ("the business of baseball"), but not to other conduct. For example, there might be an antitrust exemption for agreements concerning uniform rules of the game, schedules, and the equipment to be used because those are necessary for there to be a league at all. A similar argument might be made concerning agreements relating to rights to players, at least where there was a plausible good faith basis. The courts had not decided, however, whether the exemption extended to setting a uniform ticket price for admission, and it could be argued that uniform ticket prices across stadiums and cities are not necessary to the operations of a league. Even farther removed from the "business of baseball" would be agreements as to what prices to charge for hot dogs or tee shirts, or what brand of beer to serve. And if teams could not legally agree to eliminate competition by fixing the prices at which they sold tee shirts, they should not be able to reduce such competition indirectly by requiring all proceeds from those sales to be shared.

From the beginning everyone recognized that the best outcome would be to reach an agreement on revenue-sharing acceptable to both the Yankees and MLB without the necessity of litigation. Over the spring of 1996, as I became increasingly educated about the structure and rules of MLB, that conclusion was underscored. To begin with, Steinbrenner did not relish litigating against his fellow owners. Although baseball is today a multibillion dollar business, much of it (as was apparent from the owners' meetings I attended) is conducted in an atmosphere somewhere between that of a country club and the U.S. Senate. Personal relations matter, and matter a lot. Many of the owners were not only long-time business colleagues but friends. George was particularly uncomfortable being at odds with Bud Selig.

In addition, MLB had adopted rules that prohibited clubs from suing to challenge any MLB action; and the sanctions potentially available were deliberately open-ended—in theory MLB could suspend Steinbrenner from baseball and impose crushing fines on his team. I believed that if a court ultimately ruled that MLB's actions violated the antitrust laws it would enjoin or vacate any sanctions that MLB tried to impose for bringing the lawsuit; it would be against public policy to permit retaliation against someone for bringing a meritorious antitrust action—indeed, where (as would be the case with MLB) the retaliation itself was collusive, such retaliation would constitute a further violation of the antitrust laws. However, the issue was not so clear if a Yankee lawsuit were to fail. Collective action in retaliation for bringing a good faith lawsuit should be improper regardless of whether the lawsuit ultimately succeeds; a party should not have to risk financial ruin in order to access the judicial system. On the other hand, the law on this point was not as clear as we would have liked. Commencing litigation could amount to rolling the dice with the future of the Yankees at stake. If we won, George and the Yankees would be fine; if we lost they could be severely damaged.

In addition, even if MLB did not retaliate directly, the Yankees would face a hostile membership. The League constantly makes decisions over schedules, rights to players, rule interpretations, and financial assessments that affect the success and prospects of individual clubs. How a club fares in such situations is significantly affected by how the membership, and the MLB staff, feel about the club and its owner. Because such choices are subjective, and because courts are reluctant to second-guess the internal decision-making of associations like sports leagues, it is usually difficult to secure effective judicial review. As a result, win or lose the Yankees could face serious repercussions for challenging MLB in court.

Throughout 1996 Steinbrenner and his staff worked to reach an accommodation with the League while Robert Silver and I crafted the best case we could, should litigation become necessary. I also began representing the Yankees in other matters, including certain key player disputes. The issues were interesting, and I liked representing Sussman and Steinbrenner. David Sussman was a tough, thoughtful lawyer who worked as hard as or harder than the outside counsel he retained. Low-key in demeanor, he never seemed ruffled or tense regardless of the circumstance—an important quality for a Yankees' executive.

George Steinbrenner is as direct a man as I know. No one is ever unclear where he stands, or where one stands with him. His compulsive pursuit of excellence and attention to detail, coupled with his intelligence and extraordinary knowledge of baseball, meant that if we made a mistake, he was likely to spot it. His directness meant that if he noticed it, we would hear about it. Most of my clients are the same. Over the years I have come to have a great deal of choice as to what matters I take on. As I once explained to Steve Kroft on *60 Minutes*, everyone is entitled to a lawyer but not everyone is entitled to me. The clients I choose to represent tend to be those who care as much about winning as I do and are willing to work at it as hard. They also tend to know the difference between good, better, and best work—and to demand (and be willing to pay for) the best.

For Cravath the Yankees were a high-profile client whose significance went beyond the fees we earned and the opportunity for tickets. Although the team paid substantial fees over the course of a year, they were a fraction of what the firm charged its top clients. What made the Yankees interesting to Cravath were the bragging rights that came with representing the most successful sports franchise in history and the leading sports team in our hometown.

Although the general issue of revenue-sharing remained an important focus of our work, at the end of 1996 the prospect of litigation over it seemed unlikely, at least in the near future. The revenue-sharing that MLB was by then demanding was costly to the Yankees, but probably not so burdensome as to lead them to risk a court fight. In early 1997, however, all that changed.

★　★　★

BASEBALL CLUBS, LIKE OTHER SPORTS TEAMS, HAVE VALUABLE trademarks. Clothing manufacturers and other companies are willing to pay substantial fees for the right to use such trademarks on their products. Prior to 1997 the staff of Major League Baseball had made unsuccessful efforts to license the trademarks belonging to league members based on an agreement signed by most, but not all, of the clubs. The Yankees had not signed the current agreement, but more than three-quarters of the clubs had; and under MLB rules a three-quarters vote was arguably sufficient to authorize such licensing. Until early 1997 the question of who had the authority to license trademarks belonging to the Yankees was moot because of the inability of the league staff to negotiate a meaningful contract. (One proposed deal with Nike and Reebok would have provided the Yankees with $100,000 a year, an amount that Steinbrenner and Sussman believed ridiculously low compared to the value of the club's trademarks.)

In January 1997, however, David Sussman called to brief me on discussions about a possible ten-year deal between the Yankees and Adidas. Under the proposed agreement Adidas would pay $95 million to make and sell certain Yankees merchandise and be identified as a sponsor in advertising and at Yankee Stadium. Steinbrenner's view was that this money belonged to the Yankees and that the trademarks and other property that Adidas wished to use were the Yankees' to license. The agreement did not deal with any league trademarks or property (for example, the "MLB" mark or insignia that appears on much baseball merchandise and in many advertisements); those had been developed and were owned by MLB and were its to license. The Adidas contract dealt with trademarks developed and registered by the Yankees alone.

The first question that we analyzed was the extent to which the licenses the Yankees might grant were included in the rights that MLB had voted to market itself. If so, there could be a challenge to any contract entered into by the Yankees without MLB permission; and any proceeds would be divided (according to MLB rules) among thirty clubs equally—with the Yankees receiving one-thirtieth of the revenue from Adidas instead of 100 percent.

Second, even if MLB had not yet asserted control over certain rights (for example, the right to place advertising in a stadium), the contemplated agreement was for ten years. What would happen if during that term three-quarters of the clubs voted to expand the rights MLB purported to control? Again, it might seem odd that rights to trademarks that the Yankees clearly had in 1997 could be taken away during the term of the contract without either their or Adidas's consent. However, because of the blanket power that MLB claimed over all aspects of a club's business, the issue needed to be addressed.

A third question was whether to bring MLB into the Adidas negotiations before they were completed. There were potential advantages in doing so, including the possibility that the League would facilitate an agreement. After all, the sponsorship fee that Adidas would pay would almost certainly increase the price that other clubs could obtain for similar rights. It was likely that the amount paid for the Yankees would be higher than what a sponsor would pay for other teams, but even a fraction of $95 million would be far more than other clubs had had any reasonable prospect of obtaining prior to the Yankees-Adidas negotiations. On the other hand, there was suspicion on the part of both the Yankees and Adidas that if MLB knew of the negotiations prior to their conclusion it would try to block the transaction—a view supported by subsequent events. Neither the Yankees nor Adidas fully trusted the other to stand up to the pressure that we knew would come if the negotiations were revealed before the parties had irrevocably committed themselves. We recognized that MLB might also be displeased with a fait accompli, but concluded that it was better to seek forgiveness than permission. As a result, the talks continued in secret.

On March 3, 1997, with the deal finally done, the League and the public were informed that the parties had entered into a ten-year sponsorship agreement. Because of a confidentiality requirement, no details were provided. Adidas planned subsequent negotiations with other teams and with MLB itself; revealing the terms it had given the Yankees would give those teams, and the league, information that they could use against Adidas in those negotiations.

However, one of the first reactions of MLB was to request the specific terms of the contract. In one sense this request underscored the anticompetitive nature of what was going on. Agreements to share confidential pricing information are routinely found to violate the antitrust laws. On the other hand, if one assumed the propriety of the rule that revenues from certain licensing deals had to be shared among all teams equally, MLB had a legitimate interest in understanding whether the rights being licensed were ones over which it had asserted control. Nevertheless, the Yankees and Adidas feared that to the extent that the agreement succeeded (as we thought it had) in licensing rights over which MLB had *not* yet asserted control, releasing details of the contract would provide a road map for an after-the-fact change to the rules or their interpretation.

Anxious to maintain confidentiality, while also anxious not to offend the League more than necessary, we initially tried to describe the basic terms of the agreement to the MLB leadership in confidence. Unfortunately, a day after we revealed the amount that Adidas was to pay, the *New York Times* reported the $95 million figure based on information furnished by "a baseball official who asked for anonymity." That leak and others like it convinced Adidas that MLB could not be trusted; anything that was revealed to the League would be made public. What happened next increased its concern: MLB ordered us to turn over a complete copy of the contract and threatened sanctions if we disobeyed.

MLB described its requests and threats in detail to selected journalists, and I soon found myself advising the Yankees on their legal rights, preparing to litigate those rights, *and* responding to repeated press inquiries. My clients were colorful subjects; under normal circumstances events that would go unnoticed if they involved another sports team or owner were reported prominently if they related to George or the Yankees. The conflict between the Yankees and baseball, and between George and the other owners, made for an irresistible story. The fact that $95 million was at stake added to the drama.

I had been involved in high-profile cases before, and the press attention now did not approach that of General Westmoreland's libel action or the Texaco-Pennzoil battle. However, the Yankees-Adidas story was a challenge in that it required dealing with sports, business, and general news reporters, each with a different perspective, often on the same day. In negotiations with MLB representatives and conversations with the press I tried to be conciliatory without conceding issues important to the Yankees or their new partner. I was, I think, successful in not giving much away. I was not so successful at being conciliatory.

It soon became clear that unless we were prepared to turn over the full agreement we faced immediate sanctions, and the court fight that would inevitably follow. We still hoped to avoid litigation. Moreover, if we had to litigate, it was better to fight over sanctions against a club for licensing its own trademarks than over sanctions for refusing to provide a copy of the contract as required by MLB rules. This was, I concluded, the wrong time to fight, and the wrong issue to fight over.

I proposed to George and David Sussman that we provide the contract to selected MLB officials with an accompanying letter warning that we believed that sharing the contract's terms with other teams or with Adidas's competitors (including by making the terms public) would itself violate the antitrust laws and be a breach of fiduciary duty. Such an approach avoided sanctions or immediate litigation and at the same time preserved our position that sharing such information violated the antitrust laws. We also hoped to discourage further MLB leaks by threatening another legal claim if such leaks continued.

It would take a few days to get Adidas's approval to disclose the contract. In the meantime I did not want to take the risk of having MLB act precipitously. Accordingly, later that day when a reporter asked whether we had decided how to respond to the League, I replied by saying that while there were serious confidentiality issues

I believed it was likely that the agreement would be turned over. The next day a *New York Times* headline proclaimed: "Yanks to Detail Adidas Deal." Although the article that followed accurately quoted my more qualified commitment, the headline writer had conveyed the message we had wanted sent. It would be difficult for MLB to act precipitously in the face of public belief that they were about to get what they wanted. Two days later, with Adidas's reluctant permission, we delivered the contract.

Although we had initially avoided a fight, over the next two months it became clear that the Yankees would eventually have to choose between sharing their sponsorship money or going to court. For Steinbrenner, dividing up the $95 million with his competitors was not an option. The club's success and popularity made its name and trademarks among the most valuable in sports. Their value was part of what Steinbrenner bought when he purchased the club from CBS in 1973 and what he enhanced over the next quarter century.

From 1973 through 1996 the Yankees had won more games than any other team in baseball. During the eight years beginning in 1996 the Yankees would win six American League Championships and four World Series. Such a record would have been impressive in any period; in a time of free agency, with the Yankees competing against teams owned and bankrolled by major media conglomerates, it was extraordinary. That record was the result of George's leadership and investment; no owner had cared more, invested as much, or been as effective. He would fight to keep what he had earned.

Litigation carried substantial risks, but even if the courts decided to adhere to an antitrust exemption for the business of baseball, the "revenue-sharing" at issue was different from any conduct that had been immunized previously. What most convinced us that litigation was necessary was MLB's position that the league claimed the right later to change its rules in such a way as to invalidate portions of the Adidas contract retroactively. We believed the contract was consistent with MLB rules as they then stood—that Adidas was paying the Yankees for sponsorship rights that MLB had not up to then claimed it controlled, and which it was not itself trying to market. Nevertheless, the League asserted the power (by a vote of three-fourths of the teams) later to decide that it, not the Yankees, controlled the sponsorship rights covered by the Adidas contract. We asked MLB to agree that if the rules were changed, the new rules would not apply retroactively to this contract. Initially, Bud Selig seemed agreeable. However, Greg Murphy (president of Major League Baseball Enterprises, the entity responsible for MLB's collective marketing of trademark licenses) was opposed to any concession to the Yankees. Murphy's hostility may have been rooted in a desire to maintain maximum flexibility for his business; it may also, as the press suggested, have been influenced by resentment over the rejection by the owners of his own proposed deal with Nike and Reebok—a rejection led by Steinbrenner. Whatever the reason, opposition to our proposed compromise prevailed.

Accordingly, on May 6 Adidas and the Yankees filed a lawsuit in federal court in Tampa. Adidas was represented by Jonathan Schiller, a partner in the Washington, DC, office of Kaye Scholer. One of the country's leading trial lawyers specializing in high-stakes litigation, a year earlier he had collected a nine-figure jury verdict against AT&T for breach of a complicated contract related to cellular spectrum rights.

Because we could sue in any state where Major League Baseball did business, and because the Yankees and MLB did business in every state with a Major League team, we had many choices where to file our lawsuit. There were, however, only two serious alternatives—New York, the Yankees' hometown, and Tampa, where Steinbrenner had a home and where the Yankees trained. On the surface, New York was the obvious choice. However, there were three concerns. First, there was the danger that New York City would be perceived as *too* favorable a forum for our side. This could lead a court to lean over backward in favor of the League or even to consider transferring the case to a more neutral site.

Second, a case in New York, the media capital of the world, could be expected to generate maximum press coverage—which might result in further polarizing MLB. In addition, the Yankees would be at a disadvantage in any media battle. The early stories might be neutral, or even positive, but the more intense the coverage, the more reporters would search to find something new, different, and usually negative to say. Even leaving aside the antipathy to the team—and to George Steinbrenner—felt by many writers, the League had far more PR personnel on the payroll, with many more favors to offer friendly reporters.

Third, and most important, it was critical to the Yankees that their case proceed to trial quickly. The longer it dragged on, the longer the club would be in a legal limbo subject to sanctions. The federal court in New York has many judges; some could be expected to expedite the case, with a trial in less than a year, but others would take three to five years or longer. Because cases are assigned to judges randomly there was no way to predict whether we would draw a fast or slow judge. In addition the federal court in New York City has a relatively heavy caseload, which could delay the case even before an expeditious judge. The federal court in Tampa had a smaller caseload and a reputation for moving to trial relatively promptly.

We chose Tampa. This was not a dumb decision, but it certainly turned out to be a wrong one.

The first week after filing was spent in drafting discovery, fielding calls from the press, and preparing a motion to enjoin MLB from suspending George. Thursday afternoon I flew to Las Vegas for a long weekend. I was pleased with the case we had prepared and looking forward to several days of relaxation with David and Jim.

★ ★ ★

I GO TO LAS VEGAS THREE OR FOUR TIMES A YEAR. I ENJOY Atlantic City and Atlantis in the Bahamas, and I have visited casinos from Monte Carlo to Hong Kong, but Las Vegas, with its combination of sun, shows, and high-stakes gambling, remains my favorite. Casino gambling is different from poker, bridge, and the other card games that I play in that the house has an edge on virtually every bet available (which, of course, is why it is profitable for casinos to build elaborate palaces, put on great shows, and provide free food, wine, rooms, and even air fare). The only even-money bet is the so-called "odds bet" at the dice table, which is one of the reasons I favor craps.* Another reason is that dice is a social game. There is time to relax and talk, and virtually everyone at the table is focused on a common goal. Sensibly played, even at high stakes, dice is no more expensive than most forms of entertainment, particularly given the free rooms, dinners, and shows—and there is always the chance for a big payoff.

Craps and litigation have their similarities. It is necessary to manage your exposure while taking risks. It is critical to be patient and not get carried away. Luck plays a key part. Every hand, short or long, eventually ends. And the result of every new roll, like the result of every new case, is independent of the last.

When I went to my room at Caesar's Palace Friday afternoon to check for messages, I found one from Sam Butler. Sam was Cravath's presiding partner, and my relations with him were complicated. There was, I believe, considerable mutual respect, and he and I had often worked together to improve the firm. We also had much in common: both of us were native Midwesterners, had been promoted to partner ahead of our contemporaries, and had unusually prominent practices that contributed significantly to the firm's revenues and reputation. There were also many differences. I was considerably more liberal, more informal, less risk-averse. For more than twenty years Sam and I had disagreed over who should make partner, and when; the kind of cases to pursue; what organization and structure was best for Cravath in the twenty-first century; and the proper scope of *pro bono* work.

---

*The catch is that the odds bet can only be made following an initial bet on which the house has a 2% advantage. However, since the odds bet can be between two and a hundred times larger than the initial bet (depending on the casino) the overall edge of the casino can be reduced to between 1% and less than one-tenth of 1 percent. Overall, craps is the game where the house has the smallest advantage.

When I returned his call, Sam got right to the point. Gerald Levin, the CEO of Time Warner, Cravath's largest client and a company the firm had represented since it was founded more than half a century ago, had called to object to our representation of the Yankees. During the time I was the Yankees' lawyer, Time Warner had acquired Ted Turner's Turner Broadcasting System, a company that among other things owned the Atlanta Braves. Cravath had never represented the Braves, and representation of a corporation does not necessarily prevent a firm from suing one of that company's subsidiaries, particularly one unrelated to the firm's work for its client.

Nevertheless, while Time Warner had no legal right to require Cravath to abandon its Yankees representation (and although the canons of ethics forbid a law firm from dropping a client during litigation merely because it wants to represent a larger client), I immediately recognized the bind we were in. Not only was Time Warner important to Cravath's financials, but the firm felt a deep-seated loyalty to a client it had represented for six decades. When I asked Sam why Time Warner was complaining now, he said that they had found out only the day before that I was representing the Yankees against MLB. In view of the widespread press coverage of the dispute over the prior sixty days, and the fact that I had personally been repeatedly quoted as the Yankees' lawyer, I found Time Warner's explanation difficult to believe. "Have they been living in a cave?" I asked.

I looked for a compromise. We had been planning to name most of the teams as well as MLB itself as defendants. However, only the League was a necessary defendant, and I offered to ask Steinbrenner to drop the Braves as a defendant if this would make Time Warner more comfortable. Sam agreed to raise the proposal, but he also asked me to tell George that the firm might have to withdraw from representing the Yankees. I said that I did not believe we were free to do so without the Yankees' consent.

I sympathized with the position in which Sam (who had personally represented Time Warner for more than twenty years) found himself, but it was clear to me that I could not responsibly abandon the Yankees, or George, at such a critical time. Steinbrenner and

Sussman had brought this action on my advice, accepting the risk involved on the assumption that I would see it through. As I walked from my room to the casino to join David and Jim Miller at the dice table, I thought about the firm's difficult choice between offending our largest client and incurring the legal and ethical complaints that the Yankees could make if Cravath withdrew in midstream.

It took me about six minutes to travel from my room to the craps table. By the time I got there, there was only one solution that seemed acceptable—I would have to leave Cravath. In one sense it was unthinkable; but in another it seemed inevitable. My leaving would preserve the firm's relationship with Time Warner, avoid a fight with Sam over whether to abandon the Yankees in mid-litigation, and enable me to fulfill my responsibilities to my clients. Over the next few days I would experience many emotions as my career at the only firm I had ever known unraveled; but for the moment I was doing for myself what my clients paid me to do for them—analyzing a difficult situation objectively and dispassionately and choosing the best of imperfect solutions.

It was, however, a difficult choice. Mary and I had from time to time discussed the possibility of my leaving. Sometimes those discussions had been triggered by my dissatisfaction with the firm's direction. On two occasions they followed an offer from another large law firm. However, each time Mary and I had decided that the combination of professional opportunities, financial security, and personal relationships that Cravath offered was too good to leave.

Before Sam's call the prospect of my leaving had seemed remote. I had turned 56 the previous March, and it seemed more a time to enjoy my success than to strike out in a new direction. That night I called Mary to tell her about my conversation with Butler. "What are you going to do?" she asked. "I don't know," I temporized. "I may have to leave the firm." After a pause long enough for her to realize I was not going to soften my comment with a laugh, she said: "There has to be another way."

"You may be right," I told her.

Six weeks later, while riding bikes through France, Mary said that she had realized then that my career at Cravath was probably over. "Whenever you say, 'you may be right,'" she said, "what you mean is that you've made up your mind and you're not interested in further discussion." All she said the night of May 10 was, "I know you will do the right thing, and I know whatever you do we will be happy." She was not, at the time, entirely convincing.

I returned to New York Saturday night, a day earlier than planned. I wanted to talk things over with some of my partners, and I had depositions in Virginia on Monday and in New York on Tuesday in cases other than the Yankees litigation. Before flying to Richmond, I spoke again to Sam, Tom Barr, and several of my other partners. I discovered that my proposed compromise was not acceptable to Time Warner. No one liked the idea of my leaving, especially under these circumstances; Tom and Frank Barron in particular tried to explore alternative solutions. In the end, however, no one could think of one that worked. We said that we would sleep on it.

We all agreed that we wanted to avoid any public controversy. Trying to explain our positions in public risked being drawn into mutual recriminations. I did not want to be seen as being at odds with my partners; the firm did not want to be perceived as caving in to pressure from a large client to abandon a smaller one. None of us, we said, would comment publicly until we reached an agreement.

It was not to be. The next day Mary called me in Richmond to tell me that an article in the *New York Times* reported that the firm intended to withdraw from its representation of the Yankees. Moreover, Butler was quoted as suggesting that Cravath's Yankees representation had somehow been a mistake on my part, of which the rest of the firm had been unaware. Mary, always my fiercest defender, was infuriated by the implication that I was at fault. Although I too was concerned about Sam's comment, I thought there was little chance that anyone would take seriously the idea that Cravath was unaware that I was representing the Yankees against the remainder of Major League Baseball; even leaving aside the firm's procedures and records, there was all the publicity.

"Sam must have been in the same cave as the Time Warner folks," I joked.

When I spoke to him, Sam assured me that he was not the source, and that the reporter already had the story when he called so under the circumstances he felt he had to say something. He did not explain why he had made the particular comments he did.

One unintended consequence of the article was that reporters contacted several experts, including the country's two leading legal ethics professors, Geoffrey Hazard of the University of Pennsylvania and Stephen Gillers of New York University, both of whom confirmed that there was no ethical prohibition to Cravath's continuing to represent the Yankees. The published opinions of such experts confirmed George and David's view that the firm was improperly pursuing its financial interests at the expense of its obligation to the Yankees.

I had explained to George over the weekend that the one aspect of the case that Time Warner might credibly claim to have been surprised by was the fact that, in addition to MLB's being sued as an organization, the Braves themselves might be named as an additional defendant. There was no ethical conflict in suing the Braves—they were not and had never been a client of Cravath; and Cravath had never received any confidential Braves information in connection with its representation of Time Warner. However, Time Warner could understandably be unhappy to have even an indirect subsidiary sued by its longtime law firm. I had therefore asked George on Saturday to agree to drop the Braves as a defendant and he had agreed.* He could not understand why this had not ended the matter.**

---

*While it was true that a decision adverse to MLB would affect the Braves, that was something that had been known from the beginning.

**It was later reported that Fay Vincent, a former baseball commissioner and a member of the Time Warner board, had been responsible for the company's position. This made sense because Steinbrenner had been responsible for firing Vincent as commissioner and Vincent was known to harbor hard feelings over the incident.

My main concerns over Monday's article were two-fold. First, I did not want issues of potential conflicts to distract from the merits of our case or provide an excuse to delay our proceedings. Second, I knew the heartburn that the article, with its implication that Cravath and I would be abandoning the Yankees, would cause Steinbrenner and Sussman. When I spoke to them later that day, they were both angry and concerned.

I had not yet raised with either of them the possibility of my resigning from Cravath; it was a big step, and I was not ready to discuss it outside the Cravath family and my own. I told George that I would be returning to New York late that evening and would call him the next morning. George felt exposed; he knew the pressure that was being put on Cravath and on me to cut him adrift. However, he was sympathetic to my personal situation and did not press me to tell him what I thought the ultimate outcome would be.

When I got home that night Mary was waiting for me. Over a glass of wine we reflected once more on why I saw my leaving as the only principled choice available. The previous weekend Mary had continued to express many concerns about my leaving, most of which I shared. However, with the decision behind us, we were able to focus on what the future might bring. With my greater tolerance for uncertainty, I was the more sanguine. But what Mary lacked in appreciation for the prospect of striking out in a new direction at a time when many couples are planning retirement, she more than made up for in determination. Having failed to protect me from myself, she was doubly determined to make the best of what was to come.

Actually, part of my confidence about the future was based on what I had seen Mary do. When in 1985 our second, and my sixth, child (Alexander) was born, she had resigned her position as a vice president at CBS to be with the children. A year later we sold our apartment in New York City and moved to what had been our weekend retreat in northern Westchester County, forty miles to the north. Mary liked being at home, but she missed practicing law. There had to be something, she reasoned, between the intense work

schedule that she was used to and giving up paid employment altogether. The solution she found in 1988 was to open up a law office
three miles from our house on the Village Green in Bedford Village,
New York (population 3,210).

Although Bedford was not a center of commercial activity, and
Mary had little interest in writing wills or doing real estate closings,
she soon discovered that her clients did not care where she worked
as long as she could be reached by phone and fax and was available
for meetings and court appearances. Her first clients, based on her
prior work, were broadcasting companies and airlines. By 1997 her
firm, Boies & McInnis, had half a dozen lawyers and a diverse litigation practice. Watching her I had learned that computers, word
processors, and electronic libraries had eliminated many of the
economies of scale that large firms once enjoyed, that big law firm
clients were prepared to turn to small firms in small towns if they
had the right lawyers, and that enough top lawyers preferred a Bedford environment so that Mary could hire people as good or better
than the lawyers in the big cities. I can, I thought, do what Mary
has done.

Shortly after seven a.m. on May 14, I spoke with George Steinbrenner to tell him that I would be leaving Cravath to continue to
represent him and the Yankees. He was grateful but worried about
what it meant for my future. "Take some time to think about it," he
cautioned.

When I spoke with David Sussman a few minutes later he was
even more direct. His first reaction was shock: "You don't need to
do this. It's a critical case for the Yankees," he continued, "but you
shouldn't throw away your Cravath partnership over it." He too
advised me to think it over.

I told both of them that I had, that we did not have more time,
and that I would not be comfortable with any other decision.

It was still early that same morning when I went to meet with
Sam Butler to work out the details of my retirement. The atmosphere was friendly, even relaxed. The two of us quickly agreed on
a severance package and a joint statement that fairly reflected our

mutual admiration and respect. I then went to the conference room next to my office for a deposition I was conducting. Around eleven in the morning Sam walked in with a letter of agreement for me to sign, which I did. He then went to catch a plane, and I returned to my deposition. Less than one hundred hours after he had first called me to raise his concern about the Yankees, I had retired from Cravath and embarked on an adventure the extent of which I could not possibly have foreseen.

When my deposition was over, I left to meet Mary for a long lunch at La Caravelle, one of New York City's best French restaurants and a favorite of mine for almost forty years. We began with a glass of champagne—not so much because of a celebratory mood, but because we always began that way at La Caravelle. The enormity of the step I had just taken was beginning to set in and "now what?" was on both our minds.

The first necessity was to find me a place to work—a phone, a fax, and a way to get something typed. Sam had offered to make my office and secretary available to me until I found somewhere permanent, but we both knew it would be awkward representing the Yankees (at that moment my only client) from Cravath's offices. My second requirement was to find a staff. High-stakes litigation is a team sport. Mary had demonstrated that a team could be small if it was very good, but no one could do what she and I did without support. Mary suggested that temporarily I move into her firm's space, an offer I quickly accepted. She had a well-equipped office, close to our home, and I knew her people.

We also talked about whom I might recruit to join me—lawyers, secretaries, paralegals. Two potential first recruits were Robert Silver and my son Jonathan (who had just completed his final year at Tulane Law School). In addition to his intellect and legal skills, Silver was a pleasure to work with. Although no one was more driven to win, his generosity, honesty, and sense of humor endeared him even to his opponents. Robert and I had worked well together for more than fifteen years, and I believed I could count on him joining me.

I was less certain about Jonathan. He had the intellect, people skills, and confidence necessary to practice law in a small firm taking on big cases. I also knew that he was reluctant to return to Kaye Scholer, where he had been a summer associate, and that he was interested in going somewhere smaller where he thought he would get more responsibility faster. I believed that, like Robert, he would not be intimidated by the risk of a new enterprise. But how would JB feel about working with his father?

Cravath had put out a brief press release announcing my departure, and Sam and I had agreed that I would speak to the press either with him or another Cravath partner to avoid any conflict. So after lunch I returned to the building and responded to several press calls with Evan Chesler. We tried our best to downplay the significance of my withdrawal, but I could tell that we were having limited success.

When we finished, I called Robert Silver and Jonathan. I was delighted to find that both were enthusiastic. By the time I left Cravath late that afternoon, my new firm had tripled in size.

The next morning I discovered that my decision was indeed news. The *New York Times* reported it on the front page:

> David Boies, the superstar litigator who was virtually synonymous with the premier Wall Street law firm of Cravath, Swaine & Moore, announced yesterday that he was leaving the firm because he wants to represent clients whose interests collide with some of the giant companies that the law firm represents.

Similar articles appeared in the *Wall Street Journal, USA Today,* and elsewhere. In one sense it was nice to read complimentary descriptions of my career; but a repeated theme of the articles was that Cravath had suffered a major setback. "Mr. Boies's resignation hurts the venerable Cravath," the *Wall Street Journal* reported. The *New York Times* ran this quote:

"In the legal industry, it's like it's 1956 and Mickey Mantle is suddenly a free agent," said Steven Brill, the legal publisher and founder of Court TV. "This is a terrible loss for Cravath."

I knew that the pride of my former partners would be piqued by such reports and that some of them might be tempted to defend the firm by attacking me. In the days that followed I tried to downplay my departure, and happily, with the exception of a single subsequent *Wall Street Journal* article purporting to quote critical comments from anonymous Cravath sources, the firm and I succeeded in maintaining a united front.

Wednesday, May 15, I drove the three miles from our home to Mary's office to begin work at my new firm. *USA Today* that morning had quoted me as not worrying about my future because "I've got one more client now than I did when I started practicing law." When I arrived at the office, I had a message waiting for me from Sheldon Solow, one of New York's leading real estate owners, whom I had represented while at Cravath. "Now you have two clients."

As the day went on I received calls from other Cravath clients whom I had represented, including DuPont, Florida Power & Light, and Georgia Pacific. All had the same message—we hope you will continue to be our lawyer. That was the good news. The more complicated news was that I had cases that until yesterday had occupied a dozen lawyers—but I had only myself, Robert Silver, Jonathan, and whomever I could poach from Mary. By the end of my first week I could tell that my presence in her office was becoming a problem. I was giving her associates and paralegals so much to do that her work was not getting done. Moreover, I had her phone lines and fax machines so tied up that often she could not receive calls or send or receive a fax herself; and as more and more boxes arrived, her elegant offices began to resemble the final resting place of the Ark of the Covenant in the first Indiana Jones movie.

Mary and I enjoyed working together on individual cases, and the day before I withdrew from Cravath I had proposed that we combine our practices. We had decided, however, that our objectives for a law practice, and to some extent our management styles, were sufficiently different that separate firms made sense. We also thought that it was undesirable for us to be competing for the same resources. Our limited experience over the first few days of my new venture confirmed the wisdom of our decision. Mary and I had originally thought I would camp out in her offices for a few weeks until I located space of my own. We now decided to accelerate my search.

The weekend after I left Cravath, we drove around looking at office space near our home. One of the choices was a building four miles south of our house that had several thousand square feet of loft-like space on the third floor that had recently been vacated by a phone solicitation business. Although there were no individual offices, it had everything I needed—in particular, plenty of phone, fax, and computer lines. I arranged to move in the following week. Soon thereafter Mary was quoted in the press as saying, "We were happy to have him here and we were happy to have him leave."

By the time we moved, we had been joined by Diana Clarke (a young lawyer who had been working in Robert Silver's office), Ellen Brockman (a friend and paralegal from my days at Cravath), and Jodie Egelhoff (a former paralegal at the Skadden Arps firm who was particularly adept at computers). I also called on my oldest son, David, an experienced antitrust lawyer who was a partner in the firm of Straus & Boies, for help, particularly with the Yankees litigation. And I began talking to Jonathan Schiller, my friend and co-counsel in the Adidas litigation, about joining me.

Just as Cravath had originally provided me with the opportunities to launch my career as a young lawyer, it now provided generous support to my new firm. It gave me all the furniture from my office in Manhattan, as well as extra desks and filing cabinets. Its experts helped me select computers, phones, fax machines, and other office equipment—and the firm used its vendor relationships to get me quick service and attractive prices. Partners and other personnel with special expertise helped me select software, set up accounting procedures, arrange for insurance, and understand state and federal payroll and other tax issues.

My plan was to create a firm of eight to ten lawyers. I do not like being an administrator; I wanted to do what I did best and enjoyed most—practice law. I had watched Mary's firm best Cravath and other top-notch firms in major antitrust cases while staying small. The problem was that she was a lot better at saying no than I was, or am. (Women, she told me later, have more practice.) I enjoyed my relationship with existing clients and had a hard time refusing their requests. I also had a hard time turning down a new client with a challenging problem. I knew early on that it would be difficult for me to have the discipline to stay small; I had no idea, however, how thoroughly I would fail.

During that first month I was working night and day to keep up with the Yankees litigation and the matters that I had for my other clients. Even during the long weekend we took in New Orleans for Jonathan's law school graduation, he and I spent much of the time on the Yankees case. For him it was an unvarnished introduction to what practicing law with our firm would be like. In the middle of June, Mary and I were scheduled to take a bike trip in France followed by a week at Wimbledon. We briefly debated whether it was the right time to be away for three weeks. However, the Yankee case was in the capable hands of Silver and Schiller, and our other work appeared under control. We decided to go.

Part of our reasoning was that with a new firm, and my tendency to want to take on every interesting case that came my way, we would have to stake out time to enjoy life outside the office. During my years at Cravath I had always been able to do this. While a few of my partners grumbled that I spent too little time in the office, most were happy with my results. I was, however, well aware that much of my ability to take vacations was a result of all the support the firm gave me. One test of whether my new venture would be successful would be whether I could continue to practice law at the highest level and still take time off.

After Mary and I returned home, I continued my efforts to re-cruit Jonathan Schiller. There were substantial risks for him in giv-ing up the security of his big-firm partnership. Moreover, in addition to being one of the country's top trial lawyers, he was probably the leading American attorney specializing in interna-tional arbitration.* Both of us wondered whether his international clients would be comfortable with a small, unknown firm. An-other issue arose because of Jonathan's desire to stay in Washing-ton; did it make sense for a new firm with fewer than ten lawyers to operate offices in different cities?

In the end we decided that we enjoyed working together and that we could offer clients an attractive option. It helped that nei-ther of us was risk-averse. On September 1 Jonathan resigned from Kaye Scholer and what had been David Boies & Associates became Boies & Schiller. Jonathan brought with him Bill Isaacson, a young litigation partner at his firm who, like me, had graduated from the University of Redlands. Together with two associates hired in September, Jonathan and Bill constituted our new Washington, DC, office; we were now nine lawyers strong.

★ ★ ★

THE MOST IMPORTANT ISSUES DURING THAT SUMMER WERE whether Major League Baseball would follow through on its threat to suspend Steinbrenner and whether the Yankees would be re-quired to go to arbitration rather than litigate in court. We pre-pared a motion for a preliminary injunction to prevent MLB from

---

*Arbitration, the resolution of disputes by a panel of practicing lawyers, is increasingly viewed as a faster and less costly alternative to conventional trials. Arbitration is particularly relied on in resolving disputes between parties to international business transactions, who are often suspicious of each others' courts.

suspending George, and responded to MLB's motion to compel arbitration.*

MLB's rules required any dispute to be arbitrated by the commissioner of baseball. We challenged those rules on two grounds. First, we noted that as a technical matter the League did not have a commissioner, since following Fay Vincent's removal the owners had deliberately decided not to appoint a successor. Although Selig had been named "acting commissioner" and had gradually begun to assume more of the powers exercised by previous commissioners, both he and MLB had continued to insist that he was not the commissioner and did not intend to be considered for that position.

Second, and more importantly, Selig had an interest in the outcome of the dispute: he was the owner of a club that would benefit by MLB's appropriation of the Yankees' sponsorship fees, and this bias barred him from being an arbitrator. Although originally hostile to arbitration agreements, courts today accept that parties can contract to remove their disputes from the judicial system and have them decided by arbitration. There are, however, certain limits, and one of those is that parties are entitled to have an arbitrator free from personal interest or bias.

MLB wisely decided to postpone any decision on suspension until after the issue of the arbitration requirement was clarified. If the court ruled that the Yankees were not required to arbitrate before Selig, there would be little basis for penalizing George for taking action that the court had already ruled was appropriate. If the court required arbitration by Bud Selig (or another arbitrator selected by MLB), the result was predictable, and there would be time enough to impose suspension as a penalty not for going to court but for executing and implementing the Adidas contract.

By being patient, the League and its counsel deprived us of a

---

*Soon after the Yankees suit was filed, MLB removed George from its executive council. This in itself caused no immediate harm. A much more serious step would have been to suspend Steinbrenner from baseball completely, an act that would have barred him from participating in the running of the Yankees.

likely early victory and avoided fighting on ground that would be difficult to defend—and they did so without giving up any right ultimately to take the action they had postponed. It was clear that MLB was well represented and that we could not count on our chances being improved by their mistakes.

The League also moved to transfer our claims from Tampa to New York City. This was a more surprising step, and we seriously considered agreeing. While originally we had been worried that New York might be perceived as too much the Yankees' home turf, that reason was neutralized if MLB had picked that forum. However, we were still concerned with the pace of the litigation, and at that point the judge in Tampa seemed determined to move ahead promptly. Ultimately, we too decided to be patient. We put in briefs that defended our filing in Tampa while recognizing New York's connection to the dispute.*

At the end of July Jonathan Schiller and I flew to Tampa to argue the pending motions before Federal District Court Judge Henry Lee Adams Jr., who had decided to hear both MLB's transfer motion and the issue of arbitrability on the same day. Engaging in the tea leaf reading to which most trial lawyers are addicted, both sides concluded that this meant that the court was leaning toward keeping the cases.**

---

*In effect we told the court that there was a sound basis for the case to be in Tampa (it was the plaintiff's choice; it was where the Adidas contract was signed; it was where the Yankees had offices and training facilities), but that there was also a basis for New York. We wanted to let the judge keep the case if he were interested in it, or send it to New York if he were not. Depending on his outlook, our case could be viewed as an exciting opportunity or a huge burden. If the court were interested enough in the case to keep it in Tampa, it was unlikely that he would dismiss it and require the Yankees to arbitrate their dispute; if he found the case to be an unwanted burden (too big, too long, too complicated), I would rather he send it to a court in New York than to arbitration before Bud Selig. Leaving the transfer issue open for the judge to decide either way gave him an easy escape without relegating our claims to arbitration.

**It seemed unlikely that Adams would decide the pivotal arbitrability issue in a case that he was going to transfer, and it seemed unlikely that Judge Adams would spend the time to prepare for, and hear oral argument on, the complicated arbitrability issue if he were not intending to decide it.

At the end of the argument that day, he told us, "I'll get something out to you as soon as I can." A month later we asked the Magistrate Judge in charge of discovery to permit depositions to begin. The Magistrate declined, saying Judge Adams had told him a ruling was imminent. His expectations of a quick ruling, like our own, were wrong. It was not until December 19 that the court in Tampa finally issued its decision. Seven months had passed and we had made no progress toward trial. Several brief attempts at settlement had been made, but with the case stalled, there was little pressure on MLB to make concessions. Judge Adams's decision, contrary to both side's predictions, transferred the case to New York without even addressing the arbitration issue.

To say that we were interested in which of the thirty-two judges of the Southern District of New York we would get was an understatement. The tension created by the litigation was significantly affecting the Yankees' ability to conduct routine baseball business with other clubs. (When I attended the baseball owners meeting in Atlanta as a Yankee representative, MLB's counsel read a statement critical of the lawsuit and of my presence at the meeting. Some owners laughed it off; others did not.) We had believed that a prompt resolution was important at the time we commenced the litigation. Events since then had confirmed how right we were.

I was having lunch with Mary at Sparks Steak House in Manhattan when I received a call telling me that the judge assigned to our case would be John Martin. When I later spoke with George Steinbrenner and Lonn Trost (who had become the Yankees' general counsel after David Sussman left to become general counsel of MTV), I told them that Martin was a conscientious, no-nonsense judge who would move the case quickly and fairly. I could not predict how he would ultimately decide the merits of the case, but I thought it unlikely that Martin would require arbitration before an interested party.

"You will get a trial and you will get it promptly," I told Steinbrenner. "What that means is that if you're still interested in settling your right to keep the Adidas sponsorship payments, you should have your chance soon."

I explained that I believed Martin's reputation was well known and that MLB's counsel would be giving their client pretty much the same assessment of the judge. I also told George that MLB would be crazy to risk litigating its antitrust exemption in this case if it did not have to. Because the merchandise rights at issue here were so peripheral to the business of baseball, and because there were substantially less anticompetitive ways for MLB to accomplish any legitimate baseball objective it might have, this was the wrong case for the League to test the continued viability, and possible limits, of its antitrust exemption.

If I was right, Steinbrenner would soon have the chance to lock up his right to the Adidas millions. "The question," I told him, "is what is your objective? Is it to win this battle, or to limit or eliminate baseball's antitrust exemption?" There were, I explained, a number of future collective actions that might be adverse to the Yankees' interests, actions whose validity would depend on the existence and applicability of an antitrust exemption. Just as this was a poor case and a poor judge for MLB to litigate the viability of its antitrust exemption, this was a good case and a good judge for us to litigate those issues if our objective was to circumscribe the antitrust exemption generally. George was firm that if he could resolve the Adidas issue by negotiation he wanted to. He had repeatedly said that he had filed the case as a last resort, and he was clear that he did not want to use it to establish limits on baseball's antitrust exemption.

Not long after this conversation, Judge Martin scheduled a status conference in which he made clear his intention to complete pretrial proceedings promptly. Shortly after that, settlement discussions began in earnest. We had talked about settlement before without much progress. Now, however, with the spur of Judge Martin we began to make headway. If we had been willing to compromise and share any significant amount of the millions due from Adidas, we would have reached agreement immediately. The prob-

lem was that we insisted as a matter both of principle and of economics on receiving all the money. The League was therefore put
to a choice—give up its claim in this case and preserve its antitrust
exemption until the next dispute (which might well have facts more
favorable to its position), or roll the dice now with all the risks that
entailed.

Ultimately MLB capitulated on the key issue in dispute and
agreed that at no time during the life of the Adidas contract would
it challenge the contract or seek a share of the $95 million.*

There was one difficult issue remaining: MLB wanted the
Yankees to agree not to challenge in court baseball's merchandis-
ing, revenue-sharing, and other rules in the future. Under no circumstances, I said, could the Yankees agree. Initially Selig and his
staff were firm that they could not give the Yankees what they
wanted on the Adidas contract, then have us turn around and
bring a new suit on another issue. As a compromise MLB's lawyers
proposed that we dismiss our complaint "with prejudice," which
would arguably preclude relying on the same claims in the future.
Although dismissals with prejudice are common in many settlements, I did not want to do anything that would preclude or limit
subsequent litigation. I recognized, however, that no settlement
was possible unless Selig became comfortable that no new litigation was likely in the near future; I would have felt the same way
had I been in their position.

We considered an agreement not to sue for a particular period.
However, courts might not enforce such an agreement, and both
sides were troubled by the implication that litigation was expected
at the end of that time. In the final analysis the settlement went
forward without any formal commitment by the Yankees because
Selig became comfortable with George's personal assurances that
he intended to avoid further litigation if possible and my point that

---

*Major League Baseball also agreed itself to give a contract to Adidas that would allow
the company to use the logos of all thirty MLB teams, and the Yankees agreed to pay MLB
several hundred thousand dollars in costs.

if we had any present intention of further litigation we would not be settling this case.

On April 29, 1998, Adidas, the Yankees, and Major League Baseball officially settled their differences, leaving the question of baseball's antitrust exemption for another day. For the present, baseball preserved its antitrust exemption, the Yankees kept their $95 million, Adidas got the right to sponsor the Yankees and sell their merchandise, and George was reinstated to baseball's executive council. The Yankees went on to win the World Series in 1999 and 2000. I went on to practice law in a firm that, in a way, Ruth built.

3

A Twins' Ransom

WHEN I LEFT CRAVATH THERE WAS ONE CLIENT IN addition to the Yankees whom my partners insisted I take with me—a woman whose children had been abducted by her former husband and whose efforts to get them back forced her, and me, to battle the government of Guatemala, unscrupulous lawyers, indifferent judges, and the United States Department of State.

José Habie was born rich and Jewish in a country that was overwhelmingly Catholic and poor. His father, Alberto, was heir apparent to an agricultural and textile empire built by José's grandfather that would have made the family wealthy by U.S. standards; by the standards of their native Guatemala, they were one of the country's royal families. José's mother, Sara, had left high school to marry Alberto when she was fifteen. By the time she was twenty, she had three children—José, the middle child, and his two sisters. Sara was entirely subservient to her husband and accepted his unfaithfulness and occasional violence as an undesirable, but natural, part of her life.

The only son in a male-dominated society, José was indulged from the moment he was born in November 1956. By the time he was a teenager, he was given the run of the family business, where he treated the employees, and they him, as though they were his serfs.

At that time, Guatemala was a violent place with rebels and government-aided death squads competing to intimidate and kill not only each other but each other's natural allies—and with organized gangs whose specialty was kidnapping wealthy Guatemalans and their children. The Habie family's wealth and position made them a natural target, and from his birth José was isolated from society at large for his protection. Even among the children of other oligarchs, he was separated by his religion.

After graduating from the American School in Guatemala City, where he had been sent for security purposes and to learn English, he went to North Carolina State, where he earned a degree in textile engineering, then to the University of Pennsylvania's Wharton School for a master's degree. In college he said his name was Joey, and he used that name thereafter in Guatemala as well as in the U.S.

In February 1980, while Joey was at Wharton, his grandfather died of natural causes. Three months later his father was assassinated as he drove onto the grounds of his textile plant. The reason for the assassination and the identity of the assassins were never determined. It was whispered that the murder was the work of Sara's relatives, who were angry at Alberto's treatment of her, but most were inclined to blame the guerrillas. At the age of twenty-three, Joey inherited the family empire. He was rich, handsome, and powerful. He was also alone and insecure, sleeping in a house with armed guards, a loaded rifle on top of the television in his bedroom.

Amy Robin Weil was born February 7, 1961, the third child of Irvin and Rhea Weil of Birmingham, Michigan. Irvin was a successful interior designer and Amy grew up in a comfortable, upper-middle-class environment. She was as intelligent as she was attractive, and her security at home and popularity with classmates bred a sense of safety even when she was reckless.

Bored with high school and the boys she knew, she skipped her senior year, entering Michigan State at seventeen. In 1979, the year before Alberto Habie was gunned down, Irvin Weil dropped dead of a heart attack in Florida where he and Rhea had moved when Amy entered college. In September 1980 Amy transferred to the University of Florida to be closer to her mother. She graduated in 1982 and went on to earn an MBA in finance and a masters in health administration two years later.

Three days before Christmas 1983, Amy Weil and Joey Habie went out on a blind date. By all accounts, including their own, it was love at first sight. Joey had dated attractive women for years, but he had never met anyone like Amy. Where other women had been diffident in the face of his wealth and power, she was confident and challenging. Amy herself had dated many attractive men, but in addition to his intelligence and wealth Joey had an air of mystery that she found irresistible. The two were inseparable from the night of their first date until Joey returned to Guatemala seven days later. A week after that he came back to Florida and proposed. On June 30, 1984, they were married at Temple Beth El in Boca Raton. The reception for 350 guests from Guatemala and the U.S. was held at the elegant Boca Raton Hotel.

Amy knew from the beginning that Joey's business was in Guatemala, and that they would spend much of their time there. Unable to speak a word of Spanish when they met, she threw herself into learning her new husband's native language and culture. The couple maintained residences in both Guatemala and Palm Beach, Florida, dividing their time between them. Their home in Guatemala City was a sprawling mansion surrounded by high walls; guards armed with assault weapons stood at the gate and patrolled the grounds.

Amy preferred Florida. Not only did she continue to consider it her home, she began to find that Joey treated her differently in Guatemala. When they were living or working in the United States (where most of the major customers for Joey's textile business were located), Joey gave her the same consideration and respect as when they first met. However, in his native country his attitude changed. Although he respected her business ability and the two of them came to run the family textile business jointly out of a shared office, he insisted on controlling all their money and bank accounts, requiring Amy to get his approval for even trivial expenses. Moreover, when they were out with friends or Joey's family, he would correct, criticize, and occasionally ridicule her. When she disagreed with him in public, he would become angry, even if she was defending herself against his barbs.

In 1985 Amy convinced Joey to start a distribution company in the U.S. They named it Liztex USA, and set up offices in New York and Florida. They agreed that Amy and certain Liztex USA employees would own the stock and that Amy would be paid a salary based on earnings. She was an excellent businesswoman, and the new company prospered; for the first time she began to earn money that was hers alone.

A few years into their marriage, Amy believed that Joey was involved with a woman who worked in the family business. Amy's mother-in-law (now in her mid-forties) and women friends sympathized but advised her that this was to be expected of a man in Joey's position. Amy had a hard time accepting this, but for a while she did her best to adapt. She recognized that Joey did come from a different culture; but mostly she was still too much in love to contemplate leaving him.

On November 17, 1989, Amy gave birth to twins Alexandra and Daniel in Boca Raton, Florida. It was a difficult delivery, and Amy was hurt that Joey did not come to join her until after the children were born. The couple's relationship improved briefly after she returned to Guatemala with the twins but soon again began to deteriorate. Their arguments increased in both frequency and intensity, and about a year later Joey hit Amy for the first time. She was outraged—and frightened. She had been troubled by Joey's treatment of his employees and others, but now she felt his temper turned on her. She might have left then, had it not been for the twins and the fact that she was still in love. Although she had discovered a disturbing side of her husband, he was still the most charismatic and powerful man she had ever met. And he was capable of moments of great generosity, tenderness, even vulnerability. Moreover, Amy knew she could not stay in Guatemala if she and Joey separated, and she did not want her children to grow up a thousand miles away from their father.

In January 1991 the two argued about whether Amy needed a new car. She tried to end the shouting by saying she would buy the car with her own money. Instead of resolving the matter, this infuriated Joey who felt that his wife was threatening to use the money that he allowed her to earn to disobey him. Amy, in turn, realized that her husband expected her simply to do what she was told and that she was losing her independence and self-respect.

The marriage went downhill fast. Joey made less and less effort to control his temper, his verbal abuse increased, and he demanded that Amy give him control of the money she was earning. In the summer of 1991 he struck her again (this time because he apparently believed that Amy was herself seeing someone else); and Amy increasingly feared for her physical safety. The final straw came on November 21, 1991, when Joey's armed guards on his orders shot out the tires of the car Amy was driving to stop her from driving to the office after Joey had told her not to. In the emotional aftermath, Joey told her that if she was unhappy living in his house under his rules, she should take the children and leave.

Joey believed with good reason that Amy had no realistic alternative but to submit. He had already given his banks instructions not to honor any checks or transfer requests she initiated. He also believed he had the power to destroy Liztex USA by refusing to ship the products the company distributed. It was not the first or last time he was to underestimate Amy's resolve. Unknown to him, in the months following the quarrel over the new car, she had been setting aside money in anticipation of something like this— enough to get out of Guatemala and support herself and the twins until she could find a new job.

The day after her car was shot at, she took her children and flew to Florida. There followed forty-eight hours of phone calls from Joey and his Guatemalan lawyer, Mario Permuth, in which they tried to cajole and coerce her to return. On November 25, Amy retained Jeff Wasserman, a local attorney in a small firm, to commence an action for divorce. Wasserman got an emergency court order freezing the couple's assets in the United States, including bank accounts held in the name of Joey's wholly owned companies. These accounts contained approximately $30 million. While this was only a fraction of Joey's wealth, it assured that substantial funds would be available to satisfy any final court order concerning alimony, child support, or other issues.

Wasserman's action came just in time. As soon as Joey learned that Amy had left the country, he made plans to move all the couple's assets to Guatemala, where he was confident that his influence with the government would prevent Amy from enforcing any Florida court ruling against him. The court's freeze order was entered, and the banks notified, just one hour before they received Joey's instruction to transfer the funds. When he discovered that he had been preempted, Joey sent his bank a backdated fax purporting to confirm his transfer instructions, adjusting the fax machine's internal clock so that it printed a phony date and time. The bank refused to take part in the fraud, and the doctored fax would come back to haunt him in the litigation that followed.

Although Wasserman was a respected trial lawyer with some experience in divorce cases, he recognized that he needed help to counter the lawyers Joey had retained. As a result, he recommended that Amy retain my friend, James Fox Miller, as co-counsel. Jim is the best matrimonial lawyer in Florida and perhaps the country. For a number of years he had specialized in representing parties in very high net worth divorces, including the CEOs of several Fortune 100 companies (or their spouses). Initially Amy was reluctant to agree to the expense of an additional counsel, but she was ultimately persuaded by Wasserman's advice and by her own interview of Miller.

I first learned of the Habie matter the week after Christmas 1991 when my family and Jim's were in Cancun for our annual December vacation. He told me he was being retained in an unusual divorce case and asked my views about some of the issues. We often discuss each other's cases, and I had no hint at the time that I would ever get involved. Then in late January Jim called me to say that Joey was challenging the jurisdiction of the Florida court on the ground that neither he nor Amy was a resident there.

Because of their dual residences the issue was complicated. Could I, he asked, take Joey's deposition on this question? I told him I could, if my partners at Cravath agreed, which they did.

The deposition, which I took on February 25, 1992, was not difficult. We had accumulated detailed evidence of Amy's residence in Florida, including the home she and Joey owned, tax returns Amy had filed there, the parties' registration of cars and boats in Florida, checking accounts in the state, and magazines and credit card bills sent to their Florida home. In addition Joey, who was not used to having to respond to questions he did not want to answer, lied repeatedly, and badly, under oath. "He has to settle," I told Jim after the deposition, "he can't let a judge read his testimony." Joey was represented by Aaron Podhurst, one of the top lawyers in Miami, and I was confident he would not let Joey go to trial with the record we had made.

The most interesting part of the five-hour deposition was watching Amy and Joey together. Despite the circumstances, she was protective of him. She would frown, and she twice passed me a note when I was sharp with him or confronted him with evidence that he was lying. "You don't have to embarrass him," she wrote once when the only embarrassment stemmed from his increasingly tortuous attempts to avoid admitting a fact that she, he, and I all knew was true. She also brightened whenever he walked into the room. "She's still in love with him," I told Jim.

"No way," he replied. "Not after what he's done and is trying to do to her."

"Jimmy," I quoted, "what you don't know about women is a whole lot."

Joey was also still obviously obsessed with Amy. (Sometime later, when their battle had become even more bitter, he confided to a friend: "What can I say? I still love the bitch.") After the deposition, counsel met in Podhurst's private office to discuss possible settlement. When the lawyers came out, they found Amy and Joey clasped in a decidedly nonplatonic embrace.

A day after I returned to New York, Jim called to say that, as I had predicted, the case had settled. Amy received $5 million out-right and the income from a $3 million child support trust; she also kept the approximately $1 million she had accumulated. Custody was never an issue; both parties agreed that if Amy were to go through with the divorce the children would reside with her in the States during their formative years and Joey would have unlimited visitation rights. It was not as good a financial result as I believed Amy could have achieved in court; given Joey's extensive wealth and his wife's contributions toward building his businesses, she could well have been awarded all the $30 million in seized assets and per-haps much more. However, the settlement guaranteed that Amy would be able to provide comfortably for herself and the children, and it was clear that her priority was peace.

During the divorce proceedings Amy had hired off-duty police officers to guard her and the children, afraid that Joey would try to harm her or seize the twins. Almost immediately after the divorce, Amy relaxed and the guards were released. She and Joey even be-gan dating again in Florida, and they talked about the possibility of her visiting Guatemala. The two went to a marriage counselor (or, if there is such a thing, a post-marriage counselor). Unfortunately, the same issues and attitudes that had broken down the marriage the first time conspired to frustrate their hopes. Joey returned to Guatemala and Amy began to rebuild her life.

A week later on April 11, 1992, Joey flew to Boca Raton in his private jet to see the children. He had asked Amy's permission to take the twins, by now two-and-a-half, to Disney World in Or-lando for several days and she had agreed. On April 13 Joey, Alexandra, and Daniel took off from Fort Lauderdale airport, but the destination was not Orlando. That night Amy received a phone call: "I have the children in Guatemala," Joey told her. "Now get your ass down here and come be a wife and mother."

Amy's first instinct was to take the first flight to Guatemala, an action that Jim Miller successfully counseled her against. We later discovered that had Amy gone there that April, she could have found herself in jail. Joey had filed criminal charges against Amy in

Guatemala for kidnapping based on her having taken the children to the U.S. in November 1991, and he had used his influence with the Guatemalan government to have himself appointed as prosecutor. It was a striking corruption of justice. In the U.S., or any society with pretensions to fairness, even a legitimate prosecutor would be required to step aside in a matter involving the prosecutor's personal life. To permit a private citizen to borrow the state's power to pursue a personal vendetta was shocking even for a country as lacking in fundamental due process as Guatemala was then. The next worse thing to being an enemy of the state in a third-world dictatorship is being an enemy of a friend of the state.

Jimmy reached me on April 15 to tell me what was happening. "Let me know if there's anything I can do to help," I told him. I was later to wonder whether I had spoken too quickly. This kind of problem was far removed from the cases I normally handled. In addition, although Cravath had been paid for my two days of work during the divorce proceeding, I knew that Amy could not pay the fees I normally charged for the work that would be required to battle the legal resources Joey could muster. Ordinarily my *pro bono* work involved representing someone who was indigent, taking on an important unsettled issue of law, or both. Amy was not indigent, and there initially was no obvious legal issue. What led me to offer my help was in part my friendship with Jim (whose small firm would have been overwhelmed by Joey's legions of lawyers) and in part my outrage at what Joey had done.

The kidnapping violated state and federal law as well as a court order entered at the time of the divorce that forbade Joey from taking the children out of the country. As a result we were initially optimistic that things would be worked out quickly. Our hopes were reinforced when Aaron Podhurst told Jim that he would see that Joey returned the children promptly. Joey, however, ignored Podhurst's advice, and Podhurst (a lawyer of unquestioned integrity) refused to participate in the effort to force Amy to give up her rights to her children. Unfortunately, Joey had little trouble hiring other lawyers without Aaron's scruples.

More bad news followed. As part of the divorce settlement the $30 million in frozen funds was to have been released, the $5 million lump sum payment to have been made, and the $3 million child support trust to have been funded. However, while the $30 million had been unfrozen and the $5 million lump sum paid, the $3 million trust had not been funded. Permitting the $30 million to be returned to Joey without having a funded trust in place was a lapse for which Miller, Wasserman, and I were all responsible.

When it became clear that Podhurst's reassurances were ill-founded, Jim filed an emergency motion requiring Joey to return the children immediately and for sanctions against him. Since the abduction violated a court order and was a felony under Florida law, we had expected the court to act swiftly and decisively—particularly since the children had been taken to a foreign country. It was therefore a great surprise when the judge assigned to the case, Gary L. Vonhof of the Palm Beach County Circuit Court, would not even grant a prompt hearing. Even more surprising, when Vonhof did grant one—eight days after the kidnapping—he claimed he had "not yet had an opportunity to take a look" at the applications we had filed and so was not in a position to make a decision. Vonhof did not have an unduly heavy schedule; even if he had, he should have found time to deal with this emergency. The next occasion Judge Vonhof saw us was May 18, over a month after the children had been abducted. Again the hearing ended without the judge ordering that the children be returned.*

---

*At the hearing Leon Margules, one of Joey's new lawyers, argued as possible justification for the kidnapping that the children had been "sexually and physically abused" while in Amy's care. It was a preposterous claim. Moreover, even if true, the allegation would not have justified the kidnapping. The children, after all, had been with Joey at the time and would have been with him for more than a week. The twins had been in no danger, and if there had really been any evidence of abuse, the issue could have been promptly brought to the court before Alexandra and Daniel were even scheduled to return to their mother. Moreover, both Joey's mother and sister owned houses in Florida. Joey could have taken the children there until any issue was resolved. There was no justification for taking the children to Guatemala.

On May 20 the judge finally issued an order directing Joey to return the children. However, he still did not make any finding of contempt or impose any sanction. At a hearing two days later, in an effort to convince the judge to continue delaying the sanctions, Joey's counsel Alvin Entin announced, "I can tell your Honor that we are trying to comply with this court's order to return the children." Entin represented that Mr. Habie went "to the embassy in Guatemala yesterday seeking exit documents for the Habie children" and that "passports cannot be obtained in one day." He argued, "You cannot hold him in contempt because of the fact that he is doing everything possible that he can to comply with this Court's order."

Entin's statement was simply not true, as the next seven years would show. Even if it had been, it did not justify Joey's violation of the court order. Yet still Judge Vonhof continued to delay. Ten weeks after the kidnapping, Vonhof entered an order finding that Joey had acted unlawfully and without any justification. He ordered Joey to return the children immediately, but still did not impose any sanctions. Two years later Joey was to tell me that Vonhof's delay, and his failure to order sanctions, had convinced him that he had little to fear from the U.S. courts. It was not to be the last time that the American justice system would fail Amy, Alexandra, and Daniel.

After Judge Vonhof made his ruling he appointed a lawyer friend of his, Michael Sheinvold, as a "guardian *ad litem*" for the children to investigate and report what was in their best interests. There were three troubling aspects about this. First, guardians are customarily appointed where there is some doubt as to what custody arrangement should be ordered, not when an existing custody order has been clearly violated. Second, guardians are customarily

---

More importantly, as the court would eventually emphasize, there was "*no* evidence" of abuse. Most judges would have sanctioned a party, or a party's lawyer, who made such baseless charges. Although Vonhof did not seem impressed by the allegations, neither was he inclined to discipline Joey or Margules for making them.

appointed from a list of trained personnel; Sheinvold had no significant experience in such matters. Third, Vonhof directed that Joey pay the guardian's fees and put no limit on what those fees should be.

The order appointing the guardian provided for him to perform his work after the children were returned to the U.S., but following consultation with Joey and his lawyers Sheinvold began while the children remained in Guatemala. Also with Joey's approval, Sheinvold added his brother (a psychologist in Pennsylvania) to the payroll, and the two men were ultimately paid more than $300,000 by Joey—all while the children remained in Guatemala. Joey paid Sheinvold more both in total and on an hourly basis than he had received from any client in his entire career.

Eventually, Vonhof's continued lack of action, and the discovery that he was engaged in *ex parte* communications with Sheinvold (conversations that took place without our knowledge or ability to be present), convinced us that we had to have the judge removed.*

Vonhof's replacement, Judge John L. Phillips, appeared totally

---

*Amy had wanted to move to recuse Vonhof earlier when she was told that the judge himself had been through a divorce and custody dispute. Her concern escalated when the judge delayed action, then appointed as a guardian a friend who was also a divorced father. At the time Jim Miller and I convinced her not to take action. In retrospect it was a mistake.

However, I am always reluctant to make such a move. First, most judges make a genuine effort to decide cases without regard to their personal biases. Second, even when a judge appears to be acting improperly, as a group they are notoriously protective of each other, and a new judge will often begin with a strong predisposition against the party who has had the temerity to accuse his or her colleague of bias. Third, if the recusal fails, the judge may make it his or her personal mission to exact revenge. All in all, recusal motions are a last resort.

Eventually Judge Vonhof's *ex parte* communications with Sheinvold, who by then appeared increasingly influenced by the payments he and his brother were receiving, left us with no alternative. By then, however, much damage had been done.

unaffected by our recusal of his colleague, perhaps in part because the Florida Court of Appeals had already commented on the "peculiar circumstances" surrounding Vonhof's guardian appointment and noted that the actions of Vonhof and the guardian were "questionable events which may give rise to reversible error." Judge Philips proceeded to hold prompt hearings, issued an order requiring Joey to return the children to the U.S. at once, and imposed substantial fines for every week he delayed. He also discharged the guardian, finding that his actions appeared to corrupt his office.

By then, however, Joey had already embarked on a legal campaign to pressure Amy into abandoning her efforts to reclaim her children. That campaign would ultimately entail more than a dozen separate legal claims against Amy, her mother, and her lawyers in both federal and state courts in New York and Florida. The basic thrust was to accuse Amy and her mother of "stealing" money from the companies the Habies had run. Throughout their marriage Joey and Amy paid themselves from company accounts whatever amounts they needed to support their lavish lifestyles. Since the companies were owned by Joey, and since he had approved all payments, there was no basis for complaint. However, in order to construct a lawsuit, Joey created the fiction that the companies were really owned by his mother, and that the money had been taken without her permission. No matter that what Amy was accused of taking was in large part used to pay for household expenses, fuel for Joey's jet, and other joint costs, or that Sara Habie was not the real owner. Joey produced employees prepared to swear under oath that his mother was the owner of the companies and even fabricated documents to support his claim. He also asserted that Amy had acted illegally in 1991 when she set cash aside that she ultimately used to fund her escape, even though the money was clearly owed to her as part of her Liztex USA earnings.

The many lawsuits that he filed against his former wife posed two major threats. First, there was the risk that she might lose one of them. Even though the contention that Joey's mother was the owner of the companies was a lie, proving the ownership of a Guatemalan bearer-stock corporation was not easy.* Second, even if Amy ultimately won each of the lawsuits, the legal fees required would exhaust her assets. Joey, in fact, made clear that this was his intent.

When I agreed to help Jim Miller recover Amy's kidnapped children, I had not foreseen the time and money that that effort would require. Defending Amy from Joey's lawsuits while at the same time seeking sanctions against him required hundreds of hours of my time (as well as that of several other lawyers) for several years. Over those years, my representation of Amy Habie would worry my family, strain my relationships with my partners at Cravath, burden my new firm, and subject me to a variety of personal and professional threats. If I had known at the beginning what I knew at the end, I might well have told Jim that I could not help. I became a lawyer wanting to do justice, but I had long since learned that there was a limit to how much justice many clients could afford to buy or that I could afford to contribute. There were many other worthy causes that could have profited from the time and money we devoted to the Habie litigation. On the other hand, few causes are more important than preventing the legal system from being used by the rich and powerful to subvert rather than deliver justice. And perhaps I would have taken on Amy's cause and Joey's challenge even with full knowledge of what lay ahead.

But the question was academic. I had agreed to represent Amy, and that was not a commitment I could walk away from merely

---

*A bearer-stock corporation is one owned by whoever holds the stock certificates. Corporations in the U.S. and most industrialized countries register the owners of their shares. However, in many third-world countries and first-world tax havens, bearer-stock corporations are used to conceal ownership.

because the going got tougher than I had expected. A lawyer has a choice of what clients to take on. However, except when a client fails to fulfill its own obligations, a lawyer does not have the choice of abandoning a client in the middle of a case. Three years after the kidnapping, with no end in sight and with Sam Butler increasingly restive about the time I was devoting to the litigation, Mary asked me, "What if the firm simply tells you, you have to stop representing Amy?"

"The firm won't do that," I assured her.

"But what if they do?"

"They won't, but if they did I couldn't agree. They could have told me no in 1992. Part of being with a firm is giving up the right to decide unilaterally what cases to accept. But once I take a case, I'm stuck with it."

Mary claims she does not roll her eyes. But occasionally she does.

In their effort to find some judge somewhere who would take their claims seriously, Joey's lawyers brought cases before two different state judges in Florida, two Florida federal judges, and a federal judge in New York. In some cases his lawyers sued Amy's mother as well as Amy. On one occasion Joey's lawyers sued Jim Miller and myself for our role in keeping the Habies' U.S. assets frozen during the divorce proceeding. The claim was brought in the name of a Panamanian company named PTS Trading Company.

Depending as it does on the quality of judge one draws, justice is much more unpredictable than we like to pretend. Florida state court judges vary widely in intelligence, ability, fairness, and judicial temperament. In the *PTS* case we were lucky to get Judge Robert M. Gross of the Palm Beach County Circuit Court. Gross was at the time one of the best trial judges in Florida, and has since been elevated to the court of appeals. After giving Joey's lawyer more discovery than we thought necessary, he granted our motion and dismissed the case. Joey and his lawyers appealed, but the

Florida Court of Appeals affirmed and rebuked both Joey and his lawyers for their abuse of the legal system.*

In addition to his efforts to use civil lawsuits to put pressure on Amy, Joey engaged in three other tactics. He hired lawyers willing to argue to U.S. criminal prosecutors that Amy had "stolen" money from his mother's companies. These claims were rejected; but again Amy faced the cost of having to defend herself. Joey, with his lawyer's assistance, also mailed vicious "newsletters" to thousands of residents of Palm Beach County, where Amy lived and worked, accusing her of everything from drug use to attempted murder. The mailings stopped only when we subpoenaed and threatened to sue both the printer and the lawyers who helped pay him.

In some ways the most extraordinary effort Joey made to coerce Amy into submission was to have the Guatemalan government indict her for "kidnapping" for taking the children to Florida in November 1991. The fact that she had had his explicit permission, that the Florida court had awarded her custody, and that Joey himself had expressly agreed that Amy should be the primary custodial parent did not deter him. No claim was too outrageous for Joey to make, no action too irresponsible for his Guatemalan government retainers to take on his behalf. Guatemala had made little progress

---

*The court noted that Joey had "kidnapped the children from their home in Florida and took them to Guatemala" in violation of state and federal law as well as his own agreement, and that "he has had corporations which he controlled . . . wrongfully maintain . . . lawsuits against Mrs. Habie." The court held:

"There is only one conclusion which can be drawn from this case, and that is that Mr. Habie intends to use his financial resources in order to punish not only his former wife, but her lawyers as well, and to discourage counsel from taking on the representation which his former wife will surely need in the future."

The court went on to award us attorney's fees "because there was a complete absence of (1) a justifiable issue of either law or fact raised by this complaint, and (2) good faith, based on the client's representation."

Unfortunately, few appellate courts were willing to be as tough on frivolous claims, and few trial courts prepared to move as expeditiously as Judge Gross. We were also disappointed that the Florida Bar failed to take any action to discipline Joey's attorneys despite the court's pointed suggestions that it do so.

toward the rule of law in the decades preceding 1996. Violence remained pervasive. Government-aided death squads continued to operate, and government officials continued to do the bidding of the nation's oligarchs. The Clinton administration was making efforts to reduce human rights violations in the country, as elsewhere in Latin America, but the limits on those efforts would soon become apparent.

When Jim, Amy, and I first discovered that Joey had gotten his government to indict her (and to have himself appointed to prosecute her), our outrage was tempered somewhat by the dark humor of the situation. The indictment, of course, prevented Amy from visiting her children in Guatemala, but there would have been no real chance of her entering the armed compound where they were held even had she been able to go. The indictment was certainly outrageous and a troubling illustration of Joey's power in his country, but it seemed not to threaten Amy in the U.S. Our lack of concern turned out to be a conceit that almost resulted in disaster.

In June 1994 I was in my New York office when my long-time assistant Linda Carlsen told me I had a call from someone who worked in the U.S. Attorney's office in Florida who did not want to give a name.

"I am calling about Amy Habie," the caller began, "the woman whose children were kidnapped by their father and taken to Guatemala. Are you still representing her?"

I said that I was, and waited to see what came next. Particularly in uncertain situations, silence is often a dual opportunity—to learn something if you keep quiet for a moment, and to avoid making a mistake by speaking too quickly. "Are you still also representing the FDIC?" the caller asked. I said that my case on behalf of the Federal Deposit Insurance Corporation against Drexel Burnham and Michael Milken had been completed.

"You certainly did a great job for the government and taxpayers. Everyone in the office admired your work."

"Thank you" was the most noncommittal thing I could think to say.

"I was still in law school when you tried the *Westmoreland v. CBS* libel case," the anonymous voice continued.

"It seems like it was longer ago than it has been," I temporized as I tried to figure out where the caller was going. I had not been given a name, and there wasn't an easy way to ask for one.

"How is the mother holding up?"

"It's very hard on her, but she's not going to give up trying to see her children," I said. "Unfortunately our legal system gives her former husband a lot of opportunities to harass her, and he is safely in Guatemala, where he feels he is above the law."

"You don't know the half of it," the caller went on.

"What do you mean?"

"I probably shouldn't be calling you at all, but it's not like it's classified information." The pause that followed was only a few seconds, but it seemed much longer. I was afraid to say anything for fear of spooking a caller who was already obviously ambivalent about contacting me. I was also afraid that, if the silence lasted too long, that also might scare the caller away. Finally, the voice continued.

"You know that the kidnapper has accused your client of being a kidnapper herself?"

"Yes," I said, laughing. "Fortunately or unfortunately, that's the least of our problems."

"You don't know," the caller said slowly in a lowered voice. "You don't have any idea."

Maybe a couple dozen times in my life I've actually felt my skin tingle with apprehension. The first time was in 1962 when I realized that I was about to be in a knife fight with someone who actually wanted to kill me. Another time was a phone call sixteen years later when I was told that my oldest son, David, was in the hospital, the victim of a gang attack. A third occasion was the afternoon my daughter Mary was to be born when the doctor after fourteen hours of labor suddenly said, "There appears to be a problem with the baby's heart. I want to do a Cesarean immediately." All of those occasions, and other less significant incidents, turned out well. But I remember the alertness that sudden concern brings, and I had a similar feeling now.

"I probably shouldn't be talking about this," the caller repeated. "But you need to know. The State Department has begun to process a request from the Guatemalan government to extradite your client, and it's serious enough for our office to have been contacted. The FBI has been asked to monitor your client's whereabouts so that she can be picked up if the decision is made to proceed."

"That's not possible" was my first reaction, but even as I said it I knew that it was—and something about the caller made me believe everything I was being told.

"Is there anything more you can tell me?" I asked.

"No."

"Is there any way for me to contact you?"

"No, I've already said enough."

After a moment I said, "Thank you. Thank you very, very much."

The last thing the voice said was "Good luck." I never learned the caller's name.

Jim Miller and I immediately began to try to find out whether this new information was accurate. After numerous phone calls and meetings with State Department representatives, FBI agents, and U.S. Attorney personnel, we found the phone call to be depressingly on target. Guatemala had asked the U.S. to extradite Amy for kidnapping. We were told that the President of Guatemala had personally raised the issue on a state visit to Washington, and that the State Department was treating the application seriously.

I was outraged. It was bad enough that the State Department had done little to protect the interests of three American citizens and that no political or other pressure had been put on a country continuing to benefit from America's economic and military support to return two kidnapped American children to the United States. Now to be told that the State Department was considering deporting one of its own citizens to face the corrupt justice of Guatemala to curry favor with a regime we should not have been supporting in the first place, was almost more than I could comprehend.

I felt certain that the Secretary of State, Warren Christopher, could not be aware of what was going on. Chris was an old friend and professional colleague, as well as a fellow alumnus of the University of Redlands. We had worked together in the past, including representing IBM. He was a thoughtful, careful lawyer whose long career in court and in government epitomized integrity. I trusted him to do the right thing for the right reason, but I was equally certain that, if I were wrong in my judgment as to how he might balance justice in an individual case against the needs of international diplomacy, neither he nor the Clinton administration would be prepared to take the political heat that a public airing of this issue would create. Amy had been determined to avoid publicity. She did not want to put her children in the spotlight, and she knew it might make any reconciliation more difficult. She had not replied in kind even in the face of Joey's mailings. However, we would do whatever was necessary to stop her deportation to a Guatemalan jail.

I began by sending a detailed letter to Warren Christopher. I felt certain what he would do, but the issue was too critical to rely on my opinion of any individual; I also made appointments to brief congressmen and senators from Florida, New York, and elsewhere about the situation. Soon after my letter, a meeting was arranged where Amy, my partner Phil Korologos, and I met with State Department representatives in Washington, D.C. We were unable to get anyone from the department to address the question of how the request could ever have been treated seriously, but we did receive the assurance that was our primary concern: no attempt would be made to extradite Amy.

We left the meeting relieved but troubled. "What," Amy asked, "would have happened if someone hadn't warned you of what was under way? Or if I didn't have a lawyer who knew the Secretary of State and who could get appointments with members of Congress?" I said to her that in the end our government would probably have done the right thing even without the warning and our resulting efforts, but I had then, and have now, enough doubt to make me worry.

★　★　★

BY 1997 WE HAD SUCCEEDED IN TURNING BACK ALL OF JOEY'S efforts. Each of the cases brought against Amy and her mother had been dismissed, and Joey and his companies had been ordered to pay millions of dollars in damages and sanctions. We had also succeeded in obtaining funding for the $3 million trust that Joey had agreed to establish as part of the divorce settlement. The money was held by Aaron Podhurst's firm, which was prepared to turn it over if authorized to do so by a court. Unfortunately by the time this issue was to be decided, the case had been transferred again, this time from Judge Philips to Judge Kathleen J. Kroll, a friend of Judge Vonhof, who lacked Judge Philips's attention to our case. Once more we were delayed in obtaining hearings and decisions. Ultimately Kroll issued the necessary order to fund the trust, but her long delay gave further encouragement to Joey to believe he had little to fear from American judges.

Despite our successes in court, we still had not succeeded in achieving our primary goal of securing the return of the children. Following the kidnapping, felony warrants were issued for Joey's arrest. However, Joey stopped traveling to the U.S. and his influence with the Guatemalan government prevented his extradition. He also removed his assets from the U.S. to prevent enforcement of the damage awards.

In an attempt to create some support for his claims in a case before New York federal judge Sonia Sotomayor, Joey had resorted to forging and backdating a number of documents. Amy at once recognized from their contents that the records had to have been made up after the fact. But how to prove it? Our first evidence was a sequence of pages, all purporting to deal with transactions in a three-month period. Two of these were dated four years later than the others. Either the later documents (which were dated the year they were submitted to the court) had been erroneously given a future date or all the other documents had been backdated. It sometimes happens that a person will write last year's date in error, or even an earlier year; but it would be extraordinary to write a future year by mistake. We thought the implication was clear: the person fabricating these documents in 1995 had mistakenly written "1995" on a couple of them instead of the backdated year that they had planned to use. Nevertheless, we felt we needed more definite proof.

The American legal system generally does not deal effectively with litigants who are prepared to lie and fabricate documents. Lawyers are reluctant to believe that their client is actually lying and are generally prepared to present to a court whatever "evidence" their client gives them. Judges, often facing busy schedules and almost always loath to believe that litigants and their lawyers will lie and fabricate evidence, are equally reluctant to act; when one side makes a charge of extreme misconduct and the other hotly denies it, courts have a hard time concluding that a party has simply made things up. As a result, many courts do not like to hear charges of serious misconduct and tend to believe that such charges are more likely false and interposed for tactical reasons. Charges of misconduct that cannot be clearly proven can end up hurting the litigant making them, even if they are true.

The documents submitted to the court were photocopies; to test their authenticity we needed the originals. Joey's lawyers fought a pitched battle to convince the court not to allow this. Ultimately, Judge Sotomayor ordered their production, and the second phase of our analysis began. We tried to hire an expert to examine the ink used to see whether it was of a kind in use at the time the documents were dated. We discovered that the three leading private experts had all been retained by Joey or one of his companies soon after we had made our motion for the production of the original documents. We asked the court to require Joey to release at least one of the experts, but the court refused to do so. We then hired an expert who examined the documents with infrared light and other techniques that revealed changes to the surface of the paper not visible to the naked eye. He found that the documents had been subjected to high temperatures, which produced an aging effect. His examination also revealed lines caused when a document is written on while another document is underneath it, thus indenting the paper on the bottom. As a result we were able to show that certain papers were prepared after documents that purported to be dated later.*

It was clear from comments made by the judge that she was now considering serious sanctions. These would be against Joey's lawyers, who, unlike Joey, were present in the U.S. so the sanctions could be enforced. Shortly after our arguments had been submitted, I received a call from Guatemala. The proposal was simple. If we would drop our motion for sanctions, Joey would agree to withdraw the fabricated documents and to permit Amy to visit her children on a weekend of our choice.

The first part of the offer gave us nothing that we were not already certain to achieve; with or without Joey's agreement, the fabricated documents were history. In addition, we were virtually certain to be awarded sanctions, which would provide both a financial benefit and punish conduct that decidedly deserved to be punished. On the other hand, the offer was the only practical way Amy, who had not seen her children in more than three years, would be able to do so in the foreseeable future. In the previous year Joey had largely prevented Amy from even speaking to them by telephone. Not only was she desperate to see them, but she feared that if she did not reestablish contact soon their memory of her would fade. Although it frustrated all of us to allow Joey yet again to get

---

*We also eventually hired someone who purported to be an ink expert, and he concluded that the ink used in writing the documents was not available the year the documents were dated. However, serious doubts about the expert's reliability raised during discovery ultimately led us not to rely on his findings.

Even without ink-dating evidence, the proof we had of document falsification was overwhelming.

away with an abuse of the legal system, it was not a close decision. Money and retribution meant little compared to the chance for Amy to be reunited with her children, if only temporarily.

We agreed to Joey's proposal and began making preparations for the trip. Our primary concern was that Guatemala was such a violent place Joey could have her harmed without leaving any clear proof he was responsible; ultimately, however, we concluded that the risk was worth taking. There was no doubt that Joey was capable of violence. A year earlier he had sent us pictures of a battered and bleeding former employee of Amy's Liztex USA business after Joey had personally beaten the older man. However, killing or kidnapping an American citizen on her way to visit her abducted children might awaken even the somnolent American State Department, and that possibility might discourage Joey and his henchmen. Moreover, he loved his children and knew that if anything happened to Amy in Guatemala they would eventually come to know that he had been responsible, and that knowledge would drive a permanent wedge between them. Over the years I had also come to believe that Joey had good qualities as well as bad and that there were limits to what he would do even if he could get away with it.*

Two years earlier I had tested that belief. Over Mary's objections and the concern of my children I had flown to Guatemala City to take a court-ordered deposition of Joey at the Camino Real Hotel. The deposition was tense, as might be expected. At the end of the first of two days I asked him to deliver cards and small presents for the children that Amy had given me. I did not have any real expectation that he would agree, or if he did that the gifts would actually reach the children. (A courier service had once written to Amy that her packages addressed to the children had been refused by Joey, who claimed that the children no longer lived in Guatemala.) Joey's response caught me off guard. "If you

---

*It is always a chancy thing to conclude that someone is bad but not *that* bad; and for that reason I would not have wanted to rely on my instinct in the absence of other factors.

would like to join me at my house for dinner, you can give them to them yourself," he said with a smile.

He could have asked me that question five times and gotten five different responses. As it was, my immediate reply was: "Can you give me a ride?"

"It's the only way you'll get there."

To the court reporter who was still in the room listening to us with open mouth, I said, "Please let my office know where I'll be if there is an emergency, but ask them not to tell anyone else." I could just imagine the response had my family found out where I was going, but I wanted my office on alert just in case.

Joey drove me himself in his black, armor-plated Chevrolet Suburban, with me in the passenger seat and two guards armed with assault rifles positioned behind us. Joey's residence was a 22,000 square-foot house surrounded by seven acres of grounds and encircled by a twenty-foot-high wall. Armed guards stood at the entrance. When we arrived, the gate, as high and solid as the wall itself, rolled to the left to reveal half a dozen more guards standing by.

Joey was a gracious host, showing me around the house that he and Amy had built. Although he was recently remarried to a woman from Argentina, his conversation was punctuated with references to Amy. Pointing out an overgrown tennis court that had obviously not been used in years: "I had this built for Amy. She loved to play tennis. Does she still?" Noticing my interest in a rifle on top of a television in his bedroom: "Amy never liked me to have guns visible in the house, especially after the children were born. But the children need to learn sometime." With respect to particular furnishings: "Amy ordered this from a decorator in Florida. I never gave her a budget. I trusted her completely."

When Joey, his new wife, Marianna, the twins, and I sat down to dinner, I found Joey's tastes mirrored my own—simple food, few sauces. "If I had known you were coming, I would have ordered diet root beer," he joked, reminding me how much he knew about me. I spent most of the meal talking with the children, occasionally answering a question from Joey or Marianna, or asking one myself. There were no guards present (or at least visible) and the evening was almost relaxed.

By far the best part was seeing the twins, who were six years old at the time. Once they got over their initial shyness, Daniel and Alexandra were active, happy children. Although clearly more fluent in Spanish, they spoke English whenever I was present, except to ask their father how to say something in English. When they were told I was their mother's lawyer, they attached themselves to me for the evening. They asked me many questions about myself and the United States and spoke easily of their mother in front of Joey. However, I noticed that they only asked directly about their mother when Marianna was out of the room. A quiet, attractive woman about the same age as Amy, Marianna treated Joey with practiced deference. It was clear that he had found a second wife who, unlike his first, would not dispute his authority. She was not a weak woman; her obedience came from a sense of her role and place.

Both children were absorbed in the cards and presents. Daniel in particular studied Amy's card for a long time. When he showed me his room, he put the card in the second drawer of his dresser, underneath what was already there.

The fact that Joey clearly loved the twins, and they him, tempered the harsh feelings that his conduct had built up. I was also encouraged by the love the children had for a mother whom they had not seen in nearly four years. However, I also noted the way Marianna's mouth tightened whenever Amy's name was mentioned, and the extent to which the children's openness evaporated when she was present.

The next day I completed my deposition and returned home.

Although Amy's sister Susie had agreed to accompany Amy to Guatemala, I believed that I should go too. In the event that Amy was confronted with any demand, it would be important to have someone on hand to advise her. Also, the more American citizens affected by any action Joey might take (particularly if someone with my visibility was involved), the greater the threat to Joey that the American government might intervene with its Guatemalan client-state—a threat that might discourage Joey from acting at all.*

My decision to accompany Amy was not greeted with enthusiasm by Mary or my older children, but they were as supportive as their concern for my safety would permit. Amy, Susie, and I flew to Guatemala from Miami in February 1996. It was a beautiful day both in Miami and in Guatemala. It was not, it turned out, a good omen.

Throughout the plane ride, Amy could barely contain her excitement. When we passed through customs, I noticed her looking around in the hope that the children might have been brought to greet her. We took a taxi to the Camino Real Hotel, where we checked in—Amy and her sister into a room under Susie's name. There was a message waiting for me to call Mario Permuth, Joey's Guatemalan lawyer. Permuth was a smooth character with sufficient connections to travel to the U.S. on a diplomatic passport. He was not in his office so I left a message for him to call me back. It was approximately two p.m. when he rang. After exchanging pleasantries, I said, "Amy is, of course, anxious to see her children. When will they be arriving?"

"Why don't you and Amy come meet us at the Jewish Community Center at around four this afternoon?" Permuth replied.

"This was not what we agreed," I complained. Being in Guatemala was bad enough, but at least at the Camino Real we were in a public place with many witnesses, including visitors from the U.S. and Europe. I knew the Jewish Community Center. Located in a residential section of Guatemala City, it was a virtual fortress, surrounded by thick walls; the only ways in or out were a reinforced steel door for pedestrians and a solid ten-foot-high steel gate. Next to the center, also behind the walls, was a synagogue. Because of the walls, neither the center nor the synagogue was visible from the

---

*There was, of course, still the issue of the Guatemalan criminal charge against her. However, I was convinced no action would be taken to arrest her unless Joey wanted her arrested.

street, and many residents of the city were unaware they were there. I had discovered from previous visits to Guatemala that Joey and his guards had the run of the place. Once inside, Amy would be entirely at Joey's mercy without any witnesses (or at least any not under Joey's control).

While I continued to believe that Joey would not harm Amy, there were limits to the risks she should take. Equally important, even if nothing bad actually happened, the palpable threat would make it impossible for her to relax with her children and might cause her to break down. I was also conscious of the fact that the last time Amy was in Guatemala, the same guards that were with Joey now had shot out the tires of her car with her in it.

"Why can't the children be brought to the hotel?" I asked.

"Joey wants to talk to Amy before she sees the children. He thinks if he and Amy meet alone, they can work things out."

"Are the children at the center now?"

Permuth paused before replying. "Not at the moment, but they can be brought there as soon as Amy and Joey finish talking."

There was nothing that could not be discussed, more comfortably and safely, at the hotel. Moreover, the purpose of the visit was to let Amy see her children. Nothing was likely to be accomplished until that happened. I was pretty sure that Amy would never go to the center if the children were not there. Even had she wanted to, I was not certain I would let her. But I decided against telling any of this to Permuth. If Joey intended to harm or seize Amy, I didn't want to give him the opportunity to make alternative plans—including, possibly, to have her picked up or arrested at the hotel.

"This is not what we agreed," I repeated, "but if you are determined I will see you at the center at four."

Amy and Susie were downstairs in the hotel lobby waiting for the children to arrive. Before going to give them the bad news, I called my office. Prior to leaving New York I had arranged a variety of contingency plans, one of which involved leaving the country unexpectedly. Concerned that the phones in the hotel might be tapped, we had agreed on a simple code. If I called and said we might stay in Guatemala a little longer than planned, my office was to make reservations for the three of us to leave on the next plane out. From my airline guide, which I had brought for just such an occasion, I knew that we had already missed the last flight to the U.S. for that day but that there was a plane to Costa Rica later that afternoon.

"This may take a day or two longer than we planned," I told my office. "Make us some backup reservations. And check to see whether it would be easy to come back through Costa Rica. I've never been there, and since I'm this close maybe I'll take advantage of the opportunity."

When I told Amy the news, she sagged as if she had had the wind knocked out of her. After a minute she said softly, "I was afraid I couldn't trust Joey. This has all been a plot to get me in a position where he can pressure me into signing away my rights to the children." Such an agreement if signed under duress would not be enforceable. However, proving duress might be complicated. Moreover, Joey could use such a document to try to convince the children that their mother had abandoned them.

"I'm not going to that place," Amy told me.

"Of course not," I replied.

Amy and Susie could easily make the plane to Costa Rica. "Go to the airport, check in, and go to the gate," I told them. "Board the plane as soon as you can, and if you're asked to get off for any reason, make a scene that everyone will remember. Use a pay phone at the airport to confirm to my office that you're boarding and that the flight is on time. If everything goes smoothly, ask my office to tell me that my schedule has not changed when I call from the center."

Without checking out of their room, Amy and Susie took a cab to a prominent shopping area, and another cab from there to the airport. I stayed behind. I wanted to see whether Joey and Permuth had anything useful to say. More important, by occupying them until Amy and her sister were safely on their way I would lessen whatever chance there might be that they would go looking for Amy before she had escaped. I arrived at the center shortly after four p.m. From the outside the compound looked like the fortress it was, with no visible indication that behind its walls was a house of worship. I knocked on the metal door, which opened to reveal two thugs with assault rifles.

"Funny, you don't look Jewish" I said with a nervous attempt at humor entirely lost on my hosts. In response to my subsequent "*Señor Habie, por favor*," they motioned for me to follow them into the guardhouse that abutted the sidewalk. We passed through a metal detector that they set off but I did not, then proceeded past the synagogue and into the Jewish Community Center, where Joey and Mario Permuth were waiting.

Almost immediately they asked, "Where is Amy?"

I explained truthfully but incompletely that we wanted to understand what was on their minds before she met with them. As we talked, it became clear that the answer was nothing new. Their argument was that Joey was untouchable in his own country, that the American courts were a joke, and that the only way Amy would be able to see her children was to visit them in Guatemala. If she would only agree to give Joey custody, help get the U.S. criminal charges against him dismissed, and repay some of the money she had left from the divorce settlement, he would arrange to have the criminal charges against her dismissed and allow her to visit the children in Guatemala. In response to my obvious points that Amy could not spend enough time in Guatemala to sustain a normal relationship with her children, that the children (native-born American citizens, like their mother) deserved to be able to spend time in the U.S. during their formative years, and that I could not recommend that Amy give up the money that remained, Joey would stare and Permuth would shrug.

After about ninety minutes I called my office in New York— to remind my hosts that people knew where I was and to confirm that Amy and Susie were on their way to Costa Rica. Half an hour later I told Joey and Permuth that it was clear that we were not going to make any progress and that I needed to get back to my hotel for a seven p.m. conference call. When Joey said he still wanted to speak with Amy privately before she saw the children, I told him that I had explained his position to her, that Amy was not prepared to meet him prior to seeing the children, and that consequently she was returning to the U.S. Both Joey and Permuth were visibly taken aback.

"When is she planning to leave?" Permuth asked.

"She may have already left," I replied as naturally as I could. Neither man seemed to know how to react. When I asked if someone could take me to my hotel, Permuth offered his car. As we drove back to the Camino Real, he asked me what I expected to happen next.

I told him that we would explain to the court what had happened and that I assumed we would then proceed to litigate the sanctions motion that we had given up for the visit that never happened. Beginning to recognize the consequences for Joey's American lawyers, Permuth (who had become affiliated with Joey's Miami law firm and who was personally being sued by Amy) changed his tune. It had been a "mistake" for Amy to leave. There had been a "misunderstanding"; he had not meant to imply that Amy *had* to speak with Joey before seeing the children, or that the children could *only* be seen at the Jewish Community Center, but just that that was what he and Joey "recommended."

"If it was a misunderstanding, it was certainly an unfortunate one," I told him. "But both you and Joey seemed quite clear." As he drew up at the hotel, he invited me to join him for dinner, and I accepted. Each hoped to learn something from the other in a more relaxed atmosphere. Each of us was disappointed.

I returned to New York the following day to find a series of increasingly desperate messages from Joey's lawyers. If we would pick a weekend, Joey would pay all our expenses to return to Guatemala, and they would guarantee that everything would go smoothly this time. I told them that I wanted both them and Permuth to give those assurances to me and to Judge Sotomayor.

They readily agreed. On a conference call, Sotomayor made it clear that she expected Joey's promises to be kept this time. On April 13, 1996, four years to the day after Amy's children had been taken, I again accompanied my client to Guatemala.

This time everything did go smoothly. When Daniel and Alexandra came to meet Amy, she was momentarily overcome. Quickly recovering when she saw the look of concern in their eyes, she began what she told me that night was one of the three happiest days of her life. (The other two were the day her children were born and, ironically, the day she married Joey.) The twins were much closer to her, and much more natural with her, than I had expected given their relatively young age at the time of the kidnapping and the years that had gone by. Initially they were more guarded when Joey was present; however, as they saw their parents acting in a friendly way with each other, and when they saw that Joey did not disapprove when they showed affection for their mother, they became relaxed even in his presence. When it was time to say good-bye at the end of the first day, Daniel hugged his mother and said, "I love you, Mommy. Can I see you tomorrow?" Assured that he would, he scampered off to the SUV where Joey waited for him. Alexandra was more subdued. "Good-bye, Amy," she said. "Thank-you for the presents." I could tell that being addressed by her first name bothered Amy, and as I walked Alex slowly to Joey's vehicle, I told her gently that in the U.S. young children do not usually address their parents by their first names. "I'm supposed to," she replied. "Did your father tell you that?" She shook her head. "Did Mariana?" After hesitating for a moment, she slowly nodded.

The second day both Amy and her children were conscious that in twenty-four hours Amy would return to the U.S., and that consciousness created a palpable tension. It was nevertheless a good day, and seeing Amy, Alex, and Danny together made me determined to find a way to break the impasse that separated them. Joey's apparent decency, and even occasional kindness, led me to hope that something could be worked out. And for several months Joey permitted Amy to resume telephone contact and allowed visits to the children by Amy's mother and sister.

However, in 1997 Joey reasserted his original demands on a take-it-or-leave-it basis, cut off visits and began to limit phone calls to pressure Amy to agree. By the fall of 1997 matters had returned from bad to worse. On October 16, I returned home to find several increasingly distraught messages from Amy on our answering machine. When I finally returned her call, she was in tears. The night before she had been trying to phone her children when Joey picked up the line. He told her that her calls were upsetting the children and that he was going to cut them off entirely.

Jim Miller believes that Joey's ostensible softening was never more than a ploy—to bail him and his lawyers out when they were caught fabricating evidence, and as part of his psychological warfare against Amy. As Jim saw it, Amy's brief contact with her children would only make the pain of separation more unbearable—which was exactly what happened. Amy's suffering when she was again cut off from her children sent her into a depression that would have destroyed someone with less strength. Jim's position was also supported by something Joey said to me two years later.

"I thought," he told me, "that if she saw how wonderful the children were, she would agree to our proposals so that she could talk to them on the phone and visit them in Guatemala." I pointed out that if Amy had agreed, she would have been entirely at his mercy over future contacts with her children. His response was both natural and chilling.

"As long as she behaves herself, I would have no reason to cut her off. But she has to learn that she can't have her own way. She has no power. That is the fact. She simply refuses to recognize it."

Another possible explanation for Joey's hardening was Mariana's growing influence. Both Mario Permuth and Mel Schwartz (a Florida lawyer who represented Joey's mother) warned me that

Mariana saw Amy as a threat to her relationships with both Joey and with the children.*

Another development that may have encouraged Joey to take a harder line was that he had found an ally in Florida. In March of 1996 Amy purchased a Palm Beach lawn care and landscape business from its owner, Scott Lewis, for $800,000. Scott Lewis signed a five-year noncompete agreement and for several months stayed on as a consultant. That fall, however, Lewis left Amy's employ and began to compete with her, signing up most of the customers he had serviced before selling the business.†

What caused Lewis to do what he did was not certain. He claimed that because Amy had not paid certain disputed consultancy fees she had "defaulted" and that he was therefore relieved of his noncompete obligation. There was some speculation that Joey had put him up to it, but both Joey and Lewis denied this. Amy believed that Scott was angry because she had spurned his romantic advances. (Lewis first denied under oath that he ever had, or tried to have, a personal relationship with Amy; later he asserted and repeated under oath that he had slept with Amy. Amy was outraged by the latter claim. "I wouldn't worry," Jim Miller tried to reassure her. "Any way you look at it, it's clear he lied under oath. No one who matters is going to pay any attention to what he says.") Whatever the cause, litigation ensued and at least by 1997 Mel Schwartz, the Habie family's lawyer in Palm Beach, was in contact with Lewis's lawyers, and Joey and Lewis were talking

---

*Later, parents of the children's classmates in Guatemala who knew Amy from her time in Guatemala would call her to tell her of critical and unpleasant remarks about Amy that Alexandra had heard Mariana make (and which, as children so often do, Alex repeated to classmates). Later still, we discovered that Mariana had called these parents to yell at them for talking to Amy. A trained psychologist, Mariana had the intelligence, skills, and tenacity to do great damage.

†Since the hard assets that Amy had purchased were worth well under $200,000 and most of the value of the business she had purchased were the customer contracts and relationships, Lewis's actions threatened to deprive her of what she had paid for.

directly.* How much the prospect of Lewis opening up a second front against Amy played in hardening Joey's position I do not know; but by the end of 1997, the impasse was as great as ever.

★   ★   ★

IN SEARCHING FOR A WAY TO BRING JOEY BACK TO THE BAR-gaining table, the only avenue that we had not pursued to conclusion was a case that we had brought a year earlier against Joey's mother, Sara Habie, for aiding and abetting Joey's destruction of Amy's U.S. textile company, Liztex USA. The case had originally

---

*Lewis proved almost as litigious as Joey. In addition to repeated claims and cross-claims against Amy, he brought a bar complaint against Amy's lawyer Skip Smith (dismissed for no probable cause), a bar complaint against Palm Beach lawyer Ted Leopold, who later represented Amy (also dismissed for lack of probable cause), an initial bar complaint against me (dismissed for lack of probable cause), and a second bar complaint against me (also dismissed). Lewis also brought a claim against me before the Federal Elections Commission, which too was dismissed (but not before Lewis convinced the *Wall Street Journal* to report the claim on the *Journal*'s front page).

The Lewis litigation was originally assigned to Judge Wennett. Wennett had a reputation for being slow but fair, and both parts of his reputation were borne out in the early stages of the litigation. However, as the case progressed, Skip Smith became concerned that Wennett's rulings appeared to favor Lewis and the attorney, Jack Scarola, whom Lewis had hired. Scarola, who had been criticized by a federal judge for unethical behavior, was not a lawyer who would be expected to have much credibility with most judges. However, when it was revealed that Wennett, while our case was pending before him, had attended a dinner at the home of Scarola's partner without advising Smith of the relationship, Smith asked the court to consider recusal. To his credit Wennett recused himself without apparent bitterness.

Ironically the case was then assigned to the same Judge Kroll who had been so derelict when she was responsible for the kidnapping case. Kroll was also recused after it was discovered that she had had secret conversations with Scarola during the pendency of the Scott Lewis case before her; in those conversations she had asked Scarola for financial assistance in her campaign for reelection—and Scarola had promised to give it. Making matters worse, neither Kroll nor Scarola advised Amy or her attorneys of their *ex parte* communications. Unfortunately, before her recusal Kroll made several rulings in favor of Lewis that subsequent judges who heard the case would not reexamine. It was not the Florida judiciary's finest hour.

been brought to close the loophole that Joey had created by his claim that it was really his mother who owned the business.

Our plan was to use this case to put financial pressure on Joey to negotiate custody. He had succeeded in stymieing the collection of the large money judgments against him by pretending that his mother owned all the Habie family assets. It was, of course, not true, and if the properties had been in the United States, a U.S. court would have pierced that fiction. But, the assets were in Guatemala, and as long as we had a judgment only against Joey, he and the compliant Guatemalan courts could hide behind the fig leaf of his mother's asserted ownership.

We hoped that a judgment against Sara would be the last, critical piece to the puzzle. With judgments against both Joey and his mother, there would be no excuse for not attaching the Habie family assets, and if the Guatemalan courts refused to recognize U.S. awards without any excuse, it could threaten the country's U.S. trade and aid objectives. It was likely that Guatemala would decide that those objectives were more important than protecting Joey Habie from his just desserts. I was convinced that, faced with that threat, Joey would negotiate rather than risk Amy's capturing a significant part of his empire.

It had been evident over the last few years that Joey had two overriding objectives in addition to keeping the children—to safeguard his fortune and to impoverish the woman who had left him. Even though Joey had given up attempting to force Amy to return to him, he did not want her rich and successful without him. Losing tens of millions of dollars would be bad enough; having it go to his faithless former wife would be unbearable. A judgment against Sara could provide us with the ransom we needed to reunite Amy with her children.

We thought we had the opportunity to try the case in November or December 1997. However, there was a problem. When I left Cravath, the firm made clear that any further representation of Amy Habie was my responsibility; Cravath would no longer provide any assistance. It was an entirely reasonable position. Over the five years that I had represented her on a pro bono basis the firm had contributed not only my time but that of several other lawyers—time that by May 1997 was valued at approximately $3 million. In addition, although Amy had paid Cravath a significant amount for its expenses, the firm had spent more than $300,000 that had not been reimbursed. It was one thing for Cravath to indulge my commitment to Amy Habie's cause when I was a productive partner, quite another for me to expect such support after I left.

The problem was figuring out how my new firm, with a total of nine lawyers, could take on a pro bono litigation of the magnitude of the Habie controversy. Even at Cravath I had told Amy and Jim Miller that I could not be responsible for the Scott Lewis litigation, at least to the extent that it remained an ordinary commercial dispute. That litigation was manageable, and Amy could afford to pay lawyers to handle it. However, the battle with Joey was another matter. Amy could not begin to match the resources that Joey threw into his campaign against her. He had repeatedly said that she would eventually have to give up because she would run out of money. He had failed only because Cravath had stood in the way. I was determined not to let him succeed now, but balancing the needs of the litigation with the resources of my fledgling firm was a challenge.

Three other lawyers at the firm (Robert Silver, Diana Clarke, and Jonathan Boies) agreed to contribute their time, working extra nights and weekends to help. Tara Verkuil, who ran a graphics firm that my firm often used to prepare trial charts and demonstrative exhibits, contributed her services. Mary and her firm also pitched in, and my daughter Caryl agreed to come to Florida to help me try the case against Joey's mother.

Five foot two with blue eyes and blonde hair, Caryl does not look like a courtroom killer. However, in the eleven years since she had graduated from law school, she had honed her skills (including during several years at the San Diego office of Milberg Weiss, one of the most successful plaintiffs' firms in the country) to the point where she was an excellent trial lawyer. When I left Cravath, I tried to convince her to join her brother Jonathan and me in New York. She made it clear at the time that she had no interest in moving permanently to any place where it snowed in the winter, but when we spoke in September about the Habie case, she volunteered to take a leave of absence and come to Florida to help. Jim Miller's son Charles, himself a capable young lawyer who practiced with his father, also joined the team.

We knew that the case against Sara Habie would be complicated. She did not, after all, really own or control Joey's companies, and we had little admissible evidence of anything she had personally done to harm Amy's business. We also faced arguments by Sara's lawyers that evidence related to the children's kidnapping should be kept from the jury. The court had limited our case for damages to economic loss, holding (wrongly, I thought) that damages could not be awarded for the loss that Amy had suffered by being deprived of her children. This gave Sara's lawyers the argument that the kidnapping was irrelevant to our remaining claim and that evidence related to it would be severely prejudicial.

In addition, our best evidence came from assertions Joey had made in an attempt to deflect responsibility from himself, but those statements were hearsay unless we could bring Joey to court—and he, of course, remained in Guatemala, beyond the court's subpoena power. It was obviously unfair to have Joey elude us by claiming that his mother was responsible, then to have his mother escape by saying Joey was responsible without being able to confront Sara with her son's statements. Nevertheless, this was the result of rules of evidence established to protect litigants from having statements used against them without their having an opportunity to cross-examine.

The right to cross-examine witnesses against you and not to have your fate dependent on hearsay is engrained in our justice system and (at least for criminal cases) protected by the Bill of Rights. There are, however, exceptions. Certain out-of-court statements are considered sufficiently trustworthy that they are admissible even if the person who made them is not available to be cross-examined.

One example is a "dying declaration"—a statement made by someone who knows he or she is dying. Another example is "business records"—papers prepared in the ordinary course of business containing information that the business needs to know in order to operate. If we were to be able to use Joey's hearsay statements against his mother, we needed to bring them within a recognized exception.

There is no hearsay exception for statements by family members, probably for good reason, but there were two exceptions that we thought might be applicable. Statements by a party's "co-conspirator" are admissible even if the co-conspirator cannot be cross-examined. Conspirators are people who act together in an attempt to achieve an unlawful goal. Courts reason that each conspirator should be bound by what other conspirators say in the course of the conspiracy. To justify admitting Joey's statements as those of Sara's co-conspirator, we would have to establish that mother and son were engaged in a common undertaking, that the undertaking was unlawful, and that the statement was related to the undertaking.

A second exception to the hearsay rule that might apply was for statements made by a litigant's agent. An "agent" is someone whom you agree to have act for you, whether paid or unpaid. Statements by a litigant's agent are admissible even if the agent is not available for cross-examination because courts reason that someone who authorizes another person to act for her should be bound by what that person says or does. To justify admitting Joey's statements as those of Sara's agent, we would have to prove that Sara let Joey act in her name.

It was critical for us to find a way to convince the court to admit Joey's prior statements. We did have a few statements from Sara herself, as well as some documents purporting to bear her signature (some Joey had submitted to various courts, others we had subpoenaed from banks where Sara did business), and we had Sara's deposition. However, the documents were limited, Sara's statements even more so, and the deposition was taken at a time when we were attempting to show that Joey, not Sara, was primarily responsible.

Another problem was that we risked our credibility if we were seen as contradicting our repeated statements that Joey, not Sara, owned and controlled the companies that had been harassing Amy. In addition, except for Amy herself, who had little personal knowledge of what, if anything, Sara had done, we had no witnesses who could testify to the facts we needed to prove. Our case was primarily a "paper case," and paper cases are often difficult for a jury.

As we prepared for trial, we identified three key themes. One was that Joey was Sara's agent. This made Joey's statements admissible. A second theme was that either Sara owned and controlled the companies that had been harassing Amy (in which case Sara was liable directly), or Joey owned and controlled them and Sara's support of his denial of ownership made her his co-conspirator (in which case she was also liable). A third theme was that the motivation for Joey and Sara's efforts to destroy Amy's business was to force Amy to submit to Joey's custody demands. This helped explain why they would have destroyed Amy's business and helped rebut Sara's defense that the actions taken were simply "commercial" decisions. This argument also enabled us to make relevant, and hence admissible, the facts related to the kidnapping.

As our December trial drew near we also focused on possible ways to call Sara Habie herself as a witness. A party to a civil trial is ordinarily not required to be present. Accordingly, the only way to force someone to appear is to serve them with a subpoena. The problem was that such a subpoena could be served only in the State of Florida or within one hundred miles of the courthouse. Thus we had to find Sara in Florida or on a boat within one hundred miles of Miami. We had managed to serve her to commence our action by staking out the Florida home of her daughter as well as Miami boutiques where we knew she liked to shop based on credit card records we had subpoenaed. Although we correctly figured that she and her lawyers would be too smart to let her be caught a second time, we went through the stake-out exercise for several weeks just in case.

Our judge in Miami was Ursula Ungaro-Benages, a fair-minded, intelligent jurist who could be expected to apply the law strictly. She was exactly the kind of judge I would ordinarily hope to draw. However, in this case, if we could not find a way to force Sara Habie to trial, we might end up with a gap or two in our evidence—gaps that Ungaro-Benages would be unlikely to bridge regardless of how sympathetic our case. Judge Ungaro-Benages could also be expected to hold us to the trial date she had set.

Sara's lead lawyer, Mel Schwartz, was loud and aggressive, telling Caryl and me at every opportunity how weak our case was and urging us to drop it. When it became clear a week before trial that we were unpersuaded, he asked us to agree to a short adjournment. We ourselves were not completely ready and I had other things to do that month, but we sensed that Schwartz was in worse shape than we were. Moreover I had just agreed to represent the Department of Justice in its investigation of Microsoft, so 1998 was already shaping up as a busy year. Better, I thought, to try the case at the end of 1997 than in early 1998. We declined Schwartz's proposal.

Two days later he notified the court that he was suffering from chest pains and had a note from his doctor saying it would be inadvisable for him to proceed with our trial. We were deeply suspicious, and the judge seemed skeptical as well. However, when the court asked for our position concerning a one-month delay, Caryl, after consulting with me, said that we did not object, but that we did not want to be in the same position a month from then. We asked the court to require that Schwartz have another lawyer prepared to try the case at the beginning of January if Schwartz were not prepared to proceed himself. The court readily agreed.

We used the extra month to refine our preparation, but we still could not figure out how to get Sara Habie to show up. At our annual end-of-the-year Caribbean vacation Mary, Caryl, Jimmy, and I all agreed that our best chance was to make such a point of Sara's absence that Schwartz would feel he had to bring her to court. Juries tend not to appreciate litigants who do not give the same priority to a trial that they themselves are required to give.

I believed that on balance the right choice for Schwartz was to keep Sara out of the courtroom and take whatever heat our tactic generated—Sara on the stand could end up offending the jury even more than an absent Sara, and there was a plausible chance that without her available we would not be able to offer sufficient evidence even to get our case to the jury. My goal was to put Schwartz under enough pressure that he might make a mistake.

When on January 5 we showed up to pick a jury, we learned two things. First, it was Schwartz's colleague, Lawrence Duffy, who would be trying the case. Duffy was a good lawyer, and I calculated that his low-key approach would be more effective than Schwartz's bluster. Second, in response to the judge's question as to whether the defendant would be present for the trial, Duffy said that they had not yet decided, but that she was available. Sensing uncertainty, I pounded on Sara's absence at every opportunity during jury selection and my opening statement. My efforts were rewarded when, the morning Amy was to take the stand as my first witness, there at the defendant's counsel table was Sara Habie.

In anticipation of the possibility of Sara showing up at some point, Caryl had a subpoena prepared and waiting in her briefcase. As she handed me the paper and I walked toward the table where Sara and Duffy sat, they recognized the blue-backed document for what it was. Sara was trapped, and she knew it. Having been served with a trial subpoena, if she failed to appear the court would enter judgment against her.

Amy's testimony went well; she explained how she had developed and grown her U.S. textile business, how bright its prospects for the future were, and how it had been destroyed following the kidnapping. The main gap in her testimony, which Duffy skillfully exploited, was her limited ability to tie Sara to any of the events that destroyed her company. Amy was able to cite chapter and verse as to Joey's responsibility, but she had mostly hearsay knowledge of Sara's role, and this Ungaro-Benages excluded.

As soon as Amy's testimony was completed, I called Sara to the stand. It is always a gamble to call your opponent as an adverse witness, and I generally avoid doing so. However, in this case I needed evidence that only Sara could provide. Whether I could extract that information remained to be seen.

In his opening statement Duffy had tried with some success to distance Sara from Joey's conduct. He told the jury that she did not know what her son was doing at the time and disapproved of it when she found out. Amy had told me that Sara was basically a decent but weak person who believed she had no choice except to support Joey in whatever he wanted to do. Amy knew (and had testified) that Sara did not actually own or control the Habie family companies. My job was to convince the jury that this basically decent mother should be held liable for helping her son. To do so, I would have to show the jurors a deceptive, manipulative side of Sara that would cause them not to trust her and to believe that it was fair to impose substantial liability.

Right from the outset, I was aided by Sara herself. Although Spanish was her native language, she spoke and understood English reasonably well—and better than one or two of the Hispanic jurors. Yet she feigned an inability to understand me and asked for an interpreter. She, and perhaps Duffy, saw this as a way to disrupt the flow of my questioning and to give her time to think. The problem was that it quickly became apparent that her lack of understanding was an act. I showed her numerous bank documents, involving large dollar transactions, which she had signed—all in English, and many quite complex. "Did you understand what you were signing?" I asked. If she said no, she would lose credibility with jurors who would not believe that anyone would sign financial documents involving such large sums without understanding what they were signing. When she admitted that she did, it was clear that she understood English perfectly well.

I also brought out that she traveled in both the U.S. and Europe, alone and without a translator, and that she regularly conversed and transacted business in English. As the pace of the examination picked up, she would sometimes begin to answer in English without waiting for the translator, to the amusement of the judge as well as the jury. Once I used my limited Spanish to ask a short question in Spanish. As the puzzled translator paused, not exactly sure what to do, Sara answered—in English. Out of the corner of my eye I watched the Spanish-speaking members of the jury explain to the other jurors what I had said. As I paused and glanced at the jury, one of them winked. Unnecessarily, and with no benefit, Sara had thrown away her credibility.

As the examination progressed, I caught her in a number of inconsistencies with documents she had signed and statements that she had made at her deposition. When she would pause over a document purporting to bear her signature, I would ask, "You're not suggesting that this document your son's counsel produced to us in discovery is a forgery, are you?" The answer was always a quick no. I was trying to establish a pattern that would hold when I came to one of my most important documents, a letter purportedly signed by her to Aaron Podhurst. The signature did not look like other examples of her signature, and I suspected that Joey had actually signed her name.

"Now, this is another document you signed, correct?" I began.

Her answer actually came back quickly, although the two or three seconds it took seemed longer at the time. "Si."

The letter contained numerous statements inconsistent with her testimony and with her counsel's contentions—statements made to support Joey's arguments, such as that she owned and controlled the Habie family companies. Sentence by sentence I took her through the letter. "Was that true?" I would ask. Again, she was trapped and again she knew it. She did not want to say the statements were true; if she did, her defense self-destructed. On the other hand, there was no good explanation why she would have signed something flatly untrue. I could almost see her mind wishing she could take back her initial admission that the signature on the letter was hers. Her only explanation was that she had signed the letter only because Joey had asked her to. But that explanation was itself a trap. "Did you always sign whatever he asked you to sign, even if you knew it was untrue?" I asked with a note of incredulity. "Yes," she answered, not waiting for the translator.

When I sat down, I saw that Caryl had written me a note: "No more gaps." She was right. We now had from the defendant's own mouth the admission that she had knowingly signed false statements to help Joey. That was enough evidence of conspiracy to get past a motion for a directed verdict and permit the case to go to the jury. As the jury saw more of Sara and learned more about what Joey had done to Amy with Sara's support, I felt confident about what their decision would be.

Our next witness was a damages expert, William Chandler, who had conducted a study of the value of Amy's business and calculated the loss caused by Joey and Sara's conduct. The trial was going well, and this was our opportunity to win our ransom. There was one problem. Duffy had made a motion to exclude our expert's testimony because we had allegedly not filed the "expert report" required by the federal rules. The purpose of an expert report is to set forth the substance and bases of an expert's expected testimony so that the other side can prepare its rebuttal. Duffy did have a technical point—we had not formally filed the report in connection with Amy's claims against Sara. However, because we had filed the identical report in a related case, and Duffy had received it in discovery, and Chandler was on our witness list for Sara's trial, Duffy had not been prejudiced by our having failed to file it formally a second time. I did not think he would win his motion.* I was wrong.

---

*The claims against Sara had been consolidated with those against Joey and various companies, including Liztex S.A. (Indeed the name of the case against Sara was *Amy Habie v. Liztex S.A. et al.*—Sara was one of the "ct al.") The damages we claimed from Sara were the same damages claimed from Joey and Liztex S.A. In the case against Joey and his companies Chandler had filed his report calculating Amy's damages and setting forth in detail what his testimony would be concerning the value of Amy's business and her loss as a result of Joey and Sara's conduct. The business was the same; the value was the same; the conduct was the same; the loss was the same. Although the report had not been separately filed in Sara's case, a copy had been furnished to Schwartz and Duffy as part of the discovery process in preparing for the trial against Sara. Duffy argued that even though Chandler was on our witness list as an expert for our trial of Sara's case, even though we had no other damages expert listed, even though Chandler had no personal knowledge and could only testify as an expert, and even though he had received Chandler's report during discovery, he had not understood that Chandler expected to testify to the contents of his report during the trial against Sara.

At the end of the day, just before Chandler was scheduled to testify about his damage calculations, Judge Ungaro-Benages ruled that he could not do so because of our failure to file his expert report. That decision left us without a damages expert and without any apparent way to prove damages. It looked as if we would win the case but get no recovery. I was surprised by the decision, but I had to agree that the judge had a basis for it: we had been careless.

At dinner I concluded that our only chance was to put Amy on the stand to give the testimony that we had planned to have Chandler provide. Of course we had not filed an expert report for Amy either, but the difference was that because it was her business, she could testify about its value as a "fact" witness. The rules require an expert report for expert witnesses, but no comparable report needs to be filed for fact witnesses. In general, the distinction makes sense because expert testimony is more complicated and requires more time to rebut than fact testimony. Although the distinction did not make a lot of sense in our case, where the testimony to be given was essentially identical, this time we had the technical rule on our side. The same strict adherence to form that had cost us Chandler's testimony now opened up the way for Amy to present the same material.

The next morning, over Duffy's objections, Amy began her damages testimony. The subject matter was complicated, she had had only hours to prepare, and I knew she was scared that she would make a mess of things. However, she was clear and convincing on direct examination and equally strong during cross. In the middle of her direct, when she was dealing with calculations of net present value, and particularly complicated net income formulas, Duffy objected that she had no basis for giving that testimony herself and that she was improperly parroting the expert testimony that had been excluded. The objection might have prevailed except that among Amy's other accomplishments were a master's degree in finance and service as the chief financial officer of a corporation where she made the same kind of calculations. "A plaintiff is entitled to testify to the value of her business and the loss suffered," Judge Ungaro-Benages ruled. "I'm afraid you have to take the plaintiff as you find her. If she has the background to use certain calculations, she is entitled to use them."

As soon as Amy was off the witness stand and the jury had filed out of the courtroom, I gave her a big hug.

"Thanks for bailing us out. It's nice to have a client who can double as a financial expert."

The way things worked, Amy's testimony was more effective than Chandler's would have been. One of Duffy's arguments had been that she was a poor businesswoman and therefore her company was of little value regardless of what Joey or Sara might have done. After listening to Amy, no juror could question her competence.

Duffy made a last desperate attempt to undercut her credibility by calling Carol Lewis, Scott Lewis's wife, but it backfired badly. Carol Lewis, who had worked as a secretary in the lawn care business's office for several months after Amy took over, was called to testify about conversations she claimed to have had with Amy at that time. Unfortunately for Duffy, nothing she had to say had much to do with the issues at trial, and her obvious hostility toward Amy made her a horrible witness. Even worse for Duffy, during cross-examination Carol Lewis admitted that Joey and her husband spoke by phone and exchanged faxes. Two of the jurors shook their heads in apparent disgust. Jurors normally conceal their emotions during trial, but occasionally something happens where it is simply human nature to react. The idea that Scott and Carol Lewis were cooperating with a kidnapper because of their commercial dispute with Amy was understandably disturbing, and the fact that Duffy had tried to rely on such a witness to attack Amy's credibility cost Duffy his own. He was also damaged when on cross-examination Carol Lewis identified Mel Schwartz, co-counsel with Duffy representing Sara, as Joey's attorney. Duffy's strategy had been to separate Sara and Joey. Now here was testimony that Sara's lawyer was secretly Joey's attorney as well. Up to Carol Lewis's testimony, despite his unattractive client, Duffy's professionalism had earned the jury's respect. After the trial a juror would say that Carol Lewis's testimony made jurors think that they had been wrong about Duffy.

The lowest point for both Lewis and Duffy was when she admitted that she had approached one of Amy's employees on the street and told him to pass on to Amy the false news that Joey and his new wife were going to adopt the twins. Carol Lewis initially denied remembering having done this. Eventually, however, she admitted:

> Q And what did you say to him?
> A I said Joe wants Amy to know that he's adopting the children.

> Q And what was the purpose of your telling this to an employee of Amy Habie?
> A It was the only way I knew to get the message to her.

At this there was an audible gasp from the jury box. Here was a mother publicly taunting another mother about the threatened loss of her children, and willingly delivering that message at the request of the kidnapper himself. I think that if the jury could have awarded damages against Carol Lewis, they would have.

As the trial drew to a close, I had one important worry unrelated to how the case was going. I was scheduled to start a six-week trial in New York City representing Banque Indosuez on Thursday, January 23, 1998, and it was clear that I would not be finished with the Sara Habie trial until the following Monday or Tuesday. The trial in New York was before Justice Beatrice Shainswit. She was known to be tough on scheduling issues, but based on the simple proposition that I could not be in two places at once, I hoped she would postpone the trial a few days—particularly since the overlap had resulted from the delay in the start of the Habie trial due to circumstances beyond my control. Once again I was wrong.

At the end of the day on Wednesday, while I was arguing a legal issue to Judge Ungaro-Benages, Caryl handed me a note saying

that Judge Shainswit had denied our application for a postponement: the trial would start the next morning. I explained my
dilemma to Judge Ungaro-Benages, who graciously agreed to postpone closing arguments until the following Monday, when Justice
Shainswit did not hold court. Caryl and Amy drove me to the Miami airport, where I caught the next plane to New York.

We picked a jury for the Banque Indosuez trial on Thursday and
opened on Friday. I returned to Miami Sunday night and closed to
the Habie jury on Monday. The closing went well, and I felt reasonably confident as I flew back to New York. Juries, however, are
unpredictable, and no trial lawyer likes to be a thousand miles away
when one of his juries is deliberating. Juries sometimes come back
with questions during deliberations. Also, when a jury files into the
courtroom in the morning and out at night, it notices your absence.
No trial lawyer wants to risk a jury's concluding that its trial is not
the most important thing that lawyer is doing.

I need not have worried. Three days later, while I was in court
in New York, my son Jonathan brought me a note that the Habie
jury had returned a verdict for Amy in an amount several million
dollars more than the $51 million we had asked for. In the movies,
and with some judges, we could have expected to keep the jury's
award. In this case I predicted (correctly) that Judge Ungaro-Benages would cut the verdict back to the amount requested.

The verdict was a satisfying victory that could have made Amy
a wealthy woman. However, money had never been her objective.
The question on her mind, and ours, was whether the verdict
would provide the leverage we needed to reunite her with her
children. We got our answer several weeks later. Joey fired both his
and his mother's lawyers and retained Barry Levine and Bruce
Holcomb of Dickstein, Shapiro, Morin & Oshinsky, a firm with a
stature and reputation quite different from that of his previous counsel. I had worked with Bruce closely in the past and trusted him. I
knew Barry only by his reputation, which was excellent. In our initial conversations they told me that they had taken on this representation only because they were convinced that Joey genuinely wanted

to settle. Although Jim Miller was suspicious, I believed them. With judgments against both Joey and his mother now in hand, Amy had a realistic chance of collecting $50 million or more of her ex-husband's money. Although that was only a fraction of Joey's wealth, I knew he would want to reach a settlement that would avoid a large payment.

The problem from Amy's standpoint was that even though she had gained substantial economic leverage, she couldn't force Joey to share the children unless he were willing to trade custody for money. Barry and Bruce quickly made clear that he was. If Amy would give up her judgments against Joey and his mother, Joey would agree to joint custody, with the children dividing their time between Guatemala and the U.S. For Amy it was an easy decision. All she had ever wanted was to be reunited with the twins. We proposed that Joey pay the lawyers' out-of-pocket expenses, the fees owed to Jim Miller, and the money Amy had spent defending the various meritless claims brought against her—a total of approximately $3 million; Amy would give up the remainder of the $51 million. Ultimately Joey agreed, and we began to negotiate the details of how the children should divide their time between their two parents. By the fall of 1999 we had an agreement in principle and Amy was permitted to visit Alex and Danny in Guatemala. Barry Levine gave me his personal assurance that Joey would cooperate in helping Amy reestablish her relationship with the twins and that if he did not, Barry would support me in seeking sanctions from the court.

On November 30, 1999, I once again accompanied Amy to Guatemala City, where Joey had made us reservations at the Hyatt Regency Hotel, which he owned. He agreed to let Danny and Alex spend the night with Amy—the first the children had spent with their mother in over seven years. Once we had reached agreement on the terms of custody (which had the children continue their schooling in Guatemala but spend all vacations, long or short, with their mother, and which gave Amy the right to visit the children in Guatemala), the civil judgments in the U.S. were vacated (subject to being reinstated if Joey violated the terms of the custody agreement), and Jim Miller and I worked with Barry Levine to resolve all criminal indictments of which we were aware. Dismissing the Guatemalan indictment of Amy was as easy for Joey as getting it had been in the first place; persuading the state criminal authorities in Florida to give up their charges was more complicated, but nevertheless achieved.

I discussed with Barry Levine the possibility that there was a sealed federal indictment of Joey in existence of which no one was aware. Barry checked with his contacts in the Justice Department and reported back that he was sure that there was not. I tried to convince Joey and Barry to bring the children to the U.S. for a visit before their next vacation. I believed the sooner the children were reunited with their mother the better. I also believed that if there were a sealed indictment the best way of convincing prosecutors to dismiss it was to be able to point to the children in the U.S. Joey, however, was determined to find out for sure that he could travel unimpeded in the U.S. before he would release the twins. Accordingly, he and Mariana flew to Fort Lauderdale to test his newly negotiated freedom to travel. It was a short test.

As Joey walked to the terminal from his private jet, he was arrested by the FBI and taken to jail in handcuffs. There had indeed been a sealed indictment and the FBI had been tracking his plane. Although, in the years immediately after the kidnapping, the FBI's commitment to the Habie case left something to be desired, all that changed when a dedicated new agent, Martin Ruiz de Gamboa, was assigned to the matter. Ruiz de Gamboa and the FBI had built up a substantial file on Joey and his travels, apparently almost succeeding in having police apprehend him in other countries he visited.

I learned that Joey had been arrested just before I began a lecture in Houston. Immediately after the address I excused myself and flew to Palm Beach. When I arrived at the courthouse, I found Amy, Mariana, Joey's sister and brother-in-law, Barry Levine, Jim Miller, and numerous reporters waiting. The U.S. Attorney and the

U.S. Magistrate refused to set bail because of the obvious flight risk Joey represented. That meant that he was going to stay in jail unless something radical could be done. Barry and Joey's brother-in-law asked me whether I thought they should bring Daniel and Alexandra to the U.S. They knew the answer themselves, but I did not hesitate to confirm it for them.

"The longer the children stay in Guatemala," I said, "the harder it will be to talk to the prosecutors." Jim Miller had already asked the prosecutors if they might be open to some resolution of the charges against Joey. "We're not even interested in talking until the children are returned to the United States," he had been told. Within hours the children were on a plane for their first visit to their mother in her home country since April 1992, seven years before.

At Barry Levine's request I accompanied him to visit Joey in his cell. The Palm Beach County prison may well be to other jails what Palm Beach is to other counties, but it is a jail nevertheless and Joey was understandably overwhelmed by his captivity. "I have to get out of here," he told us.

To Barry he said, "Do whatever it takes, agree to whatever you have to, but get me out of here. If Amy wants sole custody of the children, she can have it."

Barry and I told Joey, as I had told Mariana and Joey's sister earlier, that it was not going to be easy, but that we would do what we could. "Amy has told me that she doesn't want you in jail," I reassured Joey. "She and I are scheduled to meet with the prosecutors tomorrow to try to get you released."

As we left, he said, "Tell Amy thank-you."

Amy had given me many reasons to admire her strength and decency over the years that I had represented her. Although I once saw Nelson Mandela from a distance, I have never actually met a saint. Amy was not a saint and, like everyone else I have known, from time to time made mistakes and acted badly. Moreover, the years of tension, conflict, and separation from her children had taken their toll, emotionally as well as physically. But her single-minded pursuit of what she believed was in her children's best interest was remarkable. This was most evident during the twenty-four hours after Joey was arrested. It would have been natural for Amy to take satisfaction in seeing Joey punished, even to use the leverage his arrest gave her to increase her time with the children or to recut the financial settlement.

Joey was in jail and the children were back with her in the United States. As long as Joey stayed in prison, her time with the children was safe, and she was wise enough to know that once he was released, custody conflicts would eventually reappear. In the face of all this, she never wavered from two simple propositions. It was bad for her children to have their father in jail, and she would not use the leverage Joey's arrest had given her to renegotiate. Amy was not naive; she had been through too much for that. Nor was she selfless. It was simply that her most important goal was to establish as normal an environment for her children as possible. To her that meant not leaving their father in jail, not interfering with their having time with their father, not abruptly removing them from the only school they knew, and not doing anything that would unnecessarily cause conflict with Joey or his family.

Hers was not the only possible approach. The children's interests might well have been best served by keeping them in the U.S., bringing them up with Amy's values undiluted by Joey and Mariana, and leaving their father in jail until he and the twins realized how wrong his conduct had been. But that was not how she saw it.

Amy and I made her case to the prosecutors. She was more thoughtful, passionate, and persuasive than I was. Barry Levine almost blew it when he tried to argue that the charges should be dismissed without even a period of probation because otherwise Joey and the children might blame Amy for his arrest. "They really don't get it, do they?" one of the prosecutors remarked. At the end of the day, however, it was agreed that Joey would plead guilty and be placed on five years' probation with no jail time. He did not spend a second night in jail.

I wish I could say that Amy has been rewarded for her forbearance by cooperation from Joey and his family in rebuilding her relations with her children. It is certainly true that her time with them is substantial and that (allowing for the parental/child tensions inherent when children become teenagers) her relations with Danny and Alex are remarkably good given the years of separation. At the same time, both Joey and Mariana have showed that any gratitude they may have had for Amy's actions following Joey's arrest does not prevent them from being difficult and even occasionally mean. Just getting compliance with the orders Joey agreed to when he was released has been a constant struggle, with Amy subject to thinly veiled threats to turn the children against her if she complained to the court or the probation department. Joey again retained counsel in Florida to do what Barry Levine and his firm were uncomfortable doing, but Levine continued to represent Joey and, unlike Aaron Podhurst, did not appear to take a stand against his client's actions.

This was a case where the good guys and the bad guys were easy to identify. The bad guys, in addition to Joey, included judges who, for whatever reason, delayed justice in a case where justice delayed was justice denied; the Guatemalan officials who, at Joey's bidding, indicted an innocent woman for kidnapping; the Guatemalan rabbi who turned his religious center over to a kidnapper and his armed thugs; the lawyers who took Joey's money and abused the legal system; and the State Department personnel who considered deporting an innocent and aggrieved American citizen to promote relations with a government that had no respect for the rights of its own citizens let alone the rights of Americans. There were also many good guys—dedicated FBI agents, prosecutors, and judges who did their job and more. And, of course, there was Amy.

It is harder to assess the extent to which the American legal system itself functioned well or poorly. It failed Amy and her children for too many years, but at the end of the day it was the only reason her children were eventually reunited with her. We like to say we are a government of laws, not of men or women. But our government, and our justice system, are dependent on the quality and integrity of the people who administer those laws. No case I had ever been involved in made that point more clearly than the Habie kidnapping litigation.

4

Conversations with Bill Gates

I N NOVEMBER OF 1997, MICROSOFT WAS POSSIBLY THE
most successful company in history. Founded as a partnership
between Bill Gates and programmer Paul Allen in February
1977 when Gates was twenty-one, Microsoft in twenty years had
become the most valuable company in the world, eclipsing IBM,
GE, and Exxon in market capitalization. Gates had become the
world's richest man with a personal fortune that would briefly exceed $100 billion. In addition to their wealth, Microsoft and
Gates were celebrated for their creative and successful software
and for their vision that had helped create the personal computer
industry. Microsoft was repeatedly ranked as America's most admired company, and Gates the most admired business executive.
As *Fortune* reported in February 1998, "Americans love Microsoft. They love its products. They admire its CEO."

About three months before that article appeared, I received a call
at home from my new partner, Jonathan Schiller, that began a chain
of events that was to put me directly in the path of the Microsoft
juggernaut. Some years earlier Jonathan had been a partner of Joel
Klein in the Washington firm of Rogovin, Huge & Schiller. By
November 1997, Joel was the assistant attorney general in charge of
the Antitrust Division of the Department of Justice. He had called
Jonathan to ask whether I would be willing to represent the De-

partment in connection with a possible monopolization suit against Microsoft under Section 2 of the Sherman Antitrust Act.

Although "monopoly" technically means "single seller," the law has long defined it as a seller with sufficient market power to raise (and keep) prices significantly above competitive levels even if it is not the only supplier. In general, a company with a stable market share of more than 75 percent will have such power. However, the antitrust laws do not outlaw monopolies per se. Since the laws are intended to require competitors to compete, the company that competes successfully should not be penalized even if that success results in its achieving monopoly power. The Sherman Act therefore outlaws monopolies only if the monopoly was obtained by acquiring independent companies, or if the monopolist secured or maintained its position by anticompetitive practices. The Department of Justice had in fact investigated Microsoft for monopolization five years before, but had settled for a vaguely worded decree that the company subsequently interpreted as essentially meaningless. Now the department was both investigating whether Microsoft had violated that decree and beginning an investigation to see whether new charges should be brought. The question of whether Microsoft had violated the earlier decree was relatively limited. It was the issue of a possible new antitrust case that Klein wanted to discuss. I would, I told Jonathan, call Klein.

That Klein was reaching out to me was on the surface surprising. The Department of Justice historically had rarely hired private lawyers to represent the U.S. in court. Retaining anyone from the outside was certain to result in some criticism within the department, as well as from Microsoft and its political allies. In addition, there was my role in defending IBM in its thirteen-year antitrust battle against the same Antitrust Division that Klein now headed. That case, which was dismissed after a trial that itself lasted more than six years, was widely viewed as the department's worst defeat in decades of antitrust enforcement, and I was identified as one of the architects of that defeat. *United States v. IBM* was referred to, inside and outside the government, as "the Antitrust Division's

Vietnam." Retaining me would be viewed by some as the equivalent of the U.S. Army's recruiting a former Viet Cong general.

The failure of the government's case against IBM had led many to question whether it was wise to invest the department's resources in monopolization cases. If the department took Microsoft to court, it would be the first major monopolization trial since the IBM dismissal. Joel explained that he believed that my antitrust experience outweighed the issues raised by retaining an outside lawyer, and that he believed that my role in the IBM litigation was an advantage, not a disadvantage.

"You know how they think," he said. "You know their playbook and how to counter their plays. You can keep them from dragging this case out the way you dragged out IBM."

There was no point in arguing that the IBM suit dragged on not because of our tactics but because the government lacked a coherent theme and strategy. In any event, part of what I might bring to a case against Microsoft would be the ability to develop such themes and strategy.

There were many reasons for me not to take the case. My new firm was just getting started. In October 1997 we had opened a four-lawyer office in Orlando to concentrate on our representation of Florida Power & Light and now had fifteen lawyers in three offices, with the resulting overhead. Although the firm had many exceptionally talented lawyers, I was the magnet for many of our major clients. How would they react, I wondered, if I were occupied by a multiyear battle against Microsoft? In addition, Mary was concerned that any case against business and cultural icons like Microsoft and Gates was likely to be viewed as a wrongheaded attack on success. In the end, however, I agreed with Jonathan Schiller's analysis: "This is not a case that you can turn down."

I had written and lectured on antitrust issues for three decades. The legal questions, including whether the antitrust laws should be applied to computer software and other high-tech markets, were among the most important antitrust issues being debated. What happened in the personal computer industry was critical to consumers and the country. In addition, if a case against Microsoft ever went to court, it would be one of the most important, and exciting, trials of the century. I had made a commitment to Jonathan and the other lawyers who had joined us, and if they had felt I should not take on the Microsoft project I would have said no. However, with Jonathan's support, I enthusiastically accepted Joel's offer.

In the fall of 1997 both Joel Klein and I were of the view, contrary to the arguments of Microsoft and many others, that the antitrust laws should be applied to software and other high-tech markets. We also felt that Microsoft, whose "Windows" software had for years controlled between 80 to 95 percent of the personal computer operating system market, had monopoly power.* The critical issue appeared to be how Microsoft had achieved and maintained its apparent monopoly—an issue about which we were undecided.

During December I began my review of voluminous materials from publicly available sources and from the department's files. When our family left for our annual end-of-the-year trip to the Caribbean (this time to Anguilla), I carried with me two boxes of papers to read on the beach. I continued my work on weekends and occasional evenings in January during the four-week Habie kidnapping trial.

I learned that Microsoft's success was based on the operating system it had created for the IBM personal computer. The application programs that customers actually run (for example, word-processing programs, accounting spreadsheets, games, tax preparation programs) all rely on the computer's operating system (or OS) to translate and implement their software into commands that the hardware can execute. An operating system is

---

*There are circumstances where even a company with a very high market share may not have monopoly power—for example, where entry into a market is so easy that if an existing firm raises prices new competitors will offer consumers an alternative so quickly that the existing firm will not be able to maintain the increase. However, the evidence suggested that barriers to entry into the operating system market were likely to be high.

often described as the level, or "platform," that exists above the hardware and below the applications program to which the program is connected or "interfaced."

In the late 1970s IBM dominated the computer business. When in 1980 Apple began to market the first commercially successful home computer, IBM initially dismissed it as a niche product unrelated, and unthreatening, to its dominance of the computer industry. It believed that the demand for home computers would remain small because of their limited capabilities and relatively high cost, and that there was little chance that its business customers would find practical uses for the new machines. It was not that IBM did not recognize the demand for a desktop device to perform word-processing, graphics, and data-processing functions in individual workers' offices; it was just that it was convinced that that demand would continue to be met most effectively by terminals connected to large mainframe computers.

The company's projections were grounded in three undisputed facts. First, terminals, or "workstations," connected to central processing units had been the way the power of the computer had been brought to individual workers on a real-time or interactive basis since the 1960s (when IBM had introduced the System 360 model 67). Second, there were significant economies of scale in having many workers able to use the power and memory of a single large CPU. Third, the capabilities of the early Apple products were too limited to be useful in a business context.

What IBM ignored was that the cost of processing power and memory was continuing to decline rapidly, and as it did so the significance of economies of scale declined as well—making it practical to load more and more functions into a stand-alone desktop computer at a price that would compete with the central-computer-with-terminals business model. IBM, like virtually everyone else including Microsoft, also greatly underestimated the home market for desktop computers—in part because it did not recognize how the increase in disposable household income made it practical for millions of consumers to invest thousands of dollars in devices that enabled them to do things that they had never done before. It is easy to predict the market for something that is primarily a replacement product, one that enables people to do the same things they already do cheaper or better. It is much harder to predict the market for a product that offers people the opportunity to do many new things. IBM also underestimated the extent to which creative software would enable home computers to do more, better, easier than anyone imagined.

Microsoft's initial success can be traced to five decisions by IBM in 1981. The first was to develop an IBM "home computer." When Apple's success and the expanded potential of what was still referred to as the home computer became apparent, IBM raced to introduce a product of its own.

The second decision was to subcontract the computer's operating system. In order to bring what IBM named the "personal computer" or "PC" to market as fast and inexpensively as possible, the company subcontracted the major components of its new product—including the "chip" that provided the computer's processing to Intel and the computer's operating system to Microsoft. Historically IBM, with one of the world's greatest programming staffs, had developed such software itself. However, the company believed that subcontracting would be both faster and less expensive than developing its PC operating system in-house. Also, it continued to underestimate both the importance of the PC to its future and the importance of the operating system to the PC. IBM's decision to outsource the development of its personal computer software gave Microsoft the opportunity of the century.

Third, Microsoft took advantage of this opportunity by convincing IBM that it was the right company for the job, and then proving that it was. IBM's decision about who its sub-contractor should be was the only one Microsoft could influence, and influence it Microsoft did. In winning the contest, it showed the combination of technical innovation, marketing superiority, and customer focus that was to characterize its future success.

IBM's fourth decision was to license its PC operating system to manufacturers of what were initially referred to as "IBM compatible personal computers"—a decision that soon permitted IBM's design to overtake Apple as the standard for desktop computers. An important reason for IBM's decision, and a principle that was to play a significant role in our antitrust analysis, was the fact (sometimes called "network effects") that the value of certain products increases the more widely they are used. For example, the value of a telephone to a user increases the more other users there are to call. The same is true for computers. Any operating system that achieves dominance for a significant period will benefit from a self-perpetuating cycle. Applications writers will want to write their programs for the operating system that is most widely used because it increases the potential market for their software, which will increase the operating system's dominance still further because of users' demands for the most and best applications. This will in turn further increase the incentive to develop applications for that operating system, and so on.

The fifth IBM decision, and in some respects the most interesting, was to permit Microsoft to retain the right to license that software to companies that might manufacture copies of the IBM PC. IBM's policy of licensing its PC operating system to other potential manufacturers made a lot of sense, but the decision to permit Microsoft to license the software in competition with IBM, and to develop new products based on the underlying code, was considerably less obvious. IBM's approach was rooted in its concern that, given its then dominant position, the antitrust laws restricted the extent to which it could control who was granted a license to use its operating system.*

Microsoft's initial success was the result of IBM's decisions and

---

*Years later during the Microsoft trial, Jeff Blattner and other Justice Department lawyers remarked on the irony that had it not been for the antitrust laws, Microsoft might have remained simply another successful IBM subcontractor.

the skill with which Microsoft exploited the opportunity it had been given. If there was an antitrust violation, it would have to be found in conduct after Bill Gates's company had achieved its dominant position.

By February 1998 I was in the second week of the eight-week Banque Indosuez trial in New York State Court. In my spare time I continued to study documents and was in almost daily telephone discussions with department lawyers who had been concentrating on the case, in some instances for several years. I also talked with representatives of twenty state attorneys general who were conducting a parallel investigation of Microsoft.

An important focus of our investigation was the Internet browser. Two years earlier a small start-up company named Netscape had developed a pioneering product, the Netscape Navigator, that enabled PC users to "browse" the Internet easily. Few products grew as fast in distribution and use as Netscape Navigator in its early years, and despite its far greater size and resources, Microsoft initially had great difficulty convincing consumers to use its own browser, Internet Explorer, or IE.

In late 1996 Microsoft began a concerted campaign to increase the distribution of its browser at the expense of Navigator. To the extent that the company was merely trying to compete on the merits, there was nothing wrong; indeed such competition was exactly what the antitrust laws sought to foster. However, beginning in 1997 the Department of Justice became concerned that Microsoft was using its market power to require customers, suppliers, and other industry participants to enter into agreements that blocked Netscape from distributing its product and customers from using it. Such conduct, when combined with monopoly power, would establish a violation of Section 2 of the Sherman Act. (It might also violate Section 1 of the act, which prohibits anticompetitive agreements even if the parties do not have monopoly power.)

Our investigation indicated that through contractual provisions and some design choices, Microsoft had effectively tied* the use of its browser to the availability of its Windows operating system. Since there was no practical alternative to Windows, this meant that personal computer manufacturers (like IBM, Hewlett Packard, and Dell), Internet service providers (like America Online), applications program developers (like Intuit), and ordinary computer users would have to use Microsoft's browser even if they preferred Netscape's. Although Netscape still had a substantial share of browser usage, that share was declining and could be expected to fall sharply with the shipment in June of Windows 98, a new version designed to prevent replacement of Microsoft's browser with Netscape's.

The suppression of Netscape's browser would eliminate an important threat to Microsoft's operating system monopoly. The popularity of Navigator was leading more applications developers to write programs that ran on Navigator. Since Navigator could in turn run on a variety of operating systems, this multiplied the number of "cross-platform applications programs" that could run on both Microsoft and non-Microsoft operating systems. Because the inability of non-Microsoft software to compete effectively with Windows was based on the self-reinforcing network effects that resulted from having many more applications available with Windows than were available for use with other operating systems, the success of Navigator threatened Microsoft's OS monopoly.

Another concern was Microsoft's efforts to block the distribution and use of Java, a software distributed by Sun Microsystems that, like the Netscape browser, acted as "middleware" (programming between the operating system and applications software). Applications written to connect to Java applications programming

_____

*"Tying" refers to the practice of requiring a customer to take a product it doesn't want (the "tied product") in order to get a product that it needs (the "tying product"). Where customers have limited competitive alternatives to the tying product, the practice may violate Section 1. If the seller has monopoly power and the practice protects or extends such power, it will ordinarily violate Section 2 as well.

interfaces, or APIs, like programs written to connect to the APIs of
the Netscape Navigator, could run on many operating systems, not
just Windows. Again it appeared that Microsoft had used its market
power to limit the use and distribution of Sun's Java.

In addition to our other evidence, we had identified e-mails
from Gates personally and several of his top executives in which they
recognized that Navigator and Java threatened Window's dominance, and discussed how to eliminate those threats.

At the end of March 1998, I completed my closing argument in
the Banque Indosuez case and, while the jury was deliberating, flew
to Washington to review the status of our investigation and discuss
our strategy with Attorney General Janet Reno. After I had finished
my presentation, the attorney general asked me to outline what I
thought Microsoft's best response would be and how I would answer that response, which I did. As we were leaving, she drew me
aside. Did I have enough resources? I said I did. Could the department effectively take on Microsoft in court if that ultimately proved
to be the right decision? I said it could. "The subject matter is complicated, and Microsoft will try to make it seem even more so," I
said. "But this is really not that hard a case to try."

We still had much work to do. There were key people in the
antitrust division itself who opposed a suit against Microsoft. And
even if there were ultimately a recommendation to the Attorney
General to go forward, she would make the final decision. Nevertheless, we were far enough along that it was time to give Bill
Gates and his team a chance to meet with us to discuss our preliminary analysis.

Before commencing major antitrust litigation, it is standard
practice for the government to give a prospective defendant an opportunity to convince it not to proceed. In part this is done because the mere bringing of such a lawsuit by the Justice
Department can affect a company and its business, and before imposing those consequences the government in fairness needs to
make sure that it has fully heard the other side. Such meetings are
also done in the department's self-interest to avoid making a costly

and embarrassing mistake. I had expected Janet Reno's question, and had given considerable thought to what Microsoft's best arguments were likely to be. However, the company had many more lawyers and much more information than I had and might well make a better defense of its actions than I would.

Doug Melamed was Joel's chief deputy. Dan Rubenfeld, a professor of economics on leave from his university, was Joel's deputy in charge of economic analysis. The evening of April 17 Joel, Doug, Dan, and I met with Bill Gates, his general counsel Bill Neukom, and Sullivan & Cromwell partner Richard Urowsky at the latter's offices in Washington, D.C. Such a meeting would ordinarily be held at the Justice Department, but Microsoft had asked to meet at its lawyers' offices, and Joel was not one to stand on ceremony. A couple of the younger lawyers on Joel's staff groused about Microsoft's "arrogance" at asking the department to come to them. Joel laughed it off. "I can listen as well at their offices as in mine," he said. Also on our mind was the publicity that might be generated were Bill Gates spied entering the Justice Department's offices.

My back was painfully reflecting months of too much travel, too little sleep, and too many heavy suitcases filled with paper. My condition was sufficiently obvious that we spent several minutes at the beginning of the meeting with Gates and his lawyers offering practical advice. They knew that "less travel, more sleep, and fewer papers" was not at that time meaningful advice, and their suggestions were both appreciated and useful. When we turned to substance, the meeting started well for Microsoft. Gates was a passionate, articulate, and fact-laden defender of the company he had founded, at his best describing Microsoft's many accomplishments, including how it had initially achieved its position at the expense of larger, better-financed, and better-positioned competitors. His problem came in responding to questions. There is much to be said for staying on message, but when you seek to persuade, you must address the concerns of the people you are trying to convince. As the evening wore on it sometimes seemed as if Gates were attempting to win the hearts and minds of a nonexistent audience rather than persuading us. Although prior to the meeting we had given his lawyers an outline of our key conduct issues Gates kept returning to the argument that Microsoft lacked monopoly power. About two-thirds of the way through the meeting I tried to redirect the focus.

"I know you feel strongly that Microsoft does not have monopoly power, and that that should be the end of our analysis," I said. "I am not asking you to abandon that position. However, you should understand that it is likely that we will conclude that Microsoft does have that power. We are much more uncertain which, if any, practices of the company are improper. It would help us if you would concentrate on the issue of Microsoft's practices."

Gates's immediate reaction was to tell me that any thought that Microsoft had monopoly power simply showed how little we knew about the industry. We did have some discussion of practices, but the focus remained on monopoly power. At one point, arguing that all that mattered in the industry was people, and that people were mobile, Gates said, "Give me any seat at the table. Give me Sun, give me Oracle,* give me IBM, even give me AOL, and I will come out on top." As we left the meeting, I almost believed him. He was as smart, thoughtful, creative, articulate, and driven as anyone I had met. Nevertheless he did not help his company that evening, as his lawyers later acknowledged.

Microsoft soon launched a public relations offensive that was one of the toughest I had seen. Gates was quoted by *Fortune* as describing our investigation as "this stupid thing." Steven Ballmer, Gates's right-hand man and the person who would succeed him as CEO before the case was over, told a software developers conference, "to heck with Janet Reno." We had informed Microsoft that we believed that its planned Windows 98 operating system should

---

*Oracle and Sun, together with IBM, were viewed by Microsoft as its leading software competitors. Apple was a distant also-ran.

continue to permit users to remove the IE browser. The company responded

> Holding up the release of a major software innovation like Windows 98 would be like telling General Motors they cannot come out with new cars this fall, or telling Paramount they can't come out with any new movies on July 4, or telling Wall Street they can't issue any new stocks.

"That is so totally unfair," a Department of Justice lawyer complained. "They know we don't want to hold up Windows 98, and that all we want is for them to continue to allow users a practical choice of which browser to use."

"Of course they do," I replied, "and of course it is. But it's not their job to be fair."

The company also hired PR firms around the country to submit pro-Microsoft opinion pieces to local newspapers without identifying them as having been paid for by Microsoft. When the *Los Angeles Times* reported this story, the state attorneys general who were investigating the company were furious. They were similarly displeased by Microsoft's attacks on their competence. "Bill Gates has said he can't believe he will be regulated by people who didn't pass high school physics," one complained to the *Washington Post*. "We can't believe we have to deal with someone who didn't pass high school civics."

Microsoft's efforts were not the "public relations fiasco" that *U.S. News & World Report* described them as, and they probably did not cause either the Justice Department or the states to take any action they would not otherwise have taken, but they certainly did not help Microsoft either.

I had drafted an initial complaint as early as February, in part to set out what I thought had to be supported in order to bring a case. Over the following weeks our discovery had revealed evidence for most of the points that I had outlined. My original complaint had claims under all three of the major antitrust provisions: Sections 1 and 2 of the Sherman Act and Section 7 of the Clayton Act.

The heart of the complaint, and what made the case important, was the Section 2 monopoly maintenance claim. The primary purpose of Microsoft's browser war, as revealed by its internal documents, was to eliminate a potential threat to its operating system monopoly. If the government's action were to match the alleged illegal conduct, it was necessary to proceed under Section 2. Persons who opposed bringing any suit at that time argued that if a case were brought it should be a narrow browser-only case for Section 1 tying and, perhaps, attempted monopolization of the browser market. By contrast, I was more confident in our ability to win the broad monopolization case.* I also believed that in order to get a court to intervene in the dynamic and successful personal computer market we had to convince a judge that something important was at stake.

Ultimately Joel and then Janet Reno came to the view that a Section 2 monopoly case was appropriate. The concern at the department was that such a case would take years to prepare and perhaps additional years to try. "If the judge is willing," I told Janet Reno, "this case can be prepared for trial in less than a year. The trial itself could be anywhere from two to six months, but not more if we do our job of focusing on the key issues."

Probably the biggest mistake plaintiffs' lawyers make is complicating their case with unnecessary issues and evidence. I had already reduced our case to six key themes.

---

*All the conduct at issue was relevant to a Section 2 monopoly case, and the standard that had to be met for establishing improper conduct was easier in a Section 2 monopoly case than in either a Section 1 case or a Section 2 attempted monopolization case. A Section 2 monopoly case, unlike the other claims, required proof of monopoly power; but of all the issues to be tried that was the issue about which I was most confident. I believed there was merit to including a Section 7 claim both because the effect on competition that had to be shown to make out a violation was less and because a Section 7 violation made it easier to justify divestiture if the department concluded that was appropriate.

First, Microsoft had monopoly power because PC manufacturers had no practical alternative operating system to Windows. This power in turn gave the company control over Internet service providers and software developers.

Second, Microsoft's power was protected by what we labeled the "applications programming barrier to entry"—the self-reinforcing cycle of networks effects that led consumers to want a computer that would run the largest number of applications, and applications developers to write programs to run on the operating system with the greatest market share.

Third, Netscape's browser and Sun's Java threatened this barrier to entry by enabling applications developers to write programs that could then be used with a variety of systems.

Fourth, Microsoft used its control over access to Windows to force PC manufacturers and Internet service providers to distribute its browser instead of Netscape's, to induce applications developers to write for Microsoft's browser instead of Navigator, and to discourage the use of Java.

Fifth, by preserving its monopoly, Microsoft was able to charge higher prices and exercise more control over what choices were offered consumers than would be possible in a more competitive market.

Sixth, Microsoft's conduct deprived ordinary computer users of a free choice of which browser to use, and new companies were being deprived of the opportunity to compete on the merits that Microsoft had enjoyed—with the result that consumers would be deprived of still more choices in the future.

It was not a simple case, but it could be readily understood in a matter of days or weeks, not months or years. I expected Microsoft to try to complicate and delay. Most defendants seek to do this, believing that a delay is as good as a win, just less permanent. The problem is that such temporary respite often comes at the expense of making permanent victory more difficult. Defendants usually have both more resources and greater access to evidence than plaintiffs; in such a case, preparation time benefits the plaintiff more than the defendant. In addition, a judge will often react badly to delaying tactics. Even so I expected Microsoft to stick to the conventional defendant's playbook and try to draw the case out. I knew that to prevent that tactic from succeeding we would have to identify understandable themes from the outset and stick to them.

We had planned to file our complaint on May 12, 1998. However, on May 11 Joel Klein called Microsoft general counsel Bill Neukom to give a heads-up on our plans. A series of telephone calls lasting well into the night between Joel and Bill Gates followed, at the end of which we believed an agreement in principle had been reached to settle. I had ambivalent feelings. On the one hand I thought that the changes the company was agreeing to were useful, that we would achieve those changes immediately, and that we would avoid the risk of a trial. On the other hand I thought that we should, and probably would, win at trial and that we could then expect significantly greater relief.

We put off filing the complaint until Monday, May 17, and Bill Neukom and his team flew to Washington to draft an agreement. The department's negotiating team was led by Jeff Blattner, who was as knowledgeable as anyone other than Phil Malone as to the facts and issues. While Jeff and others negotiated, Chris Crook and I and our trial team used the time to refine our complaint and supporting evidence. Phil Malone had to divide himself between the two efforts since both Jeff and I needed his support. Late in the afternoon, Phil returned to our war room from a negotiating session.

"Unless they're playing a game," he said, "there's not going to be a settlement. Neukom has cut back on what Gates offered Joel." We both suspected this might be a negotiating ploy to test our resolve. It turned out that it was not. When Jeff stuck to what he believed Joel and Gates had agreed to, the negotiations ended. Perhaps Joel and Gates had misunderstood each other in the early-morning hours of their long-distance telephone negotiations. Perhaps Microsoft had changed its mind. In either event we were going to trial. Neither Phil nor I was disappointed.

We had our first hearing before Judge Thomas Penfield Jackson on May 22. The initial reaction of the press in general and legal commentators in particular indicated we were decidedly the underdogs. Virtually everyone expected the case to take years; most people expected that when we did get to trial we would lose. The *National Law Journal*'s headline read, "No Precedents Squarely Cover Software Cases," a point that was to become central to Microsoft's defense. The *Wall Street Journal* joked: "Good thing Bill Gates is still a young man. He might live long enough to find out how the case against his company turns out." *Time* predicted "a long and costly battle" and reported that "many legal scholars" thought we would "have a tough time winning." *Newsweek* reported that "most experts think" that we had a "tough case" to win. Numerous articles drew an analogy between the case just filed and the IBM litigation.

I appreciated the many letters and e-mails I received from consumers and others cheering me on. Someone sent me a quotation from the beginning of the movie version of *A Civil Action* in which John Travolta says:

> Lawsuits are war. It's as simple as that. And they begin the same way: with a declaration of war—the complaint . . . When you're a small firm and they're a big one it's easy to be intimidated. Don't be—that's what they want . . . I don't run away from bullies.

In general, I think the analogy of litigation to war is overdone. While there are similarities (including the critical importance of planning, discipline, and logistics), you can't get hurt in litigation unless your charts fall on you. Nevertheless, before the Microsoft case was done I knew what Travolta was talking about.

I had appeared before Judge Jackson fifteen years earlier when he was presiding over my discovery of the CIA and National Security Agency in connection with General Westmoreland's libel case. I knew both from that experience and from Jackson's reputation that he was a good and experienced trial judge. Ronald Reagan's first appointment to the federal district court in the District of Columbia, he was conservative and would begin with a disinclination to meddle with a company as successful as Microsoft. On the other hand Jackson was himself a former trial lawyer with respect for the rule of law. I believed he would find the facts fairly (in a government antitrust case there is no jury) and that if they added up to an antitrust violation, he would rule in our favor.

Appearing for Microsoft were John Warden and Richard Urowsky. Richard is a brilliant antitrust theoretician. John is a trial lawyer of the very first rank whom I have known for thirty years. When he was a young lawyer, John had succeeded in reversing a major antitrust award against Kodak, and he had gone on to several other significant successes. Particularly with the back-up provided by Microsoft and Sullivan & Cromwell—widely regarded as one of the best large law firms in the country, and the firm my son Christopher chose to join when he graduated from Yale Law School—the two men were a formidable team.

Before the hearing we had filed a motion for a preliminary injunction that would require Microsoft to give Windows users a choice of browsers either by making its own removable or by distributing Netscape's browser with Windows. Such an injunction is designed to maintain the status quo until a full trial. In asking for one here, we were giving the judge an alternative. If you do not grant us an early trial, we were saying, at least require Microsoft to provide a practical choice of browsers while the trial is delayed. Our motion also presented Microsoft with a dilemma. The longer any delay, the stronger our case for an interim injunction; conversely, the more it argued against the injunction the better our argument for an early trial became.

The hearing started with my explaining why it was important that the case move quickly. John Warden argued that any trial date before 1999 was unrealistic. After hearing from each side, Judge Jackson said that he would not grant a preliminary injunction but would set September 8, 1998, as the trial date. John protested loudly, but Judge Jackson noted that he knew from prior experience that large law firms and the Justice Department could prepare big cases in a relatively short time if the judge held their feet to the fire. Nevertheless, the court continued, "Come back to me later on after you have made the effort to get ready to take this case to trial. And if you can convince me that you should be given more time, I will try to listen with an open mind."

Both sides now turned to the nuts and bolts of pretrial "discovery." The purpose of discovery is to further the search for truth by providing equal access to facts and evidence and by eliminating "trial by ambush," where one side hides evidence it wants to spring at trial on an unsuspecting opponent. The three basic tools of discovery are document demands (by which a party can require someone to produce all their documents and records relating to the case), interrogatories (written questions that one party can require another to answer), and depositions (in which a party can require a witness to answer oral questions under oath before trial).

Discovery works reasonably well when you have two relatively equally matched opponents (either two large parties, each of which can afford the costs of extensive discovery, or two small ones, neither of which has many resources, and for whom discovery is therefore limited to the essentials); it works much less well where one party has the power and resources to overwhelm the other. Here both sides had the resources to do whatever was necessary. Although Microsoft had three times as many lawyers as I had and spent more than eight times what we did, we were relatively evenly matched. My trial team of a dozen department lawyers made up in hard work, commitment, and ability what we lacked in numbers, and the government has powers of investigation that no private party can match. In addition, at critical times I was able to enlist Bob Silver in crafting our legal analysis and my partners Steve Neuwirth and Mike Brille in preparing important witnesses. Neither side was going to overwhelm the other.

Discovery started in earnest in June, and my team crisscrossed the country reviewing documents and taking depositions. There is sometimes a tendency to think of government lawyers as less capable than their much more highly paid counterparts in big firms. Somewhere there are mediocre lawyers in government, just as there are in private firms, but my Microsoft trial team was as good as any I have ever had.

Three weeks into discovery the U.S. Court of Appeals handed down a decision that, on the surface, hit us hard. Late the previous year the Department of Justice had moved to have Microsoft held in contempt for violating the 1994 consent decree by tying its IE browser to a new release of its operating system, Windows 95. Judge Jackson, who had approved the 1994 consent decree and hence had jurisdiction over motions for contempt, had denied the motion but did issue a preliminary injunction ordering Microsoft not to tie its IE browser to Windows pending a full trial.

On June 23, the day before I planned to fly to San Francisco to review discovery and trial preparation plans with the lawyers there, the court of appeals reversed the injunction, holding that the consent decree did not prohibit Microsoft's proposed action. Since the claim that Microsoft had violated the antitrust laws by tying the IE browser and Windows was an important part of our complaint, Microsoft (and many commentators) were quick to interpret this decision as our death knell. In particular, they pointed to a portion of an opinion by the two-judge majority cautioning that "the limited competence of courts to evaluate high-tech product designs and the high cost of error should make them wary of second-guessing the claimed benefits of a particular design decision."

This is what Microsoft had been arguing all along, and it was quick to assert that the ruling "cut the heart out" of our claim. The *Financial Times* reported the opinion as a "significant victory" for Microsoft; the *Washington Post* agreed, adding that "legal experts said the ruling would force Justice to rework the strategy" of its case. *U.S. News & World Report* said the decision "fell on Justice like an anvil to the head" and "severely impairs Justice's ongoing antitrust suit."

As I flew to San Francisco the following morning, I read and reread the court of appeals decision. I knew I had to figure out how to deal with the ruling before I next appeared before Judge Jackson. It was also important not to let the trial team get discouraged or have potential witnesses give our case up as a lost cause.

By the time I was over Nebraska, I thought I understood the majority's opinion; by the time I landed in San Francisco, I was certain how I would deal with it. When I walked into the large conference room at the Justice Department's offices at 450 Golden Gate Avenue, the faces of the assembled team were glum. It was clear that it was not only Microsoft that saw the opinion as a body blow to our case. However, it was also clear that no one was prepared to throw in the towel.

I noted at the outset that we had to accept the majority opinion as the law for planning purposes. It was true that it was a two to one decision, and that the majority consisted of two of the most conservative judges on the court of appeals. However, Judge Jackson would consider himself bound by the ruling unless and until it was reversed by the court of appeals itself or by the Supreme Court, and there was no realistic chance that either was going to happen before trial.

Our first argument was that the ruling interpreted the 1994 consent decree, and as the decision itself made clear, our issue of whether the tying was illegal under the antitrust laws was a separate question that it had not addressed.

Second, the majority opinion emphasized the lack of evidence to support the district court's decision. This fact, together with the first point, emphasized the need for us to identify the elements of an illegal tying claim under the Sherman Act and to be sure that we had extensive evidence of each such element. That work was already under way.

Third, the opinion effectively recognized that Microsoft had monopoly power. This was significant because under Section 2 once monopoly power is established a company is prohibited from many acts that companies without monopoly power are permitted. Tying the browser to the Windows operating system software might not violate the consent decree, but it could well violate Section 1 and almost certainly violated Section 2 if monopoly power was assumed.

Fourth, the opinion was concerned exclusively with product design, an area in which the courts have historically been reluctant to get involved. By contrast, much of our case related to Microsoft's agreements with PC manufacturers (OEMs), Internet service providers like AOL (ISPs), software developers, and content providers. Such agreements raised garden variety antitrust issues.

By the end of our meeting I knew that my audience in San Francisco agreed with my analysis. We now had three more difficult audiences to convince. There were potential industry witnesses who were unlikely to come forward unless they were convinced we would win; then we had to convince Judge Jackson at trial; and ultimately there was the court of appeals.

The evidence that we uncovered that summer gave me additional building blocks with which to construct our case. Microsoft was active in cross-examining witnesses we deposed, but while it took some depositions of its own, they were surprisingly few. Nor did it undertake massive discovery of the federal government itself. The U.S. government is the world's largest user of computers in general and personal computers in particular. During the IBM litigation much of our best evidence turned out to be documents that the government produced in response to our demands—and admissions by government employees in depositions. Representing the U.S. in civil litigation is a two-edged sword. There are many advantages, but one important disadvantage is the many documents and witnesses you are stuck with. There would be, I believed, government documents and employees on each side of the case. I had expected Microsoft to undertake a major effort to mine the government for evidence helpful to it. When it did not, it freed us from the need to rebut our own documents and witnesses.

There were two depositions in which I wanted to participate.

One was Microsoft's examination of Jim Barksdale, Netscape's CEO. Netscape was a central part of our case, Barksdale was a critical witness, and Microsoft had made it clear that attacking his credibility was a priority. The other deposition was that of Bill Gates. Probably not since John D. Rockefeller and Standard Oil had a dominant company so reflected the personality and decisions of a single person. Gates had built the company and personally dictated the practices that were now under attack. Particularly with his charisma and credibility, I thought he would be the most important single witness of the trial; I knew from firsthand experience how strong an advocate he could be. This was a deposition I needed to do myself. I also did not want to pass up either the challenge or the opportunity of an extended dialogue with one of the most interesting business executives of our time.

I had reserved the month of July for a cross-country Jeep trip with my youngest son, Alex. The Gates deposition was not scheduled until August. However, the Barksdale deposition was set for July 17 in Mountain View, California, just north of San Jose. Since Alex and I were planning on visiting our ranch in northern California anyway, we agreed that I would interrupt our trip for a day to sit in on Barksdale's examination.

I began taking cross-country trips with my children in 1980 when Christopher and Jonathan were twelve, the same age that Alex was when our 1998 trip started. The Jeep that Christopher and I drove to Aspen in 1980 was an old CJ-5 with no top and no doors. Although the CJ-5 had been replaced and replaced again, it became a tradition over the years to leave the top and doors behind even when we had a Jeep that had them. We also typically left on July 1, the day after Mary's birthday.

Sometimes we plan where we are going in advance, sometimes not; sometimes when we do plan in advance, the plan changes en route. Our favorite destinations are Colorado and California, but we have visited each of the contiguous forty-eight states on one Jeep trip or another. We stay off the interstate highways and take our time.

This time our path was in part dictated by our desire to watch the All-Star Game (played that year in Denver), explore Bryce Canyon and Yellowstone Park, and visit our ranch, which was located 100 miles north of San Francisco. We arrived in San Francisco after two weeks on the road. The doorman at the Fairmont Hotel was a little disconcerted by our appearance (and the appearance of our vehicle); however, once he was assured we did in fact have a reservation and had not wandered in by mistake, he was quite friendly. After spending the following day at Fisherman's Wharf and on a cruise around San Francisco Bay, we headed to Mountain View.

I spent several hours at the Barksdale deposition (which went well and was somewhat shorter than expected), while Alex was entertained by Netscape techies. The following morning we continued on our trip. When we returned home two weeks later by way of the Grand Canyon and the St. Louis Arch, I found the case progressing well toward trial.

My examination of Gates was originally scheduled for August 10, and when I arrived in Seattle, I was shown a copy of a front-page article in the *Seattle Times* that described the upcoming deposition as a "battle of titans" for which they should sell tickets. Karma Giulianelli, a bright young Justice Department attorney who was helping me prepare for Gates, was amused by the piece. "Little do they know how boring it's likely to be," she said.

I too was amused, but I also wondered what effect the hype would have on Gates. By all accounts he was someone used to being in command. He was also very competitive. ("I'm looking forward to this," he told a friend. "I enjoy depositions.") I knew that Gates would not be able to control his deposition; no witness can in the hands of an experienced lawyer, because the examiner controls the subjects, questions, and pace. I also knew how disastrous it is for witnesses to fence or compete with examiners; they almost always come off as arrogant, evasive, or both. In their preparation of Gates, I expected that his lawyers would warn him of this. But I wondered whether the press hype would interfere with Gates's willingness to follow that advice—and how I could make following that advice difficult.

At the last minute the examination was postponed because of a controversy over whether the press would attend. There was a statute that appeared to mandate that examinations in antitrust cases brought by the government be open to the public. Judge Jackson had reluctantly so ruled, denying the company's request to bar the press. On the eve of the scheduled deposition, however, the court of appeals handed Microsoft what looked at the time to be a victory, barring reporters until it heard the case. Since the court set its hearing after all the depositions were to be completed, the decision effectively meant that the press could not attend any deposition. Some of the trial team saw the court of appeals stay as just another example of that court going out of its way to protect Microsoft. I wasn't so sure. The stay was certainly unusual, and appeared to contradict a congressional command; but the court of appeals for the District of Columbia had a record of being concerned about the intrusiveness of the press, and I was inclined to view the decision as more antimedia than pro-Microsoft. In any event the more interesting question to me was what effect the decision might have on Gates, including whether the absence of reporters would make him more or less aggressive.

The deposition was rescheduled to start August 27. When I arrived in Seattle the day before, Phil Malone and Karma Giulianelli were already at a motel in Kirkland, Washington, with several boxes of documents. After checking in to the motel, I walked around the neighborhood thinking about themes I wanted to develop the following day. Some lawyers take a deposition from a detailed outline, questioning the witness about every event and document that appears relevant. In general, I try to identify basic themes, then engage the witness in a conversation designed to establish and support them. Individual facts, events, or documents may serve as tools, but I may go an entire day without showing the witness a document or asking about a specific fact.

In virtually every case there are truths that favor each side. The examiner, by controlling the questioning, is able to focus on those that favor his client. Witnesses are then forced to make uncomfortable choices. They can admit fact after fact, knowing they are building the examiner's record, or they can try to deny or evade. The goal of the examiner is to press and cajole witnesses into taking positions as absolute as possible in which they either give up more than they should or stake out a position that is ultimately not sustainable and ends up damaging their credibility—and hence their ability to provide effective testimony against the examiner's interests. The goals of witnesses are to provide balanced answers that give the examiner what he is entitled to (and will probably be able to prove in any event), while providing the qualifications and context that limit the usefulness of the concessions—and to avoid staking out positions in terms so stark or absolute that they cannot be sustained.

I normally videotape depositions, and we had set up to do this with Gates. A tape captures the mannerisms, delays, and inflections that a cold transcript misses; it also tends to restrain some of the obstructionism and coaching that lawyers sometimes engage in when trying to keep a witness from giving too much away. If a witness does try to play games, a videotape captures such activity in living color.

When I got back to the motel, I stopped by Karma's room to ask her to pull together what she thought were the five to ten most helpful documents authored by or sent to Gates. Back in my room, I turned on the television and found that *Tombstone*, a movie about the Earp brothers, was about to start. In the middle of the film Karma brought me a package of about fifteen documents, saying she had difficulty narrowing the list further. As I glanced through them I could see why; there were so many helpful statements. Thursday was going to be an interesting day.

We arrived at the Microsoft campus in Redmond, Washington, to be greeted by a mixture of suspicion and hostility that reminded me of the reception I had received in Mississippi courtrooms in the 1960s when I was representing civil rights workers.

"Are they always like this?" I asked Phil, who had already taken a number of depositions there.

"Pretty much."

We were ushered into the conference room where the deposition was to be taken to discover that Gates would be represented by not one but three lawyers—Richard Urowsky, the Sullivan & Cromwell partner who was the architect of Microsoft's defense; Bill Neukom; and David Heiner, one of Neukom's deputies. It was understandable that both Neukom and Urowsky would want to see how Gates performed. It would, however, be interesting to see who would be responsible for making objections and giving Gates advice, and whether the other two could restrain themselves. Having a single coach advising you in the middle of a game is hard enough; it is really difficult to have more than one.

My examination was scheduled to begin after lunch. When Gates came into the room, it was clear that this was not the confident, dynamic executive I had met four months before. He moved quickly to his chair, nodding briefly in our direction but avoiding eye contact. While seated, he rocked slightly back and forth. As I typically do, I began my examination by saying good afternoon to the witness. For the first time in more than thirty years of taking depositions, I got no response.

Someone wandering into the deposition would not have thought anything important was under way. The space itself was nondescript, with bare walls and none of the solemn trappings of a courtroom. The papers scattered across the table, and the boxes of documents that surrounded us, gave an air of informality. Gates and I, each dressed in our inexpensive suits, faced each other across a simple wooden table, speaking for the most part quietly and without emotion. Nevertheless, the stakes could not have been higher.

Microsoft had already told the press that Gates would be one of their key witnesses at trial. If he was as effective as I believed he could be, he would have a powerful impact, particularly on a judge predisposed to be suspicious of government interference. On the other hand, because Gates so personified Microsoft, it would be stuck with any admission he made, and any credibility hit he took would damage the entire company. I did not think much about it until the deposition was already under way, but it was also true that, because of the central role Gates played, if he could not give a satisfactory justification for conduct that we challenged, any explanation by one of his lieutenants would carry little weight. Many corporate CEOs can claim lack of knowledge and let a subordinate defend what was done. At Microsoft the buck started and stopped with Gates.

I was only minutes into the questioning when Gates began to engage in a pattern of verbal fencing that came to characterize his deposition in court and in the popular press. He was doing nothing different than what thousands of deponents have done over the years. Only he was not just any witness; he was the most important witness in an unusually important case.

Gates also fell victim to a tendency to make broad, colorful statements that probably made sense to him when he said them but proved impossible to sustain. For example, in an attempt to show that Microsoft was not as dominant as we suggested, he would go to the unnecessary extreme of asserting that people two years earlier had considered the company "on the verge of doom." Phil immediately passed me a note that Microsoft in that year, 1996, had recorded over $2 billion in after-tax profits. Juxtaposing that fact with Gates's assertion not only disposed of the assertion but began the process of eroding the witness's credibility.

What is going on? I wondered. Haven't his lawyers prepared him? Is he refusing to follow their advice? Where is the man who blew me away last April? And how do I keep him from reappearing?

My early themes with Gates were that Microsoft believed Netscape and Sun's Java represented competitive threats, that it analyzed how to cripple the two companies, that it undertook a program of weakening Netscape and Sun by depriving them of the revenue they needed to support their products, and that it used its power to force other industry participants to stop supporting its two rivals.

In my first afternoon I showed Gates documents that suggested Microsoft wanted to create a negative impression of Netscape among financial analysts. I showed him an article from *Business Week* that reported him as saying, "Our business model works even if all Internet software is free. We are still selling operating systems." The magazine went on: "Netscape, in contrast, is dependent on its Internet software for profits, he points out."

Gates began by claiming not to recall making such comments. His testimony in this respect could well have been true, in that busy executives do not remember every interview. However, since the thoughts attributed to him were consistent with his own e-mails, it would have been easy to say, "I don't remember saying this specifically, but I probably did, and it certainly reflects my views." Instead his response made it appear that he was trying to run away from what he had said at the time, giving more emphasis, and a more negative cast, to the statements than they otherwise would have had. At one point his failure of recollection extended to not knowing what was meant by "Internet software."

As it became clear to me that he would contradict the written record, I began to use more documents than I ordinarily would have. I found that Phil and Karma had an uncanny ability to pull just the right document from their boxes for me to bait the hook.

I showed Gates a 1996 memorandum to his top executives about combating Netscape in which he wrote, "At some point financial minded analysts will begin to consider how much of a revenue stream Netscape will be able to generate." Unable to reconcile this focus with his present testimony all he could say was, "I can't reconstruct my state of mind in 1996."

The more he was pressed the more unresponsive his answers became.

Q In 1996, did you want, desire, financial analysts to have
   a poor or pessimistic or negative view about Netscape?

A Well, as we, during 1996, were improving our product and demonstrating our products and talking about what we thought customers were interested in, there were several elements of feedback that we'd get including what customers were saying about our Internet strategy and our Internet products, and the analysts, likewise, were a form of feedback . . .

Either a simple yes or a simple no would have been better. When I asked him about what Microsoft sought to accomplish, he again avoided answering.

Q Let me be sure my question is clear. Was any part of Microsoft's actions with respect to its browser or, as you sometimes refer to it, browser technology, motivated by a desire to drive Netscape's revenues from users of Netscape's browser down to zero?

A Well, I think you're getting a little bit psychological there.

At the end of my first afternoon I turned to meetings that were held in May and June 1995 between Netscape and Microsoft representatives. In our May 1998 complaint we had alleged that Microsoft had tried to get Netscape to agree to limit competition with Microsoft, a clear violation of the antitrust laws. When I raised the topic, Gates surprised me by asserting that he had never heard of any allegations concerning the Netscape meetings until a recent *Wall Street Journal* article. How could that have been the first time, I asked, when it is in our complaint? He replied that he had never bothered to read the complaint, and no one had ever told him it was in there.

When I talked to Joel Klein, and later that evening to Mary, I told each of them that it was hard for me to believe that Gates would be a witness at trial. "He's a different person from the man we met with in Washington," I told Joel. "He would be a disaster as a witness if he acted like this before Jackson. Even if they're able to clean him up for trial he's locking himself into positions he can't escape."

"It is almost," I later mused to Mary, "as if they have forgotten that everything he says now is being recorded and will be played back at trial."

It was an understatement to say I was puzzled by Gates's performance; he had all the tools to be a great witness and had some of the best lawyers in the world to help him. I was also puzzled by his counsel. When a witness of mine begins to damage himself the way Gates was doing, I will either interrupt the deposition for a break to get the witness on track or admonish the witness on the record to listen to the question, be responsive, and not volunteer. Richard and Bill had sat silent; when David Heiner had spoken, it was to defend what the witness was saying. At one point when I suggested that Gates was evasive or nonresponsive, Heiner told Gates that he "should continue" his pattern of responses. I can understand a lawyer's inclination to defend his witness, particularly someone who was his boss's boss. But if, as it appeared, David had been given the assignment of representing Gates and Microsoft at this deposition, he was not serving either client well by not taking control of the situation. And if he was unable to control Gates, a distinct possibility, somebody needed to intervene. Maybe, I thought, they were waiting for the evening recess to regroup.

To my surprise the second day of Gates's deposition mirrored the first. Again my ritual "Good morning, Mr. Gates" was met with silence, and I waited a moment as the videotape recorded the scene.

I began with the subject of Java. Because of its ability to reduce Microsoft's applications programming advantage, Java was widely referred to within and without Microsoft as a major competitive threat to its dominance. Gates initially fenced over the use of the word "threat."

Q When you talk about having a view that what Sun was doing was a competitive "activity," do you use the term "activity" to mean the same thing that you meant before when you used the term "threat"?

A You were the one who used the term "threat." I'm not quite sure. It was competitive. Is something that is competitive always a competitive threat? I'm not sure.

Q Mr. Gates, I think the record will show, and if necessary we can go back to it, that you used the term "Java runtime threat." Do you recall doing that?

A Yes.

Q Okay. Now—

A That's not the same as "competitive threat."

Q Well, when you used the "Java runtime threat" phrase, what did you mean by threat?

A I meant that it was competitive.

Q And so you were using, in that context, "threat" and "competitive" to mean the same thing?

A Yes.

I then turned to the issue of what Microsoft did to respond to the threat Java posed.

Q What did you do to try to respond to what you have described as the Java runtime threat?

A The same thing we always do, just innovate in our products and use the customer feedback to delight them so they choose to license our products . . .

Q Did you do anything else?

A I'm not sure what you mean. I mean our whole activity here, everything we do really comes under what I just described . . .

> Q Well, sir, does trying to undermine Sun come within the activity you've just described?
>
> A I don't know what you mean by that.

> Q You don't?
>
> A No.

I could tell by the way Heiner and Urowsky began to shift in their seats and look at each other that they knew all too well where I was going. I showed Gates an e-mail he had sent to his top executive Paul Maritz in which he asked: "Do we have a clear plan on what we want Apple to do to undermine Sun?"

> Q Did you send this e-mail, Mr. Gates, on or about August 8, 1997?
>
> A I don't remember sending it.

> Q What did you mean when you asked Mr. Maritz whether or not "we have a clear plan on what we want Apple to do to undermine Sun"?
>
> A I don't remember.

He might not remember, but I did. Microsoft's "Office" software was probably the single most important applications program, and being able to use that application on their computers was important to a large number of Apple customers. If Microsoft stopped offering Office for use on Apple desktops, it would cripple Apple's sales. I began with that truth, which I knew Gates would eventually have to accept.

> Q And was it your understanding that Microsoft Office for Macintosh was believed by Apple to be very important to them?
>
> A I really have a hard time testifying about the belief of a corporation. I really don't know what that means.

> Q Well, sir, in making the decisions as to what you would ask of Apple, did you believe that what you were offering

Apple with respect to Microsoft Office for Macintosh was important enough to Apple so that they ought to give you something for it?

A I have no idea what you're talking about when you say "ask."

I showed Gates an e-mail from Microsoft executive Don Bradford to Gates, Maritz, and others dated February 13, 1998. The first paragraph reads: "Getting Apple to do anything that significantly/materially disadvantages Netscape will be tough. Do agree that Apple should be meeting the spirit of our cross license agreement and that Mac Office is the perfect club to use on them."

Q Do you have an understanding of what Mr. Bradford means when he refers to Mac Office as "the perfect club to use on Apple"?

A No.

Q The second sentence of that paragraph, the one that reads, "Getting Apple to do anything will be tough." Was it your understanding in February of 1998 that Microsoft was trying to get Apple to do something to disadvantage Netscape?

A No.

Q Did you ever say to Mr. Bradford in word or substance in February of 1998 or thereafter, "Mr. Bradford, you've got it wrong, we're not out to significantly or materially disadvantage Netscape through Apple"?

A No.

Q Did you ever tell Mr. Bradford or anyone else in February 1998 or thereafter that they should not be trying to get Apple to do things that would significantly or materially disadvantage Netscape?

A No.

It was becoming increasingly clear to me that I was never going to have the chance to examine Gates at trial. Whatever Microsoft's plans had been before this deposition, John Warden and Richard were too smart to let me have an opportunity to repeat this in front of Judge Jackson. Accordingly, I began to treat the examination as if it were the last word. Most depositions are designed to prepare for trial, and you try to develop the building blocks you will use then rather than explicitly combining those blocks to establish your case at the deposition itself. However, where a key witness is not likely to appear, the deposition becomes a substitute for trial testimony. I therefore decided to go into the Apple story in more detail.

> Q Did you ever discuss within Microsoft threatening Apple that you were going to cancel Mac Office?
> A You wouldn't cancel—no.

I wanted to prove that Microsoft had used the threat of canceling Mac Office to force Apple to stop supporting Java and Navigator. I was confident I could do that with the documents Phil and Karma had given me. The reason I did not begin with them was that I wanted to give Gates the opportunity to take positions that would undercut his overall credibility. Once I had him locked in, I moved to the documents, beginning with an e-mail Gates had received.

> Q Now, in the second paragraph of this e-mail to you, the second sentence reads, "The threat to cancel Mac Office 97 is certainly the strongest bargaining point we have, as doing so will do a great deal of harm to Apple immediately." Do you see that, sir?
> A Uh-huh.

> Q Do you recall receiving this e-mail in June of 1997?
> A Not specifically.

I then showed him an e-mail he himself had written six weeks later.

Q It is clear from your August 8, 1997, memo that you are still attempting to get Apple to do additional things, is it not, sir?

A No.

Q Well, sir, let's read it. It's only three lines. You write, "I want to get as much mileage as possible out of our browser and Java relationship here." And when you talk about "here," you're talking about with Apple, are you not, sir?

A I'm not sure . . .

Q The very first sentence is, "I want to get as much mileage as possible out of our browser and Java relationship here." Second sentence says, "In other words, a real advantage against Sun and Netscape." The third line says, "Who should Avie be working with? Do we have a clear plan on what we want Apple to do to undermine Sun?" Now, do you have any doubt that when you talk about, "I want to get as much mileage as possible out of our browser and Java relationship here" you're talking about Apple?

A That's what it appears.

I then went to an e-mail written by Gates more than a year earlier to show that the original idea of getting Apple to help Microsoft in limiting Netscape and Java had been his.

Q In the second paragraph you say, "I have 2 key goals in investing in the Apple relationship—1) Maintain our applications share on the platform and 2) See if we can get them to embrace Internet Explorer in some way." Do you see that?

A Yeah.

Instead of accepting what could not be denied and providing the most helpful context he could, Gates again tried to avoid what he himself had written.

Q Do you agree that in June of 1996 the two key goals that you had in terms of the Apple relationship were, one, maintain your applications share on the platform, and two, see if you could get Apple to embrace Internet Explorer in some way?

A No.

As I continued to press him with his own words, Gates began to search for ever more strained ways to limit what he had said.

Q So you're writing a memo to Paul Maritz, a senior vice president, and Brad Silver, an officer of some kind, and you're sending copies to four other people on the subject of the Apple meeting, and you say, "I have 2 key goals in investing in the Apple relationship."

A That's quite distinct than any goals I might have for a deal with Apple. It says, "I have 2 key goals in investing in the Apple relationship," not "I have 2 key goals for a deal with Apple."

Q Well, sir, does it say at the bottom of the e-mail that you are proposing something with Apple and you are identifying what Apple would get under your proposed deal and what Microsoft would get under your proposed deal?

A Yeah, that's at the bottom of the e-mail.

Gates was trapped; both he and his lawyers knew it, but there was now no escape.

Q In fact, at the bottom of the e-mail talking about a proposed Apple-Microsoft deal, you say, "The deal would look like this," and then you have got a column

"Apple gets" and a column "Microsoft gets" and a column "Both get"; right, sir?

A I'm reading that.

The e-mail made clear that the "goals" that Gates had written about, and which he was now trying to avoid, were exactly what he wanted to achieve in his proposed "deal" with Apple. If I believed Gates would be a witness at trial I could have waited to drive home the point. As it was, I continued.

Q Your e-mail begins, "Last Tuesday night I went down to address the top Apple executives;" correct, sir?

A That's right.

Q And down at the bottom when you're introducing the deal, you say, "I proposed." Now, you're referring to what you proposed to the Apple top executives, are you not, sir?

A Yes.

Q Okay. And what you proposed was "the deal" that you then describe at the bottom of the first page and the top of the second page; correct, sir?

A That's right.

Shortly after this exchange Gates's lawyers spoke up to suggest that I was wasting time on unimportant points. The usual rule is that only one lawyer can speak for a party at a deposition, and some lawyers might have asked them to decide among themselves who that would be. However, there was no point in being testy; besides, I was interested to see whether Gates interpreted their statements as support for him to continue what he was doing. Perhaps he did, or perhaps he was already set in his approach.

Q My question, Mr. Gates, has to do with what your goals were, what your stated goals were. Now you say here, "I have two *key goals* in investing in the Apple relationship, one of which is to get Apple to embrace Internet Explorer technology in some way." Did that continue to be a goal that you had after 1996?

A It wasn't a goal in investing in the Apple relationship in terms—in the sense I meant it here. It was a goal for our overall dealing with Apple. One of many.

Q Okay. Was it your key goal?

A I'm not sure what you mean by "key." It was a goal.

Q What I mean by "key goal" is what you meant by "key goal" in your June 23, 1996, e-mail, Mr. Gates.

He went on to testify that the actual deal was reached in 1997 and that it was somehow "a separate thing" from his 1996 efforts. The problem was that we had an e-mail from 1997 as well. This one was from Microsoft executive John Ludwig and the subject was "conversations with BillG last night."

Q And the BillG referred to there is you; correct, sir?

A Yes.

Q And it begins, "I attended the exec staff meeting last night." Can you explain for the record what the exec staff meeting was?

A He is referring to a regular get-together four times a year of the Microsoft executive staff.

Q And he goes on to say that "There were three interesting exchanges with Bill and the whole group about Apple." Do you see that?

A I see it.

Q And No. 1 is, "Bill's top priority is for us to get the browser in the October OS release from Apple. We should do whatever it takes to make this happen. If we are getting shut out, we should escalate to Bill. You should make sure that we are engaging deeply with Apple on this

one and resolving any and all issues." Do you recall con-
veying to your executive staff in or about August of 1997
that your top priority was to get Microsoft's browser in
the October OS release from Apple?

A   No, I don't recall that.

I then showed him another 1997 e-mail, this one from Don
Bradford, also on the subject of "conversations with BillG last
night." The message said that Mr. Bradford "will take the lead on
working out the Apple bundle deal."

Q   The last sentence of the second paragraph says, "Bill was
     clear that his whole goal here is to keep Apple and Sun
     split. He doesn't care that much about being aligned
     with Apple, he just wants them split from other poten-
     tial allies." And that relates to Java, does it not, sir?

A   I don't have a direct recollection. If you read the sen-
     tence in front of it, that paragraph seems to relate to Java
     runtime.

Q   Do you have a recollection of telling your executive staff
     on or about August 21 that your whole goal with re-
     spect to Apple related to Java runtime was to keep Ap-
     ple and Sun split?

A   No . . .

Q   Do you have any reason to believe he would make up
     anything about what your statements were?

A   No.

Next I turned to Microsoft's deals in which content providers
agreed to limit the extent they did business with Netscape. Gates
admitted that he knew that Microsoft had given content providers
inducements to agree not to pay Netscape for access to certain
Netscape services.

Q   As you sit here now, can you think of any legitimate rea-
     son why Microsoft would be getting content providers to

agree not to pay Netscape? I'm not talking about getting
them to try to use your channel bar. I'm talking about
getting them to agree not to pay Netscape.

A You'd have to ask somebody else why they put that in the
agreement, unless you're asking me to speculate wildly.

If Bill Gates could not come up with a legitimate reason for
getting content providers to cut off Netscape's revenue, it was going to be difficult for Microsoft to convince the court that it was
anything other than an attempt, in the colorful language of another Microsoft executive, to "cut off Netscape's air supply." The
same result flowed from Gates's practice of dealing with documents that he had sent that were hard to explain by saying that he
did not remember them, and of dealing with similar documents he
had received by saying that he neither remembered them nor remembered being told what they said. Many lawyers advise witnesses wherever possible not to remember harmful documents.
However, this approach gives up what may be your best chance to
explain the document and put it in context. In addition, if the
document is one that a judge or juror is likely to think the witness
should remember, an asserted failure of memory undercuts the
witness's overall believability.

In order to show the exclusionary effect of Microsoft's agreements limiting the extent to which Apple and others could promote Netscape or Java, we needed to establish the importance of
what was referred to as "usage share." The threat to Microsoft
posed by middleware in general, and by Netscape and Java in particular, was that applications programmers would write their programs to connect to middleware APIs instead of those of Windows.
Programs written to Windows APIs would, in general, only work
with Windows; programs written to middleware APIs would, in
general, work with many operating systems. Since the dominance
of Windows depended on its having many applications that could
work on it but not on other operating systems, middleware posed
a major threat to Microsoft's market power.

A computer user could only use an application that connected to middleware if the consumer was using that middleware. Microsoft's conduct was therefore directed at discouraging the use of Netscape Navigator, Java, and other middleware—and we had good evidence that Microsoft was succeeding. Its lawyers, however, tried to obscure the significance of this conduct by emphasizing the extent to which Netscape and Sun were able to distribute copies of their products over the Internet, by direct mail, and by other means. Consequently it became important to establish that distribution by itself was not enough; what mattered was whether distribution resulted in the consumer using the product—measured, for example, by the relative use of Navigator compared to Microsoft's browser, or "usage share."

I began by having Gates explain the importance to Microsoft of a broader distribution of APIs.

> Q Am I correct that the broader distribution of the APIs is something that makes writing those APIs more attractive to independent software writers?
>
> A If users are choosing to use the software that those APIs are present in, it makes it easier to convince software vendors to write to those APIs.

As I tried to figure out how to follow up, I temporized by essentially repeating my prior question. But this time I got a better answer.

> Q Let me ask the question this way. Why were you interested in having Apple distribute your APIs?
>
> A Well, the key issue wasn't about distribution at all. The key issue was usage share by Mac users of the various browsers that were available on the Macintosh.

There is, as every trial lawyer knows, no substitute for luck, and there are few things luckier in a case than a witness from the other side whose lawyers let him try to educate you.

With respect to Netscape, Microsoft's approach was to use its

power over its operating system to induce other industry participants to agree to restrict the ability of consumers to use Netscape's
browser. With respect to Java, Microsoft had a dual approach—
first, to reduce the usage of standard Java as distributed by Sun, and
second, to gain control over Java by encouraging the use of a modified version of Java distributed by Microsoft. Gates initially denied
having either goal.

I showed him an e-mail written to him on April 14, 1997, by
the Microsoft executive, Ben Slivka, responsible for its Java efforts.
The subject of the e-mail to Gates was "Java review with you."

Q And he lists what he describes as some pretty pointed
   questions that you, Mr. Gates, had about Java. Do you
   see that?
A Well, I'm not sure those are the pointed questions. It says,
   "I want to make sure I understand your issues/concerns."

Q Well, that's actually the last part of a sentence that begins,
   quote: "When I met with you last you had a lot of *pretty
   pointed questions* about Java, so I want to make sure I understand your issues/concerns." That's what the sentence
   says; correct, sir?
A Right.

Q And when Mr. Slivka says, "I met with you last," he's
   talking about you, Mr. Gates; correct, sir?
A Yes.

Q And when he says, "You had a lot of *pretty pointed questions* about Java," he's again talking about you, Mr. Gates;
   correct?
A Right.

Q And then he lists . . . "1. What is our business model for
   Java? 2. How do we wrest control of Java away from
   Sun?" Do you see that?
A Uh-huh.

Gates admitted that Microsoft's efforts to "wrest control of Java away from Sun" had led to a lawsuit by Sun, which had resulted in a preliminary injunction against Microsoft. But he testified he did not know what Sun claimed in the lawsuit. He also testified he did not know what "control of Java" meant. Indeed, Gates testified that "we were glad to have people use" the Java APIs distributed by Sun. This did not seem consistent with the last e-mail. In addition, we had a July 14, 1997, e-mail to Gates from Group Vice President Paul Maritz.

> Q Mr. Maritz writes to you in the third sentence, quote, "If we look further at Java/JFC being our major threat, then Netscape is the major distribution vehicle." Do you see that, sir?
> A Uh-huh.

> Q Do you recall Mr. Maritz telling you in words or in substance that Netscape was the major distribution vehicle for the Java/JFC threat to Microsoft?
> A No.

It was clear that Microsoft was not, contrary to Gates's earlier testimony, "glad to have people use" what Maritz had described to Gates as "our major threat." I next showed Gates an e-mail to him dated August 25, 1997, that dealt with a Microsoft version of Java called J/Direct.

> Q That says, quote, "So, we are just proactively trying to put obstacles in Sun's path and get anyone that wants to write in Java to use J/Direct and target Windows directly," close quote. Do you see that, sir?
> A Uh-huh.

> Q Do you recall being told in or about August of 1997 that Microsoft was trying to put obstacles in Sun's path and get anyone that wants to write in Java to use J/Direct and target Windows directly?
> A No.

Q Do you know why Microsoft was trying to put, quote, "obstacles in Sun's path," close quote?

A I don't know what that means.

There followed one of the more amusing efforts by Gates to avoid the plain meaning of his e-mails, one that left Judge Jackson shaking his head when it was played in court.

Q Now, Mr. Slivka here says that Microsoft is going to be saying uncomplimentary things about JDK 1.2 at every opportunity. Do you see that?

A Where's that?

Q That is, "JDK 1.2 has JFC, which we're going to be pissing on at every opportunity."

A I don't know if he's referring to pissing on JFC or pissing on JDK 1.2, nor do I know what he specifically means by "pissing on."

Q Well, do you know that generally he means by "pissing on" that he's going to be saying and Microsoft is going to be saying uncomplimentary things?

A He might mean that we're going to be clear that we're not involved with it, that we think there's a better approach . . .

Q Yeah. And as the chief executive officer of Microsoft, when you get these kind of e-mails, would it be fair for me to assume that "pissing on" is not some code word that means saying nice things about you, that it has the usual meaning that it would in the vernacular?

A I don't know what you mean in this kind of e-mail.

Although our primary focus was on Netscape Navigator and Java, there were other middleware issues. One was Microsoft's efforts to discourage Apple from distributing its media player, QuickTime, and to support Microsoft's media player, NetShow.

Again, since QuickTime had the potential to encourage applications writers to write to QuickTime APIs instead of to Microsoft's
proprietary APIs, producing applications that could then be run
on non-Microsoft operating systems, it was a potential threat to
Microsoft's applications programming advantage. I began with a
question that was later widely reprinted during the trial.

> Q Do you believe that QuickTime software competes
> with any software distributed by Microsoft?
> A Depends on what you mean by "compete."*

The answer should, of course, have been a simple "yes," as Microsoft later admitted. Eventually Gates agreed that his company
had made an effort to convince Apple to develop jointly a common media player based on Microsoft APIs instead of developing
new versions of its own. (An Apple witness would ultimately testify colorfully that Microsoft tried to induce Apple to "knife the
baby.")

Microsoft had asked to stop the second day of the deposition at
4:00 p.m., and at 4:03 p.m. we did. In our discussions after Gates
had left the room, Heiner and Neukom said they assumed that I
was done.

I was free to go on for three or even four days.† However, with
the tape in my bag, I should have left well enough alone. Earlier in
the day I had called Mary at the lunch break. When she asked me
how the deposition was going, I told her that I was now convinced
that Microsoft would never call Gates at trial.

---

*We had a similar exchange concerning Netscape:

Q In or about January of 1996 or thereafter, did Microsoft try to study Netscape
  to determine how you could reduce Netscape's ability to compete?
A I don't know what you mean by that.

†Originally Microsoft had asked the court to restrict Gates's deposition to one day. In
an attempt to resolve the matter without the court's deciding the issue, I offered to limit it
to two days, if Microsoft would agree. It had refused my compromise, and the court had ultimately refused to restrict the time I spent with a witness as critical as Gates.

"It's bad enough to have this happen on videotape," I said. "Can you imagine what this would be like in open court?"

Whether Gates would come to trial would affect how I could use the videotape. Judge Jackson had already indicated that he would not spend time reviewing videotaped deposition testimony of people who were going to testify in person. However, if Gates did not come in person, I could play the videotape at will; and as the tape now stood it was devastating.

If we continued on to September 2 (the next available date for Gates), his lawyers would have several days to clean up his testimony and demeanor. They could also ask him softball questions after I was through to enable him to explain away his missteps. If I then played the tape, they would have the right to then play this additional testimony—which would be the last impression the judge would have of Gates. Microsoft could not totally rehabilitate their boss, but they could do a lot. I knew from my meeting with him in April how effective he could be when properly prepared.

What I could not understand was whether he had not been prepared for this deposition, or was ignoring his preparation—and if the latter, why his lawyers weren't doing something about it. Something had certainly gone wrong, but I could not assume that whatever had happened would happen again.

Taking another day of Gates is the kind of mistake that is made by an inexperienced lawyer who believes that because things have gone well so far, the good times will continue to roll. It was therefore with a mixture of amusement and chagrin that I reflected, as I flew back to New York that evening, that that was exactly what I had done. There were some additional points worth covering. But the potential gain was not remotely worth the potential loss.

Over the weekend I decided that if Microsoft's lawyers called to convince me not to take a third day I would graciously agree. (I decided not to make the offer myself, since it might alert them to my concern.) By the morning of September 1, when I was scheduled to leave New York to return to Redmond, no one had phoned.

Since the Microsoft lawyers were usually relentless in trying to avoid discovery, this reinforced my sense that this third day might be a trap.

When the deposition resumed, I was alert for any signs that Gates had changed. He continued to respond with silence to my "good mornings," he avoided eye contact, and he again continued to rock back and forth as he thought and spoke. However, he seemed more relaxed, more confident—and more dangerous.

It soon became apparent that nothing had changed. Gates testified that Microsoft charged IBM higher prices for Windows than it charged other large PC makers because IBM had declined to do certain "promotional things." However, apparently sensing that it would be harmful to link retaliation against IBM to anything to do with browsers, he again tried to avoid recognizing the browser as a distinct item. Eventually, however, he had to admit:

Q Well, sir, the term "browser" is a term that is widely used within Microsoft, or at least was until this year; correct, sir?

A We use the term "browser," yes.

Q Including by you; correct, sir?

A Yes.

Once Gates abandoned his attempt to avoid using the term browser, we moved to a discussion of the importance Microsoft attached to overtaking the lead that Netscape had achieved in browser market share.

Q Are you aware of documents within Microsoft that describe browser share as the company's number one goal?

A No. I'm aware of documents within Paul Maritz's group that may have stated that . . .

Q Now, did you ever tell Mr. Maritz that browser share was not the company's number one goal?

A No.

Gates tried to say that Maritz's views were limited to his particular group. Even if true, that would have been an important group, since it had responsibility for both Windows and browsers; but it was not true.

Q Mr. Gates, isn't it the case that you told Mr. Maritz that browser share was a very, very important goal and that's why he believed it?

A I guess now we're delving into the inner workings of Paul Maritz's mind and how he comes to conclusions?

Q Well, let me try to ask you a question that won't require you delve into anybody else's mind. Did you ever tell Mr. Maritz that browser share was a very, very important goal?

A I know we talked about the browser share being important.

I next showed him an e-mail that he had written January 5, 1996.

Q And the first line of this is, "Winning Internet browser share is a very, very important goal for us." Do you see that?

A I do.

However Gates remained determined not to admit that Microsoft was concerned with Netscape, testifying that in the period around June 1995 he had "no sense of what Netscape was doing." He seemed to believe that the more he admitted that Netscape was a threat to Microsoft, the more credible our claims that Microsoft had acted to exclude Netscape would become. The problem was that he could not make the evidence that Microsoft believed Netscape was a threat go away; all he could do was damage himself trying.

It had been widely reported in the trade press that Netscape threatened to "commoditize the OS"—that is, reduce the applications programming advantage of Windows by making applications available to all operating systems. Gates tried to deal with this by asserting that it was merely a bold, and unsubstantiated, claim. However, we had memos from both Ballmer, one of Microsoft's top two officers, and Gates himself warning that Netscape threatened to "commoditize" the OS. And so it went.

In a March 13, 1997, memo, Microsoft executive Brad Chase had written to Gates, Ballmer, Maritz, and others describing Microsoft's browser battle as a "jihad." Gates might have tried to dismiss the document as just an example of overly colorful language; his actual approach was more creative.

Q   Now, when Brad Chase writes to you and the others "we need to continue our jihad next year," do you understand that he is referring to Microsoft when he uses the word "we"?

A   No.

Q   What do you think he means when he uses the word "we"?

A   I'm not sure.

Q   Do you know what he means by "jihad"?

A   I think he is referring to our vigorous efforts to make a superior product and to market that product.

Q   Now, what he says in the next sentence is, "Browser share needs to remain a key priority for our field and marketing efforts"; is that correct?

A   Yes.

Q   The field and marketing efforts were not involved in product design or making an improved browser, were they, sir?

A   No.

The reason why "browser share" was "a key priority" for Microsoft was emphasized in a memorandum prepared by Paul Maritz that Gates had distributed to a number of people in Microsoft on

April 6, 1995. The title of the memo was "Netscape as Netware" (Netware being a program distributed by Novell), and the memo stated, "The analogy here is that the major sin that Microsoft made with Netware was to let Novell offer a better (actually smaller and faster with simpler protocol) client for networking. They got to critical mass and can now evolve both client and server together." This document substantiated our contention that Microsoft had set out to use its power to stifle Netscape before it could achieve critical mass.

Gates tried to avoid the document's thesis that crippling Netscape was intended to eliminate the threat posed by the company's browser by disputing that Netscape posed a browser threat. In the process he gave testimony so at odds with the evidence that it caused the courtroom to erupt in laughter when it was played.

> Q Well, sir, in April of 1995, insofar as Microsoft was concerned, was Netscape primarily a browser company?
> A No.
>
> Q It was not?
> A No.

This was not going to be a good document for Microsoft under any circumstances, but Gates was hardly making it better.

> Q My question is whether, as you understand it, what Mr. Maritz is saying here is that Microsoft should not make the same mistake with Netscape's browser as it did with Novell's Netware?
> A Does it say "mistake" somewhere?
>
> Q Okay. Do you think that when Mr. Maritz uses the term "major sin" that Microsoft made, he is referring to what he thinks is a mistake?
> A Probably.

If a witness fights too hard, when he does give in he often gives up more than he might otherwise have done. Thus it was that Gates finally admitted not only that Netscape competed with Microsoft's IE browser, but also that he and Microsoft viewed the Netscape Navigator "as competing with Windows broadly" and not merely with IE.

Q When did you first consider Netscape's browser to be your primary or most important non-Microsoft browser with which Internet Explorer was competing?

A I think by late 1995 we thought of Navigator as competing both with—well, competing with Windows broadly, including the Internet capabilities of Windows.

Our Section 2 monopolization case was premised on the fact that, by stifling Navigator, Microsoft had acted to preserve its Windows operating system position. To show this we needed to establish that Navigator was a competitive threat not merely to IE but to Windows itself. We believed the evidence bore this out, but now we had Gates admitting it.

Near the end of the deposition I showed Gates an e-mail he had sent to his top executives dated August 15, 1997, on the subject of IBM and Netscape.

Q You type in here "Importance: High."
A No.

Q No?
A No, I didn't type that.

Q Who typed "High"?
A A computer.

Q A computer. Why did the computer type in "High"?
A It's an attribute of the e-mail.

Q And who set the attribute of the e-mail?
A Usually the sender sets that attribute.

Q Who is the sender here, Mr. Gates?
A In this case it appears I'm the sender.

Q Yes. And so you're the one who set the high designation of importance, right, sir?

A It appears I did that. I don't remember doing that specifically.

Q Right. Now, did you send this message on or about August 15, 1997?

A I don't remember doing so.

The exchange produced a sad shake of the head by Judge Jackson when it was played in court. Microsoft's lawyers tried to dismiss exchanges like this as irrelevant to the issues. In a sense they were right; much of the testimony did not establish any substantive point, and the games Gates played were no different from what many deponents have done. In another sense they could not have been more wrong. In order to justify what Microsoft had done, they would try to convince the judge of numerous facts, including the reasons the company did or did not do certain things; they would also want to convince Judge Jackson that what was said in Microsoft documents meant something other than the most natural interpretation. Both would require the judge to trust the defendant's witnesses. If the judge did not believe Gates, Microsoft would have lost its most effective voice. Moreover, because of the extent to which Gates personified Microsoft, if the judge concluded he could not trust Gates, he might well be suspicious of Microsoft's motives and witnesses generally.

Finally I had enough sense to stop. It was now 3:16 p.m. Microsoft's lawyers waived their right to question Gates. It was a sensible decision if they planned to bring him to trial, since he could give then whatever testimony he might give at his deposition. However, if Gates were not to testify, Microsoft had just lost its chance to rehabilitate its most important witness.

As I flew back to New York, I reflected on what had happened. Had the court of appeals done us a favor by barring the press from Gates's deposition? If the press had been present, would he have behaved differently? What accounted for the Gates at my deposition, so different from the man I'd seen before? What were his lawyers thinking? How could they have stood by while this happened? How lucky was I that no one had used the break between the second and third days to repackage the witness? And, if I was right and Gates could not be a witness at trial, why did his lawyers pass up the right to question him at the end of my examination?*

Back in New York I now turned to one of the most difficult tasks of the entire case. From the beginning of our investigation, industry participants had been more than willing to tell us privately of Microsoft threats, bargains, and retaliation that constituted anticompetitive conduct under the antitrust laws. Except for Netscape, however, none was willing to talk in public. Somehow I had to convince some of them to become witnesses.

Joel Klein and I had spoken to personal computer manufacturers, Internet service providers, software developers, and content providers. Over and over again they told us "off the record" of Microsoft's power and misconduct, then somewhat guiltily explained that they could not afford to testify because of the fear that the company would retaliate against them. "Microsoft's control over Windows gives it the power to destroy our profitability," one PC manufacturer explained, "simply by delays, lack of cooperation, and failure to provide us what it provides our competitors. We would know it was happening, but it would be hard to prove." It was a point industry participants made repeatedly.

"If I were confident you would win, it might be worth the risk," we were told by an important content provider. "But Microsoft has always beaten the government. Why should I believe it will be different this time?" Although the words varied slightly, this point was made repeatedly as well. Even companies who had been

---

*I also thought about my decision to take the deposition myself. A trial is a morality play, and presentation is important. A deposition, by comparison, is usually a test of patience and preparation. In the case of Gates, because of his central importance, I had decided to take his deposition myself even though I knew that Phil Malone was at least as patient and better prepared. He could certainly have asked all the questions I did. Would, I wondered, Gates's responses have been the same?

publicly critical of the defendant were reluctant to testify. Microsoft might tolerate occasional carping, they believed, but it would never forgive lending aid or comfort to the government. As the *Wall Street Journal* put it with atypical understatement, "Few Microsoft foes dare to fight firm in Washington—most competitors fear retaliation in the marketplace."

As we tried to convince, cajole, and shame potential witnesses to say under oath what they were telling us privately, one fact became clear. No one wanted to be the first or only person to testify. If we could get a few witnesses, we might be able to convince others to join them; but landing the first one sometimes seemed a mission impossible.

For several reasons IBM was high on my list. With both major hardware and software businesses, it had much to gain from limiting Microsoft's anticompetitive practices; and as my deposition of Gates had indicated, IBM was already the least favored major PC manufacturer and hence had less to lose than others. In addition, the company had a long tradition of being committed to legal and ethical behavior and would be inclined to believe it had an obligation to come forward now. My personal experience with the company also made it easier to talk with them and gave IBM confidence that when I said this time the government would not back off, they could believe it.

It was still not easy. Less than two weeks before our witness list was due I had just finished helping our daughter Mary move into her dorm at school when I checked with my office before heading back to Armonk. I was told that the IBM lawyer I had been dealing with had called. When I returned his call, I was told that IBM vice president John Soyring would be available to testify. It wasn't as dramatic a moment as the Gates deposition, but it was a turning point in the case.

AOL was another logical possibility. It had firsthand knowledge of Microsoft's efforts to get Internet service providers to boycott Netscape. Moreover, while AOL had benefited from those efforts, it knew that, unless checked, Microsoft would in the long run extend its dominance to all aspects of the Internet. It also helped that AOL's executive vice-president and general counsel was George Vradenburg. George and I had been friends since we were young associates together at Cravath more than a quarter of a century earlier. He had gone on to become general counsel of CBS (where he retained me in the Westmoreland libel case), then of Fox before becoming general counsel of AOL. He would not, of course, let AOL do something simply out of friendship for me. However, the fact that we could trust each other helped. In particular, we were able to discuss the possibility of an AOL witness and the topics such a witness might address without either of us being concerned that what we said would be repeated. Mutual trust allowed us to begin a process that ultimately led to AOL providing a witness, a process that without that trust probably would not have ever started.

We were able to convince Sun Microsystems to join IBM and AOL in making a witness available to testify and, with the safety in numbers represented by those three, persuaded executives from Apple, Intel, and Intuit to testify as well. The most unexpected witness was Steven McGeady from Intel, Microsoft's long-time partner in the PC business. So closely did the two companies work that their efforts were sometimes referred to as if they were a single enterprise, "Wintel." Intel's management was not happy that one of their executives was cooperating but did not feel that they could stop him. They did, however, prevent us from meeting with him privately.

On Friday, September 11, John Warden and I argued Microsoft's motion to dismiss our case before Judge Jackson. This was the last chance that Microsoft had to avoid a trial, and several hundred members of the press and public lined up for a chance to watch. Every previous occasion in which Microsoft faced a government antitrust challenge it had managed to avoid a trial. What, people wanted to know, would happen this time?

John Warden was well prepared, and he made a polished and impassioned argument, asserting that Microsoft's conduct was nothing more than normal, aggressive competition. He also argued that the antitrust laws were not well suited to software and other high-tech business, in which one company would inevitably dominate until it was replaced by a new dominant company. I emphasized the evidence we had accumulated that Microsoft's actions went considerably beyond normal competition; that Microsoft's power imposed limits on what the company was permitted to do to destroy smaller rivals; that there was no exemption in the antitrust laws for software or high-tech markets, and if there was to be an exception, it had to come from Congress, not from the courts; that it was not inevitable that there be a single dominant company in browsers or operating systems; and that even if the nature of a market meant that there would be only a single dominant company, it was important that which company survived be determined by competition, not anti-competitive agreements.

This was the first test of our legal theories and of the evidence we had assembled. A decision to deny Microsoft's motion would not mean that we had proven the facts we asserted, only that we had enough to justify a trial; however, it would mean that Judge Jackson agreed with our basic legal theories. If we survived this motion, two significant hurdles remained—a trial, at which we would have to prove our facts, and an appeal, in which an appellate court would reexamine our legal theories. However, as everyone in the courtroom and many outside it knew, this first test was critical. If we lost, we were out of court. If we won, for the first time Microsoft would have to defend its aggressive brand of competition at trial.

I expected to win this round, but the tension was still high as we waited for Jackson's decision. When the judge refused to dismiss the case, we took time for a celebratory dinner before returning to work. We had a month to go (Jackson had granted Microsoft an additional three-week delay of the trial until Thursday, October 15—later postponed until the following Monday by agreement of the parties), and I spent the time talking to actual and potential witnesses, refining our legal arguments, designating what portions of the depositions that we had taken we would offer into evidence, and personally selecting the documents we would use. By the time the trial commenced, I had read every deposition that had been taken and every document that anyone proposed as an exhibit.

We had taken only five months after the complaint was filed to get our case to trial, an accomplishment unprecedented in the history of government antitrust cases. Equally remarkable, I remained optimistic that we would win. Many in the press and elsewhere continued to deride our prospects, but they had not yet seen our evidence—including the Gates deposition. I did not underestimate the obstacles that lay ahead, but the first step in winning a World Series is getting there. We were there, and we were prepared.

5

The Trial of Microsoft

I T WAS DUBBED BY *FORTUNE* AND OTHERS THE "TRIAL OF the Decade," and the line of people hoping to watch wound its way around the courthouse halls. Seats for the opening day of *United States v. Microsoft* were at such a premium that even many of the lawyers representing the parties had to stand in line to get in.

The weekend before my opening statement I decided that, in addition to our primary themes, I would try to juxtapose the evidence we had accumulated with the denials of Microsoft officers, particularly Gates. For example I would show Gates denying any intention to harm Netscape, then show a document quoting Gates asking AOL in a private meeting: "How much do we need to pay you to screw Netscape?"

I would show testimony of Gates asserting that he was unaware of any attempt to get Netscape to limit its competition with Microsoft and that when asked to consider putting money into Netscape he had refused, saying it "didn't make sense to me." I would then show a document in which he suggested that Microsoft "could even pay them money as part of a deal buying some piece of them or something" in order to convince Netscape to limit or delay competitive initiatives.

We had constructed a giant screen in the courtroom with computer-driven displays that could show videotaped depositions, documents, or (when I wanted to highlight inconsistencies) both at the same time.

My approach was not without risks. Taking Gates on in open court would be seen as challenging a popular and respected icon. Moreover, if it looked to Judge Jackson that I was attacking Gates unfairly, I knew he would be offended. However, it was important to show that Microsoft's conduct represented the corporate philosophy of the company, not the isolated acts of lower-level staff. The best way to do that was to begin with Gates's own statements.

I completed my opening in midafternoon of October 19, 1998. It was impossible to discern any reaction from the judge, who took notes with a poker face, but the reaction of what had up until then been a somewhat dubious press corps was encouraging. Jackson gave John Warden the option of beginning then or waiting until the next day; John opted to delay. If I had been in his position, I would have been reluctant to let the judge dwell on my statement overnight without any rebuttal, but such things are less important in a bench trial (that is, a trial without a jury) than they are with a jury.

John Warden's opening statement the next day was the detailed, comprehensive argument that I had expected, with one possible exception: he did not deal directly with many of the key points, particularly the inconsistencies between Gates's testimony and his e-mails, that I had emphasized. Perhaps he felt it was important to concentrate on his positive points rather than rebutting mine, or perhaps he had not expected my attacks and was not certain how to respond. Whatever the reason, much of what I had said went unchallenged.

With opening statements completed, we turned to the actual evidence. As often happens in a bench trial, Judge Jackson had ruled that each party would submit the direct testimony of their witnesses in written form, followed by cross-examination by the other side. This meant that the first oral testimony the court would hear from a witness would be on cross-examination. The judge, with the consent of the parties, had limited each side to twelve witnesses. Ours represented a virtual who's who of the country's most respected technology companies. In addition to two economists, computer scientists from Princeton and the University of Pennsylvania, and an industry expert, we had executives from AOL, Apple, IBM, Intel, Intuit, and Sun Microsystems—and, of course, Netscape.

Our first witness was James Barksdale, the CEO of Netscape. As a leadoff witness you need someone who will put some points on the board and do no damage; you do not want to take a risk. If your first impression with a judge or jury is not good, your case is in trouble. You also want a witness who can explain the overall case and put matters in context. Jim Barksdale was a natural choice—smart, careful, and articulate, with a down-home accent and sense of humor that reflected his Arkansas background. His credibility was enhanced by his wide business experience; prior to being selected to run Netscape, he had served as president of Federal Express and of Mc-Caw Cellular. I thought it unlikely that even as experienced a trial lawyer as John Warden would make much headway.

In his written testimony, Barksdale had described Netscape's enormous initial success, the threat its Navigator and Java posed to Microsoft, a June 1995 meeting at which Microsoft tried to convince him to agree to limit Netscape's competition, the subsequent efforts Gates's company made to exclude Netscape from the market, and the success those efforts had had because of Microsoft's monopoly. Although John spent four days trying, he was unable to move Barksdale off these central contentions.

Prior to the commencement of trial Joel Klein and I agreed that I would keep a low profile, speaking to the press on background inside the courthouse (where cameras were barred) but generally not participating in the daily televised interviews on the courthouse steps that we expected would characterize the trial. Our resolve lasted less than twenty-four hours. After Microsoft's aggressive (and, we believed, inaccurate) interpretation of the first day of the Barksdale cross, Joel decided that someone needed to respond, and that I was in the best position to do it. Thus it was that every day after trial, and sometimes at the luncheon recess, I made myself available for a no-holds-barred press conference fifty feet from the courthouse.

A bench trial is always a two-front war as lawyers try to per-suade the trial judge while at the same time building a record for an appellate court to consider. With Microsoft the press offensive almost represented a third front. In nearly every high-profile case, lawyers and their clients try to spin the evidence. Usually this reflects little more than the natural desire to have people who don't know us (or who do but are highly impressionable) think well of us.* In some cases, however, the view outside the courtroom on how a case is going may be critical to whether witnesses are prepared to come to court and how forthcoming they are prepared to be. U.S. v. Microsoft was such a case.

Although Microsoft had more people and resources devoted to the PR battle than the government, we more than held our own. Part of the reason was that, as in the courtroom, Microsoft tried to spin too much. It characterized the first day of court as "a good day for Microsoft"; and, no matter how badly it had actually gone for the company, every subsequent day was also "another good day for Microsoft." For a time journalists reported neutrally whatever either side said, but soon "another good day for Microsoft" be-came a running joke.

Microsoft also tended to treat each news cycle as a separate era, saying whatever its PR people thought would generate a good story that day (or half day) without any apparent thought to how that fit with what would happen next month, next week, or even the next day. Lawyers cannot afford to shade their evidence in a long case; eventually the truth comes out, and lack of candor will only make a neutral situation bad or a bad situation worse. The same is true when dealing with the press.

An additional reason for our relative success with reporters was

---

*In a jury trial lawyers are also concerned that jurors will disregard their instructions not to read anything about the case and will be influenced by what the media reports.

that, confident in Joel's support, I was freer to respond openly to their questions. Always looking over their shoulders at what the reaction in Redmond might be, and never fully understanding what was happening in court, the Microsoft PR representatives had little choice but to pass on an increasingly stilted message.

After the first week of trial several reporters arranged to have drinks with the PR representatives of Netscape and Microsoft. They invited John Warden and me to join them. I accepted; John declined. At the end of each week through the rest of the trial, the press corps, Microsoft's PR representatives, and I would gather at a local bar to relax and talk about our mutual obsession. Gina Talamona, the Justice Department's press liaison, faithfully joined us—more, I thought, to watch over me than to participate. The discussions were strictly off the record, and nothing said in any of our more than two dozen evenings ever got printed. We enjoyed each other's company, and there was no one else who was as knowledgeable about the case as we were—and hence no one else with whom we could debate the esoteric points that fascinated us. We also did it because each time we got together anyone who was willing to listen learned something. I did not believe that anyone there knew more than I did, but many of the journalists* knew something different than I did. We all had different sources, different facts, and (perhaps more important) different points of view. The give and take as the evening wore on offered insights as to how neutral observers reacted to particular witnesses, arguments, and evidence. There was no guarantee that any individual reporter, or the press as a whole, was a reliable proxy for what Judge Jackson was thinking, but it was the best proxy we had— and much better than simply talking to people who already agreed with you.

---

*Particularly such experienced and well-connected reporters as Ken Auletta (*New Yorker*), Joe Nocera (*Fortune*), John Wilke (*Wall Street Journal*), Steve Lohr and Joel Brinkley (*New York Times*), Jim Rowley (*Reuters*), Paul Davidson (*USA Today*), and James Grimaldi (*Washington Post*).

Our second witness was AOL Vice President David M. Colburn. One key point Colburn had made in his written direct testimony was that Microsoft had used its Windows monopoly to force AOL to boycott the Netscape browser. I knew that Warden would attack this assertion, and before Colburn testified I wanted to bolster his testimony with evidence that Microsoft had engaged in similar conduct with other companies. Accordingly, I had asked Barksdale about Apple's 1997 decision to abandon Netscape's browser and to adopt Microsoft's. Barksdale testified that Apple had agreed to drop Navigator and instead ship Internet Explorer because of threats from Microsoft. To corroborate his testimony I introduced a handwritten note setting forth the views of Apple's chief financial officer. "Apple needed to ensure that Microsoft would continue to provide MS Office for Mac or we were dead," the note said. "They were threatening to abandon Mac." This document fitted with those from Microsoft that I had used in the Gates deposition and in my opening.

Although Warden did indeed attack Colburn, contending that AOL picked IE because of its superior technology, the witness held his ground. Warden tried to raise questions about Colburn's objectivity by noting that in 1995 AOL president Stephen Case had referred to Microsoft as AOL and Netscape's "common enemy" and "the Beast from Redmond that wants to see us both dead." Warden also tried to pull the sting of our market division allegations against his client by emphasizing that in 1995 AOL and Netscape had also discussed ways in which AOL might compete less with Netscape and cooperate more.

The problem with John's first point was that the more the judge believed AOL viewed Microsoft as the "enemy," the stronger the inference that AOL must have been forced to choose the "beast" instead of its natural ally. The problems with John's second point were that in software development neither AOL nor Netscape had anything like Microsoft's power, and that even had AOL been wrong, that did not make Microsoft right. A problem with both points was that neither rebutted Colburn's central assertion—that

Microsoft used AOL's need for access to Windows to force AOL to boycott Netscape.

One subplot to the Colburn cross was, when would it end? I had originally said I would play the Gates videotape after Barksdale's testimony. However, to accommodate Colburn's schedule I postponed the videotape until after Colburn. Warden then took so long with his cross of Colburn that when court ended for the week on October 29 the tape had still not been played. To say that the press was frustrated by our failure to get to the Gates tape was an understatement. The videotape was under seal until it was played in court. Microsoft had historically exercised tight control over which reporters had access to Gates, what he would answer, and how long he made himself available. The prospect of a tape of no-holds-barred questioning of the world's richest man by an experienced examiner had the media salivating.

I had selected several hours of testimony, and Microsoft had chosen several additional hours. In total the time required was more than a full court day. In an attempt to prepare reporters for what they would see, Microsoft had begun telling them that they should not pay too much attention. This, of course, only fanned the flames.

Our third witness, Apple Senior Vice President Avadis Tevanian Jr. was scheduled for Monday, November 2. Tevanian's written testimony asserted that Microsoft's 90 percent market share and its monopoly power in PC operating systems meant that when Microsoft required customers to take an additional software product as a condition of getting Windows, they had to agree. He testified that this was what happened with browsers. He agreed with Barksdale that Microsoft forced Apple to stop promoting Netscape's browser by threatening to cancel software applications critical to Apple's computers, and also explained how Microsoft had asked Apple to stop marketing its QuickTime media software "cross platform" (that is, in a way that enabled developers to write programs that could be used with both Microsoft and non-Microsoft operating systems).

"Microsoft made it clear that if Apple refused to relinquish the playback market, Microsoft would use its monopoly power to drive Apple out of the entire multimedia market," he said.

The Saturday before Tevanian's testimony Mary and I drove to Connecticut to watch Mary Regency in a soccer game. On our way back we debated whether to play the Gates video at the start of the proceedings on Monday. Doing so would delay Tevanian's cross and, since there would be no court on Tuesday because of Election Day, possibly delay the completion of his examination until the following week. Lawyers are always reluctant to leave one of their witnesses hanging over a weekend—it gives the other side too much time to prepare their cross. On the other hand, I was eager to have Judge Jackson watch Gates on the big screen.

Mary had asked, "Do you have to play all the videotape at the same time?"

"I'm afraid so," I had said at the time, but the next day on my way back to Washington I began to rethink my answer. Why not play only those portions that related to the topics Tevanian would address and keep the rest for later? We would have to play both our and Microsoft's selections related to those topics so that they could not claim anything was out of context, but I did not see any legal reason why we had to follow the normal practice of playing all designations relating to all topics together.

When the following Monday morning we sought to present selected portions of the videotape, Microsoft objected that the videotape should not be played at all and that we should be limited to introducing the typed transcript of the deposition; the company did not object at that time to our offering only excerpts related to Apple. Judge Jackson had little patience for the argument that he should not be able to see the witness's demeanor, and off we went to the movies.

The videotape may have been tame by the standards of prime time network television. It did not, however, as Microsoft had predicted to the press, "bore everyone in the courtroom to tears." In fact Judge Jackson, the press, and public spectators appeared fascinated. Occasionally even Jackson departed from his normal dead-pan to chuckle or shake his head. The Gates on the tape was particularly disconcerting in the light of his reputation as the brilliant strategist who had micromanaged Microsoft's rise to power.

It had not been my purpose, but after the tape Microsoft's cross-examination of Avadis Tevanian was anticlimactic. Tevanian stuck to his guns and Microsoft made little headway. Thereafter we adopted the practice of playing Gates excerpts in between each of our witnesses, selecting passages that dealt with topics our next witness would address. Gates's admissions bolstered each witness's testimony. Where he denied a fact or asserted lack of knowledge, it gave our witnesses a dramatic way of making their points.

On Thursday, November 19, after several installments of the videotape, Microsoft made an effort to stop our playing excerpts before each of our witnesses took the stand, arguing that we should be required to play all the remaining selections at once. This was the objection Warden might have raised when we began, but now it was too late—partly because we had found cases supporting our approach; partly because the judge found it "useful" to have Gates's statements juxtaposed with our witnesses' testimony.

"If anything," Jackson told Warden, "the trouble is with your witness."

The following weekend, with our case more than half completed, we were feeling pretty good. Monday, November 23, however, brought news that made me wish the trial had kept to its original schedule—to begin September 8 and be finished before mid-November. AOL, headlines announced, had agreed to acquire Netscape for approximately $4 billion.

Microsoft predictably argued that this merger assured that Netscape with AOL's sponsorship would continue to compete effectively and that Microsoft had been right to worry about its competitors ganging up against it.

The acquisition ultimately turned out to be a non-event for the lawsuit, because we were able to demonstrate that nothing that AOL could do now would reverse the effects of Microsoft's anti-competitive actions concerning browsers, and that the acquisition was irrelevant to our claims relating to Microsoft's anticompetitive behavior with respect to Java, Intel, and Apple. Still, the announcement shook things up for a couple of weeks.

There was no court on December 7, so I spent the day at the Justice Department's offices preparing for the completion of the testimony of Sun's James Gosling. Late that afternoon I received a call from *Wall Street Journal* reporter John Wilke. "How do you feel about Gates's comments?" he asked. I did not know what he was talking about, initially supposing incorrectly that he was referring to the old news of Gates's recent congressional remarks.* It turned out that Gates, John Warden, and Bill Neukom had held a press conference to attack the Justice Department's case in general and me in particular.

"Boies," Gates had asserted, "made it clear that he is out to destroy Microsoft and make us look very bad." Warden chimed in with apparent indignation that my deposition of Gates had been designed "for the sole purpose of turning this case into a personal attack."

There was no point in replying in kind, and I was more amused than offended. My immediate response, which the *Wall Street Journal* quoted the next day was:

> "What Mr. Gates says about this case outside of court, not under oath and not subject to cross-examination, is irrelevant to the trial. What Mr. Gates says about me personally, in or out of court, is irrelevant to the trial."

I probably should have stopped there. Mary would have stopped me there. But Mary was not with me. I continued:

> "If Mr. Gates's attorneys call him as a witness at trial, and I am sure they will if he asks them to, Mr. Gates will have

---

*During the early days of the trial Gates had testified before a congressional committee investigating Microsoft's conduct.

another opportunity to testify under oath, and I will have another opportunity to cross-examine him."

The next day Joel Klein said to me, "You know, you're daring him to testify." I had to acknowledge that I probably was.

"Is that because you don't want him to, and you think that your dare will scare him off? Or is it because you want him to and you're trying to make it impossible for him not to show up?"

I was wondering the same thing myself. However, it is always better if your client thinks you have a plan, so I simply smiled and changed the subject.

We recessed for the holidays after court on Wednesday, December 16. Thursday morning, after a longer than usual end-of-the week evening with the press corps, I flew back to New York to do my Christmas shopping and try to make my way through all the work that had accumulated over the past eight weeks. When our family flew to Cancun the day after Christmas, I carried with me a box of materials relating to the cross-examination of Microsoft's witnesses who would testify in January. This time I actually studied them.

We had two of our witnesses remaining—Intuit CEO William Harris and Professor Franklin M. Fisher from MIT. We had high hopes for both, but afterward Joe Nocera would write with his usual bluntness, "the government closed its case with two witnesses, one powerful, one pathetic."

The "pathetic" witness was William Harris of Intuit, who wilted under cross-examination. I did not think he did as poorly as the press reported, but he did suffer by comparison to the unusually effective witnesses who preceded him. I was glad we had not left him for last.

The "powerful" witness was our economics expert, Professor Frank Fisher, one of the country's leading economists. I first met him in 1970 when we were looking for an expert in the IBM litigation. Frank had never testified, but Carl Kaysen, then head of the Institute for Advanced Studies at Princeton, recommended him. I flew to Boston to meet him, liked what I saw, and for the next decade worked with him off and on to demolish the government's economic arguments. Since the IBM litigation I had retained him as a witness in several major antitrust cases. Initially there had been reluctance among some people at Justice to retain Fisher because they believed it would underscore the anomaly of my representing the Justice Department after the IBM litigation.

"There is no one better at explaining the differences between this case and the IBM case than Fisher," I countered. "Also, I need someone I can trust and who can get ready in weeks, not months or years."

Frank is a quick study, and I knew that our history of working together would cut through a lot of the routine that is usually involved in preparing an expert witness. At trial Frank did not disappoint. He was careful and credible, and did not overstate; he also drilled home each of our key points with detailed economic and factual support.

We completed his testimony the morning of January 13. After the luncheon recess Steve Holtzman offered the last of our documents and deposition excerpts, and at about 2:45 p.m. I informed the court that "the United States rests." It had been less than fourteen months since my first call from Joel.

We felt good about the proof we had developed. Our witnesses had survived with their basic points and credibility intact. We had also assembled a strong case from documents, including Microsoft's own e-mails, and from our depositions (including, of course, Bill Gates's). We were farther along at this point than anyone outside our trial team had expected. On the other hand, as I cautioned my trial team, we were supposed to be ahead at this stage. The record consisted primarily of witnesses, documents, and depositions we had selected. Where would we be when Microsoft finished its turn?

Usually (particularly in a jury trial) plaintiffs win or lose based on the strengths or weaknesses of their evidence. In this case, however, despite our accomplishments, I was convinced that Judge

Jackson was waiting to see what evidence Microsoft would present to counter ours. Joe Nocera fairly summed up where we stood: "Gates & Co. have been embarrassed, but the government has not landed a knockout blow."

If the evidence ended up roughly equally balanced, we would lose—because, as a legal matter, we had the burden of proof and because, as a practical matter, a cautious and conservative Reagan appointee was unlikely to outlaw the actions of a company as admired as Microsoft unless the evidence against it were overwhelming. We had, I hoped, brought Jackson to the point where he was open to our arguments. In order to persuade him, however, we needed to do what is the hardest task in a trial—make your opponents' witnesses support your case.

First at bat for Microsoft was Dr. Richard Schmalensee. Like Fisher, Schmalensee was a brilliant economist with numerous publications and honors. He was also an articulate and charming speaker. On the surface, the company could not have chosen a more capable advocate. Even so, their choice to begin with Schmalensee was something of a gamble. Economics testimony in an antitrust case is critical, and parties ordinarily call their expert after several fact witnesses have testified. If Schmalensee were effective, he could blunt our momentum and open the door for the witnesses who followed. However, he was Microsoft's only economics expert; if he stumbled, it would be hard for the company to recover. At one level I admired the boldness and confidence shown in opening with Schmalensee, but it seemed to me an unnecessary risk. Microsoft did not need to catch up on our entire case in one stroke, and it might have used a less critical witness to draw the initial fire of our cross-examination.

Even more questionable was Microsoft's decision to have Schmalensee testify that the defendant did not have monopoly power. It wasn't necessary to win that point to win the case, and the chances that Microsoft could pull it off were slim. It had plausible arguments that even with monopoly power it was entitled to compete in the ways it had; however, its argument that it lacked that power was weak. If Jackson concluded that Schmalensee's testimony that the defendant lacked market power was unreliable, it could undercut the witness's ability to convince the court on Microsoft's primary argument.*

Predictably, I began my cross by attacking Schmalensee's monopoly power testimony. Also predictably, Schmalensee was soon on the defensive. What was not predictable was the extent of the rout that would ensue.

I began by establishing that the normal way to analyze market power was to define a relevant market, measure the defendant's share of that market, and (at least if the defendant's share were substantial) determine if there were barriers to entry. Schmalensee, knowing that such an analysis would suggest that Microsoft possessed monopoly power, tried to assert that this was only one approach and, while it was "useful in some circumstances," it was "not terribly informative" here. I then confronted him with his testimony just three months earlier in *Bristol v. Microsoft* where he had testified that the analysis I had suggested was "the traditional and most common approach" and the one he followed. Schmalensee shifted uncomfortably in his chair, and Judge Jackson interrupted his notetaking to look at the witness.

Schmalensee went on to testify that, even though he knew that we claimed that the relevant market consisted of personal computer operating systems, he "did not investigate and did not feel a need to investigate whether there was or was not" such a market. He was, I knew, trying to avoid being drawn into the dilemma of either admitting there was such a market or having to explain why there was not. The problem was that his cure was worse than the disease; in saying he did not even investigate this central issue, he looked indifferent to the facts. And the problem was about to become worse.

Schmalensee had testified previously for Microsoft in *Caldera v.*

---

*Even if, for client relations or other reasons, it had been necessary to argue that the company did not have monopoly power, it would have been better to have that issue addressed by a second economist, so that Schmalensee's personal credibility was not impaired.

Microsoft, and he had admitted to me earlier in the day, before he saw where I was going, that he considered *Caldera*, *Bristol*, and this case all part of "one big matter" with common issues. I now confronted him with the written record of his *Caldera* testimony that desktop operating systems *did* constitute a relevant market. In court, as on the radio or television, five seconds of dead air is a long pause; fifteen seconds can seem like an eternity. Schmalensee stared at his words for twenty seconds before responding. His explanation when it came was that the *Caldera* case dealt with "actions taken by Microsoft around 1990, 1991" and dealt with "competition before the emergence of Java, before the emergence of Netscape." His testimony, he added, had to be limited to "that time period." It was a creative response, but creating explanations extemporaneously on the witness stand is risky.

I next showed him testimony from the *Bristol* case in which, in late 1998—only a few months earlier, and long after the emergence of Netscape and Java—he had again testified to the existence of a personal computer operating systems market. Schmalensee was trapped, and he and Judge Jackson knew it.

The witness was likewise unable to reconcile his testimony in the *Bristol* case—that software at issue in that case used to enable applications to run on both Windows and Unix operating systems did not constitute "platform competition"—with his testimony now that Java and Netscape did. Judge Jackson interrupted:

> What I'm trying to find out is whether or not what you have said here in the *Bristol* case is consistent with the way in which you defined the platform competition in this case. I'm having difficulty at this point.

So was Schmalensee.

The witness was also embarrassed when, late in the afternoon, he was forced to admit that during a recess he had been given information to help him respond to my questions by one of Microsoft's lawyers. At my request a visibly disturbed Judge Jackson instructed that during cross-examination "there should be no conversations with the witness" by any Microsoft representative.

It was a glum Dean Schmalensee who left the witness stand that afternoon.

After court recessed for the day, John Warden tried to convince Judge Jackson to permit Microsoft to talk with its witness during breaks. I understood John's point; lawyers always work with their witnesses, particularly their experts, to help refine their testimony. However, in my experience that was not ordinarily done during cross-examination and in any event the court had already ruled. Trying to change the ruling was, I believed, a lost cause, and pursuing it risked raising the court's suspicions that Microsoft did not trust what its witnesses would say unschooled.

"I don't want you woodshedding a witness on cross-examination," Judge Jackson now warned. "I don't want witnesses, when they are on cross-examination . . . to be conferring during recesses and overnight adjournments to improve the quality of their testimony."

The following day I continued to probe at Schmalensee's monopoly power conclusions. I asked him whether Microsoft's persistent high profits were evidence that it had monopoly power. Initially he disagreed, asserting: "You cannot infer from profit that it is monopoly power." I then showed him a copy of a 1984 *Harvard Law Review* article he had written in which he had said in part,

> . . . persistent excess profits provide a good indication of long-run power. They show clearly that there is some impediment to effective imitation of the firm in question. The deadweight loss caused by such a breakdown in competition, and the resulting market power available to individual firms can be roughly estimated from the observed excess profits.

Dean Schmalensee stared long and hard at what he had written, looked up at me, then returned to his article. Finally he raised his head and with a wan smile said, "My immediate reaction is 'what could I have been thinking?'"

The spectators laughed, Judge Jackson shook his head slightly, and everyone in the courtroom could sense Dean Schmalensee's remaining authority slipping away.

A witness who fights battles he or she cannot win, and who is consequently embarrassed, will often end up giving up more than is necessary. An increasingly uncomfortable Schmalensee agreed that his "conclusion that Microsoft did not have monopoly power depended on his conclusion that there were not substantial barriers to entry" and that such barriers existed. Equally striking, he admitted that because of the applications and other support for Windows, PC manufacturers "have no commercially viable choice but to license Windows," and there was at present nothing "that would count as viable competition." He also admitted that the middleware of Netscape or Sun, by "creating cross-platform applications," had been "a significant potential platform threat," but that following Microsoft's actions there was no longer any possibility that they would ever become a competitor.*

As my cross-examination progressed, the faces of the Microsoft lawyers became increasingly grim. Unable to talk with their witness because of the judge's orders, they could do noth-

---

*Schmalensee also admitted that "most applications are written for Windows first and sometimes only"; that "the applications programming alleged barrier to entry is something that does, in fact, make it more difficult for people to enter the business of supplying operating systems"; that "in general, a clear signal of low barriers is provided only by effective viable entry that takes a nontrivial market share"; that during the years the government alleged that Microsoft had monopoly power, no one had successfully entered the PC operating systems business; that Microsoft had no existing serious threats"; that "if you have entry on a small scale and not any expansion so that you put . . . real pressure on established firms' profits, you infer that there is something preventing the expansion"; and that "a barrier to entry is any factor that permits firms already in the market to earn returns above the competitive level while deterring outsiders from entering."

These admissions themselves established our monopoly power claim. After the case was over Dr. Schmalensee conceded to Ken Auletta that he had been opposed to the decision to have him address the issue of Microsoft's monopoly power.

ing except sit and watch as their most important witness first lost
his credibility, then admitted their case away. They were, I knew,
wishing that it would all end, and I too was ready for it to be
over. The easiest way to spoil an effective cross-examination is to
keep it going too long. By definition the witness being crossed is
not on your side. An expert has been hired to hurt you, not help
you; and particularly with someone as smart and articulate as
Schmalensee, there is a serious danger that he will succeed.

But I wanted to end on a high note, and I generally try to reserve one good point for the end of any cross. The one I reserved
for Schmalensee turned out better than I hoped.

I had planned to end by returning to the issue of Microsoft's
profits, and I began by asking Schmalensee whether he had sought
to determine what the company's operating system profits were. I
expected him to answer that he had not and to explain that he did
not believe that the level of those profits were relevant to his analysis. It would not have been a great answer, but it would have been
a safe one. However, apparently still smarting from prior embar-
rassments, he did not want to say he had not investigated this issue;
instead he said that he *had* tried to find out what the profits were.
If, as happens in presidential news conferences, he had had the
ability to cut off follow-up questions, all might have been well.
But he could not avoid the follow-up, and since he did not know
what Microsoft's operating system profits were, he now had to explain why not.

His answer was that Microsoft had told him that the company
itself had no idea. My next question, with a tinge of amused dis-
belief, was "And did you accept that explanation at face value, sir?"
For a moment the witness froze—perhaps realizing the increasingly tangled web into which he was being drawn. If he answered
yes, he made himself look foolish; if no, he was calling his client a
liar. His answer ended up being

I was surprised, but I will be honest with you; the state of
Microsoft's internal accounting systems do not always rise

to the level of sophistication one might expect from a firm as successful as it is.

I did not emphasize the irony of the witness's assertion that he would "be honest," a claim judges often associate with the opposite. What I did was to press him as to what he had (and had not) done to confirm Microsoft's claim that it did not have any records that showed how profitable its operating system was. As it became clear that he could not point to anything concrete that he or his staff had done, Schmalensee became progressively more uncomfortable and more desperate to end this line of questioning. My last question was:

> Just to be clear, you were told that Microsoft doesn't have any records that show how profitable their operating system is, doesn't have any records that show what ancillary revenues or profits it receives, and you accepted that on face value; correct?

He replied:

> Mr. Boies, they record operating system sales by hand on sheets of paper. Under those circumstances, I accepted the absence of a detailed cost allocation system absolutely.

I paused a moment to let the absurdity of his answer sink in. Then, with a slight smile and an even slighter shake of the head, I walked back to the plaintiff's table, advising the court as I did so, "Your Honor, I have no more questions."

Schmalensee's testimony that the most computerized company ever, staffed by some of the most advanced techies the world has known, kept the multibillion-dollar sales of its most important product "by hand on sheets of paper" stunned everyone in the courtroom.

When, after a brief recess, Richard Urowsky began his redirect, he essentially ignored the concessions the witness had made on cross, concentrating instead on Microsoft's affirmative points. In testimony that lasted the balance of the day and well into the next, Schmalensee testified that there were many ways for Netscape to distribute its browser other than through OEMs and ISPs, including direct mail; that Netscape's share was declining because IE was a superior product; and that most operating system suppliers (including IBM and Apple) bundled a browser with their software.

The first point was disposed of by the witness's earlier admissions that the OEM and ISP channels, which Microsoft had blocked, were "the most important" forms of distribution; that it was usage, not mere distribution, that mattered; and that most consumers used the browser they got with their PC or online, not what they got in the mail. The second point was disposed of by Microsoft's own assessment that until recently Netscape's browser had been superior, that even now the most knowledgeable users preferred Netscape, and that the best that could be said for Microsoft was that as of today the browsers were comparable.

The third point, however, was important and potentially damaging. Urowsky had introduced a chart listing eight PC operating systems suppliers, each of which bundled a browser with their OS software. As Urowsky skillfully took his witness through the chart Judge Jackson was paying close attention. At a break a reporter asked me the question I suspected was in the judge's mind. How could we complain about Microsoft including its browser in Windows if everyone else did the same?

One answer was that companies with monopoly power are not free to engage in conduct that is permitted for companies without monopoly, but that was not very satisfying: if everyone independently decided to include a browser maybe there was a significant benefit to doing so that would be lost if Microsoft were forbidden to do it. Another answer might be that everyone was simply following Microsoft's lead, but the evidence on this was disputed. A third response was that none of the other companies had entered into the contracts that Microsoft had to require industry participants to disadvantage a competitor. This was a powerful point, but it still did not address why, as we claimed, Microsoft's combining its browser with its operating system was independently improper.

We had to have a better solution. It came because of what I had learned about IBM's OS/2 operating system when preparing for John Soyring's testimony. One of the operating systems on Schmalensee's list was IBM's OS/2. While IBM did distribute a browser with OS/2, it, unlike IE, was readily removable. Our central complaint about Microsoft's design was not that it distributed a browser to Windows users but that it had deprived its customers of an effective choice of which browser to use by preventing either OEMs or others from removing IE. I whispered to John Cove to find out in which of Schmalensee's other examples the browser was also readily removable. By the time I had my turn to cross-examine the witness again, I knew that half his examples were removable browsers, and I suspected they all might be.

I took Schmalensee through his chosen list, one system at a time, beginning with the ones I was sure about. In every case, he admitted that the browser was, unlike IE, removable. What had started out as a positive point for Microsoft ended as irrefutable evidence for the government.*

★   ★   ★

MICROSOFT'S SECOND WITNESS WAS PAUL MARITZ, A GREAT bear of a man who was one of Gates's two top executives, and the one directly responsible for Windows and the IE browser. With intelligence and confidence to match his girth, Maritz was proba-

---

*Fortune magazine's report on the beginning of Microsoft's case featured a large, full-color cartoon showing Schmalensee sitting in the witness chair hanging himself with a noose as Judge Jackson and I looked on. It accurately reflected how much of the damage done to Microsoft's case was self-inflicted. In a sense the problem was not the witness's; he had simply been sent out to take a bridge (in fact, several bridges) too far.

bly Microsoft's most effective witness. For three days I cross-examined him. For three days I would knock him down only to have him come back swinging. His testimony (that Microsoft was threatened by alternative operating systems, that the company did not consider Netscape a threat at the time it took certain critical actions, and that Microsoft's designs were motivated entirely by how to make a better product for consumers) was contradicted by a raft of internal e-mail and prior admissions, but Maritz stayed on message—and he did so, for the most part, recognizing and dealing with the opposing evidence rather than ignoring it. He was combative, but he preserved his credibility.

When he finally left the stand, we were both exhausted. I had, I thought, fought him to a standstill, and I had gotten one important new substantive admission. Microsoft's lawyers had begun to argue that no one had to worry about the possible disappearance of Netscape's Navigator because there were many other new browsers appearing. Maritz admitted that because those new browsers all adopted Microsoft's proprietary architecture, none of them posed a competitive threat. But if Microsoft had more witnesses like Maritz, I was in for some hard work. Judge Jackson seemed to be enjoying the show. At one point, when Urowsky rose to object to my pressing Maritz, Jackson overruled him, noting in a matter-of-fact tone, "The witness is awfully difficult to get an answer from."

When Martiz finally left the witness box, he walked directly to our table. Extending his hand to me, he said with a smile, "I'd love to meet you sometime under different circumstances."

"So would I," I replied.

★   ★   ★

MICROSOFT'S NEXT WITNESS WAS JAMES ALLCHIN, PRESENTED by Steven Holley, one of John Warden's partners. Allchin held a doctoral degree in computer science and was, after Maritz, the top Microsoft executive in charge of Windows; if possible, he was even smarter and more knowledgeable about the key issues in the case. Before my cross-examination, Allchin had presented a videotape that showed in a dramatic way three key points. First, Windows with Microsoft's browser did seventeen important things much better than Windows could do without IE. Second, Windows' performance suffered when Netscape's browser was used with it. Third, if a program designed by our witness Professor Edward W. Felten (intended to show that it was practical for Microsoft to offer users the option of turning off IE)* were run, Windows' performance was further degraded.

I was impressed, as were the press and courtroom spectators, and I had no doubt that Judge Jackson was too. First Maritz, and now the Allchin tape. It was late in the game but Microsoft seemed on the verge of putting on the quality defense I had expected from the beginning.

In cross-examining Allchin, I was counting on my horde of e-mails to bring him to heel. There were, however, two other factors that I did not then know that turned out to be at least as important. There was something about the Allchin tape that would deal Microsoft a blow from which it never fully recovered. And there was something about the witness himself.

Allchin had a reputation for a toughness that belied his soft-spoken, casual manner. However, Microsoft's lawyers and others would tell me later that while he could be tough, even harsh, in e-mail communications, he recoiled from personal confrontations. I did not know it at the time, but during my prior cross-examinations Allchin had been in the court watching intently, and just before his testimony had expressed concern about what lay in store for him. I also learned that his discomfort during my cross had been noticed by virtually everyone except me and the lawyers at our table. *Fortune's* Nocera reported:

---

*The purpose was to undercut Microsoft's argument that they could not give consumers the choice of whether or not to run IE.

Allchin was in court last Tuesday morning—the day Maritz was being pummeled by Boies. He sat with the Microsoft PR staff, but didn't talk to them much. He spent most of his time staring at his shoes, his hands tightly clasped. He looked like a lobster who's just been informed that he's next in the pot.

It is generally a good idea to let a witness get a sense of what cross-examination will be like, but where the experience begins to be unsettling, it has to be coupled with advice and reassurance. I assume that Microsoft's lawyers did what they could, but it was not enough.

I began my cross by turning to the first of the seventeen claimed benefits of integrating IE into the Windows 98 version of Microsoft's operating system in such a way that it could not be removed. I established that the purpose was to show the benefits and "rich experience" that Microsoft claimed could be achieved only by designing IE and Windows as a single, integrated package.

The problem was, as I had discovered and as Allchin soon admitted, exactly the same "rich experience" could be obtained by combining Windows 95 (without a browser) and a stand-alone IE browser that Microsoft sold at retail and was available for download over the Internet. The benefit came from adding the browser, not integrating it. This was critical because it meant that there was no justification for combining the browser and operating system together in such a way as to prevent their separation. The very benefits Microsoft identified could equally well be obtained by combining two separately available products.

Q And that combination of two retail purchase products would do exactly what you're describing here on this video; right?

A That's correct.

Consumers could have both the choice of which browser to use and the opportunity, if they chose, to enjoy whatever particular benefits IE offered. Microsoft's argument—that depriving consumers of an effective choice of which browser to use was justified by benefits that could not be obtained if the products were kept separate—was refuted by its own witness.

I proceeded to go through the seventeen examples one by one. In each case I would play the part of the video that claimed the improvement resulted from integration, then force Allchin to admit that "a user who had an original version of Windows 95 without any web browser at all, and who added to it the retail version of IE 4.0 would have exactly the same experience as is described here for a user with Windows 98."

Seventeen times I drove home the point that Microsoft had no justification for depriving consumers of browser choice by designing its operating system to include a browser that could not be removed. Consumers had the same benefits available either way, but in one case they had an effective choice of which browser to use and in the other they did not. Seventeen times I drove home the point that the impression the video had originally given was misleading.

I then turned to the statement on the video that Caldera's operating system had a "built-in browser." Allchin quickly admitted, as had Schmalensee, that the Caldera browser was removable. He also admitted that by "built-in" he meant only that the browser was distributed on a CD that was included in the same box as the CD that contained the operating system.

By now Allchin was in full retreat. He admitted that he "believed that Netscape's web browser was a serious potential platform threat to Microsoft." He accepted, after some hesitation, that integrating the browser into Windows was, in the words of his fellow Microsoft executive Ben Slivka, "a response to that platform threat." He admitted that he believed that to win the browser war Microsoft "must leverage Windows more," by which he meant using "the huge installed base of Windows" to require computer users to take the Microsoft browser.

At the end of the afternoon Microsoft's lawyers were desperate to work with Allchin overnight to get him back on track. John Warden again stepped in to try to persuade Judge Jackson to let Holley talk to the witness during the evening recess. Jackson again refused. Meanwhile our side was continuing to study the video-tape Allchin had introduced.

The next day I turned to the videotape's claim that running the so-called Felten program designed to turn off IE degraded the performance of Windows. Allchin's video tried to discredit the Felten program on the ground that its use prevented Microsoft's operating system from working effectively. With the help of Professor Felten and two of his associates, I had discovered overnight both that the tape was wrong and how to prove it.

I played the Allchin tape where a frozen system is shown and the narrator says, "It is taking a very long time, however—unusually long—to access the web site. That's a result of the performance degradation that has occurred because of the running of the Felten program."

I then emphasized what Allchin's tape was representing.

Q Now the clear implication of this video is that what the
    viewer is seeing right now is Windows 98 running after
    the Felten program has been run, correct?
A Yes.

I got Allchin to agree that the way one knew whether the Felten program had been run was that before it was run the so-called "title bar" at the top of the Windows 98 computer screen included the words "Microsoft Internet Explorer" but that after the Felten program was run the words "Microsoft Internet Explorer" disappeared, to be replaced with the words "Windows 98."

I then replayed the tape, freezing the frame at the point where the narrator purports to demonstrate the degradation. I pointed out that the title bar showed "Microsoft Internet Explorer."

Allchin himself froze, and the courtroom fell silent. Judge Jackson looked at the frozen videotape, stared hard at Allchin, looked again at the tape, then back at Allchin. I continued

    Q This is the portion of the clip where you are saying that after the Felten has been run, that the performance of Windows is degraded, right?

    A He is saying that.

All of a sudden the narrator of the Allchin tape had become a "he."

    Q Right. He is saying it and you are vouching for it?

    A Yes.

    Q Well, sir, if you look up here, it says 'Microsoft Internet Explorer,' correct, sir?

    A It does.

    Q And you've already testified that you know that that means that the Felten program has *not* been run, correct?

Allchin looked stricken. As he hesitated, he looked over to the Microsoft counsel table. No one met his gaze; Holley in particular was intently studying his notepad, which from where I was standing looked blank. Finally Allchin said, "That's right."

Having admitted that, contrary to the videotape's representation, the Felten program had not been run, Allchin's only explanation was that there must have been a "mistake." But he had no answer to my follow-up:

    Q Okay. People make mistakes. I can understand that. But how in the world could your people have run this program, calling it the Felten program, when they at least knew it wasn't?

He did not fare much better when confronted with his e-mails that contradicted the points he had made in his written testimony.

Again, he had no explanation except that he had been "wrong"—
"unfortunately, I was wrong"; "as I say, I was wrong"; "Mr. Boies,
this is just wrong"; "What I wrote here was wrong."

I ended my cross early Tuesday afternoon without using many
of my best Allchin e-mails and without exploring a question that
had been nagging both Professor Felten and me about the Allchin
tape. The tape showed that Windows 98 performance was degraded when run with the Netscape browser. Felten in his tests
had not been able to duplicate Allchin's results, and we were suspicious that the tape had been manipulated in some way. However, I had no clear proof and decided not to pursue that issue and
risk giving the witness a chance to regain some of his confidence.
I also decided not to use my remaining e-mails. I expected Holley to do a redirect examination, and I wanted to have some key
ammunition for recross. Both Allchin and his tape had been dis-
credited; if Holley surprised me and did not do a redirect, I could
live with that.

Holley did examine the witness for the last few hours on Tuesday, but it was uneventful, and had he stopped at the end of the day
the witness would have been free to go with no further questions
from me. Holley did not stop, a decision that both he and Allchin
would come to regret.

At an early dinner that evening Phil Malone, John Cove, and I
asked ourselves the same question that was probably haunting
Allchin—how had all this happened?* Despite the day's events,
Allchin seemed to me basically a decent man. Had he knowingly
got on the witness stand to sponsor under oath a videotape that he
knew was inaccurate? If not, who had set him up? And did they
really think they would get away with it? I found it hard to believe
that Steve Holley would have participated in consciously presenting

---

*When Allchin and his wife left the courthouse that afternoon he tried to avoid the
press by slipping out a side exit. When he was spotted by a photographer, Allchin tried to
hurry away, covering his face with his arm.

an inaccurate tape. But if not, how was it he did not know about the tape's inaccuracies?

After dinner I met Jonathan Schiller for a drink at the Prime Rib restaurant to discuss various firm matters. We had been there only a few minutes when someone called to tell me that Microsoft was telling reporters that I had ignored a key part of the videotape dealing with the performance of Windows 98 using the Netscape browser. Holley, reporters were told, would emphasize this point in his redirect Wednesday morning. I left Jonathan and hurried back to the office. When I arrived, I found Professor Felten and his associates already at work analyzing again the portion of the tape on which reporters had been told Holley would rely.

Part of me doubted that Holley would really revisit the Allchin tape, since doing so would remind the judge of Tuesday's fiasco. Was this work necessary? I wondered. Indeed, the thought crossed my mind that this was a clever feint to cause us to waste time on an unnecessary exercise. However, as Felten, I, and everyone else was aware, this was not a dress rehearsal; as Waylon Jennings used to tell his people, this was the big time and we were professionals. Microsoft was on the ropes, and if Holley were bold enough to return to the Allchin tape, we had a chance for an early knockout.

I went to bed as Felten and his associates energetically worked away; when I returned the next morning, they were still there. We did not have a complete answer yet, so they continued to work while I went off to court.

Holley did in fact return to the videotape. Allchin claimed that he too had worked late into the night and was now convinced that the video was accurate after all.

Q Mr. Allchin, can you explain to the court how it is that the machine used in the demonstration exhibited the behavior that you have just described?

A Yes, because there were many demos being done, they did a rehearsal run. They started with a base build, and then they ran through the software that they were going to show, and then they did the removal of the software through the "Add and Remove Programs." And in this particular case, Prodigy during that remove doesn't—it removes that key which, on a regular Windows 98 system, would make no difference. And then they eventually did the demonstrations that were shown, so it was as part of the rehearsal of just, you know, going through what was on the tape, which is the Prodigy system changed that title.

Allchin's explanation had everyone in the courtroom confused. In addition, if this were true, why had Allchin given the testimony he had the day before? Holley seemed to be taking a huge risk for little potential gain. The best he could hope for was that Judge Jackson would believe that Allchin had not understood the tape he had vouched for, or how it had been prepared. And if it turned out that there was a problem with this new explanation, "mistake" would not be an excuse: Allchin, Microsoft, and even its lawyers would be seen as having tried to put one over on the court.

I had some difficulty understanding the rest of Holley's redirect as well. At one point he asked Allchin whether other suppliers distributed a browser. This merely set Allchin up for a reprise of my earlier cross-examination of Schmalensee.

I began my recross of Allchin midmorning.

Q Is Microsoft, to your knowledge, the only OS vendor that prevents customers from removing the browser, if the customer wants to?

Holley immediately raised an objection—which was overruled and only served to underscore the importance of the inquiry. Next Allchin, like Schmalensee before him, tried to temporize. "I don't know," he began, "it depends on what you mean by 'remove.'"

A few minutes later, however, he gave up.

Q Would you agree that every other operating system vendor, except Microsoft, permits a customer who wants

to, to remove the browser that comes with the operating system?

A   Yes.

As my examination continued, his discomfort became palpable. At one point I interrupted a nonresponsive answer.

Q   Do you understand the question I am asking?
A   Maybe not.

I went on to use the e-mails I had saved just in case Holley
brought the witness back. I showed Allchin where he had sought
"to tie IE and Windows together," where he had said that winning
"the browser battle" depended on integrating IE into Windows,
and where he had said that one of Microsoft's reasons for preventing removal of IE was that OEMs were reluctant to ship more than
one browser with their PCs and that therefore tying IE to Windows 98 would mean that "Netscape never gets a chance on these
systems." The witness who was supposed to defend the consumer
benefits of Microsoft's design decisions was revealing those decisions to have been driven by an effort to prevent users from choosing between the Microsoft and Netscape browsers on their merits.

Allchin, who had recovered some of his composure during
Holley's examination, now looked worse than yesterday. Shortly
before the lunch recess one of my trial team passed me a note:
"Holley to Schmalensee: What could *I* have been thinking of?"

It was about to get worse. At the recess Malone and Felten had
briefed me on their conclusions about the Allchin tape. There
were a number of unanswered questions, but I had enough to
work with. "What *was* Holley thinking of?" I asked Phil. And
what, I wondered, was going on with Allchin?

It was about four o'clock when I finally turned to the tape.
The portion of the video comparing the performance of Windows 98 with IE and with Netscape was about four minutes long.
I began by playing those four minutes from start to finish to give
the court context and to dramatize its importance. The tape pur-

ported to show a single computer, and the voice-over declared, "We have not made any other changes to this computer or Windows 98 except to run Dr. Felten's programs." That was not true, as I was about to demonstrate.

I had already established that Allchin claimed personally to have checked the videotape and that he was satisfied "that the demonstration was, as near as you could tell, fair and accurate." After playing the video through once, I started again from the beginning and, after about twenty seconds, froze the tape. I pointed out to Allchin and the court that in the second column on the screen, where program icons were listed, there were two icons indicating the presence of two separate programs.

I then played the tape for another two minutes before once more freezing it.

> Q Now, do you notice that in the second column, where we used to have two icons, we now only have one icon?
>
> A I see that.

> Q Now, that indicates that something has happened to this in the last two minutes, right?
>
> A Yes.

Allchin looked stricken; Judge Jackson looked stunned; the courtroom was silent as a tomb. It was suddenly clear that the tape did not show a continuous demonstration of a single machine. Microsoft had spliced together pictures of different machines running different programs to try to make the point they wanted.

I again ran the tape, and again froze it. This time I paused before asking a question. Every eye in the courtroom went immediately to the column showing program icons. The second icon had reappeared. In the silence I heard a Microsoft lawyer whisper, "Oh, shit."

When it became apparent where I was going, a shocked Judge Jackson had asked Allchin, "You mean, this wasn't run on the same machine?" Initially Allchin said he did not know. As I continued and Allchin repeatedly said, "I don't know" and "I can't tell," Jackson became exasperated.

> THE COURT: How can I rely on it if you can't tell me whether it's the same machine or whether any changes have been made to it? It's very troubling, Mr. Allchin. And I would feel much better about it if you had made the test yourself, if you had been there.
>
> A   Yes sir, I have made the test.
>
> THE COURT: Yeah, but that's not what I'm seeing here.

When finally Allchin admitted, "there were multiple machines involved," he was accepting what I had known since the noon recess. Jackson shook his head, observing, "It simply casts doubt on the reliability, entire reliability, of the video demonstration. It's difficult to make a finding as to what it reveals."

When I finished my examination, a chastened Steve Holley asked to speak to the judge privately to "apologize" and ask for an opportunity to redo the tape one more time. Judge Jackson agreed, on the condition that the government had a representative present. That evening, Jim Allchin, Steve Holley, and as many Microsoft technical people as could be gathered tried until six-thirty the following morning to recreate the performance results shown on the original tape. Unable to do so, Allchin's only explanation was that the performance comparison "has to be done in a controlled lab environment, and I do not have that here . . ."

Microsoft still had eight witnesses to go, but its defense never recovered. Some of the remaining witnesses were better than others, but none was able to make much progress in the face of the documents, e-mails, and admissions we had accumulated. All of them added admissions of their own. (For example, Microsoft executive Cameron Myhrvold admitted the company did not want users to have both its and Netscape's browsers on a PC because "we thought we would lose in a side-by-side choice"). And at least one remaining witness dissolved on the stand as badly as Schmalensee and Allchin.

Daniel Rosen was the Microsoft executive who led the team that met with Netscape in the middle of 1995 to discuss possible business arrangements. These were the meetings in which, according to the testimony of two Netscape executives, Microsoft proposed an agreement to limit competition—and threatened that, if Netscape did not, Microsoft would drive its smaller rival out of business. Such an agreement would be a clear antitrust violation. Rosen's only purpose as a witness was to deny that charge. Since we had the burden of proof, it was likely that if Rosen simply said it did not happen and survived cross-examination with his credibility moderately intact, Judge Jackson would rule for Microsoft on this claim.

Rosen testified that he was unaware of any "browser war" or competition between Microsoft and Netscape and claimed that he never considered Netscape a platform threat. His thought process appeared to be that he could not be accused of dividing markets with a company that he did not believe competed with, or threatened, Microsoft. The problem, of course, was that numerous documents and e-mails, and every prior witness, had said that Microsoft did consider Netscape a platform threat. The opening seemed too good to be true. As I confronted Rosen with document after document and prior admission after prior admission he looked as bad as Allchin and Schmalensee.

Shortly before lunch I showed Rosen one of his own e-mails, in which, just before a key meeting with Netscape, he himself had labeled the rival company a serious threat. "Did you believe that, sir, at the time you wrote it?" I asked. When Rosen replied, "No, sir," the courtroom erupted in laughter. Rosen's explanation was that the e-mail was "a draft" in which, for reasons he could not explain, he wrote down assertions he did not believe. After I pointed to the fact that the e-mail showed a date and time the message was sent to two Microsoft executives, Rosen maintained it had never gone out.

The explanation did not seem credible to me or, I thought, to Judge Jackson. In any event, I thought there was nothing more to be done. During the noon recess I began working on the balance of my cross. Just before the afternoon session John Cove and Phil Malone handed me evidence that caused me to return to the "draft" e-mail. Suspicious of Rosen's explanation, and more creative than I had been, they had used the ninety-minute recess to research from where within Microsoft the "draft" had been produced. What they discovered was a Sullivan & Cromwell letter confirming that the document had been found not in Rosen's files but in those of the two addressees.

The "draft" *had* been sent—it was not a draft at all; Rosen's elaborate explanation was a fabrication. He was caught, and he knew it. Judge Jackson was visibly angry, but he did not (as some judges would have done) cite the witness for contempt or refer the matter to the U.S. attorney for a perjury investigation.

When Warden's younger partner Michael Lacovara rose to examine Rosen and try to rehabilitate the witness, Jackson said, not unkindly, "Mr. Lacovara, it is always inspiring to watch young people embark on heroic endeavors." Michael made the best effort he could, but with 20/20 hindsight it would have been better to let the witness just slip away. Their problem was that, as I had done with Allchin, I had held back something to use on recross, expecting that Microsoft would not have the discipline to write the witness off without attempting a further examination. My recross, when it came, was short.

I wanted to establish that Rosen had had access to the Netscape browser code before his May and June 1995 discussions with Netscape. Access to that code would demonstrate once and for all that he knew Netscape posed a platform threat and would provide the motive for the June attempt to divide markets. Rosen (who admitted to having come to Washington thirty days before his scheduled testimony in order to prepare to be cross-examined by me) saw where I was going and asserted with conviction that he had not had access to the code until July 1995. In fact, he emphasized, he distinctly remembered a Microsoft executive telling him in May that they had just received an early version of the code, and that Rosen himself did not receive the code until July.

"You don't remember that, do you sir? You're just making that up, aren't you?" I was rarely sharp with a witness, and all attention was now focused on Rosen.

"No," he replied without conviction, "I remember it."

I then handed to the witness and to Judge Jackson a document that showed that the code had been given to Microsoft in April— and that Rosen had been present at the meeting. As I waited for the contents of the document to sink in, Judge Jackson looked at the paper in his hand, glanced sharply at the witness, slapped the paper down on his bench, and turned his back on Rosen.

"I stand corrected," Rosen said weakly, without waiting for a question. There was nowhere for him, or his company, to hide. It was late Tuesday afternoon, and Microsoft was scheduled to complete its case by Friday. Since there was no court on Thursday, and there were three witnesses to go, it would have been impossible to finish on schedule if any one of these three took the time previous witnesses had used up. However, everyone seemed to accept that the case was now effectively over, and we all worked to fit the remaining evidence into the time available. We even finished early on Friday.

The end-of-the-week party with the press corps, which this time was joined by several Microsoft lawyers, was like the last night at camp. It had been an arduous four months, but I sensed that I was not the only one who would miss it. We were scheduled to resume the trial to hear rebuttal witnesses, but after twenty-four witnesses in person, more than fifty by deposition, and several thousand exhibits in evidence no one expected that the rebuttal would change the outcome.

I took the weekend off and then turned to catching up on my other cases. During April and May I divided my time between preparing for the rebuttal, working on Garry Shandling's case against Brad Grey (see chapter 7), preparing for a September jury trial of environmental claims against W. R. Grace (see chapter 8), negotiating a settlement with defendants in the price-fixing case we had brought against vitamins manufacturers (chapter 6), and representing the State of Alaska in connection with British Petroleum's announced acquisition of ARCO/AMOCO.

The rebuttal case began June 1 and, as expected, produced few surprises. When it ended on June 23, Mary and I flew to California. I spent a good part of July with my family at our ranch in Lake County, California, during which time I recruited my son Christopher (Jonathan's decidedly non-identical twin brother) for our new firm.*

We submitted our proposed findings of fact on August 10.† Two days later I flew to Greece for a three-week family vacation. As we sailed from Mykonos to Santorini, I tried occasionally to think about what Microsoft could say in response to our proposed findings. After Labor Day Joel and I met to discuss the upcoming argument. Neither of us could understand why Microsoft had not made any serious effort to settle. If the court ruled that it had violated the antitrust laws, then any private party could rely on that judgment in any subsequent case brought against Microsoft—a principle called

---

*Christopher, having moved to Credit Suisse First Boston from Sullivan & Cromwell, was working as an investment banker. In August 1998 he joined the firm to establish a corporate department, initially specializing in mergers and acquisitions, project financings, and related transactions.

†Following a bench trial, the parties generally prepare proposed findings of fact and conclusions of law, which they submit to the trial judge for his consideration. These submissions, which attempt to marshal all of the facts and law that each side believes favorable to its position, are the next to last chance a party has. Thereafter the court usually schedules an oral argument at which the judge has an opportunity to ask questions raised by the submissions and each side takes its last shot at presenting its case.

Judge Jackson adopted a somewhat unusual approach whereby the parties would submit proposed findings of fact, argue their proposals, receive his findings, and only then submit proposed conclusions of law (followed by oral argument related to those conclusions, followed by his final decision). It was a sensible approach: our proposed conclusions could be much more focused if we already knew what facts the court would rule had been proven. It also gave the parties one last chance to settle. The oral argument on the findings of fact was scheduled for September 21.

"collateral estoppel." In addition, such a judgment would almost certainly cause antitrust regulators in Europe to challenge the company. Regardless of what remedy, if any, Judge Jackson imposed, these effects would impose a heavy burden. The only way this could be avoided would be to settle before judgment was entered. Although that would not occur until after Jackson's conclusions of law, still three or four months away, if the findings of fact effectively nailed Microsoft, whatever limited remaining bargaining power the defendant still had would be gone.

At the September 21 hearing my argument mirrored our trial presentation; my main difficulty was selecting which pieces of evidence to use. John Warden had a more difficult task, but he rose to the occasion. His presentation was as strong as the evidence would allow. He asked the court to ignore the fact that Microsoft's witnesses had been embarrassed and to focus on the fact that the company's success was based on cool technology and tough competition. The government, John argued, was attacking Microsoft for being too innovative, too competitive; it was an attack on success designed to benefit Microsoft's less capable, less successful competitors—competitors who had provided key testimony for us at trial.

Judge Jackson asked few questions and for the most part maintained his poker face. Thereafter there was nothing more to do but wait. Although I was mainly occupied by the Grace trial in New York City, I was soon spending a moment or two every weekday morning wondering whether that day would be the one Jackson would issue his findings.

I had many reasons to be confident in the outcome. The evidence cited in our proposed findings of fact was, I believed, overwhelming—and not effectively countered in Microsoft's submissions. However, we were asking Jackson to make findings that only a handful of judges had made during the 110 years of antitrust enforcement.

Waiting for a decision is never easy; the longer the wait, the harder it gets. Finally, on the morning of Friday, November 5, I received a call from Phil Malone: Judge Jackson's clerk had telephoned to say that the court would issue its findings that afternoon. I caught a one p.m. plane to Washington. When I arrived at Joel's office, everyone was speculating on what Judge Jackson would do. Shortly after three p.m. Phil Malone left the Justice Department to go to court to wait for the release of the decision. He carried a cell phone so that he could call us as soon as he got the opinion. Microsoft, of course, also had a lawyer there. In addition the press had been informed that a decision was imminent. Judge Jackson's courtroom and the second-floor hallway outside were jammed. Camera crews and satellite trucks filled the grounds and streets outside.

Part of the reason Joel and I had stayed at the Justice Department offices was to avoid the necessity of reacting on the spot to whatever the court decided. If either of us had been present it would have been hard to decline any comment to the assembled reporters, and Joel and Janet Reno wanted to have a chance to reflect on what Judge Jackson had done before making any statement about as important a decision as this.

Shortly after four Phil called. "We won."

I walked out of the conference room to call Mary with the news, then returned to join Joel and the others in waiting impatiently for Phil to arrive with the opinion. He must have run all the way, because he was back in under five minutes. Joel and I divided up the decision, with me reading the first half and him the second. As either of us came to a particularly important sentence we would read it out loud. It was soon apparent that we had indeed won. In 412 separately numbered paragraphs Judge Jackson set forth findings that detailed Microsoft's monopoly power, its anticompetitive conduct, and the harm to competition and to consumers that resulted. Although the conclusions of law would not come for two or three months, it was clear that the findings of fact compelled a conclusion that Microsoft was guilty of violating the antitrust laws.

Early that evening Joel and I joined Janet Reno and the attorneys general of Iowa and Connecticut to discuss the decision at a Justice Department press conference. Attorneys General Tom Miller of Iowa, Richard Blumenthal of Connecticut, and Eliot Spitzer of New York had led the litigation for the nineteen states that had worked with the Justice Department on the case. There had been a time when their efforts had been given little chance of success; but despite the political pressures brought to bear by Microsoft (pressures that had driven the attorneys general of Texas and South Carolina out of the case), they had persevered.

On Thursday, November 18, Judge Jackson called both sides to his chambers for what we assumed would be a conference to set the schedule for briefing and arguing conclusions of law, and perhaps to discuss issues of remedy. Saying he had "something of a surprise" for us, he proposed that the parties, having shown that they were unable to reach a settlement on their own, enter into mediation using Chief Judge Richard Posner of the U.S. Court of Appeals in Chicago as a mediator. Judge Posner was a brilliant judge and a noted antitrust scholar. He was also one of the most conservative figures on the federal bench.

Judge Jackson's choice was as inspired as it was unexpected. Because of Posner's intelligence and conservative outlook, if Microsoft would listen to anybody it would be him. At the same time, both sides would have to recognize that Posner's views on remedy might well correspond to Jackson's. We quickly agreed to try mediation. No one wanted to offend the judge, who still had conclusions of law to enter and a remedy to determine. Besides, as both Warden and I agreed, if anyone could craft a mutually acceptable settlement it would be someone like Posner.

Initially I (and, I believe, Judge Posner) had some hope that the mediation might be successful. Sharing a taxi on our way to O'Hare after our December 6, 1999, mediation sessions, Joel Klein, Jeff Blattner, and I felt that for the first time since May 1998 Microsoft might be serious about a realistic settlement. A week later we returned to Chicago and early the following morning caucused at the Justice Department's Chicago offices

with Attorney General Richard Blumenthal and other representatives of the states. It was difficult for us to assess where Microsoft really stood, in part because Judge Posner met with each
side separately. Also, Bill Gates, who would make the final decision for Microsoft, had not been heard from. Would the court's
findings of fact encourage him to compromise or spur him to
circle the wagons?

Despite our uncertainty over whether there was any real movement on Microsoft's part, we agreed to take the initiative in proposing settlement terms. At Judge Posner's urging we had also agreed to
propose settlements that did not include requiring that Microsoft be
split up—what is called "divestiture." We also sought to tailor the
remedies we sought so that the defendant's ability to innovate and
compete was not compromised. Consumer choice and a level playing field were our objectives, not hobbling Microsoft.

While the mediation was under way, Steve Ballmer was named
CEO of Microsoft, replacing Bill Gates. Initially we thought this
might signal a more pragmatic approach to the litigation. However,
despite several weeks of effort, no settlement was obtained. Judge
Jackson heard arguments on conclusions of law on February 22,
2000, and on April 3 entered his final judgment which, as we had
expected, found that Microsoft had violated the Sherman Act. That
evening, following a joint appearance on the *Charlie Rose Show*,
Richard Blumenthal and I briefly discussed what a sensible remedy
recommendation might be—the beginning of an intensive debate
that occupied both the Justice Department and the states for the
next few weeks.

Judge Jackson sought to postpone a decision on remedy until
after the appellate courts had ruled on his February decision. A
postponement would have permitted him to tailor a remedy based
on what the appellate courts ultimately held. However, both sides
objected, and on June 7, 2000, the court issued an order requiring
the company to change its business practices and to separate its operating systems and applications programming businesses into separate companies.

We immediately began preparing for Microsoft's inevitable appeal. The appellate courts would give great deference to the trial court's findings of fact, accepting them unless they were clearly contrary to the evidence; however, the court of appeals would make its own decision on disputed issues of law, giving little if any deference to Jackson's rulings. Most of the critical issues were issues of fact—did Microsoft have monopoly power; were its practices anticompetitive, what were the effects of its conduct, and what were any justifications?

There were, however, a few key issues of law that would ultimately have to be decided on appeal. Were the antitrust laws applicable to New Economy high-tech industries? Did the fact that Microsoft's power was derived from copyrighted software insulate it from antitrust attack? Was there any limit on the extent to which a monopolist could manipulate product design in order to disadvantage competitors?

We soon had another question to consider. We learned that while the judge was considering what remedy was appropriate, he had spoken to several reporters about the case. This innocent-seeming act turned out to be a timebomb. Jackson had refused all requests for interviews during the trial, and he only spoke now to reporters on condition that they would not publish anything based on their interviews until after his remedy decision. But judges are limited in what they are supposed to say outside of court about the merits of a pending case, and we were immediately concerned that Microsoft would seek to exploit the court's comments.

The substance of what Judge Jackson said was based on the trial record and was not significantly different from what he had earlier said in open court and in his opinions; and Jackson's attempt to explain to reporters how he had reached his decision in this well-publicized trial was understandable. However, Microsoft had a record of attacking judges if given an opening (indeed Judge Jackson had been selected for the case after the previous judge, Stanley Sporkin, had been removed at Microsoft's request). I was worried that these press interviews would give them that opening.

If the company could convince an appellate court that Judge Jackson's statements to the press reflected an anti-Microsoft bias, the court might reverse his findings and order a new trial.

Ordinarily an appeal from a federal district court goes to the U.S. Court of Appeals and then, if the Supreme Court decides to hear the case, to the U.S. Supreme Court. However, by statute, government antitrust cases may bypass the court of appeals and go directly to the Supreme Court if the district court and the Supreme Court both approve. The court of appeals for the District of Columbia had thus far shown itself sufficiently favorable to Microsoft that there was strong sentiment at the Justice Department to seek a direct appeal to the Supreme Court. I did not see how the Court of Appeals could reverse Judge Jackson's careful findings of fact, or how, if those findings stood, the court could reverse Jackson's conclusion that Microsoft had violated the antitrust laws. However, I agreed that a direct appeal would accelerate a final resolution of the case and hence favored it.

The game of legal chess continued. On June 13, 2000, Microsoft filed its notice of appeal with the court of appeals in an attempt to preempt the Justice Department from going directly to the Supreme Court. It also asked Judge Jackson to stay his order requiring the company to change its practices until the appellate process was completed. The next day the Justice Department asked Judge Jackson to certify the case for direct appeal to the Supreme Court. On June 20 Jackson did so (and at the same time granted Microsoft's motion for a stay pending appeal).

In the meantime the court of appeals, acting the very same day it received Microsoft's notice of appeal and without waiting for a response from the government, issued an order that said that the appeal would be heard *en banc* (that is, by all of the court's judges sitting together rather than in a randomly selected three-judge panel) on an expedited basis. Federal courts of appeal rarely sit *en banc*, and virtually never do so until an appeal has first been heard by a three-judge panel. The unusual action was widely interpreted as an attempt to convince the Supreme Court to let the court of appeals have the first crack at Judge Jackson's opinions.

Ultimately the Supreme Court declined to hear the case directly. As is usual in such decisions, the Court did not explain its thinking. The fact that Microsoft's appeal would be heard by the court of appeals was seen by most observers as favoring the defendant. The *USA Today* headline was typical: "Microsoft Case to go Before Full U.S. Court of Appeals—Largely Conservative Panel Has Sided with Software Giant in Past." Holman Jenkins, the *Wall Street Journal's* indefatigable defender of antitrust violators (he defended price-fixing by Sotheby's and Christie's on the ground that they cheated only rich people and museums and defended Microsoft on the ground that "antitrust sins aren't found in the Bible or the Code of Hammurabi") was ecstatic. Jenkins told friends that he was certain the court of appeals would rule that Microsoft had not violated the law. Notwithstanding such views, I continued to believe that while the court might (as Judge Jackson himself had) question some elements of our claims or the particular remedy imposed, I believed it should uphold the district court's findings of fact.*

Nevertheless I could not predict how the court of appeals would rule on Microsoft's legal arguments that the antitrust laws should not apply to copyrighted intellectual property such as computer software in a market characterized by constant change and innovation, and that the antitrust laws did not constrain design decisions. I was also concerned about how the court would react to Jackson's press interviews.

---

*In fact I viewed the court of appeals' unusual action of immediately trying to take control as slightly positive. The appellate judges certainly knew the perception of the public and the legal community that they had previously exhibited a pro-Microsoft orientation. If they now reached out to take and reverse the case, this would further reduce the public's perception of their neutrality. This did not, of course, mean that they should or would affirm a decision they thought was wrong. However, if they had already been inclined to reverse, it would have been far safer not to have taken the unusual step they had. I believed the judges had an open mind, and I hoped that they would decide, as Judge Jackson had, that the support for his findings of fact was strong.

As the time for presenting the appeal approached, it began to look as if I would have to entrust the defense of my trial victory to other lawyers. At the press conference following Judge Jackson's remedy ruling, Joel Klein had suggested that I would lead the argument in the court of appeals as I had in the district court. However, Microsoft succeeded in convincing the court to schedule oral argument at the end of February 2001, and by that time it was, as the New York Times reported in late December, apparent there would be a change in administration and that I would probably not be the Justice Department's choice to argue the appeal:

Mr. Boies's very public performance defending the Gore campaign during the Florida recount battle makes it highly unlikely that the Bush administration would retain him on the Microsoft case—or any other.

Attorneys General Miller, Blumenthal, Spitzer, and others were concerned about reports in the New York Times and elsewhere that "the Bush administration seems willing to walk away from the resounding court victory the Justice Department won in the antitrust case against Microsoft." They, and I, were particularly concerned when aides to the president-elect told the Times shortly before Christmas 2000 that "a Bush administration would never have filed the suit to begin with and will drop it under certain circumstances—or settle under terms far more generous than the present administration would have offered."

When it became clear that I would not argue for the Justice Department, Attorneys General Tom Miller and Richard Blumenthal asked me if I would argue in the court of appeals on behalf of the states. I told them that I would be willing to do so if the department consented. The department did not, effectively ending my involvement in the case.

At the oral argument three facts were clear: the Court of Appeals judges were thoroughly prepared, dubious of Microsoft's broad attempt to carve software/high-tech/intellectual property/product design exemptions to the antitrust laws, and upset that Judge Jackson had given interviews to reporters between the liability and remedy phases of the trial. With two possible exceptions, the Justice Department lawyers did an excellent job. The first problem was that since they had not been present at trial, they were unable to respond completely to certain questions from the bench.* The second problem, at least from my perspective, was their unwillingness to defend or put in context Judge Jackson's comments to the press. I understood the lawyers' reluctance to fight the appellate judges who were upset with Jackson, particularly over an issue that they probably viewed as peripheral. But Jackson was not there to defend himself, and I thought that someone should have answered Microsoft's charges.† In addition, undermining the court of appeals' confidence in Jackson risked undermining Jackson's ruling.

The court of appeals released its decision on June 28, 2001. It was unanimous; and it was *per curiam,* which means that it is not the work of any single judge. My concerns proved unwarranted. The court affirmed each of Judge Jackson's findings of fact and ruled that Microsoft was guilty of monopolizing the personal computer operating systems market in violation of Section 2 of the Sherman Act. The court rejected the conclusion that Microsoft was guilty of attempting to monopolize the separate browser market because, it said, Jackson had not made sufficiently specific findings concerning that market. It also remanded the issue of whether Microsoft's combination of its browser and operating system was a violation of Section 1 of the Sherman Act; Jackson had decided that the combinations were per se unlawful,

---

*The two Justice Department staff attorneys who were assigned to argue the case (neither of whom had been involved in the trial) were well-regarded appellate specialists and effective advocates. However, by blocking me from participating, and by ignoring my suggestion that Phil Malone (who knew the record better than anyone) at least share the presentation, the Justice Department was making Microsoft's life considerably easier.

†For example, the court of appeals opinion noted: "At oral argument, plaintiffs all but conceded that the judge violated ethical restrictions by discussing the case in public."

while the court of appeals held that the combinations should be tested under a "rule of reason" standard.*

The court's affirmance of our broadest claim but not our two narrower ones may have reflected the compromises necessary to get seven judges to agree to a unanimous opinion in a complicated and controversial case. Whatever the explanation, it was a vindication of our decision to pursue the broad Section 2 claims and not merely the narrow ones.†

The court remanded the issue of remedy back to the district court for further consideration. It held that Jackson's interviews gave an appearance of partiality, that he should therefore be replaced as the trial judge, and that his remedy order, which had followed his interviews, had to be vacated. (The appellate court also ruled that Judge Jackson had erred in not holding a separate evidentiary hearing on remedy and had not adequately explained his reasons for ordering divestiture.) Despite that criticism, the court praised his fair handling of the trial itself, affirming every one of his several hundred findings of fact and most of his conclusions of law relating to Section 2.

The appellate ruling was an important antitrust precedent. The court held that Microsoft had monopoly power in the personal computer operating systems market. The court went on to rule

---

*If an act is per se unlawful, no justification is permitted. If an act is tested under a "rule of reason" analysis the competitive harm is balanced against any efficiency or pro-competitive effects.

†The court's remand of our Section 1 tying claim for a rule of reason analysis made sense; we had originally sought findings under both a per se standard and a rule of reason, but Jackson had not entered any rule of reason findings. Although I disagreed with some of the court's reasoning concerning our "browser market" attempt to monopolize claim (for example, the court's complaint that Jackson had not "entered detailed findings defining what a browser is"), I had to agree that we had not focused on that issue at trial nearly as much as we had on our primary claim, and that, as the court's opinion noted, the Justice Department's briefs and oral argument responses to the court's questions had failed to point to the evidence in the record that did exist. In addition, the court's decision on our primary claim of actual monopolization of operating systems made the browser market attempt claim unimportant.

that the company had engaged in a wide variety of illegal anti-competitive conduct, including:

- restricting the ways in which personal computer manufacturers could promote rival browsers;
- requiring AOL and other Internet access providers to use and promote IE exclusively and/or to restrict their use and promotion of other browsers;
- requiring that program developers agree, in order to get early access to Windows, to favor IE over other browsers and to favor Microsoft's proprietary version of Java over Sun's cross-platform version;
- agreeing with Apple that Apple distribute and promote IE and limit its distribution and promotion of other browsers;
- deceiving Java developers by falsely representing that using Microsoft's proprietary version of Java would not result in Windows-dependent applications;
- threatening and inducing Intel to agree to limit its cross-platform interfaces;
- designing Windows 98 so that its IE browser could not be removed by the "Add/Remove Programs" function applicable to other Windows software; and
- unnecessarily combining and intermixing browser code and other Windows code to further make removal impractical.

What was most important for the personal computer industry and antitrust precedent was that the court of appeals decision had affirmed the applicability of the antitrust laws to high-tech and intellectual property markets ("Microsoft's primary copyright argument borders on the frivolous") and had affirmed that Microsoft's conduct in restricting the growth of potential competitors through both contracts and product design had violated those laws.

The *Washington Post* (which had been sympathetic to Microsoft's position before the trial) observed: "Microsoft was—as U.S. District Judge Thomas Penfield Jackson had earlier found—a monopolist that had serially violated the law, including through acts that the company deemed improvements to its products." The *New York Times* similarly editorialized:

> The core of yesterday's decision affirmed United States District Judge Thomas Penfield Jackson's ruling that Microsoft had illegally maintained its monopoly in the market for computer operating systems. This is an important victory for antitrust enforcement and sufficient basis for the government to continue pressing for a meaningful remedy in the case.

I had two concerns with the opinion. First, I thought it was unduly harsh toward Jackson. The judge had been subject to relentless criticism from Microsoft, and I believed his comments were best understood as an attempt to explain in response what he had done. I also knew—and several reporters mentioned privately to me—that judges often talk to the press off the record or for "background" about their cases. A judge less straightforward than Jackson might have avoided the pickle in which he found himself by making sure his remarks could not be attributed to him.

My second concern related to what the Bush administration would do with the case. It was an oversimplification to say that the Clinton administration was pro-consumer while the Bush administration would be pro-business, but I knew there was enough truth to the idea to make it unlikely that Bush would have brought the prosecution. Whether the new administration would abandon an existing case was another matter. The enforcement of our nation's laws is supposed to be free from political influence, particularly when a case is ongoing. Nevertheless, it is not always so.

I was encouraged by Attorney General Ashcroft's statement the day of the opinion: "We believe this is a significant victory in terms of the determination made by a unanimous court that Microsoft had engaged in illegal conduct." But I remembered the unnamed "Bush aides" who had told the *New York Times* at the end of December 2000 that the Bush administration never would have brought the case in the first place and could be expected to resolve it favorably to Microsoft if given a chance. The court of appeals remand could be that chance in that by sending the case back to the district court for further proceedings the Bush Justice Department would have an opportunity to cut back on the remedy or even drop claims. Ultimately, it did both.

The new head of the Antitrust Division was Charles James, a likable antitrust lawyer who had served as an Antitrust Division attorney when Charles Rule, now representing Microsoft, was in charge of the division. The first two decisions Ashcroft and James made were to abandon the effort to separate Microsoft's two businesses and the claim that Microsoft's tying of IE to Windows violated Section 1. They defended their decisions on the grounds that the Section 1 tying claim was unnecessary in light of the court of appeal's monopolization ruling (which included the holding that the tying violated Section 2) and that the court of appeals opinion, while not deciding the issue, expressed some doubt about separating Microsoft's businesses.*

If Ashcroft and James used their monopolization victory to pursue aggressive conduct remedies prohibiting the company from engaging in future anticompetitive conduct and undoing the effects of past violations, then I would be comfortable with their decisions

---

*However, as the court of appeals opinion noted, price bundling (providing an operating system and browser at the same price as an operating system alone) was an element of the Section 1 tying complaint but not of the monopolization complaint; this claim was now lost. In addition, with respect to divestiture the court had noted that the district court had wide discretion in framing a remedy. Moreover, whatever the court of appeals later ruled, the issue would ultimately be decided by the Supreme Court (which, on antitrust issues at least, was considerably more liberal than the District of Columbia Court of Appeals). Finally, unilateral disarmament in the face of as aggressive an opponent as Microsoft struck me as questionable. If the department intended to settle with Microsoft, it would be good to keep as much leverage as possible.

on tying and divestiture. But what, I wondered, did those decisions say about Ashcroft and James's willingness to pursue aggressive conduct remedies? The more I heard from the Justice Department career staff, the more I worried.

As the department's negotiations with Microsoft progressed during 2001, I was repeatedly told that the staff felt that James lacked either the ability or the will to negotiate effectively with Microsoft. ("They're in over their heads." "They don't have a clue about the trial record." "We're asking for less than even the court of appeals ruled was unlawful." "James just won't confront Rule." "We've got no one who can stand up to Microsoft." "We're focusing on the concepts, Microsoft's focusing on the words—this is how we got screwed in the last Consent Decree.")

The settlement that the Justice Department ultimately negotiated was, as Bush aides had predicted in late December, much less than we would have settled for, and less than the Justice Department could have obtained in court. There were a number of lapses, but one of the more striking was that, despite the fact that the court of appeals had found that Microsoft had illegally combined browser and operating system code, Microsoft had no obligation under the settlement to revise its design or to avoid engaging in similar conduct in the future.

Nine states, including Iowa and Connecticut, vowed to press for broader relief. It was an effort doomed from the outset. Few if any judges were going to upset an antitrust settlement negotiated by the Justice Department, particularly one as complicated as this. Indeed, it is precisely because of the latitude and discretion given Justice Department prosecutorial decisions that it is critical that they be made properly.

At the hearing on whether the Justice Department's settlement should be approved, Bill Gates came in person to testify. By all accounts he was an impressive witness. After some tightening of the decree the department had negotiated, Judge Colleen Kollar-Kotelly approved the settlement.

At the end of the day, was anything achieved by the prosecution of Microsoft? In fact, quite a lot. Although the remedy negotiated by the Bush administration did not address every violation found by the court of appeals, it forced Microsoft to make important changes in its practices—and went significantly beyond what we had been prepared to settle for in May 1998. The court's judgment also permitted private companies hurt by Microsoft's illegal conduct to sue for damages and additional injunctive relief without having to reestablish liability.

The court's rulings also established important antitrust principles—including that there were limits on a monopolist's right to manipulate product design to disadvantage competitors, that the use of power derived from copyrighted intellectual property was subject to the antitrust laws, and that the antitrust laws, with their protection of competition and consumer choice, apply to the New Economy as well as the Old. And, not insignificantly for the cause of antitrust enforcement, the case demonstrated that the government could effectively try a monopolization case.

6

Fixing the Price of Health

IN MARCH 1998 BOIES, SCHILLER & FLEXNER FILED A major antitrust action against vitamins manufacturers for price-fixing. The case was the result of a year-long investigation that was more a detective story than a legal research project.

Vitamins are an essential element of human health. Vitamin tablets and capsules are taken daily by millions of Americans. In addition, most foods (and most animal feeds) are vitamin-enriched. Only a small number of international corporations actually manufacture vitamins. The hundreds of other companies that sell vitamin tablets or vitamin-enriched food (or feed) purchase vitamins in bulk from these few manufacturers and then repackage and resell them to consumers.

In late February 1997, when I was still at Cravath, Jonathan Schiller had shared with me evidence he had uncovered that Swiss chemical giant Roche, the world's largest manufacturer of bulk vitamins, appeared to have discussed its prices with competitors. While this by itself is not necessarily illegal, it is often an indication that the competitors have agreed to prices or pricing parameters, which *is* illegal.

This was a case Jonathan and I would have liked to pursue. At the beginning of the last century, Congress provided successful antitrust plaintiffs with treble damages and attorneys' fees. Recognizing that the incentive to fix prices was pervasive, that price-fixing was difficult to detect and prosecute, and that government enforcement resources were limited, legislators sought to encourage customers and competitors (who would often be in the best position to know if the law was being broken) to sue for redress. It was hoped that these "private attorneys general," as Congress referred to them, would supplement the Justice Department's efforts to catch, prosecute, and deter wrongdoers. The prospect of treble damages plus attorneys' fees makes antitrust cases attractive ones to bring, and the congressional intent of encouraging private lawsuits has been successful. Nevertheless, while treble damage awards can be very large, the profitability of price-fixing has meant that companies continue to do it despite the consequences.

The manufacture and sale of bulk vitamins is a multibillion-dollar industry. If there were price-fixing going on, it was likely that U.S. consumers had been overcharged in excess of a billion dollars. The problem is that while price-fixing is highly profitable to the companies engaged in it (at least until they are caught), the amount of overcharge to any single customer may not be large enough to justify bringing a lawsuit. Suing to recover damages requires a client to pay significant attorney's fees and expenses. (Our investment in the *Vitamins* case ultimately exceeded $10 million in lawyers' time and $2 million in out-of-pocket expenses.) While a successful antitrust civil plaintiff will eventually recover "reasonable" attorneys' fees and expenses, there is no reimbursement for the client's own time spent responding to discovery demands. In addition there is a risk that the customer will ultimately lose a case that appears strong at the outset. Moreover it will often be three years or more until fees and expenses are paid. Most people are reluctant to tie up hundreds of thousands (or millions) of dollars for two or three years to recover a relatively small amount. Since attorneys' fees and expenses are not reimbursed with interest, most individual customers would not sue even if ultimate recovery is viewed as certain.

Long ago the law developed a class action procedure to deal with cases like this. An individual plaintiff or several plaintiffs can bring a lawsuit on behalf of themselves and "all others similarly sit-uated," all of whom are collectively called "class members." Any recovery is divided among all class members in proportion to their individual claims. Class members are not liable for any attorney's fees or expenses. If a case is successful and a recovery achieved, the attorney's fees and expenses will be paid by the defendants directly or deducted from the recovery before it is divided among class members. If there is no recovery, the attorneys get nothing and class members are charged nothing. Although class action attor-neys bear all the risks of an unsuccessful action, representing a class is often an attractive assignment because the class action aggregates a large number of claims. The total amount at issue can be very large even if each individual claim is small, and the lawyers for the class ordinarily receive a percentage of the total recovery. Particu-larly where a large recovery is relatively certain, as where a com-pany has admitted price-fixing, selection as class counsel is a much sought-after plum.

Despite the many purposes served by class actions, there are potential problems. Class counsel are ordinarily not subject to effective control by their clients. The clients individually have rel-atively small amounts at stake, and neither the incentive nor the abil-ity to control the class's lawyers. Moreover many in whose names class actions are brought are small companies with whom the lawyer (or a friend of the lawyer) has a long-standing relationship; such a company may serve as "class representative" as a favor to the lawyer or in exchange for an under-the-table reward if the litigation is suc-cessful. While class counsel are subject to court supervision, the court's time is limited, its caseload is large, and it often does not have the knowledge necessary to review lead counsel's judgments effec-tively. This means that class counsel can be free to act in a way that suits their interests, but not necessarily those of the class.

In one sense class counsel's interest is aligned with the inter-est of the class because, in general, the larger the recovery, the larger the fee counsel can expect. This is particularly true in courts that award fees as a fixed percentage of the amount recovered. Some courts, however, award fees based in whole or in part on how much time class counsel has devoted to a case. In such courts class lawyers have an incentive to multiply depositions and other discovery until they have spent enough time to "justify" the fee they want.

Another potential problem is that by aggregating hundreds of thousands and sometimes millions of small claims, class counsel can threaten defendants with exposure so great that they are reluctant to take the risk of going to trial even if they believe they have good defenses; even a small risk of a very large loss may be one the defendant is unwilling to take. For this reason some class action lawyers privately joke about being in the business of selling "insurance." At the same time plaintiffs' lawyers may also be reluctant to risk a trial, since they get nothing if they lose. They often conclude that a settlement that provides them with a good profit is better than investing resources in a trial, even where the fair value of a case is more than defendants are offering. The result is that few class actions go to trial and class action lawyers are often specialists in pretrial procedures, discovery, and settlement but not in trying cases to verdict.

Despite the potential for a class action against vitamins price-fixers, both Jonathan and I recognized that it was likely that his firm (Kaye Scholer) and mine (Cravath) would not agree to such a case. Many corporations resent class actions, viewing them with some justification as often being used to extort large settlements for dubious cases. The big, established law firms whose primary business is representing large corporations tend to shy away from taking the plaintiffs' side in a class action for fear of offending their clients.

I believed that as long as a lawyer took on cases only where the law was clear and the evidence of violations substantial, there was no danger that another client's legitimate interests would be harmed. Moreover, in many cases the plaintiff is right, just as in many lawsuits the defendant is right. If a firm restricts itself solely to defendants (or solely to plaintiffs) it will give up the chance to be on the right side in many cases. I also believe that representing plaintiffs in class actions gives a lawyer experience, relationships, and credibility that can actually make him more effective when representing defendants. However, I know that my view is a minority one.

Since Schiller and I knew neither of our firms would be willing to take the vitamins case, in March 1997, Jonathan and I had dinner with Mary and my oldest son David at Chin Chin on East Forty-ninth Street in Manhattan to see whether their firms would be interested in pursuing the matter. It may have been the always excellent mai-tais, or it may have been the fact that one of Straus & Boies's Alabama clients had already come to them with a related concern. In any event, David and Mary took on the case, and for the next two months they and their firms investigated whether Roche and others were actually engaged in price-fixing.

By May 1997 they had found evidence consistent with collusion (for example, lockstep prices, lockstep price increases, price increases that did not appear to be based on cost increases, and price increases that were made in the face of excess capacity), but not enough to make them feel comfortable in starting a lawsuit. Most private lawsuits for price-fixing damages follow a government investigation that has uncovered evidence of illegal conduct. One like this without the benefit of government involvement, is a long, uncertain venture that can tax the resources of small firms, such as the ten-lawyer Straus & Boies and the six-lawyer Boies & McInnis.

The weekend after I left Cravath, Mary and I had dinner at our home with David and his wife, Robin. After dinner David and Mary asked whether I would now be interested in participating with them in their investigation of possible price-fixing by vitamins manufacturers.

There were reasons to decline Mary and David's proposal. This would be a contingency-fee case, and so would not generate any fees for two or three years, if ever. I was already committing substantial resources to the Habie litigation without any realistic hope of payment in the near future, and I knew I would soon have a payroll to meet. However, I would have enjoyed working with Mary and David even on routine litigation, and would have wanted to work on the *Vitamins* case even had they not been involved. The opportunity to work with them on a major matter was too attractive to pass up.

For me, the fact that there was no pending federal investigation merely increased the case's importance. Most private antitrust class actions follow a government investigation that has already uncovered wrongdoing. They compensate victims and enrich lawyers, but contribute little to stopping illegal activity; the government has already accomplished that. By contrast, if our pursuit of price-fixing were successful, we had an opportunity to stop conduct that was overcharging consumers and farmers for a basic element of human and animal health—and to earn a substantial fee at the same time. The opportunity to do well while doing good is not that frequent and should be seized—particularly when the opportunity is presented to an old lawyer with a young firm.

David and Mary had begun interviews with purchasers of bulk vitamins to try to assess the extent to which manufacturers competed for the purchasers' business, and had hired investigators to locate and interview former employees. They had also accumulated a large volume of publicly available data regarding vitamin prices, output, and capacity, and hired an economics consulting firm, Legal and Scientific Analysis Group (LSAG), to help analyze this data.

Although during late May and early June I was able to look at some of the material, most of my time was spent on the Yankees litigation and other cases. When Mary and I flew to Europe for a ten-day bike trip in Bordeaux and the Dordogne with our friends Jim and Barbara Miller and Don and Lynne Flexner, I took with me a four-inch binder of the data that Jonathan Boies and LSAG had assembled.

My intention had been to study the materials on the plane and while relaxing in the evening. I did begin to read them on the way to Paris, but the next time I opened the binder was on the plane ride home three weeks later. For thirty years I have taken work on vacations, most of which remains unread until I return. Mary calculates that over the last three decades I have in the aggregate carried several tons of unused paper around the world.

One piece of business I did try to do was to convince Don Flexner, the head of Crowell & Moring in Washington, D.C., to join my new firm. Don was the leading antitrust lawyer in Washington. He had started with the Antitrust Division of the Department of Justice right after graduating from NYU Law School in 1967 and had risen to head the division in the early 1980s, before leaving for private practice. Both in government and in private practice he had handled many of the most important antitrust cases of the last two decades. He would be a valuable addition to the new firm. He was also a good friend with whom, I knew, both Jonathan Schiller and I would enjoy practicing law. However, Don was not ready to move right then, and it was to be another two and a half years before he changed his mind.

I also tried to convince Jim Miller to join us, but he, too, was reluctant to leave the firm he had founded. He did agree to become counsel to Boies & Schiller and to work with us on matters in Florida so long as there was no conflict. My conversation with Don and Jim probably should have, but did not, make me think about the uncertainty inherent in the adventure Jonathan and I were beginning. Mary, as she sometimes says, worries enough for both of us.

After we returned to New York in mid-July, I began work on the vitamins investigation in earnest. In its early stages, an investigation is much like assembling a jigsaw puzzle, except that new pieces keep appearing and you never know how many there will be. The data showed that throughout the 1980s the industry had behaved the way a market could be expected to act when suppliers competed with each other. Suppliers reduced prices to gain increased business; prices tended to increase when demand exceeded supply, to decline when supply exceeded demand, and to move generally in some relation to costs. The data also showed that around 1990 pricing behavior changed dramatically. For the next six years the industry was characterized by lockstep price increases—despite excess capacity and independent of changes in costs. All this was suspicious but not conclusive, and we continued to search for direct evidence of the agreement that we were increasingly convinced existed.

Interviews conducted in the spring and summer of 1997 confirmed our suspicion that something had happened around 1990. Before then, customers had the opportunity to purchase vitamins from two or more different suppliers; beginning around 1990, however, they found it difficult to get more than one major vitamin manufacturer to offer quotes on a particular vitamin. Then, that autumn, we found the first of two smoking guns.

In the second week of September 1997, David visited an animal feed supplier who purchased vitamins to mix with the feed it sold to farmers. The supplier, a long-time customer of Roche, began by describing the now familiar frustration at being unable to secure competitive bids from Roche's competitors. This time, however, the story had a twist. In 1994 the feed supplier had been able to convince a salesman for Rhone-Poulenc (a large French manufacturer) to offer vitamins in competition with Roche, and for several months he purchased from both companies. In early 1995, the Roche salesman was visiting the feed manufacturer and saw a number of Rhone-Poulenc drums.

"What's this doing here?" he blurted out. "They're not supposed to be selling to you."

Shortly thereafter the feed company got a call from the Rhone- Poulenc salesman. "I'm afraid you got me in trouble," he began. "I'm not going to be able to continue to sell to you."

This was striking evidence that Roche and Rhone-Poulenc had agreed not to compete for certain customers. By itself such an agreement was unlawful. Moreover, customer allocation agreements are often a means of insuring that parties to a price-fixing agreement do not "cheat" on each other. By assigning particular customers to particular suppliers, the conspirators reduce the incentive suppliers have to depart from the agreed price in search of more sales. We were now virtually certain that a price-fixing agreement must exist.

Before a month passed, we had proof. Our second smoking gun came in the form of a recently terminated employee who furnished us with dates and locations of price-fixing meetings and the names of several participants. In a typical investigation we might interview scores of potential sources, and try unsuccessfully to interview hundreds more, without ever finding a "deep throat" or "insider" able and willing to reveal such details. Whistle-blowers are much honored in the press but rarely escape from their good deed unscathed. In fact, our vitamins source was so concerned about possible reprisals that the person would not talk to us until we promised anonymity and agreed not to act on the information provided until we had obtained independent verification.

In effect, the source would tell us where the bodies were buried, but we had to dig them up ourselves. The source's objective, and ours, was to make sure that we would never be in a position where we might have to identify our informant to prove or justify an allegation made in court.

Having agreed to protect our source, Jonathan Schiller and I joked about colorful code names, but we ultimately settled on the prosaic label of "the Chron." "Chron" is shorthand for "chronology," a list of key facts in chronological order that lawyers typically prepare for a case. If someone were to come across a reference to information from "the Chron," the natural interpretation would be that it was to the chronology we had developed. Although a few others may have suspected, only Mary, Jonathan, David, Bill Isaacson, and I ever knew we had an inside source—and only three of us actually knew the informer's name.

Armed with the revelations supplied by the Chron, we undertook an intensive effort to verify what we were being told. With perhaps one exception, all the key meetings appeared to have taken place abroad. It is illegal under U.S. antitrust laws to meet even outside the United States if the result is to fix prices here. Conducting meetings abroad therefore did not provide any defense to the companies we would soon be suing. However, the fact that the meetings were in Germany, Japan, and elsewhere in the world did make it more difficult to uncover evidence—as the conspirators probably planned. Over the next two months we painstakingly constructed a conventional chronology from information gleaned from interviews, public records, Internet searches, and such company documents as we could legally obtain. By the beginning of December we were able to show that key representatives of Roche, Rhone-Poulenc, and BASF (a large German vitamins manufacturer) had met together in Switzerland, Germany, and Mexico City. We were also able to identify telephone conversations concerning pricing between European managers of the three companies and U.S. employers.

By December 1997 we were prepared to file our first complaint. Before we did so, however, Jonathan Schiller informed lawyers at the Department of Justice about our plans. We had contacted the department several months earlier when we first uncovered evidence of possible illegal conduct. If there was illegal conduct going on, we felt we had an obligation to bring it to the government's attention; five years later we persuaded our clients Tyco and Adelphia to follow the same approach even though the illegal conduct was by the companies' own senior management. Also, the government has powers beyond any private law firm, including the power to require companies to produce documents prior to a lawsuit and to subpoena witnesses to testify before a grand jury. The Department of Justice might be able to discover evidence we could not. And companies are less likely to destroy documents if faced with a government investigation because of the threat of prosecution for obstruction of justice.

In addition, witnesses subpoenaed by the government might decline to testify on Fifth Amendment grounds. In a criminal proceeding such a refusal cannot be used against a witness, indeed cannot even be mentioned; however, such a refusal is admissible as evidence of wrongdoing in a civil case. And if the Justice Department succeeded in getting convictions or guilty pleas, those pleas could be used to establish liability in civil cases; all we would have to do was prove damages.

We hoped that our information would lead the department to begin its own investigation, but for a while we had no way of knowing whether it had. Communications with federal prosecutors tend to be a one-way street; you provide whatever information you are prepared to give and maybe get a "thank you" for your efforts. You rarely get more, and often not even that. Eventually word began to leak out that the government was investigating possible antitrust violations in the supply of bulk vitamins. One way we were able to track what the department was doing was through our field interviews. As time went on, we increasingly found vitamins purchasers who had been interviewed by the FBI and (later) by Justice Department lawyers; such purchasers would often tell us what questions they had been asked, which in turn indicated the direction of the prosecutors' thinking and sometimes led us to evidence we had not previously identified.

We were, of course, under no obligation to give the prosecutors a heads-up about our complaint. However, it cost us nothing to keep them informed, and it is always good to be on better terms with the government.

During the months prior to December our investigation had broadened from vitamins A, C, and E to others such as B3 (niacin) and to a nutritional additive, choline chloride. Our investigation had also broadened from the initial three companies to include other manufacturers. However, the first complaint we filed was limited to Roche, BASF, and Rhone-Poulenc and concentrated on vitamins A, C, and E. Those were the defendants and vitamins we knew most about, and we could file additional suits later if the facts justified it.

David's firm filed our initial complaint in Alabama state court under Alabama's antitrust statute. It is a peculiarity of the federal antitrust laws that only "direct purchasers," people who themselves buy directly from an illegal conspirator, can sue for damages for price-fixing. The "direct purchaser" limitation, often called the *Illinois Brick* rule after the case that first announced it, is nowhere to be found in federal antitrust statutes. Instead it is entirely judge-made, designed to simplify antitrust cases. Unfortunately the judges who made up the rule, and most of those who expanded it, never had any experience in business or in trying antitrust cases. Consequently the rule sometimes causes absurd results, where for example the only people who can sue either were not damaged at all (because they passed the higher prices on to their customers) or are not willing to do so because they fear being cut off.

Price-fixing is illegal under both state and federal law, and many states have adopted the federal "direct purchaser" limitation on suits for damages. However, many others, including Alabama, allow indirect purchasers to sue if they can prove they were damaged. For example, a feed company that bought bulk vitamins directly from a manufacturer would pass on its increased prices to the farmers who purchased the company's enriched feed. Similarly suppliers of vitamin pills that acquired bulk vitamins directly from Roche would pass on their increased costs to their customers. Under the federal antitrust laws the feed company or pill supplier (who may have passed on most or all of their increased costs) can sue for the entire amount of the overcharge, while the farmers and consumers who have actually paid the overcharge are left without recompense. In states with indirect purchaser laws, farmers and consumers can sue, and it was just such an "indirect purchaser" case that we filed in December.

Federal antitrust suits are more attractive to lawyers than indirect purchaser state actions because the recoveries are much larger—for the entire country, not merely for those states that permit indirect purchaser suits, and for the entire amount of the overcharge, not merely the portion passed on. Trying a federal case is also easier; since the entire amount of the increased price can be recovered, there is no need to show how much was "passed on." The reason that we did not bring a federal suit at the same time as the Alabama case was filed was that our clients who dealt directly with vitamins manufacturers were afraid Roche, BASF, and Rhone-Poulenc would cut them off or otherwise retaliate if they sued.

By March 1998, however, we had a direct purchaser who was

prepared to become a plaintiff despite the risks. In part, we had accumulated enough evidence of illegal conduct for our client to believe that we would win and cause the defendants to change their ways. In addition, we had promised the client that if the defendants did retaliate we would seek to enjoin that retaliation as a further violation of the antitrust laws.

A month after our federal suit was filed, I met in New York City with counsel for Roche, BASF, and Rhone-Poulenc. I began by laying out in some detail what we knew about pricing data and trends and described one meeting in Germany that all three competitors had attended. I told them the date and location and identified several participants by name. I told them that we needed additional data to refine our damage analysis but that we were prepared to negotiate a settlement in the range of $300 to $400 million. What was surprising was the reaction of the defendants' lawyers—they rejected the idea of negotiating a class settlement at all and tried to convince me simply to drop our suit.

Many lawyers believe that they should stake out an aggressive position at the outset of a case. Sometimes that works; more often it does not. In my experience, lawyers and their clients should be quick to settle early and slow to settle late. By failing to resolve a case early, litigants often miss an opportunity to settle before they (and their opponents) have run up large costs, and before positions have hardened as a result of the attacks that are inherent in an adversarial legal system. At the same time, it is dangerous to lose your nerve late in the game when the terms available may be at their worst. It is rarely possible to know for sure whether a particular case should be tried or settled, and facts discovered and analysis made along the way can certainly change an initial judgment. However, it is important to make an objective analysis at the outset. If the case should be settled, do so. If you decide it should be tried, be sure you are willing to live with that decision as the trial approaches. Defendants can particularly benefit from settling before the plaintiff understands everything that is in the defendants' files and in the memories of the defendants' employees.

Despite these advantages I often find defendants denying all liability at the beginning of a case. What made these defendants' reaction bizarre was that we knew that the defendants were engaged in illegal conduct—and in our complaint and in this meeting we had laid out enough facts for them to know that we knew. They had to be aware that this was not a case that would be decided by a debate over the inferences to be drawn from ambiguous evidence; we had them cold and they had to know it. The damage demand I had made was quite reasonable given the size of the bulk vitamins market. I could understand trying to convince me that a lower number was appropriate, but to reject serious negotiations altogether made no sense. At the end of the meeting I tried, unsuccessfully, to persuade them to reconsider.

"This case is not going away," I warned them. "There's a reason why I've shown as much of my hand as I have. If your clients are being straight with you, you have to know that you can't afford to try this case. If your clients are telling you that there's nothing going on, ask them to explain the facts I've given you. Ask them about the meeting I described. If you change your mind, please call me anytime."

As we left, David remarked, "Those guys are either great actors or they didn't have a clue coming into this meeting what is going on." I was less sure. While we had laid out our facts in much more detail in our meeting than in our complaint, the complaint itself had enough in it to alert lawyers as good as defendants' counsel that their clients were in trouble.

"If their position today was a result of not knowing what was going on, we'll hear from them soon," I replied. "However, it's possible that they or their clients have made the decision to try to overwhelm us with an aggressive defense, then try to settle on the cheap. If that's their decision this may end up being a hard trip for us, but it'll certainly be an expensive one for them."

"It will be an expensive trip for us too," David observed. "Maybe they're counting on making it so expensive we quit."

Maybe, I thought. If so, it would prove to be a painful miscalculation. While it was true that our firms together had only a fraction of the resources of any one of the defendants' law firms, we had enough resources and resolve to see the case through.

"It's not going to happen," I assured him.

"I know that, and you know that," he agreed. "But how long will it take for them to know that?"

I still do not know what caused the defendants to reject our overture, although various participants have told me they would like to be free someday to tell me. What I do know is that litigation commenced in earnest after that April meeting, and we didn't hear about settlement for eight long months. During that time the defendants threw every motion they could think of at us. They objected to all our discovery. They objected to our service of process, arguing that since many of them were foreign corporations we had to serve them pursuant to a treaty called the Hague Convention— a procedure that was more expensive and time-consuming than normal service procedures. They also continued to assert that there was no merit to our claims.

We invested a lot in the case during those months, but that investment paid off in more and more evidence of illegal conduct. We were able to confirm that the price-fixing extended beyond the three initial defendants and beyond vitamins A, C, and E. We uncovered evidence indicating that the overcharge on those three vitamins was significantly greater than we had initially estimated. And new clients came forward willing to be plaintiffs and to contribute their own evidence.

The weekend of December 14, 1998, all our firm's lawyers flew to Orlando for our annual firm meeting. Although we were still small compared to Cravath with its 350 lawyers, we had grown to 30 lawyers in four offices (Armonk; Washington, DC; Orlando; and Hollywood, Florida), and this was an opportunity to review what everyone was doing. Bob Silver and Bill Isaacson led a discussion of the progress we had made in the vitamins litigation. At the end of the discussion Jonathan Schiller remarked, "We're lucky the defendants didn't take us up on our offer last April."

Just how lucky we were about to find out.

Shortly after our Orlando meeting I received a call from Scott Muller of Davis Polk & Wardwell, representing Roche. Judge Jackson had just recessed the *Microsoft* case, and I was in my office in Armonk dividing my time between glancing at mail and planning my Christmas shopping. Roche wanted to settle, Scott told me, and he thought that a global settlement involving Roche, BASF, and Rhone-Poulenc was possible.

"You understand that the price has gone up," I warned.

Scott said he did. "Just don't get too greedy," he warned. "You have a chance to make a lot of money for your class and your firm if you don't overplay your hand."

He made it clear that if we settled, Roche was prepared to come clean and share with us the full story of the conspiracy, or "Vitamins, Inc." as it came to be called. "There's still a lot you don't know," he assured me.

"Why now?" I asked. "What happened to change your client's mind?"

"We expect there will be indictments in the next six to eight weeks, perhaps sooner," he answered.

"Do you expect to try to negotiate a plea, or do you plan to fight the indictments?"

"We expect to plead guilty. We're attempting to negotiate plea agreements now, and we expect that our pleas will be announced at the same time as the indictments."

Guilty pleas to criminal indictments would change the entire focus of our litigation. We would no longer have to prove that the defendants engaged in price-fixing, only what the resulting overcharges had been. The existence of a government investigation had become widely known, and based on our field interviews we were convinced that the government was making progress. Nonetheless, we had no idea that indictments were imminent, let alone that the defendants were prepared to admit that price-fixing had taken place. We ultimately learned that Rhone-Poulenc had broken ranks with its co-conspirators and agreed to provide evidence against them in exchange for immunity from prosecution. However, Rhone-Poulenc did not receive, and the government did not have the power to grant, immunity from civil suits. And while we would not have a guilty plea to use against Rhone-Poulenc, the very evidence and admissions the company had provided the prosecutors to obtain immunity sealed its fate in the civil litigation, at least as far as liability was concerned.

Rhone-Poulenc could, of course, have tried to negotiate a settlement with us in advance of its deal with the government. At any time after the previous April we would have been delighted to settle for limited cash payments in exchange for the evidence of conspiratorial conduct Rhone-Poulenc possessed.* One of the mysteries of the vitamins saga is why Rhone-Poulenc did not come to us at the same time it approached the Department of Justice. It turned out to be an expensive decision because the company ended up paying more than $300 million in damages, about as much as it would have taken to settle the liability of all three companies back in April.

After I hung up with Scott, I immediately called Jonathan, Mary, and David to tell them the good news. I asked Mary to call Steve Fischer of LSAG to accelerate his damage calculation, which we would need for our settlement negotiations. I also asked David to set up a system to monitor the avalanche of lawsuits against vitamins manufacturers that I knew would follow the news that government indictments were in the works.

Just as it would now be easy for us to prosecute our claims, so too would it be easy for other lawyers to follow suit.

There are a number of law firms that specialize in class actions,

---

*Antitrust defendants are "jointly and severally liable." This means that a plaintiff is entitled to collect from any one defendant the total damages caused by all defendants without any contribution from the others. This in turn meant that we could be happy collecting little or nothing from Rhone-Poulenc so long as we received evidence sufficient to prove our case against Roche and/or BASF. Sometimes no single company has the resources to pay the total damages caused by an antitrust violation and it is necessary to pursue multiple defendants in order to get paid. That was not the case with Roche or BASF; either one had the resources to pay the entire damages.

and when a company admits price-fixing these firms race to file lawsuits and to be considered for class counsel. When more than one lawsuit is filed seeking to represent the same class of plaintiffs, a judge must select who will be the "lead counsel" with the power to control the litigation and the right (and responsibility) to represent the entire class in court.

In a large case—and the *Vitamins* case was certainly that—the judge will normally appoint two or more firms to work together as co-lead counsel, plus an "executive committee" of other key firms. Since lead counsel, with some participation by the executive committee, ordinarily controls the distribution of fees, the position is highly prized.

Firms seeking to represent a particular class often agree among themselves on what role each will play. The court must approve such an arrangement, but if all firms are in agreement, most courts will rubber stamp it. Where there is no agreement, competing motions will be filed by different lawyers asking the court to select them as lead counsel based on such factors as their experience, the date their case was filed, and the amount of their clients' damages.

During February, March, and April we negotiated with Roche, BASF, and Rhone-Poulenc about a possible settlement, and with six lawyers (each of whom asserted that they spoke for many or all of the firms that had recently filed cases) about agreeing on the role various firms would play. The first negotiation reminded me of a high-stakes poker game; the second of *Lord of the Flies*.

Eventually an agreement was reached with lawyers who had recently filed complaints that preserved the lead roles that Jonathan, Mary, David, and I played while at the same time integrating key representatives of the new firms into the prosecution of the case. Everyone, we assured them, would have a reasonable opportunity to contribute—and to earn a fee. Based on this agreement, all the firms that had brought cases around the country supported consolidation of their cases before Chief Judge Thomas Hogan, of the United States Court for the District of Columbia. Hogan was intelligent, careful, and fair—good qualities to have in a judge when you have, as we did here, a strong case. I knew, however, that he would be tough on us when our focus turned to defendants against whom the evidence was not as strong as it was against Roche, BASF, and Rhone-Poulenc.

Able now to speak formally for all counsel representing the class of vitamins purchasers, we continued our talks with the three defendants. The negotiations took several months. Before we could agree on a firm amount, we needed to analyze data concerning the defendants' sales to U.S. customers together with information about related prices and costs. We had accumulated a substantial dossier on vitamins A, C, E, and B3 (niacin), and on choline chloride, but there was some information we were missing and other information that needed to be checked. We also learned from Roche that the price-fixing extended to vitamins B9 and H.

Roche and BASF had also admitted that companies other than themselves and Rhone-Poulenc had participated in the price-fixing. If we settled with the original three defendants, our ability to take discovery of them would be limited. Consequently we insisted that a condition of settlement be that all three in effect turn "states' evidence" against their former co-conspirators. However, each was reluctant to agree to extensive post-settlement discovery obligations; part of what they wanted to buy was peace, including freedom from having plaintiffs' lawyers crawling through their files. The compromise we agreed to was to have the companies provide us with the information before the settlement was signed. It was a sensible solution, but it significantly lengthened the process.

Another reason for the long drawn-out negotiations was that, given what we now knew, I believed the settlement should be at least twice my March 1998 offer. We had to convince the defendants' lawyers, and they in turn their clients, that the amount needed to settle had increased dramatically.

In the middle of May 1999 we called a meeting of plaintiffs' counsel in all the cases that had been filed. Because of the numbers involved, we rented the ballroom at the Mayflower Hotel in Washington and invited everyone who had filed a case to attend. More than one hundred lawyers, representing forty-six separate firms, showed up. Bill Isaacson, Bob Silver, Mary, and David had prepared a fifty-five-page binder for each firm summarizing the information and evidence we had accumulated. It was a detailed presentation that set forth prices, costs, and potential damages for each of a dozen vitamins, together with the time, place, and participants of illegal meetings.

"It doesn't surprise me that Roche wants to settle," Laddie Montague of Berger & Montague told me afterward, "but what I can't understand is why everyone isn't rushing to do the same."

I also summarized the progress of settlement discussions, including my March 1998 meeting, Scott Muller's December telephone call, and the negotiations that had ensued. Before the meeting Jonathan Schiller and I had explained to our new co-lead counsel, Steve Susman and Michael Hausfeld, that we believed that a realistic industry-wide settlement would be in the range of $500 million to $750 million. After some discussion, Susman proposed to the group that I be authorized to accept any industry-wide settlement I thought was appropriate at $550 million or above. The proposal was unanimously and enthusiastically adopted.

Now the poker game began in earnest. A settlement of $550 million would have represented a very good recovery, one of the largest antitrust settlements in history both in absolute dollars and in terms of the percentage of the overcharge recovered. If we believed that this amount was the most the defendants would pay, there would have been a great incentive to accept it to avoid the delay and uncertainty that taking the case to trial would involve. However, I was convinced that the defendants would agree to a settlement in excess of $550 million—assuming, of course, that they believed more was necessary to settle. But how much above $550 million? Defendants guarded their card of how much they would pay if necessary as jealously as we guarded our card of how low we were prepared to go if we had to.

By the end of May we were close to an agreement with Roche and BASF in which they would pay their share of a settlement of approximately $750 million. Rhone-Poulenc, however, was balking at the prospect of paying its share. The company argued that since it had turned the others in, it deserved a break. It also argued that since it had received amnesty from the Justice Department and had not had to plead guilty, we did not have the benefit of introducing a guilty plea against them in our civil case, as we would have against Roche and BASF.

Mostly out of courtesy to the company's lawyers, and in part because Roche and BASF had not reached the point where they were prepared to make a settlement without Rhone-Poulenc, I had debated this issue with Rhone-Poulenc's lawyers as if it were a serious one since before our conference at the Mayflower Hotel. In fact none of the debate or arguments mattered. Given Rhone-Poulenc's admissions and the evidence we had already accumulated, they were going to lose if they went to trial. The only issue was how much the damages were, and the offer I was making was reasonable. Once Roche and BASF were prepared to go forward, Rhone-Poulenc had either to get on board or risk exposure not only for its sales but for the sales of its co-conspirators.

Three days before the *Microsoft* rebuttal case began, I spoke by phone with lawyers for Roche and BASF. My message to them was simple: if they wanted to settle, it was time to reach closure. We had each analyzed, debated, re-analyzed, and debated again our respective positions. It was time for Roche and BASF to tell their former co-conspirator that they were prepared to settle with or without Rhone-Poulenc. If they were not prepared to do that, we should end discussions and begin discovery and preparation for trial. Scott Muller told me they would get back to me.

Three weeks later Roche and BASF called together to say that if Rhone-Poulenc did not agree to pay its share of the proposed settlement, they were prepared to make a separate settlement, leaving Rhone-Poulenc out in the cold. Muller and Tyrone Fahner, who represented BASF, wanted to be the ones to tell their Rhone-Poulenc colleagues, which was fine with me. Rhone-Poulenc was represented by Jones, Day, Reavis & Pogue and, after hearing from

Scott and Ty, Joe Sims of Jones Day made one more effort to convince me to give his client some kind of break. He gave it his best shot, but both he and I knew a deal was about to be done and his client could not afford to be left out.

After the *Microsoft* case finished in June, I flew to Los Angeles for the *Shandling* case, then to Las Vegas to meet Mary for the Fourth of July weekend. The first morning I was there, we had what was intended to be a final settlement conference call with lawyers from Roche, BASF, and Rhone-Poulenc. The call was scheduled for nine a.m. New York time (six a.m. Las Vegas time). Before it began I was confident that we would come out of it with a settlement. I believed we had reached agreement on what the Roche and BASF payments would be and that Rhone-Poulenc was prepared to accept the inevitable. Moreover the risk of not settling for these defendants, who together accounted for approximately 75 to 80 percent of the U.S. sales of the price-fixed vitamins, seemed too great.

However, some forty minutes into the call it did not look good. We were rearguing issues that I thought had already been resolved. The defendants wanted the settlement amount to include attorneys' fees; I thought we had previously agreed that such fees would be in addition. The defendants wanted a release of all claims for sales to class members outside the United States; I thought we had agreed that the settlement covered only claims for U.S. sales. BASF wanted a release for any claims concerning choline chloride, which had not been included in our previous discussions. When Rhone-Poulenc began to reargue its entitlement to a discount, I cut the conversation off.

"We're obviously not as close to a settlement as I thought," I told them. "Your clients need to decide whether they want to take what's on the table. We've been at this six months; I've never had a settlement drag out this long. Even if it weren't this early in the morning, I wouldn't be prepared to renegotiate. As it is, I'm going back to sleep. Let us know what your clients decide."

Three days later I returned to my room at the Bellagio to find a message from Ty Fahner. When I called him back, he told me that he was confident that there was now agreement subject only to BASF's getting a release for choline chloride sales.

"We can't pay you $200 million to settle vitamins price-fixing claims, then have you sue us tomorrow for fixing the price of choline chloride," he said. "If we pay this much money—and we're prepared to—we have to at least buy peace."

He was also concerned with the affect of any choline exposure on "opt-outs." Everyone knew that once an industry-wide settlement was announced, many class members would opt out of the settlement and settle their claims separately. Most of our class members were small companies; however, a number were large corporations with substantial damages, there were many reasons for them to opt out, including that they might believe they could get a better deal on their own.*

Both plaintiffs' and defendants' counsel expected that most large vitamins class members would opt out; and although they would comprise only about 10 percent of class members, because of their size they would represent much more than half the class's purchases. We had agreed early that the settlement would be reduced by the proportion of class purchases accounted for by the opt-outs (for example, if purchasers representing 30 percent of purchases opted out, the amount paid would be reduced by 30 percent). However, because our settlement would set the floor for opt-out settlements, Fahner was concerned not only with what he paid us but what he would have to pay opt-outs based on what he agreed to pay the class.

I understood his position, but there were two problems. First, we had from the beginning distinguished between choline chloride

---

*Even for a company that opts out and immediately settles based on what it would have gotten by staying in the class, there are advantages. The money is paid immediately, while class members do not get paid until final court approval and the resolution of any appeals, which can take two years or more. An opt-out following a class settlement also gives a class member the chance to save on attorneys' fees (because the work has already been done), or to give an easy contingency fee to a lawyer or law firm with whom the class member or one of its executives has a relationship.

and all other vitamins. The choline chloride conspiracy appeared to have a different beginning and a different end and for the most part to involve different companies. (Neither Roche nor Rhone-Poulenc made choline, and the five choline manufacturers other than BASF did not make any other vitamin.)

Second, in arriving at our settlement demands we had taken each defendant's U.S. sales of all vitamins other than choline, estimated the overcharge that resulted from the price-fixing conspiracy, then increased the amount to account for the fact that at trial we would be entitled to treble damages. The amount that BASF was being asked to pay was what we believed was justified on the basis of products other than choline chloride.

Ty's reply, which on the surface was a strong one, was that while BASF made choline chloride it did not sell it in the United States. My response was that we believed that BASF had agreed to stay out of the country as part of an illegal worldwide market division agreement, so BASF was responsible for the extent to which its agreed absence had increased U.S. prices. Ty in turn responded that we could and should collect our damages from the companies who sold choline in the United States and hence profited from the illegally high prices. I answered that we could not be sure that other choline suppliers (which, unlike BASF, were relatively smaller companies) would be able to pay. And so it went.

I appreciated the position BASF was in; I would have not wanted my client to settle one claim for a lot of money and still face related claims from the same parties. I also appreciated the cooperation BASF had provided. Ty and his colleagues had been reasonable in dealing with me, and I wanted to be so with them. In addition the amount of choline chloride sales and overcharges (and hence potential damages) was a small fraction of the agreed amount; I did not want to risk a very good vitamins settlement over a small choline chloride dispute. On the other hand, I had an obligation to prosecute the class's claims, and I believed BASF should pay something for its choline release.

Our estimate of the choline overcharge at that time was approximately $25 million. We finally agreed that BASF would pay $5 million immediately, and if we did not get at least another $20 million from other choline suppliers, we could come back to them. It was a good deal for the class, and it turned out to be a good deal for BASF as well; choline suppliers who settled later paid much more, and we never had to come back to BASF.

Including the $5 million paid by BASF for choline chloride, the industry-wide settlement total from Roche, BASF, and Rhone-Poulenc was $880 million. Before we could celebrate, however, we had to complete the preparation of a definitive settlement agreement.

The work on preparing that agreement had already been under way for a number of weeks. At the same time that some of us were negotiating the settlement amount, other lawyers were working to prepare a detailed draft into which (we hoped) a final number would ultimately be inserted. The resulting agreement ended up more than one hundred pages long.

During the months of our negotiations we had discussed with other vitamins manufacturers the possibility of their participating in an early settlement. They were not interested, which was fine with me since I was already ambivalent about settling with additional companies early. Doing so would increase the money available soon to class members, but we had already recovered about as much as the class's actual damages, and it would be attractive to take the case to trial against the remaining defendants.

We were entitled to recover against any participant in the conspiracy, large or small, the class's total triple damages. Prior settlements would be offset against any judgment, but because those settlements would be less than three times the settling companies' allocable share, those defendants who were left were exposed to both their own share of triple damages and the unpaid share of prior settling defendants. (Assume a market with an overcharge of $100 million—thus damages of $300 million—and four suppliers. If three defendants, each with 30 percent of the market, settle for $40 million each, the remaining defendant, with 10 percent of the market, is liable for $180 million—$300 million in triple damages less the $120 million already received.) This puts a substantial premium on settling early.

In August 1999 I was getting ready to leave on a three-week family vacation in Greece, joined by Jonathan Schiller and his three sons, when counsel for each of three Japanese companies (Eisai, Daiichi, and Takeda) all called to say that they had heard we were settling with the three largest defendants and they wanted to discuss a possible settlement for their clients. I told them that Jonathan and I would call them from Athens.

Eisai, which was the only one of these companies that sold either vitamin A or E (where the greatest exposure existed), was represented by Stuart Meikeljohn of Sullivan & Cromwell. Stuart was persistent in pursuing a settlement and in explaining all the reasons why it made sense to include his company in the first round of settlements. First in Athens, then continuing from phones on Delos, Paros, Ios, and Santorini, Jonathan and I began serious negotiations with Stuart and with counsel for Daiichi and Takeda.

In our initial conversations we made clear that any agreement would have to be at a higher amount per dollar of U.S. sales than what Roche, BASF, and Rhone-Poulenc were paying. Although counsel for the Japanese companies groused about the asserted "unfairness" of our position, they and we knew (and they knew that we knew that they knew) that this was still a good deal. Before the holiday had ended, we had struck a deal with Meikeljohn that, if accepted by his clients would result in it paying approximately 15 percent more than Roche, BASF, and Rhone-Poulenc on a market share–adjusted basis.

My family and I flew to Paris for a few days before returning to New York. Three days later I returned to my hotel to find a fax from Jonathan (who had returned directly to the United States from Athens) informing me that a second of the three companies had signed up for the same deal and that he was working on the third. I had little doubt that he would be successful, and he was.

We signed a definitive agreement with Roche, BASF, Rhone-

Poulenc, Daiichi, Eisai, and Takeda in October. The industry-wide settlement amount from all six defendants was $1.28 billion, including $123 million in attorneys' fees. The resolution, which became public the first week in November, was front-page news as the largest antitrust class action settlement in history.

The settlement was noteworthy both for its size and for the amount of the class's recovery compared to the actual overcharges. In the usual antitrust case (particularly a class action), even though the antitrust laws provide for damages three times the amount of the illegal overcharge, the settlement amount is a fraction of the estimated actual overcharge.*

Our settlement of more than the estimated overcharge broke the mold for conventional antitrust class action settlements. We were proud of what we had accomplished, but the case was not over by any means. We had settled with about 90 percent of the market, but we had about 10 percent to go, and we knew that the last 10 percent could take years. Nevertheless, an interim celebration seemed called for, and on November 3, Jonathan, Mary, David, and I met at Chin Chin, the restaurant where the four of us had first discussed the case in March 1997. Over mai-tais and salt-and-pepper shrimp

---

*There are many reasons why this is the case. Whether there was an overcharge, and if so how much is always hotly disputed by defendants; the extent to which a jury will accept the figures claimed by plaintiffs is uncertain. A settlement in the hand may well be worth two (or even three) in the bush. Also a settlement accelerates by several years when payment is made—a cost to defendants and a major benefit to the plaintiffs. In addition, where (as in a class action) the plaintiffs' lawyers are on a contingency fee, there can be a tendency for counsel to seek a quick settlement without the risks or costs of a trial.

Rewarding counsel with a percentage of any recovery is supposed to align their interest with the class, and to a large extent this works. But the alignment can break down where counsel has an opportunity to earn a quick, large fee, then move on to another class action in the firm's inventory. This is particularly true where the recovery to any single class member from a settlement is small, but the contingency fee to counsel will be large because of the size of the class. Finally, many plaintiffs' class action lawyers are simply not in the business of trying cases; they are bringing cases to settle. Since defendants' lawyers know that such counsel lack the ability or willingness actually to take a case to trial, such counsel's leverage is reduced. It is the realistic threat of a trial against well-prepared, effective counsel that drives a high settlement.

we reflected on the risks and rewards of the *Vitamins* case. Since March 1997 each of our three firms had devoted more time to it than any other; in fact Boies & McInnis and Straus & Boies had devoted more time to it than to the rest of their cases combined. We had made a major investment, and it had paid off.

At our annual firm meeting in Orlando in December 1999, and again at our family vacation in the Turks and Caicos Islands at the end of the month, I had an opportunity to reflect with my partners and my family on where we had been and where we might be going. Boies & Schiller had grown to more than fifty lawyers and with the addition of Don Flexner had become Boies, Schiller & Flexner. Since leaving Cravath, I had had four jury trials in addition to *Microsoft*, and had successfully resolved several matters prior to trial (including an interesting case by the Czech National Savings Bank against my client Unisys and an ill-advised defamation claim against my client Don Imus). I looked forward to a more relaxing 2000 both in connection with the *Vitamins* litigation and otherwise.

If the first two phases of the *Vitamins* case were detective work and high-stakes poker, the next phase was a game of Go. From a case where almost nothing seemed linear, we moved to one where almost everything was. The placement of the stones was, of course, important and occasionally critically so; but each side proceeded one stone at a time, trying both to contain and outflank the other. We and the lawyers representing the remaining defendants settled into our respective stereotypes: we trying to get as much discovery as possible and an early trial date, they trying to avoid discovery and delay any trial. Judge Hogan listened patiently to each of the defendants' attempts to avoid discovery, denying most of them.

He also for the most part denied their motions to dismiss. One important exception was the defendants' motion to dismiss claims for overcharges on sales outside the United States. Our primary claim was, of course, based on overcharges on sales in the United States. However, there was also a claim that since the conspiracy was worldwide and since the same conspiracy resulted both in overcharges on U.S. sales and overcharges on foreign sales, non-U.S. customers of non-U.S. suppliers could sue under the U.S. antitrust laws for overcharges on foreign sales.

There was support for such a theory in both policy and the text of the antitrust laws, but limited precedent on our side. Judge Hogan decided against us. Later, the U.S. Court of Appeals for the District of Columbia reversed his decision and reinstated our claims, but if I had been a judge and not an advocate, I think based on the precedent that existed at that time I would have decided as Judge Hogan did.

As we had predicted, about 10 percent of the class members, more than 300 in total, opted out; the opt-outs included most of the largest purchasers and represented about 75 percent of all U.S. vitamins purchases from the six settling defendants. This meant, among other things, that going forward we would represent (and negotiate for) only those purchasers who had not opted out and who were allocated $370,763,368 out of the initial $1,173,325,159 settlement, including attorneys' fees. Most of the opt-outs promptly settled on the terms that we had negotiated, but over a hundred continued the litigation. The resulting case could have been an administrative nightmare, with both the class and the opt-outs suing some or all of twenty different defendants. Judge Hogan had to commandeer a special clerk and storage space to file the mountains of paper we turned out. At one point or another more than five hundred lawyers worked on the cases, and it sometimes seemed that everyone was writing or filing something.

Fortunately Hogan kept things moving. If he hadn't, the case would have taken ten years or more. He listened patiently and with apparent interest to arguments good and bad so long as the lawyer got to the point, did not repeat, and followed the rules. Even more than his colleague Judge Jackson, Hogan generally kept a poker face.

As discovery and our interviews of industry participants continued, we accumulated additional evidence against the remaining defendants. However, our task was complicated by the fact that most of them were outside the United States. Judge Hogan could order the companies to produce whatever documents they had kept (or would admit to having kept), but when the companies produced little of use in response, there was not much he or we could do. Moreover, many key participants were no longer employed by the defendants and as citizens of Switzerland or Japan could not be compelled even to give a deposition.

We had originally sued eighteen defendants. Following our initial settlement we had twelve remaining, and the two groups quickly became known as the "Big Six" and the "Little Twelve".* Class members had received in settlement an average of 23 percent of what they had paid to the Big Six for vitamins during the conspiracy period. Our goal was to collect a higher percentage from the remaining twelve. That effort would be complicated by a variety of factors. First, several of the companies had limited assets. Second, some of the companies had not been indicted by the government and denied any participation in the conspiracy—and at that stage we had no direct evidence of their participation. Third, none of the companies manufactured either vitamin A or E, the vitamins with the largest overcharges. One company, E. Merck, manufactured vitamin C, an important vitamin but one where the alleged conspiracy lasted only from 1991 to 1995 because prices were driven down by Chinese suppliers (and where damages were limited for the same reason). All remaining defendants made products with a limited market—and limited overcharges.

---

*The Little Twelve consisted of five companies that manufactured only choline chloride and that were defendants in our choline chloride price-fixing case (Akzo Nobel, Chinook, Du Coa, Bioproducts and its parent Mitsui, and UCB Chemicals), and seven companies that, along with the big six, were defendants in our "all vitamins" case. These seven vitamins defendants were E. Merck (a German company that manufactured vitamins C and H), Sumitomo Chemicals (a Japanese company that manufactured vitamins B9 and H), Tanabe (a Japanese company that manufactured vitamin H), Reilly (a United States company that manufactured vitamin B3), Lonza AG (a German company that manufactured vitamins B3 and H), Degussa AG (a German company that manufactured vitamin B3), and Nepera (a United States company that manufactured vitamin B3).

With respect to the four B3 suppliers (Degussa, Lonza, Nepera, and Reilly), all of whom had pled guilty, and the three choline chloride suppliers who had admitted guilt to the government (Bioproducts, Chinook, and Du Coa), the issues were primarily how much the damages were and the companies' ability to pay. The issues against the remaining companies (all of whom had substantial resources) were both guilt and damages.

Gradually, we accumulated a document here and a deposition admission there that provided the evidence by which we could prove in court what we knew to be true. A trial is intended to be a search for truth. Knowing what is true is a necessary first step, but it is not enough. A lawyer must prove those truths, and prove them with admissible evidence. Often when you know the facts, and the other side knows you do, a case can be settled without having to prove your case in court. That is what happened in our Big Six settlement. But the remaining defendants, as they had a right to do, were making us prove our claims. In part, they may have believed that, with a large settlement against 90 percent of the market in our pocket, it would not be worthwhile for us to devote the time and expense required to pursue the companies that were left. If so, it turned out to be an expensive miscalculation.

As our resolve became apparent and our evidence grew, additional companies began to give up. Akzo Nobel and UCB Chemicals (both foreign choline chloride manufacturers who had not sold in the United States but who were sued based on their alleged agreement to stay out of the U.S.) settled for $7.5 million and $9 million respectively—amounts considerably above the $5 million paid by BASF for choline. Niacin suppliers Degussa, Lonza, Nepera, and Reilly settled for a total of $43,430,000, representing more than 63 percent of their total sales in the U.S. to class members during the conspiracy and many times their total profits on those sales—an unprecedented level of recovery.

I was in Botswana on safari with my brothers and sisters in August 2002 when Sumitomo decided it was time to settle. There are no phone lines or cell phones within 200 miles of Kwando Concession, where we were staying. While I take a satellite phone with me for emergencies, Jonathan rightly concluded that Sumitomo's renewed interest in settlement did not constitute one. He also rightly decided not to call me even when we moved to Singita in South Africa, which does have phone lines. As a result, when I returned to the office after three weeks in Africa, I found that Sumitomo had called several times. If anything, my delay in getting back to them had fueled their interest.

They had heard that we were negotiating with E. Merck, and while E. Merck did not have much of use to give us with respect to Sumitomo, it could not be sure of that. We ultimately agreed to settle with Sumitomo for $17.5 million, which represented 82 percent of the company's total revenue from the sale of vitamins to class members during the entire period of the conspiracy, and many times its total profits on those sales. The cost of settling late is illustrated by the fact that Sumitomo, with one-third of the sales of Eisai, paid twice the amount Eisai did.

The toughest nuts to crack were E. Merck, Tanabe, and Mitsui, none of whom had pled guilty, all of whom indignantly protested their innocence, and none of whom had produced useful evidence during discovery. The defendant against whom we had the least evidence was Tanabe. If we were going to win at trial, we needed the testimony of a co-conspirator. Despite their cooperation, the Big Six had not produced a witness who could implicate Tanabe. Consequently, when E. Merck, confronted with the growing evidence against it, finally indicated that it wanted to settle, we asked their counsel: Would the company give us a witness that could tie Tanabe into the conspiracy?

Their counsel indicated that his client could help us. However, as so often is the case, there was a problem. He did not want to identify a witness and tell us what he knew until we had a deal. We did not want to do a deal until we knew what we were getting. After some discussion it was agreed that we would settle for $50 million (89 percent of the company's total U.S. revenues from class members during the conspiracy period, and many times the company's total profits from those sales). E. Merck would also agree to provide us witnesses who would testify truthfully concerning the conspiracy. We agreed that the settlement would not be submitted to Judge Hogan for approval until after the witnesses had testified. (All class action settlements must by approved by the court before they become effective; if they are not approved, they are void.) If we were not satisfied with the testimony we reserved the right to object to the court's approval. We entered into the settlement, and E.Merck provided the testimony we needed.

Armed with this new evidence, we now turned our sights on Tanabe. Too late the company recognized that its strategy of deny, deny, deny was not viable, and it sued for peace. By then, of course, the price had gone up. Tanabe eventually settled for $45 million, which represented more than forty times the company's profits on vitamins sales to class members during the conspiracy. Had it settled when Eisai, Daiichi, and Takeda did and on their terms it would have paid less than $2 million. But Tanabe had gambled that we would not be able to prove our case, and lost.

The only other defendants were Bioproducts, Chinook, and Du Coa (all of whom had admitted fixing the price of choline chloride), and Mitsui, the Japanese parent of Bioproducts. With respect to the first three, the only question was the companies' ability to pay. Mitsui took the position that it was innocent of any wrongdoing, that it never sold anything in the United States, and that it could not be held responsible for the actions of its U.S. subsidiary. In general, it is true that a parent corporation cannot be held liable for the actions of a subsidiary, even if the parent owns 100 percent of the subsidiary and appoints its officers and directors. However, if the parent can be proven to have itself known about and participated in the illegal conduct it becomes liable as a co-conspirator.

Mitsui had not produced incriminating evidence during discovery: its document production was suspiciously sparse, but we could not prove that it was hiding or destroying evidence; its executives also uniformly denied any participation in any price-fixing activity. The proof that we had against the company was of two types. First, we had circumstantial evidence. Mitsui appointed Bioproducts officers and directors, provided Bioproducts's financial targets, and (we believed the evidence showed) knew that those targets could not be met in a competitive market. Mitsui also approved Bioproducts' withdrawal from its previously profitable sales in Europe, which withdrawal had no explanation except as the quid pro quo for European competitors not selling in the U.S.

The second type of evidence was references in papers produced by other defendants that mentioned Mitsui. There were only a few, the documents were not generally clear as to Mitsui's role, and there were questions as to whether they were admissible evidence. However, they both suggested that Mitsui was more involved than it contended and raised the question as to why it had not produced any similar documents.

We had several settlement discussions with Mitsui, but the company refused to make more than a token $1 million offer. We had demanded $25 million. This could have seemed high in view of our initial estimate that the total overcharge was $25 million and the fact that we had already received $21.5 million from BASF, Akzo Nobel, and UCB. It was also true that, in denying Mitsui's motion for summary judgment, Judge Hogan had commented that our evidence against Mitsui was "thin" and that he would revisit the company's motion after our case was presented. However, we now had a revised damage estimate of $45 million, which trebled would be $135 million. This meant that if we prevailed at trial and got everything we asked for, we could collect $113.5 million ($135 minus $21.5) from Mitsui and the other remaining choline chloride defendants. There were many hurdles to overcome, but if $25 million was a little high, $1 million was absurdly low. Mitsui never made an offer above $2 million, so we went to trial.

In my opening statement to the jury I discussed the evidence we had against Mitsui in detail. When it was the defendant's counsel's turn I expected a similarly detailed explanation of all the gaps in our supposed proof. Instead he dealt entirely with generalities about how good and honest the Mitsui people were; in his entire statement he never showed the jury any evidence nor dealt with a single piece of the evidence on which I had relied.

Our first witness was the head of Mitsui USA, whom I called as an adverse witness. He seemed as unprepared for my examination as Mitsui's counsel had seemed unprepared for my opening. As I left court at the end of the first week of trial I told our team: "Enjoy this while you can; it's not going to last." But I was wrong. It did.

Our trial team (which included Bill Isaacson, Tanya Chutkan— a talented trial lawyer who works with Bill in Washington, Michael Hausfeld, and Jim Southwick) was experienced and well prepared. However, those qualities alone could not account for what happened. The defendant's cross-examination of our witnesses was ineffectual. Its own witnesses contradicted each other as well as Mitsui's internal documents. At the end, the jury returned a verdict in the full amount of our claim. Mitsui then did what it should have done much earlier; it settled. The company agreed to forego any appeal and pay $53 million.

After collecting more than $370 million from the Big Six defendants for class members who did not opt out, we obtained an additional $225 million from the remaining defendants. Since the Big Six defendants represented more than 90 percent of the market, the recovery of $225 million from the remaining defendants was an exceptional result. It was also one for which the firm earned a substantial additional fee. The defendants together had ended up paying approximately $600 million to resolve the claims of our class members, and hundreds of millions more to opt-outs.

In the beginning this had been a hard case, with much risk. We had taken it on to try to stop illegal conduct that was harming consumers, to make a lot of money, and to have fun. We succeeded in doing all three.

7

Shades of Grey

GARRY SHANDLING IS A VERY FUNNY MAN. UNLIKE some of his fellow famous comedians, he has a great sense of humor off stage as well as on. But he was not laughing when I met him in Los Angeles in late June 1999 to prepare for the trial of his case against his long-time personal manager, Brad Grey.

Originally a successful comedy writer for shows such as *Sanford & Son*, Shandling had gone on to become a star in his own right and a frequent guest host on *The Tonight Show*. Two hit comedy series on HBO (*It's Garry Shandling's Show* from 1986 through 1990 and *The Larry Sanders Show* from 1992 through 1998) had made him both a critical and financial success. He also had a well-deserved reputation as being unstinting in the help he gave other comedians, both stars and newcomers. Critics praised *The Larry Sanders Show*, in which Shandling played a talk show host, as "the best written, most daring comedy series on television," and it won the prestigious Peabody Award as well as numerous Golden Globe and Writers Guild of America honors. Chosen as Best Comedy by the Television Critics Association, it received a record seventy-eight Emmy Awards and nominations. In its final season Garry himself won the Emmy for Best Writer on a Comedy Show.

Garry's personal manager for almost twenty years had been

Brad Grey, during which time Grey received 10 percent or more of Shandling's earnings. When he started working for Shandling, Grey was twenty-one years old with no other significant clients. By 1997 Grey's drive and ability had helped propel him to the top of his profession. He was the head and principal owner of the major Hollywood firm of Brillstein-Grey and managed such stars as Adam Sandler, Nicolas Cage, and Brad Pitt as well as such other major celebrities as Rudy Giuliani and former FBI Director Louis Freeh. He was also the producer or co-producer of numerous successful shows and series, including *The Sopranos*.

Garry was a major television star; Grey was an important Hollywood manager. Grey readily acknowledged what Shandling had done for him in Grey's early days in Hollywood. Shandling for his part had genuine affection for Grey and appreciation for his ability and long service; he also took pride in what he had helped Grey accomplish. However, Shandling had a problem, and in late 1997 he approached Jonathan Schiller and Bill Isaacson for help.

A dispute with Grey had caused Shandling to seek an independent review of his affairs. That review, conducted by Los Angeles lawyer Barry Hirsch, had concluded that Grey had improperly taken advantage of his client. While there were several asserted broken promises and financial errors at issue, the most important matter for Shandling was that his manager owned a 25 percent interest in the profits of *The Larry Sanders Show*. (Grey had originally owned 50 percent but had sold the right to half his interest some time before.)

According to Shandling, Grey had received his interest without any payment or contribution other than Grey's efforts toward the show's success, which Shandling believed his manager was obligated to provide in any event because of the 10 percent management fee Shandling paid him and the additional $45,000 per episode Grey's company received as executive producer. At a minimum, Hirsch concluded, Grey should not have taken his interest in Shandling's show for himself without recommending that his client get independent advice about the terms and desirability of the deal. It appeared that not only had Grey not ensured that Shandling received that advice, he had discouraged him from seeking it.

On the other hand, Shandling had agreed to give Grey his interest in the show, and acknowledged knowing that his manager was not making any payment. Moreover, such an arrangement was not unique. Many Hollywood managers sought and sometimes obtained interests in movies or shows in which their stars appeared. The legal question raised by Hirsch went to the heart of the relationship that personal managers have with their client: to what extent are they free to use their influence to persuade a client to enter into contracts that benefit the manager at the star's expense, particularly without ensuring that the star has had independent advice?

Managers are agents and fiduciaries—that is, professionals who act for or advise someone else. Like other fiduciaries (including lawyers), personal managers ordinarily have a legal obligation to put the interests of their client above their own. However, it is unclear when a client's agreement frees the fiduciary to pursue his or her own interests. "Informed consent" is ordinarily sufficient, but how should that be defined? Shandling had certainly given his consent, and it was "informed" in the sense that he knew that Grey would be receiving a share of the revenue from his show without consideration. What Shandling might not know was whether that deal was a good or bad idea, whether it was normal or unusual under the circumstances, or whether a different (and more favorable) deal could be negotiated. Did he have a right to depend on Grey to advise him on such considerations? If so, Grey had a conflict of interest: advising Shandling not to give away an interest in his shows without consideration (or to give away less than 50 percent) might cost Grey what he wanted.

The issue was an important one, and the kind of case that Jonathan and I liked to take on. We told Shandling that we would represent him; but how and why had he come to us? Both he and Brad Grey were in Los Angeles; the case, if one were necessary, would be brought there; and there were certainly many excellent, established firms in California. We were small, new, and far away.

"If I am going to take on Brad Grey, I need the best," Shandling told us. "And people who should know say you are the best. In addition," he continued, "the best lawyers in Los Angeles succeed by getting along with the establishment. I need someone who's not afraid to take on the industry." Whatever it may mean elsewhere, in Los Angeles "the industry" still means only one thing—the entertainment industry.

We were later to discover, as we tried to line up witnesses, what Shandling meant. There was reluctance to take sides against someone as powerful as Grey had become; and even more reluctance to attack what was seen as business as usual. Powerful managers doing business with their clients was routine; attacking that practice challenged the interests of all the people, not just Grey, who benefited from the status quo. Several clients of Grey and other industry figures privately told us that they thought Shandling's lawsuit was important and hoped we would win, and a couple even directed us to helpful facts and to questions to ask Grey. But testifying for Shandling, or even being publicly identified with his cause, was a different matter.

Jonathan and I agreed that our partner Bill Isaacson would be the lawyer primarily responsible for representing Shandling. Bill had been a champion debater at the University of Redlands, and like Jonathan he divided his time between international arbitration and jury trials. His intelligence, patience, and low-key style endeared him to judges, juries, and arbitrators alike.

Bill and Jonathan spent December 1997 and the first two weeks of January 1998 analyzing the case. One key legal issue was the precise limits on the ability of fiduciaries to profit from business dealings with their clients. In dealing with the world at large, all adults are responsible for making their own decisions and, in the absence of fraud, are bound to what they agree. The law is clear, however, that clients are entitled to trust their lawyer, doctor, personal manager, stockbroker, or other fiduciary to act in their interest. Because of the potential conflicts raised when fiduciaries contract with their clients, there are rules that prescribe what needs to be done to protect those interests. The precise rules vary from state to state, so a threshold issue was to determine precisely what rules applied in California.

There was not a case or statute that specifically dealt with the issue of personal managers doing business with their clients. However, Bill found a statute (Section 16004 of the California Probate Code) dealing with the duties of trustees that provided:

> A transaction between a trustee and a beneficiary which occurs during the existence of the trust or while the trustee's influence with the beneficiary remains and by which the trustee obtains an advantage from the beneficiary is presumed to be a violation of the trustee's fiduciary duties.

It was clear to us that Grey had "obtained an advantage" from Shandling during the existence of his relationship. Nevertheless, the trustee statute did not directly apply to our case because it dealt with trusts and because an agent (including a manager) is not technically a trustee. However, both agents and trustees were fiduciaries and there was an argument that they should have comparable duties. With some additional digging Bill found authority in another context that under California law "an agent is a fiduciary. His obligation of diligent and faithful service is the same as that of a trustee." If we could convince the court that this legal authority meant that agents should be held to the same rules as trustees, the trustee statute would create at least a presumption that Grey's actions were improper. A legal presumption can be rebutted; however, if it applied, it might be sufficient to create a jury issue, and juries tend not to be kind to agents who take advantage of their clients.

Moreover, as Bill and his team combed through Shandling's and Grey's documents, we began to uncover evidence that Grey may have taken advantage of Shandling in ways other than obtaining an ownership interest in his TV show. One issue that had been resolved prior to our retention involved commissions that Grey had deducted from monies paid to Shandling, including payments from Brillstein-Grey itself. Barry Hirsch had concluded that Grey had taken $1.2 million in improper commissions, and in September 1997 Grey had returned that amount in return for a release of any claims his client had concerning those commissions. Because of the payment and release there was no possibility of pursuing the improper commission claim further. However, we believed the facts surrounding the claim might be admissible to show Grey's pattern and practice; and these would provide context for our remaining claims, and color the jurors' view of Grey.*

A second issue related to agreements that Grey and his companies had reached with media giants ABC and MCA/Universal. In April 1994 Brillstein-Grey agreed with ABC to work together to produce new television programs. The two companies created a joint venture called Brillstein-Grey Communications, to be managed by Grey, whose only producing credits for a television series up to then were Shandling's two shows. It was an attractive deal for Grey because ABC agreed to pay all the production expenses, an initial investment of between $100 and $125 million. As part of Brillstein-Grey's contribution it agreed to give ABC an exclusive fifteen-day "first look" at every program they owned or controlled, an obligation that would

---

*Indeed had we been representing Shandling in September we might well have counseled him not to settle his dispute piecemeal. If Grey were prepared to settle those claims prior to litigation, Shandling could safely presume that he would recover those commissions in an overall settlement or at trial; and the value of his other claims was many times the $1.2 million in repaid commissions. The advantage of waiting to resolve all claims at once was that if our claims to recover Grey's share of *The Larry Sanders Show* went to trial we wanted to be certain that the jury heard the facts concerning the excess commissions. Grey's lawyers would certainly argue that those facts should be excluded because, they would say, any possible relevance after the release was outweighed by the prejudice that would result. We might succeed in getting those facts in one way or another anyway, but their admission would have been certain had the claim not been settled.

include programs involving Shandling that were owned or controlled by Grey. At the time the ABC deal was being negotiated, neither Grey nor anyone else at his company advised Shandling that they were trading away rights with respect to his shows without compensation. Nor did they try to negotiate a payment (or any other type of participation or financing) to compensate Shandling for what the "first look" at future Shandling projects contributed to the deal, or to recognize what Grey's participation in *It's Garry Shandling's Show* and *The Larry Sanders Show* had contributed to making the ABC deal possible. Moreover, neither Grey nor anyone else from his company advised Shandling that Grey and Brillstein-Grey had a conflict, or that he should consider getting independent advice.

Two months after the ABC deal, Grey entered into an agreement with Shandling by which his client would receive $500,000 over an initial eighteen-month period for exclusive "consulting services." Grey's lawyers wanted to use the payments as proof that Shandling had been compensated for the "first look" obligations to ABC. However, neither in the agreement nor in any conversations with Shandling at the time did the defendants tie the consulting services to the ABC deal. Indeed, the defendants had still not revealed to Shandling the extent of their obligations to ABC nor advised him to seek independent advice. The exclusive consulting agreement arguably made matters worse, not better; here again was a contract between fiduciaries and client without full disclosure to the client and without independent advice.

Shandling candidly told us that he did not believe that the right for ABC to have a first look at his personal projects was an essential condition to ABC's willingness to do a deal with Brillstein-Grey. That might well limit the amount of the deal's value that we could claim, but it did not negate the fact that the exclusive first look on Grey's projects involving Shandling that ABC was granted had value, and that he had never been informed of the transaction or given an opportunity to negotiate its terms.

In 1996 Grey and Brillstein-Grey entered into additional agreements with MCA Inc. (the parent of many enterprises, including

Universal Pictures) under which MCA acquired a substantial equity interest in Brillstein-Grey. As part of the agreements, the defendants transferred one half of their interest in the profits of *The Larry Sanders Show* to MCA. This transfer was one of the four express "conditions" to MCA's willingness to do the deal. Shandling was not informed of the transfer nor given an opportunity to participate in the transaction; nor did Grey attempt to negotiate any compensation for his client. Again, this underscored what we saw as Grey's conflict. He had a fiduciary obligation to try to get the best deal he could for Shandling; but giving Shandling an opportunity to participate could reduce what MCA was prepared to pay Grey and his companies.

There were two aspects of the MCA deal that were important. First, Grey was using what we claimed were ill-gotten gains (his interest in *The Larry Sanders Show*) to do the deal. Second, even if we assumed that Grey had acquired his interest in the show legitimately, it was still a breach of his duty to take the opportunity to sell part of his interest to MCA while concealing that opportunity from his client.

Schiller and Isaacson filed our initial complaint on January 15, 1998. We soon learned that Grey would be represented by Bert Fields of Greenberg, Glusker, Fields, Claman & Machtinger and by Munger, Tolles & Olson. Fields and I had worked together representing 20th Century Fox some years earlier, and I knew firsthand that he was an excellent trial lawyer and the consummate Hollywood insider. Elegant in dress and understated in manner, he was as tough a litigator as I knew. Munger, Tolles & Olson was one of the most highly regarded law firms in Los Angeles, and its senior partner, Ronald Olson, was one of the best lawyers in the country. Brad Grey had assembled a formidable team.

The filing of Garry Shandling's complaint struck Hollywood like a bombshell and stirred intense debate. Writing a week after the complaint became public, *Variety*'s editor-in-chief observed:

Who can define the lines of accountability when a manager is partly owned by the very companies that employ the talent? And that, indeed, is what's giving clients a creepy-crawly feeling. In a tough competitive business, it's vital to have someone out there militantly defending your interests. But if your manager has just made a huge deal for himself with the company bargaining for your services, who's out there defending whom?

The attention to the case was increased by Grey's public relations offensive, which was every bit as aggressive as his legal defense. Garry's performance, character, and personality all came under attack, both on and off the record. He stood up to the media assault with surprising equanimity and unsurprising humor. (Responding to one particularly brutal barrage, he asked a reporter, "By the way, they're not saying that I'm not funny, right?")

Although I had limited involvement in the case in its early stages, there was one issue that was brought to me because of its sensitivity. In 1995 and 1996 Munger Tolles had briefly represented both Shandling and Brillstein-Grey in connection with claims made against them by Linda Doucett, a former cast member of *The Larry Sanders Show* (and Garry's former girlfriend), for sex discrimination and wrongful termination. Lawyers are forbidden from being adverse to a present client, or to a former client in a case related to the matter the lawyer handled. Munger Tolles was clearly adverse to its former client Shandling. The question was whether the current and former matters were in any way "related." The problem arose because the defendants had filed a cross complaint alleging that Shandling had caused them damage by erratic behavior, including behavior concerning Linda Doucett. The allegation was silly, but we knew that Shandling would be questioned about Doucett and her allegations, and he was naturally unhappy about having that done by lawyers who had previously defended him against those charges. (Doucett turned out to be very supportive of Shandling in his litigation against Grey, but we did not know that at the time.)

Jonathan and Bill came to me because they knew my regard for

Munger Tolles, and Ron Olson personally, and also knew my general reluctance to move to disqualify other attorneys. I wanted to find a way to avoid having to accuse Munger Tolles of a conflict, and initially thought I had found it. Whatever marginal advantage Grey thought he could get from Doucett's charges (which he had previously disputed) had to be outweighed by the risk of losing the services of Munger Tolles. Bert Fields was a great lawyer, but he was heavily involved in other cases; and losing Ron Olson and Munger Tolles as co-counsel would put Grey at a serious disadvantage. Accordingly I suggested that we agree that neither side would attempt to use the Doucett claims and that we would not object to Munger Tolles. Munger Tolles thought my proposal reasonable, but it was ultimately rejected by Grey.

Jonathan and Bill felt we now had no choice but to move to disqualify Munger Tolles, and I reluctantly agreed. We duly made the motion, and the issue was heard by Thomas Dau, the California Superior Court judge assigned to Shandling's case. On April 27, 1998, Dau disqualified Munger Tolles—a decision that fourteen months later turned out to be much more significant than we thought at the time.

Over the next several months the parties engaged in the document production, depositions, and motion practice typical of high stakes litigation. Experts were obtained and briefed and dozens of potential witnesses interviewed. One difference between this case and our usual work was that here many of the potential witnesses were movie stars. When Bill Isaacson, Ellen Brockman, and I would visit Garry's friends like Warren Beatty and Annette Bening at their homes, we found our families suddenly much more interested than usual in our work.

The court had originally set a trial date of May 5, 1999. In October 1998, just as the *Microsoft* trial was beginning, Brad Grey and his companies asked for a delay until June 30. Bert Fields was representing Jeffrey Katzenberg in a very public case against the Walt Disney Company that had been expected to be completed by May

1999 but that now appeared likely to continue into June. Grey wanted to ensure that Fields was available for his trial, and we did not object. Although as the plaintiff Shandling was interested in seeing his case proceed quickly, I always try to accommodate another counsel's schedule if it can be done without prejudicing my client. Shandling agreed that a two-month delay should not be a problem, and with our consent an extension was granted. Except for Grey's deposition, which we postponed pending Bert Fields's availability, discovery continued.

By April 1999 it appeared *I* might have a scheduling problem. The rebuttal case in *Microsoft* would not begin until June 1, and it seemed unlikely that we would finish the six scheduled rebuttal witnesses by June 30. I therefore asked Bill Isaacson to call Grey's counsel and ask them to agree to a sixty- to ninety-day delay.

I was in Juneau, Alaska, on April 18 meeting with the governor and attorney general of Alaska to plan our next steps in my representation of the state's interests in connection with British Petroleum's acquisition of Arco/Amoco. When I returned to my hotel room that evening, there was a message that Bill Isaacson had called. Bill told me he could not get a straight answer from Grey's counsel as to whether they would agree to a delay. Grey's position was that we should discuss the issue when we got closer to the scheduled date, that our request was premature because it was not yet certain that the Microsoft trial would continue into July. It was, of course, a tactical ploy. As Grey's counsel was well aware, if we were not going to get an extension, we could not afford to learn that on June 29. Bill Isaacson and others were put out that Grey was being so unaccommodating. The Microsoft trial seemed a compelling reason for a postponement; it was a relatively short delay; we were the plaintiff; and we had previously agreed to a comparable request. I told them not to worry: "It's a short river that only turns once."

One advantage of Grey's intransigence was that it freed us to take his deposition. Although Fields was still tied up in the *Katzenberg* case, since Grey was opposing any delay he no longer had a basis for postponing our depositions. We therefore moved to schedule Grey's examination as soon as possible.

Jonathan, Bill, and I were all in London for an international arbitration hearing on May 4 when we learned that Grey's deposition could be scheduled for May 11. It would be challenging to complete our preparation in a week, but it was to our advantage to move ahead while Fields was occupied elsewhere.

We decided that I would begin Grey's deposition myself. I returned to New York the following morning and flew to Los Angeles two days later to prepare. The night before the examination Ellen Brockman and I had dinner with Garry and Warren Beatty to review the basic themes I intended to pursue and to get their insights. Every time I met with Beatty he impressed me with his knowledge and judgment, perhaps in part because his views (whether about the role of personal managers in Hollywood or national political issues) often paralleled my own. I also appreciated how he and Annette Bening were both willing to stand publicly with Garry before it was easy to do so in Hollywood. Shandling's lawsuit against his former manager was not only the subject of numerous press stories, it was also a regular topic of conversation at Hollywood dinner parties and Century City lunches. The debate in private was sharply divided. In public, however, comments (particularly for attribution) were more muted. Few wanted to go on record defending what Grey had done, particularly as details began to leak out. Fewer still were prepared openly to rally to Shandling's attack on Grey and business as usual.

I took the first two days of Grey's deposition, and Peter Haviland, a Kaye Scholer partner in Los Angeles who was our local counsel, took an additional two days. Grey was defended by Fields's partner Charles Shepard. He was not a bad lawyer, but neither was he in Bert Fields's league. Grey provided us with what we believed were valuable substantive admissions, as well as credibility-killing assertions that would make it hard for him to be an effective witness before a jury. He responded, "I don't know," "I don't recall," or "I don't remember" approximately three hundred times to my questions; true or not, such a convenient failure of memory would not sit well with a jury. Ironically, among the details he claimed not to know was what it meant to be a fiduciary.

It is possible, of course, that Grey's deposition would have gone the same way even had he been prepared and defended by Fields; Bill Gates after all had had the best representation money could buy. However, it was more likely that Grey's deposition was the first (but not the last) penalty he would suffer as a result of the tactical decision to oppose our application to delay the trial.

Perhaps the most dramatic piece of evidence that we uncovered was an internal memo dated January 9, 1992, to Brad Grey from Brillstein-Grey executive Sandy Wernick. Wernick had originally recommended that Brillstein-Grey take a one-third interest in Shandling's shows and not the one-half interest that it ultimately took. Grey admitted he had never advised Shandling of Wernick's recommendation. The memo was evidence of Grey's overreaching—and even stronger evidence of his breach of duty. Grey never had a good explanation as to why he had taken a 50 percent share of *The Larry Sanders Show* without even discussing the possibility of a lower percentage with his client. We felt that the concealment of the Wernick proposal underscored Grey's conflict.

Another key piece of evidence, assembled through a painstaking analysis of papers produced in discovery, was an example of creative accounting that had the effect of enriching Grey's companies at Shandling's expense. In December 1991 Brillstein-Grey had entered into a distribution agreement with Columbia Pictures. Under the agreement, similar in many ways to the ABC deal, Columbia agreed to provide financing for television programs produced by Brillstein-Grey in exchange for the right to sell those programs in syndication and to collect distribution fees. (Syndication is the distribution of television programs after

their initial broadcast; for a successful program, syndication revenues often exceed the revenues from the original showing.)
The financing that Columbia agreed to provide for *The Larry
Sanders Show* was $175,000 per episode. This amount was to be
paid to Partners With Boundaries, the company that owned the
show and that, in turn, was owned fifty-fifty by Shandling and
Brillstein-Grey.

Columbia Pictures had also agreed to pay Brillstein-Grey a
multimillion-dollar advance that was to be repaid by Brillstein-
Grey at the rate of $22,500 per episode produced of *The Larry
Sanders Show.* (The amount was one-half of the $45,000 per
episode that Grey's company received for acting as executive
producer of the program). Because the advance went entirely to
Brillstein-Grey, the obligation to repay it was entirely theirs. What
we discovered in analyzing the records was that Brillstein-Grey
had engineered an arrangement whereby half its repayment obligation was borne by Shandling.

Rather than itself pay the $22,500 per episode to Columbia,
Brillstein-Grey pocketed all of its $45,000 fee and directed Co-
lumbia to deduct the $22,500 from the $175,000 that Columbia
was obligated to provide to Partners With Boundaries. That meant
that the company received $152,500 rather than the $175,000 it
was supposed to get. Since Shandling owned one-half of the show,
one-half of the $22,500 being deducted by Columbia was being
paid by him. Brillstein-Grey's practice continued for over four
years, during which time sixty-five episodes were produced and
$1,462,500 ($22,500 times sixty-five) was deducted to repay the
advance received by Brillstein-Grey. It was bad enough that Shandling had not shared in the multimillion-dollar advance; it was
worse for Brillstein-Grey to arrange it so that Shandling repaid
half of what they had received. Grey never attempted to get Shandling's consent for these deductions, nor even told his partner
about them. Because the $22,500 was deducted before Columbia
provided its financing, the books and records of Partners With

Boundaries did not show an entry for these payments, making them difficult to detect.

After the lawsuit was filed and we discovered the recoupment practice, the defendants tried to mitigate their conduct by admitting the payments were solely the obligation of Grey's companies and by offering to repay one-half (the half effectively made by Shandling) with interest. During the lawsuit they provided what they labeled a "Show-end Accounting" for Partners With Boundaries that included a "receivable" due from the defendants equal to the amount Shandling had contributed, plus interest.

This was, we argued, merely part of "Grey's pattern of offering back the goodies once his hand was caught in the cookie jar," similar to the pre-complaint repayment of $1.2 million in commission. Moreover, the incident underscored the extent to which they controlled money that belonged to Shandling, and the extent to which they used that control to benefit themselves.

Although we had developed strong evidence against Grey, we still had our work cut out for us. Mutual friends of Grey and Shandling, including industry power broker Michael Ovitz, had tried to encourage settlement. There had been a couple of brief discussions in which Grey had seemed open to paying $1 or $2 million to resolve the dispute, but we were told that paying more or returning Grey's share of the *Sanders* show was out of the question. One reason for Grey's position was that he had received several favorable rulings from Judge Dau. The most significant of these was the court's statement at a May 12 hearing that he intended to grant Grey summary judgment with respect to our claims covering the ABC transactions. Because the issues concerning the MCA transactions were similar, such a ruling seemed likely to lead to the dismissal of those claims as well. Moreover, while Dau had not yet commented on our claim to recover Grey's share of *The Larry Sanders Show*, if it were not a violation of fiduciary duty for Grey to enter into the ABC and MCA transactions (which Shandling did not know about), it might be hard to prove a violation for taking a share of *The Larry Sanders Show* (which Shandling expressly agreed to).

Judge Dau had said that his May 12 views were tentative and that we would have a chance to change his mind at a hearing scheduled for late June, just before trial. Dau had not had the benefit of my deposition of Grey when he expressed his view in May, and I hoped that the facts established there and Grey's evasiveness would influence him. I also believed that the Wernick memo and other evidence we had found were persuasive proof that Grey had breached his duty. Nevertheless it is always an uphill battle to convince a judge to change his mind, and Dau appeared to be taking a narrow view of the obligations of a personal manager.

As trial approached, we continued to be concerned whether I would be finished in *Microsoft* in time to participate, particularly in the critical first few days of trial, when it is vital for a plaintiff to establish the themes of its case. Fortunately the Microsoft rebuttal progressed faster than expected. We completed on June 23, a full week before the Shandling trial was to begin.

We soon received two other pieces of good news—one tactical and one substantive. The tactical news was that Fields was still tied up in the *Katzenberg* case and that the lead trial lawyer for Grey would be Charles Shephard. Without taking anything away from Shephard, this was clearly a favorable development for Garry. As in any zero-sum game, if one side loses an important player, the position of the other improves. That was why Grey's team thought it made sense to oppose our April request to postpone the trial; they were counting on the possibility that the *Microsoft* case might keep me out of the contest. But now the river had turned. Not only was I on my way to Los Angeles, but the *Katzenberg* case had sidelined Grey's most important player. And Grey's predicament was aggravated by the earlier loss of Munger Tolles. On the eve of trial, the Doucett issues had, as I had predicted, faded to irrelevance; but the absence of Munger Tolles was a major disadvantage.

The second piece of good news was even better. We had just

received Judge Dau's order denying Grey's motion for summary judgment. On our most important claims, Dau rejected Grey's legal arguments and ruled that we had offered sufficient evidence of Grey's misconduct to permit our claims to be considered by a jury. First and most importantly, Dau rejected Grey's argument that he was entitled to the 50 percent of *The Larry Sanders Show* because of the supposed contributions his companies had made to the show's success. It was true that some of the contributions (such as arranging for interim financing) were probably not services that were due Shandling merely because Grey was his personal manager. On the other hand, Grey was receiving producer fees for working on the show in addition to his percentage of Shandling's earnings. Moreover, even assuming that some percentage of ownership might have been fair, Grey could not establish that he did not overreach in taking 50 percent; this was particularly true in light of the Wernick memo. Judge Dau, relying on the trustee statute that Bill Isaacson had identified almost eighteen months earlier, held:

> The transaction in which the partnership was created appears to be one in which Grey had an interest adverse to Shandling, and Grey's having taken part in such a transaction violates section 16004(a) of the Probate Code.

Dau went on to consider whether Shandling's claims were barred by the applicable statute of limitations—laws that provide that if a lawsuit is not begun within a certain period of time the lawsuit is lost and cannot be brought. In Shandling's case the applicable period was four years, and over five had passed between when Grey took his 50 percent of Shandling's show and when we first sued on Garry's behalf. On the surface, Shandling's suit was barred.

There is, however, a doctrine that says if a defendant hides the fact that you have been wronged, the statute of limitations does not run out until you reasonably know you have a claim. (This is referred to as suspending or "tolling" the statute of limitations.) Defendants could otherwise deprive plaintiffs of compensation for one

bad act by the second bad act of a cover-up. We could not argue
that Shandling did not know that Grey had been given 50 percent
of the show. Instead we argued, and Judge Dau agreed, that because
Grey had not revealed the Wernick memo until after Shandling's
lawsuit was filed, the failure to disclose the memo could toll the
statute of limitations.

The court also ruled in our favor on claims relating to the ABC
and MCA transactions, holding that the trustee statute applied to
personal managers. After analyzing the evidence related to the
ABC transaction Dau concluded:

> The evidence discussed in this section shows that, had Shan-
> dling come to Grey the morning after Grey signed the ABC
> agreement, seeking advice for the presentation of an idea for
> a new television show, Grey could not have developed this
> intellectual property for television or radio without first of-
> fering it to the newly created Partnership. To have done so
> would have violated paragraph 3.A and B of the ABC agree-
> ment. Once the ABC agreement was in place, Grey could
> no longer execute agreements for Shandling's artistic literary
> material with, for example, HBO: he was obligated to give
> ABC a first look. Thus the ABC agreement limited the uni-
> verse within which Shandling's artistic materials could be
> developed by his personal manager.

This was exactly the analysis that we had set forth in our complaint
and the principle that Shandling had set out to establish. Our
client, Judge Dau ruled, could proceed with his claims

> that defendants had a duty to negotiate for Shandling to get
> a payment on the making of the ABC agreement and that
> defendants should have advised Shandling to get independ-
> ent business or legal advice in connection with the making
> of that agreement.

This ruling was particularly dramatic because it was contrary to what the judge had told the parties he intended to do with respect to the ABC transaction. Even after Isaacson's June argument, the judge had not given any indication that he would alter his earlier decision in Grey's favor, and we were not optimistic. Judges rarely change their minds, and even when they begin to doubt that what they have said or done is right, many will not admit it to themselves, let alone to others. The best judges are those who are prepared to change their views when confronted with contrary evidence and precedent. Judge Dau noted:

> The court is mindful that at the first oral argument on this motion it announced that it was granting defendants' motion insofar as Issue No. 2. That ruling had to be made in a written order to become effective. This is that written order, and it is contrary to the ruling announced at the hearing.

Dau's analysis of the MCA transaction was based on the same legal authority and came to the same result as the ABC ruling. The court held that Shandling's case could proceed on the claims against the defendants that "they had a duty to negotiate for Shandling to get a payment on the making of the contract" and that "defendants had a duty to advise Shandling to obtain independent business advice in connection with . . . the MCA agreement."

The judge's rulings made clear that Grey was in trouble. Based on the court's prior comments on the ABC claims, Grey had felt certain he would also win the MCA claims, and was hopeful of winning the rest of the case. Now the court had upheld our legal claims, and he faced a trial missing his key player. It was, as the headline in *Variety* declared the following day, a "Stunning Reversal."

"If anyone calls to discuss settlement," I told Bill, "tell them they should call me. If they try to engage you in any discussion at all, cut it off and tell them you're busy preparing for trial." I expected a set-

tlement initiative from Grey before trial, and it was important that
no one send back the wrong message. There are two ways you can
kill a potential settlement. One is by sending a signal that your demands are so high that the other side concludes that negotiating
would be fruitless. The other is by signaling that you may be willing
to settle for less than you turn out to be willing to accept—causing
the other side not to make an offer that they would otherwise have
made and that you would have accepted; by the time they realize
you will not take their lowered proposal, it may be too late. At this
critical time I wanted to control all the messages we sent.

When I arrived in Los Angeles, I took a cab to Shandling's
house, where he was meeting with Bill and our trial team. An
hour later I got the phone call I had been expecting. It came not
from Shephard but from Fields. Did it make sense for us to talk?
He wanted to know.

"I don't know whether it makes sense or not," I replied, "but I
would enjoy seeing you." Because of our schedules, up to this
point Bert and I had had almost no contact during the case. Every
time he had been at court or at a deposition, I was not there, and
vice versa. If a settlement were possible, the two of us had the best
chance of making it happen. Grey was going to have to increase
greatly what he gave up in order to avoid a trial, and Bert had the
stature to convince him to do it—so long as he concluded it was
the right thing to do.

We met at Bert's offices at Century City after an early dinner.
He opened a bottle of excellent white wine. Bert understood that
the time had come to be realistic. I understood that a good settlement was better for Shandling than rolling the dice at trial. We
both agreed that a trial with the gloves off would be fun for me
(and for him if he were doing it), but less so for our clients in
publicity-conscious Los Angeles. Bert quickly made clear that he
understood that what Shandling really wanted was to own his
show 100 percent, and Grey was ready to return the 25 percent of
the profits that he still owned. But Fields also convinced me that
even if we won at trial, we could not get back the 25 percent of

the profits that had already been traded away. We could get damages, but that was it. How then to make up for the percent of profits that we could not claw back? One possible solution was to give Shandling the percentage of his original program, *It's Garry Shandling's Show*, that Grey owned. (We had not made a claim for that interest because in that case Shandling *had* been represented by an independent adviser.) Getting back Grey's share of Shandling's earlier show was something I knew would be important to Garry, but 25 percent of the later show was worth significantly more than Grey's percentage of the earlier one.

From the beginning of our negotiations that evening, I had made clear that any settlement would have to include a substantial cash payment. Bert had initially not agreed, but he had not disagreed either. Once we reached a tentative understanding that Grey would return his interests in both *The Larry Sanders Show* and *It's Garry Shandling's Show*, we turned to the subject of what the guaranteed cash payment would be. It was this issue that consumed most of the several hours we spent together that evening and most of Bert's wine. During the discussion Bert repeatedly argued that Grey was entitled to some ownership interest in *The Larry Sanders Show* and that, as a result, if Shandling got back Grey's remaining 25 percent of that show's profits, along with Grey's percentage of Shandling's earlier show, that was enough. I argued that Grey's exposure on the ABC and MCA deals alone justified an eight-figure payment. Eventually we reached agreement on an amount we both considered reasonable.*

I called Garry from the parking lot of Bert's building to give him and Bill Isaacson the good news. Garry insisted on taking Bill,

---

*Bert was concerned that so large a payment would be embarrassing to his client, and we agreed that the amount would be kept confidential. This agreement was kept until an overzealous PR representative of Grey's convinced a *New York Post* reporter to write without checking that Grey had escaped with a nominal payment. This quickly led to the public disclosure that the settlement's value was eight figures.

myself, and the assembled team out to celebrate. As we drank champagne at the Beverly-Wilshire bar later that same night, I agreed that the result was a good one for Garry. But I also thought it was a good one for his former manager.

"If Brad Grey is as smart as I think he is," I said, "he should be buying Bert Fields a drink. This has cost Grey more than it would have had he settled earlier, but Bert has saved him from the daily public embarrassment of a trial—and the likelihood of a jury verdict against him at the end of the road."

For me the settlement was a mixed blessing. We had won my client what he most wanted, we had earned our firm a multimillion-dollar fee (we had taken the case on a contingency-fee basis), and I was now free to meet Mary in Las Vegas for a Fourth of July weekend. On the other hand, by settling I lost the opportunity to try what was shaping up as a great case. Also, while Judge Dau's opinion would stand as an important precedent regarding the obligations of managers to their clients, rulings at trial and post-trial could have advanced those obligations still further.

However, a lawyer's first obligation is not to enjoy himself or (at least when representing a private client) to make new law, but to serve his client—and looking across the table at Garry Shandling's face, I knew we had certainly done that.

As a young partner at Cravath, Swaine & Moore (1976).

With law partners from Cravath, celebrating the 1981 dismissal of the government's case against IBM; from left, Joe Sahid, Bob Mullen, Tom Barr, Paul Saunders, Ron Rolfe.

With Senator Ted Kennedy and President Jimmy Carter in the Oval Office 1978.

At the family ranch in Northern California.

With Mary on a bike trip in the Burgundy region of France.

At the helm of our sailboat.

Relaxing on the sailboat (at the far left). Mary took this picture from the top of the mast.

Biking with Mary in the Provence region of France.

In California on a cross-country jeep trip in 1983. Sons Christopher and Jonathan are in the back with me; my sister Cathie and my father are in front.

My six children: Alexander, Caryl, Christopher, Mary Regency, David III, and Jonathan in 1998.

At Victoria Falls in Zambia/Zimbabwe, Africa, with Mary Regency, Alexander, and Mary in 2000.

Peter Muhly/Reuters

New York Yankees owner George Steinbrenner, whose lawsuit against Major League
Baseball precipitated my departure from Cravath.

AP/Wide World Photos

George W. Bush with then acting Major League Baseball Commissioner Bud Selig
and Fay Vincent.

My law partner Jonathan Schiller, during a press conference in San Francisco in 2001 following a hearing in the music industry's lawsuit against Napster.

Working with my law partner Robert Silver.

Joey and Amy Habie, before their wedding, 1984.

Twins, Alexandra and Daniel Habie.

At the press conference after Judge Jackson ruled in favor of the United States in *U.S. v. Microsoft*, with U.S. Attorney General Janet Reno; Assistant U.S. Attorney General in charge of the Antitrust Division Joel Klein; and Connecticut Attorney General Richard Blumenthal.

With Mary.

Cartoon published in *Fortune* Magazine March 1, 1999, during Microsoft trial.

Microsoft CEO Steve Ballmer; Chairman Bill Gates and Corporate General Counsel Brad Smith.

Cartoon published in *Fortune* Magazine February 15, 1999, showing Microsoft's lead witness Dean Schmalensee hanging himself on the witness stand.

Cartoon published in
Fortune Magazine
March 29, 1999,
during Microsoft
trial.

Garry Shandling; Marty Beck, a William Morris Agent; and Brad Grey when Grey was Shandling's friend as well as manager.

Garry Shandling, Warren Beatty, and Annette Bening. Beatty and Bening were important allies in Shandling's successful case against his former manager Brad Grey.

Trapper FR/Corbis Sygma

The Solow Building at 9 West 57th Street, overlooking the Plaza Hotel (right) and Central Park. The asbestos-contaminated insulation of 9 West led to the lawsuit against W.R. Grace.

With Sheldon Solow celebrating the verdict in the lawsuit against W.R. Grace

Diana ("DeDe") Brooks, Sotheby's CEO from 1994–1999.

Alfred Taubman, Sotheby's Chairman (1998–2000) (center) leaving court with lawyers Bob Fiske (left) and Scott Muller (right) after criminal conviction.

Christopher Davidge, Christie's CEO (left) and Lord Hindlip, Christie's Chairman (right).

Florida Secretary of State Katherine Harris reviewing election returns
with election officials and attorneys at 5 am on the day after the
Presidential election, Wednesday, November 8, 2000,
in Tallahassee, Florida.

At a press conference explaining Vice President Gore's position, with Counsel
Warren Christopher and Gore/Lieberman Campaign Chairman William M. Daley,
November 16, 2000.

Speaking with Judge N. Sanders Sauls and Bush attorney Philip Beck, in Leon County Court, Florida.

Argument before Florida Supreme Court on December 7, 2000; Justice Leander J. Shaw, Jr., (left) and Chief Justice Charles T. Wells (right).

In court during a break in the action in the trial of *Bush v. Gore* before Judge Sauls, December 3, 2000.

8

Grace Under Fire: Another Civil Action

COMPLEX LITIGATION IS A MARATHON, NOT A SPRINT, and *Solow v. W. R. Grace* was a marathon of Forrest Gump proportions. The suit was first filed in 1986. I became involved in the fall of 1997 when Sheldon Solow asked my advice on how to move the case along. We had met a year earlier, when I was still at Cravath, as the result of a call from Arthur Liman, one of the premier lawyers in New York during my lifetime. Liman and I had been friends for a quarter of a century and had been in a number of high-profile cases together, sometimes on the same side and sometimes not. As usual, he got right to the point.

"As you know," he said, "health issues limit what I can do right now. I have represented Sheldon Solow for a number of years. He's a good friend as well as an important client. I recommended that he call you and I hope you will see him."

I waited to respond, knowing that there was more to come. Solow was one of a handful of builders and building owners who dominate New York City's real estate business and the city's skyline. Arthur himself was in a battle with cancer that ultimately took his life, but his firm (Paul, Weiss, Rifkind, Wharton & Garrison) was one of the largest and best regarded in the city. Why involve me? I wondered.

After a moment Arthur continued. "Sheldon has a number of complicated legal issues that require a great deal of judgment. I know you are busy, but it is important to me that he is taken care of. He is smart, and he listens—although you may not always realize it until later."

"Of course I'll see him," I said.

We talked for a few minutes about things more serious than the weather but less serious than his health. I still did not understand what there was about Solow's legal problems, or about Solow himself, that was leading Arthur to look outside Paul Weiss. However, we had known each other too long for me press him about his reasons. In any event, I thought to myself, if it is important, I will find it out myself.

When I met with Solow later that week, I knew immediately he was someone I would enjoy representing. Like virtually all self-made men, he had excelled at taking advantage of the opportunities that life had given him; unlike many, however, he recognized how important a role luck had played in making those opportunities available. It was clear he would be a tough, demanding client, but one who would appreciate good legal work when he got it.

W. R. Grace was a company with many environmental sins and little interest in atonement. Among its many businesses, it was one of the leading manufacturers of asbestos fireproofing. In 1972 Grace provided the fireproofing for Solow's new building at 9 West Fifty-seventh Street in Manhattan. Of all of Solow's many buildings, this was his favorite. A sweeping fifty-story, 2.5-million-square-foot tower in the heart of Manhattan across from the Plaza Hotel, the building was a commercial and architectural triumph. Even assembling the land for it was an accomplishment. To erect the uncompromising structure that Solow did was more remarkable still, particularly for a young builder with limited financial resources. But what he lacked in money he made up for in vision, determination, and creative borrowing.

Having succeeded in completing 9 West, Solow was immediately forced to fend off repeated attempts by the building's initial anchor tenant, Avon, to force him to sell what he had created. When Solow refused Avon's first offer, his tenant refused to pay any rent on the ground that the premises differed in certain details from the architect's plans—a potentially devastating tactic given how highly leveraged Solow was at the time and how dependent he was on prompt rent payments to avoid a default. Avon hoped to put enough financial pressure on its landlord that he would have no choice but to sell. Fortunately fast-track arbitration forced the company to begin paying rent, the building was saved, and a quarter century later Solow was rich and famous. But he never forgot what he had had to go through to keep 9 West, and it made him particularly sensitive to any threats to it. When in the middle 1980s he discovered that the insulation that Grace had put into his beloved building was potentially dangerous, he was outraged.

If microscopic asbestos fibers become airborne, they can be inhaled. Long and sharp, the fibers then become imbedded in lung tissue. Contrary to popular belief, asbestos is a naturally occurring substance, and virtually all human beings have some asbestos fibers imbedded in their lungs. However, excessive exposure, in which the lungs are unable to adapt to the number of microscopic spears inhaled, can cause fatal asbestosis and cancer.

When Solow was building 9 West in the late 1960s and early 1970s, the health dangers of inhaled asbestos were already known, and his original agreement with his contractors provided that the insulation was to be "asbestos-free." Grace at the time was beginning to promote Monokote 4—an insulation product that was advertised as containing no asbestos. However, when the day came to begin fireproofing 9 West, the company told Solow that Monokote 4 was not available; that Monokote 3, which was, contained only a "trace" of asbestos; and that even Monokote 3 was entirely safe because it was cement-like, or "cementitious," with its asbestos fibers "locked in." Because asbestos is dangerous only when it can be inhaled, fibers imbedded in a stable cementitious product do not pose a health hazard. Asbestos materials that release fibers are referred to as "friable"; Grace represented that the asbestos in Monokote 3 was not friable. The company also assured Solow that Monokote 4 would be used once it was available, and a portion of the building was eventually insulated with the new product.

More than a decade after 9 West was completed, New York City passed an ordinance that required strict containment of any workplace undergoing renovations if "asbestos-containing products" might be disturbed by the work; these products were defined to include Monokote 3. The passage of the law caused Solow to begin an investigation that found that the product contained 10 percent or more asbestos fibers and that those fibers could be released if the insulation was disturbed or deteriorated over time.

Solow immediately installed special systems designed to filter out any fibers that might become airborne before they could be inhaled. He also regularly tested the air in the building—tests that uniformly showed no detectable asbestos. Despite these precautions, in the late 1980s Solow decided to undertake the costly step of replacing Monokote 3 with fireproofing that was completely asbestos-free. Because of public concern about asbestos, every product containing it is a problem for a building owner. In addition it is difficult to ensure that supposedly encapsulated asbestos fibers will not eventually be released. When Solow asked W. R. Grace to pay for replacing Monokote 3, the company refused, arguing that despite the New York City ordinance the product was perfectly safe.

Although Jonathan Harr's book *A Civil Action*, which describes Grace's approach to environmental litigation, was not published until 1995, by the late 1980s the company already had a reputation for aggressively defending against asbestos and other environmental claims. If Solow were to sue Grace, he knew that the company could be expected to subject him to all the discovery the courts would allow. Responding to its demands would disrupt his business and potentially cost millions of dollars—money that could not be recovered even if Solow won his case.*

Moreover, W. R. Grace was by now in the asbestos litigation business and had a stable of witnesses that it used in case after case to dispute the claim that Monokote 3 posed a health risk. In the particular instance of Solow's building, Grace had two further advantages. First, Solow's numerous tests had not shown any airborne asbestos fibers. There were many reasons why it was important to remove asbestos products before dangerous fiber levels could be detected; however, Grace would be able to use Solow's own test results against him. Second, the rents at 9 West were the highest per square foot in the city. Grace would certainly argue that large and sophisticated tenants would not pay such rents were the building unsafe. However, Solow had been misled by Grace, and his building was, in his view, contaminated. Grace might have many times his resources, but no one was more tenacious than Solow in fighting for what he believed was right.

Solow had been represented for several years in the *Grace* case by Paul Weiss and a team led by Ed Westbrook from the Ness Motley firm. When I was asked to get involved in late 1997, I was not sure that I would add a great deal to the team; besides, I was busy with a number of other cases. I told Sheldon that I needed to think about it, which I did as I lay on the beach in the Dominican Republic the last week of 1997 contemplating my schedule for the next several months.

The Habie trial was scheduled to start January 4. As soon as it was over I was to start a six to eight-week trial for Banque Indosuez. I had a draft Shandling complaint in my suitcase, waiting for my review; and I had already broken my rule against taking phone

---

*In England and other countries, winning parties in litigation can collect their costs from their opponent. That is not true in the United States, where in general each party must bear its own litigation costs. The exception is that successful plaintiffs (but not defendants) in antitrust, civil rights, and other cases where there is a special statute do recover their costs—and either a plaintiff or a defendant can recover costs in any case if they establish that the positions of their opponent were frivolous.

calls during our December holiday to talk to Joel Klein about
Microsoft. In addition, the vitamins price-fixing case was heating up
and our firm had significant new matters for DuPont and North-
west Airlines. Stepping into the middle of hotly contested environmental litigation would be a challenge under any circumstances;
doing so in early 1998 could have seemed downright foolhardy. On
the other hand, Solow believed I could help get the stalled case
going, and it was the kind of case that attracted me. The vast majority of claims against Grace never went to trial; plaintiffs were either worn down or bought off or both. I thought I already knew
Sheldon well enough to predict that neither would happen here.
This was a matter of principle for him, and I suppose for me as well.
When I told Mary that I had decided to take on the Grace case, she
shook her head.

"It's a good thing you weren't born a girl," she smiled. "You
just can't say no."

W. R. Grace was represented by two very large law firms,
Cahill Gordon and Reed Smith, each with a reputation for defending environmental cases aggressively and well. Grace had succeeded in delaying the case with repeated motions and discovery
requests and had responded to Solow's discovery requests by turning over millions of pages of documents that had not yet been
thoroughly reviewed. Our dual challenge was to get the case to
trial as soon as possible and to make sure that by then we had completed all we needed to do.

The first part of the task proved remarkably easy. The case was
before Justice Elliot Wilk, an experienced New York state court
trial judge with a reputation for running a fair, orderly courtroom.
When in early 1998 we requested a firm trial date the following
year, he granted our request. Grace objected that there was still too
much to be done. However, noting that the defendant's law firms
had more than 500 lawyers between them, Wilk ruled that Grace
would have to complete its work in the time available. He warned
our side, however, that if we failed to meet our remaining discovery obligations he would reconsider his ruling.

The second part of our task was more complicated—making sure that we were ready for the trial when it came. We divided the work between two teams, one led by Ed Westbrook and the other led by my partner Andy Hayes. Many lawyers do not like to share a case with other firms. My own experience has been different. A multifirm team may require a bit more tact, but particularly where lawyers bring special expertise, as Ed Westbrook did in the asbestos area, such a combination can be better than what any single firm can offer.

Andy was the ideal person to lead my firm's contribution. A quick learner (an essential characteristic for anyone jumping into a ten-year-old case shortly before trial), Andy was also easy to work with. In addition, as the lawyer responsible for separate litigation that Solow had pending before Justice Wilk against Avon and J. P. Morgan, he had earned the judge's confidence.

I had been involved in only one previous asbestos claim—a case against Westinghouse by workers who had repaired the company's asbestos-insulated turbine generators. In 1996 I had been asked by Westinghouse to represent it in the New York Court of Appeals following a punitive damages verdict against it. In my argument I had conceded that everyone was now aware of the dangers of asbestos but contended that in the 1950s, when Westinghouse had manufactured the turbines in question, it had not known, and had no reason to know. Having won that appeal, I was convinced that Solow's success would depend on proving that Grace knew, or had reason to know, when Monokote 3 was installed that the product was dangerous.*

I also knew we faced an uphill battle. Prior cases in which building owners sought to recover the costs of removing and

---

*There was a legal argument that if the product was unsafe, Grace was liable for the cost of replacing it even if it did not know of the danger at the time. As a practical matter, however, I believed it was important to convince a jury that Grace knew the health risks; strict liability in the absence of fault is, in general, more favorably received by law professors than juries. This was likely to be particularly true where, as here, the evidence as to whether the product was in fact unsafe would be in dispute.

replacing asbestos fireproofing had proven hard to win. Where a person was sick or dying, a jury's sympathy could often be relied on to overcome possible weaknesses in a plaintiff's case. However, jurors were unlikely to have a great deal of sympathy for a landlord—particularly one as rich and successful as Sheldon Solow.

Because of my other commitments, Ed and Andy, with help from my son Jonathan (JB), did the bulk of the work in 1998 and the first half of 1999. Our depositions and document discovery revealed evidence that as early as 1972 Grace knew that Monokote 3 was not as safe as it was now contending. On the other hand, the defendant had established that Solow knew that the product contained asbestos, that he was concerned with its presence, that he initially refused to permit its installation, but that he ultimately accepted its use until Monokote 4 was available.

I could see that the trial would revolve around three central issues. First, we would argue that Monokote 3 was unsafe and that it was reasonable for Solow to spend millions of dollars replacing it; Grace would argue that the product was safe and that the costs Solow incurred to remove it were unnecessary.

Second, we would say that Grace knew at the time it sold the insulation that it was not as safe as the company represented; Grace would say that it believed that the product was safe in the 1970s, and still believed so today.

Third, Grace would argue that, to the extent there was a problem with its product, Solow knew it at the time of installation and hence assumed the risk associated with it. We would argue that although Solow had been generally aware of the danger of asbestos and preferred an asbestos-free product, he had been intentionally misled by Grace about the safety of Monokote 3.

During discovery we had accumulated a great deal of evidence that the insulation was not entirely safe. Some of this came from the Environmental Protection Agency; indeed both sides were able to rely on EPA documents and studies—ours, in general, from periods when the head of the EPA had been appointed by a Democratic president; theirs in general from periods when the head of the EPA had been appointed by a Republican president.*

Other evidence came from studies we ourselves had commissioned. These also indicated that Grace's product did release asbestos fibers, both when it deteriorated over time and when it was disturbed during renovations or other construction activity.

Our best evidence was of three kinds. First, we collected samples of Monokote 3 from Solow's building that, instead of being solid and "cementitious," were soft and crumbling. Looking at these samples a jury would find it difficult to believe that the asbestos was "locked in" as Grace claimed. It was also difficult to believe that the manufacturer could have concluded it was.

Second, combing through the millions of pages of documents, mostly irrelevant, that Grace produced in discovery, we found a few statements by its employees indicating they believed Monokote 3 was unsafe at the time it was being installed. Jurors typically find what a company's contemporaneous internal documents say much more believable than what a company's witnesses later say on the witness stand, so this was powerful evidence. On the other hand, there were other Grace documents from the same time saying that Monokote 3 *was* safe; and Grace could argue with some justification that each side of almost any question has someone in a large corporation that supports it.

Third, and most dramatic, we had found Grace documents in which its executives discussed the need to remove asbestos-

---

*An exception to the hearsay rule allows government reports to be admitted in evidence. This exception fails to take into account the extent to which such reports reflect the political and policy agendas, and the plausible but by no means unimpeachable points of view, of the people responsible for their preparation. Jurors tend to give government reports very heavy weight, and without the author present to be cross-examined, there is often little a party can do to counteract them effectively. It would usually be fairer to allow experts to rely on the reports (as they can rely on anything the expert finds useful) but not to allow the reports themselves to be admitted as exhibits. In *W. R. Grace*, government reports were not decisive because they were on both sides of the issue.

containing materials from buildings in which they themselves worked, despite tests showing no detectable asbestos in the air. I was in Washington, DC, on March 8, 1999, when JB called to tell me about the first such document. I had been out late the night before (Jonathan Schiller and I had taken his sons and Mary Regency to a Rolling Stones concert), and even though it was after nine-thirty in the morning I was at first not happy to be woken up. My initial ill humor disappeared as JB explained what he had. We knew that Grace would argue that the fact that Solow's repeated tests did not detect asbestos proved that Monokote 3 was safe. This document showed Grace applied a different standard where the health of its own executives was at stake. The company might explain away an occasional document by a researcher or other employee debating the safety of Monokote 3, but there was no mistaking the point of memos calling for removal of asbestos-containing materials from facilities housing company personnel. The Grace executives obviously thought the materials were not safe enough for them, regardless of what air tests showed; how could Grace's lawyers now argue that it was safe enough for Solow and his tenants—or that Grace had not been aware of the dangers?

Mary and I were scheduled to leave on a two-week family vacation the following Saturday. Since the first week would be spent at our condominium in Breckenridge, Colorado, and since I do not ski, I would have several hours to work while Mary and the children were on the slopes. While I had been planning to spend the time primarily preparing for the *Microsoft* rebuttal and negotiating a *Vitamins* settlement, this Grace development was important enough that I asked JB to collect as many of these documents as he could for me to take with me. By the time we left Colorado I believed we had an effective counter to Grace's air-test defense.

Our experience with these critical documents illustrates the benefits, costs, and limitations of modern discovery rules; it also illustrates the tactics lawyers use to take advantage of them. Without the rule that allowed us to require Grace to produce relevant documents, we never would have uncovered facts vital to our case.

None of the witnesses we deposed, for example, knew about—or at least was prepared to remember—those decisions. Grace however was able to make finding these documents both costly and challenging by burying them in millions of pages of papers of limited, if any, relevance. In order to review these documents, Andy Hayes, JB, and their paralegals spent weeks at Grace facilities poring through files for the occasional nugget. We had the resources to undertake that work, and Solow the money and determination to pay for it, but a law firm and client with fewer resources or less determination would probably never have found what we did.

Even if we established that Monokote 3 was dangerous, and that Grace had been aware of it, that was only part of the battle. There was also the company's argument that Solow had been aware of these dangers at the time he installed the material. Grace could be expected to hammer at the fact that Solow himself had originally contracted for "asbestos-free" Monokote 4 but had accepted the older version when told that otherwise he would have to delay his building several months. Why, Grace was sure to ask, did Solow originally specify asbestos-free Monokote 4 unless he was aware of the potential dangers of Monokote 3? I had to find a way to make the jury identify with the position Solow was in in the 1970s when he made the decision to rely on Grace for the safety of Monokote 3.

We completed jury selection on September 22. In federal court and some state courts prospective jurors are questioned primarily by the trial judge, with lawyers able to ask few (and, in many cases, no) questions themselves. In most state courts lawyers themselves are able to ask extensive questions, ostensibly for the purpose of probing a person's suitability. In practice we use this opportunity (the only time we are legitimately permitted to have a dialogue with a juror) to develop a relationship with jurors and to begin persuading them of the merits of our case. In most courts the questioning takes place in the presence of the trial judge. In some states, including New York, the lawyers initially question prospective jurors without the judge present.

After questioning is completed, each side makes its "challenges for cause," which are requests for the judge to excuse a potential juror because he or she is not expected to be fair. Next, each side exercises its "peremptory challenges," the right to strike a certain number of prospective jurors (usually four to six) without explanation.

Initially I, together with counsel for Grace, met with prospective jurors to question them in a conference room up the hall from Judge Wilk's court. Jury selection is part art, part science, part guess. In the W. R. Grace case, each side had invested money in "jury consultants" who had studied the issues as well as polling and other data concerning residents of Manhattan (the pool from which our jurors would be selected) and who sought to advise us what kind of juror was likely to be favorable to one side or the other. Prospective jurors were classified by age, sex, race, religion, occupation, marital status, political affiliation, educational background, newspaper and television news channel of choice, smoking habits, neighborhood, and recreational activities, among other factors. Prior to our questioning, each juror had filled out a questionnaire setting forth basic demographic information about themselves and whether they had any affiliation with any party or lawyer in the case. During questioning we each tried to identify the jurors who would relate well to us, our clients, and the case we would present. We also tried to begin the process of persuasion.

One question Grace's lawyer sometimes asked was whether a prospective juror had read or seen *A Civil Action*. I understood why he wanted to know; the book and movie cast Grace in an unfavorable light, and did so in the context of environmental litigation. Finding out who, if anyone, was familiar with *A Civil Action* was a first step in preventing that person from serving on the jury.* On the other hand, jurors who were not familiar with it might

---

*Grace might convince Justice Wilk to remove for cause a juror familiar with the book or movie on the ground that the juror might be prejudiced against Grace as a result; even if the prospective juror were not removed for cause, Grace would have the option of using one of its peremptory challenges to strike the juror.

have their curiosity aroused by the question and, if selected, seek out the book or film during the trial. Jurors are always told sternly not to read or watch anything about a case during a trial; they often disregard this instruction.

We interrupted our jury selection on September 20 to allow me to fly to Washington for the September 21 oral argument on our proposed findings of fact in the *Microsoft* case. On September 22, Justice Wilk ruled on our challenges for cause and we each then proceeded to our peremptory challenges. Either by remarkable coincidence or because Grace and their jury consultants saw things the same way we did, the defendant eliminated all three of the prospective jurors we liked the best.

In planning my opening statement, I knew that I would focus on three themes—Monokote 3 was unsafe; Grace had known this in the 1970s; and Solow had accepted its use despite his initial misgivings in reasonable reliance on Grace's assurances. The first and second themes were the most important. Unless we established the first, we were out of court; if Grace convinced the jury that even though Monokote 3 may have been unsafe, the company did not know and could not be expected to have known, we would probably also lose the case. By contrast, if the jury concluded that Grace was at fault for distributing a product it knew was unsafe, but that Solow was also at fault for using it, under New York law it would probably apportion fault, and the worst that would happen would be a reduction in the damages awarded; since even apportioned damages would be large, this would still be a good result.* As we approached trial, the evidence in support of my first two themes was pretty good; the evidence in support of my third theme was more ambiguous.

There was a certain tension between Grace's desire to defend

---

*Under New York law, if both the plaintiff and defendant are at fault, the jury apportions responsibility and damages based on relative fault—unless it concludes that one party is so much more responsible that the other party's fault can be said to be relatively slight (or "immaterial"), in which case the more responsible party is assigned the entire blame.

Monokote 3 as safe and not friable and its plan to assert that Solow was aware that the product was dangerous at the time he accepted it. If the product were in fact safe, why would Solow think it was dangerous? Grace could have admitted that Monokote 3 was not entirely safe and that everyone (including Solow) knew it; but by this admission it would have conceded responsibility for some or all of Solow's damages unless it could convince the jury that the *only* material cause of the problem was Solow's decision—that Solow fully understood the dangers and chose to go ahead anyway. Under that set of facts, Grace would not be liable for any of Solow's damages, but assuming for the purposes of planning a trial strategy that the jury would ultimately find those facts was risky.

What Grace would have liked to argue, and essentially did right up to the time of trial, was that it believed in the 1970s and still believed today that Monokote 3 was safe, but that if it were not, Solow knew it was dangerous when he installed it. This is called "arguing in the alternative." A well-worn law school example is the person who complains that a neighbor borrowed a dish and returned it broken. The neighbor replies, "I never borrowed the dish; if I did borrow the dish I returned it in perfect condition; if the dish was broken when I returned it, it was because it was broken when I borrowed it."

Arguing in the alternative is permissible in a lawsuit, and many defendants do it—particularly in the early stages of litigation when lawyers are trying to ascertain the facts and determine what their best arguments may be. However, by trial, especially before a jury, such arguments become difficult. Juries do not want to hear clever hypotheses about what the facts might be; they want witnesses, and lawyers, to tell them what the facts *are*. It is true that the plaintiff bears the burden of proof and must show that the neighbor borrowed the dish, that the neighbor returned it broken, and that the dish was not broken when the neighbor borrowed it. Jurors, in general, do understand the burden of proof and will require a plaintiff to prove its case. However, jurors have little patience with a defendant's trying to use the burden of proof to take inconsistent positions. It cannot be true both that the neighbor never borrowed the dish and that the neighbor returned the dish in perfect condition. The jury wants the defendant to tell them which it was; they do not want to think of a trial as a game where a party shifts position depending on how the case develops.

Grace had a possible way to reconcile its two arguments. Grace could argue that it believed in the 1970s, and believed now, that Monokote 3 was a good product—and a better, safer product than other insulation available at the time. The fact that Solow's air tests never detected asbestos fibers showed that the insulation was generally not friable. However, like any product containing asbestos it had some risks, particularly under unusual circumstances. That's why Grace developed Monokote 4. Solow knew about the possible problems, which is why he initially specified Monokote 4. If the jury concluded that the risks associated with Monokote 3 made it an unsafe product, Solow knew about those risks when he installed the product.

Such an approach would require Grace not to take an absolutist position about the safety of Monokote 3. However, the evidence was going to show that there was at least a serious question about its safety no matter what position the company might take, and rather than hurting Grace at trial a more balanced argument might have enhanced its credibility. It would also have permitted Grace to argue that Solow should lose either because Monokote 3 was safe or, if the jury concluded it was unsafe, because Solow knew what Grace knew.

I believed the defendant would be reluctant to make such a nuanced argument, because of asbestos lawsuits it had won arguing that Monokote 3 was safe and because of other lawsuits still pending. To the extent I could, I wanted to force Grace's lawyers to take as absolutist a position as possible. I had begun that effort in my pre-selection questioning of prospective jurors. Would they, I asked, be prepared to award punitive damages against a company that recklessly sold a product while harboring doubts about its safety?

I continued to emphasize this theme during my opening. I began by predicting what Grace's counsel was going to argue:

> One of the things that you are going to hear from the defendants is that their asbestos, the Monokote asbestos that they put in, wouldn't release these fibers and that's what they said back in the 1970s. They said, use our fireproofing even though it contains some asbestos, because the asbestos can't get out. It can't be a danger. And they convinced the people who were working with Mr. Solow putting up the building to use this product.

Throughout my argument I repeated that Grace's position was that Monokote 3 was completely safe. There was some risk in saying this because Grace's counsel might take a different tack and tell the jury that I had been misleading them, but I wanted to smoke out their stance early and lock them into that position before they saw how the trial developed. Opening statements have a great influence on juries; it is their first exposure to what a case is about, and points that are not disputed in the openings are hard to dislodge later. Grace's lawyers would now have to confront directly the issue of the safety of Monokote 3; if they did not, the jury would accept my description of the company's stance and believe that it was changing position if it made a more nuanced argument later.

During my opening statement I also went through a detailed discussion of our basic themes, played clips from videotapes, showed the jury blown-up copies of key documents, and displayed enlarged photographs of what the Monokote 3 looked like as installed at the Solow building (photographs that showed the insulation flaking and breaking off). I also tried to deal with what I knew would be key Grace arguments: that no one had ever gotten ill and that Solow's repeated air tests showed no danger. I therefore tried to explain what the case was *not* about.

This is not a health case.

Nobody is saying that anybody has gotten sick from this asbestos up to this point in time. In fact, one of the things that I think Mr. Solow is most proud of is that when he found out about this danger and understood this danger, he took extraordinary steps to prevent a health crisis from arising. One of the things you are going to hear, both in terms of what he did and in terms of our damages, is a discussion about what he had to do in order to make sure there wasn't any asbestos that got into the bodies of the people that were working in this building.

One of the things he did, of course, was to remove the asbestos when he had the opportunity to do that.

The second thing he did was to install a particular kind of air unit to help make sure that the air quality is excellent in that building.

When James Restivo, representing Grace, rose to respond, he had some difficult choices to make—and only a thirty-minute break between the end of my statement and the beginning of his in which to make them. During my opening his colleagues from Reed Smith and Cahill Gordon were passing him notes about what they thought he ought to say, and as soon as we recessed (and the jury had returned to the jury room), they all huddled in a corner of the courtroom. If it had been me, that would have been the time when I would have been off by myself deciding what to do. Maybe Restivo wanted their contributions, or maybe he thought he had to listen. But it is hard to try a case by committee.

Restivo was an effective, experienced trial lawyer, and his statement marshaled the facts on his side well. (I was particularly glad that I had addressed the issue of the air tests in my opening because he hammered at that point effectively.) However, early in his response he staked out as absolutist a position as to what the case was about as I could have hoped for:

> Point number one and the most important point is this: There is no asbestos hazard and no asbestos contamination in the Solow Building and there never has been.

He had given me the target I wanted. Now all I had to do was destroy it.

After the opening statements it was our turn to present our witnesses and evidence. We began by showing the jury documents that demonstrated how dangerous airborne asbestos fibers were. Grace did not really dispute this, but Restivo in his statement had tried to suggest that a little asbestos wasn't all that bad.

> The air we breathe everyday has asbestos in it. Indeed the average human being carries millions of asbestos particles in his or her lungs. That's because asbestos is all around us. One reason it's all around us is that it's a natural mineral. It is mined from the earth like other minerals. It's not something that is man-made. And so you find it in the air we breathe and the water we drink because it's there naturally.

This was technically true, but it appeared to discount the threat that asbestos actually posed. In response, we introduced extensive evidence of how dangerous asbestos was and why it was necessary to reduce exposure as much as possible. It was important that the jury understood why even a possibility of exposure would lead Solow to undertake the cost of replacing Monokote 3. Also, if Restivo had initially succeeded in convincing the jury that asbestos exposure was not all that serious, and we then changed their minds, they would begin to doubt whether they could trust his other arguments.

Our first witness was Richard Hatfield, an asbestos expert who had worked with the EPA and the City of New York. He had prepared a video that showed the way fibers could be released from Monokote 3, demonstrating that the asbestos in the insulation was in fact friable. On cross-examination Restivo continued to emphasize that Solow's air tests repeatedly showed no detectable asbestos fibers.

Our next witness was Dr. William E. Longo, a second asbestos expert. Longo testified that if Grace had done tests that were available in the 1970s, they would have shown that the asbestos in Monokote 3 posed a potential health hazard. Our third witness, yet another asbestos expert, was William P. Heffernan, a former employee of the EPA and of the United States Public Health Service. He had received the EPA's gold medal (the highest award the agency gave its employees) and after leaving the EPA had been retained by the Defense Research Institute to advise about asbestos hazards in buildings. As we went through the qualifications of each of our experts, we were essentially saying: if the EPA, the U.S. Public Health Service, the Defense Research Institute, and other asbestos manufacturers relied on these people, you should too. Heffernan, like Longo and Hatfield, went on to testify that he had evaluated the Monokote 3 in Solow's building and that the insulation posed a potential health hazard. He also testified that OSHA, EPA, and New York City regulations required special precautions for dealing with Monokote 3—precautions, we argued, that would not have been necessary were it not dangerous.

Following Heffernan, we called Steven Cherniak, Solow Building Company's CEO and former chief financial officer. Cherniak had the care, precision, and patience of an accountant, and I knew he would be a difficult person to cross-examine. He explained his and Solow's concern at the presence of asbestos in 9 West after the passage of New York City regulations that required special procedures for dealing with Monokote 3. He outlined the steps they had taken to determine whether to replace the material, why it was expensive to replace insulation after a building was completed, and the amount that Solow had spent on replacing it and installing special air filters. Cherniak also explained that studies undertaken by major tenants at 9 West had concluded that the Monokote 3 insulation should be removed. This last point was important because Grace's main argument was that Monokote 3 was safe and the expense of removing it unnecessary. Here were respected third parties such as Xerox and the predecessor to J. P. Morgan Chase saying that the asbestos insulation had to be removed.

Cherniak, as I had expected, held up well during cross. However, Restivo was able to remind the jury yet again that Solow's repeated air tests had given the building a clean bill of health.

On October 1 we called Michael Patti—a gruff sixty-three-year-old construction manager who had been one of the owners of the company that installed Monokote 3 at 9 West. My purpose in calling him was to establish that Grace had represented that the insulation was safe at the time it was installed. This was important because we wanted to disprove Grace's contention that Solow had known of any danger at the time of installation. In interviews before his testimony Patti had made clear that Grace had led him to believe that Monokote 3 was safe. However, he also made it clear that he did not want to get in the middle of Solow's fight with Grace, that accusing someone of wrongdoing in court was contrary to his culture, and that he did not really remember exactly what he had, and had not, been told a quarter century earlier. He was not a hostile witness, but I had to tread carefully.

I began by establishing that Patti relied on Grace for information:

Q Who told you what Monokote 3 was like?
A The manufacturer, representatives of the manufacturer.

Q The representatives of Grace?
A Of Grace.

Q And did you rely on what they told you?
A Absolutely.

Q Did you believe you could trust what they told you?
A Yes.

Thus far it was relatively straightforward. Patti could hardly have disagreed. I had shown that he was relying on Grace for information about Monokote 3, but I had not yet put the hard question: what had Grace told him?

I did not want to ask him that directly because I knew from my interview of him that he might well respond that he did not remember. The question needed to be asked in such a way that it would be hard for him to fall back on claimed lack of knowledge. I began:

Q Did they tell you that Monokote 3 was a good fireproofing product?

A Yes.

It would have been hard for Patti to have responded "No" or "I don't remember." In fact, for that reason, the question might have been objected to as "leading."* Consequently, I had to try to guide Patti as much as possible without leading (or at least doing so in such a way that I drew an objection that Justice Wilk would sustain).

Grace's lawyers had not objected to my asking whether the company had represented Monokote 3 as "a good fireproofing product," perhaps because it would have seemed odd to deny it. I might have left it there and argued that such a statement implied that it was safe. However, one of Grace's arguments was that Solow

---

*A leading question is a question, usually one that can be answered "yes" or "no," where the witness knows what answer the examiner wants and needs only to agree. Leading questions are objectionable because they result in testimony framed by the examiner, not by the witness; it is for precisely the same reason that all trial lawyers would prefer to lead whenever possible. Leading questions are permitted when cross-examining a witness called by the other side, or when examining a witness you have called if you can convince the judge that the witness should be ruled "adverse" to you (as, for example, when you call as your witness an officer of the other side). The hurdle for convincing a court that a witness is "adverse" is relatively high. You must show the court that the witness is not neutral and is trying to help the other side. I did not believe there was any way I could make such a claim about Patti.

was on notice that even though Monokote 3 was good insulation, it still possessed whatever potential dangers were inherent in materials that contained asbestos. I needed to address the safety issue directly, even though I could not comfortably predict Patti's answers. "Did they tell you whether or not Monokote 3 was safe?" I asked.

A great answer would have been "Yes, they told me it was safe." A bad answer would have been "I don't remember what they told me." A worse answer would have been "No, they never addressed safety." Patti hesitated less than five seconds, but it was long enough to raise tension in the courtroom and to make Justice Wilk look up from his notes, glance first at the witness, then at me.

"As far as I knew, it was safe," Patti finally answered.

This was not the time to point out that he had avoided my question. I assumed he believed Monokote 3 was safe; what I was asking (and what was important to the case) was whether Grace had represented the product as safe. Instead, I continued as if he had given me exactly the answer I had wanted.

Q And did they ever tell you anything inconsistent with that?

A No.

That was as good as I was going to get, at least for the moment, so I moved on. Later in the examination, however, I returned to the subject to see if I could get stronger testimony.

Q Did anyone from Grace ever tell you whether or not the safety of Monokote 3 had been questioned by anybody?

A Yes.

Q What did they tell you?

A There was a concern about having an amount of asbestos in the product.

Q And did they tell you that they believed that the product was safe?

A At the time, they believed the product was safe.

Q That's what they told you?

A Yes.

Finally I had the testimony I wanted. The last two questions (and particularly the last question) may have been leading, but fortunately there had been no objection. In many ways a trial, like sky-diving, is not inherently difficult; however, both can be terribly unforgiving of even the slightest inattention.

I had one more important point to cover with Patti. We had established earlier in the trial that as Monokote 3 aged, its tendency to crumble and flake and release asbestos fibers increased. This helped explain why even if early air tests might show no detectable asbestos, it could still be important to remove the insulation before it began to release a detectable number of fibers. In order to show that Solow should not be held responsible for knowing that insulation would inevitably deteriorate over time, I wanted to establish that Grace had represented that Monokote 3 would not change as time went by.

Q Did Grace tell you anything about how long Monokote 3
   would last in the building?

A As far as they were concerned, forever.

Q And they told you that?

A Yes.

My entire examination of Patti, including questions about his background and family, took about forty-five minutes. When it was Grace's turn to cross-examine, its lawyers again faced difficult choices with little time to think about them. Should they confront Patti with respect to the two critical points in his testimony? If not, should they cross-examine him at all? If yes, what should they ask?

Grace decided not to confront Patti directly concerning the two key points I had made. It was a reasonable decision. Once having committed himself, he was not the kind of witness to back down. However, Grace did not waive its cross-examination entirely, a more dubious decision. Most lawyers have a difficult time deciding to forgo entirely the chance to question a witness. However, Grace, who had no effective way to undercut either Patti's credibility or his key substantive testimony (and did not even try), kept Patti on the stand for significantly longer than I myself had examined him. This is almost always a mistake, and it was here.

Grace's counsel spent a lot of time establishing that Patti knew that Monokote 3 contained asbestos. However, one of Patti's answers was, "Early on, in discussions, they did tell me there was a trace of asbestos in Monokote." There was no dispute that Patti (and Solow) knew that Monokote 3 contained asbestos. All that the cross succeeded in doing was eliciting testimony that the company had minimized the amount of asbestos in its product.

At the end of the cross Grace was somewhat worse off than it had been at the completion of my examination. Moreover, by using Grace brochures with Patti to underscore that the company had revealed that Monokote 3 contained asbestos, Grace's lawyer gave me the opportunity on redirect to show Patti and the jury brochure pages that Grace had not used. I showed Patti a Grace advertisement which represented that Monokote 3 had only "minimal amounts of asbestos which are locked."

Q. Did you believe that, sir?
A. Yes.

After Patti left the stand, Ed Westbrook examined a former W. R. Grace employee, Edward Kerr. Kerr, seventy-one years old, married fifty-one years with five children and thirteen grandchildren, was an open, friendly witness who was endearingly credible. He had been a Grace district manager responsible for supervising salesmen selling Monokote insulation. Westbrook showed Kerr numerous internal Grace documents discussing the dangers of asbestos. In each case Kerr testified that Grace had not told him, or insofar as he was aware any other salesperson, of the dangers.

Following Kerr we introduced deposition testimony from William Sinacore (a former Grace vice president), called Jack Halliwell (an asbestos consultant for Solow), and introduced the deposition testimony of Reed Wright, a former Grace manufacturing manager. All these witnesses provided evidence of the dangers of asbestos generally and of the Monokote insulation in particular.

Wright also testified about a Grace practice of running manufacturing plants at night so that people in surrounding towns would not see the dark smoke and pollution, including asbestos fibers, that were being emitted. Grace had objected vehemently to the prejudicial character of this evidence and argued that it was irrelevant to the issue of whether or not Monokote insulation was or was not dangerous. However, by arguing that Grace believed Monokote 3 was safe, Grace had made its intent an issue. We were able to convince Justice Wilk that its practice of running plants at night to escape detection of illegal pollution was relevant to the company's state of mind.

After we completed the reading of Wright's deposition, Ed Westbrook examined Dr. Henry A. Anderson, the chief medical officer for Occupational and Environmental Medicine of the Wisconsin Division of Public Health. Dr. Anderson testified that even small incremental exposure to asbestos was cause for concern and provided graphic illustrations of how the inhalation of asbestos fibers hurt and killed people. He also explained how it took years, sometimes thirty to forty, before the harm caused by asbestos inhalation manifested itself—making clear that the fact that no one had yet fallen sick from exposure to asbestos at the Solow Building did not mean that there was no danger.

Finally I called Sheldon Solow to the stand. Although lacking the expertise to testify whether Monokote 3 was or was not actually dangerous, Solow was probably our most important witness. It was critical to convince the jury that Solow had not been aware of the dangers of Monokote 3 at the time it was installed. The testimony of Michael Patti and Steve Cherniak had given us a big leg up, but the jury would want to hear from Solow himself. We also needed to convince the jury that the decision to replace the Monokote insulation was a reasonable one. This should have been primarily a question of the safety or lack of safety of the fireproofing, but the jury would be influenced by whether they thought Solow (who made the ultimate decision) was himself reasonable and credible.

In addition, Cherniak might be the CEO, but Solow was the owner—it was his name on the door. It was important that the jury like (or at least respect and trust) this billionaire landlord. New York City is not a landlord-friendly venue, but we had two things going for us. One was Solow's personality. Tall, good-looking, and elegant in his tailored suits and custom shirts, he did not look (or talk) like the jurors, but he had natural warmth, honesty, and directness. Moreover, then in his seventies, he had lived the prototype of the American dream. His father was a bricklayer whose family emigrated to this country from Russia, and whose success led to his ownership of several buildings. Unfortunately, Solow's father lost his buildings in 1929, shortly after his son was born, and went back to being a mason.

Solow went to P.S. 131 in Brooklyn and worked for a general contractor as a bricklayer himself during high school and after he graduated. (I had worked as a hod carrier for a year between high school and college, so I knew firsthand how hard he had had to work in those early years.) He was still a young man when he became a general contractor himself. His first building was a garden apartment complex in Far Rockaway, Queens, that he still owns. He was just turning forty when he began assembling the land for what became 9 West Fifty-seventh. By 1999, like his friend Donald Trump, Solow was one of the richest, most successful, and best-known builders and owners of high-quality commercial and residential properties in New York City. But his humble beginnings, generosity (he had given millions to charities), and grandfatherly demeanor were an antidote to the natural gulf between him and the jurors.

Another thing we had going for us was that the jury did not have to embrace Solow; they had only to like him better than Grace. If we could not accomplish that, I told him the evening before his testimony, he should go back to laying bricks and I should go back to carrying them.

Despite my confidence in Sheldon, I had waited until late in our case to call him. Grace had more material to use on him than it had for our earlier witnesses, and I did not want to risk an early setback. I wanted the jurors already convinced of the facts to which he would testify before he took the stand. Indeed, Solow was such a crucial witness that had he testified early, before his testimony had been bolstered and confirmed by others, and if the jury had concluded that he was not believable, our case might have been lost.

After covering Solow's background, I began with the decision to install Monokote 3.

Q And did they talk with you about the fireproofing that had been selected?

A They did because there was a sentence in the contract that mentioned something about Monokote 3 and Monokote 4, and I knew nothing of Monokote 3 or Monokote 4. And I asked what it was about.

And they said, well, Monokote 3 has some small traces of asbestos and for some reason Grace is now going to produce Monokote 4 which does not have any asbestos at all.

I said, well, it says in here when it's available. Well, they told us, it's going to be available very soon.

I said, are they both safe? They said yes.

Q Why was it important to ask them whether or not the fireproofing was safe?

A I was wondering why there was the change, why did they want to go from 3 to 4. They said they are both safe.

Q Was it important to you to know that fireproofing was safe?

A Absolutely.

Q If they had told you that the fireproofing was defective
in any way, what would you have done?
A I would not use it.

I then turned to the question of when and why Solow had concluded there was a problem with Monokote 3. He explained that in
the middle 1980s New York City had passed Local Law 76, which
established strict procedures for dealing with asbestos-containing
materials, defined to include Monokote 3. He promptly retained
experts to examine the issue, and they reported that Monokote 3
did pose health risks, which would increase over time as the insulation deteriorated. He also testified that major tenants independently
hired experts to investigate the safety of Monokote 3 and that they
too called for its removal.

Solow held up well under cross-examination. Whenever
Restivo pointed out that he had known that Monokote 3 contained
asbestos, he was able to emphasize that he had been told that it was
safe, and that the asbestos in it was "minimal" and "locked in."
Restivo's best points were that the air tests never showed any detectable level of asbestos fibers, and that Solow and Cherniak had repeatedly assured tenants that there was no danger. Solow's answers
were: first, it was important to remove the asbestos before there was
any actual harm; and second, even before the insulation deteriorated
or was disturbed by renovations, asbestos fibers would be released if
the insulation were subjected to water (resulting, for example, from
a leak or burst pipe) or an accidental fire.

As we approached the end of our case, we had established two
of our three themes—that Grace had represented that Monokote
3 was safe and that Solow had believed those representations. We
had also introduced substantial evidence that Monokote 3 was not
safe, and on balance I believed we were ahead on this theme as
well. However, even with our witnesses, Grace had managed to
introduce some evidence supporting the safety of Monokote 3,
and I knew that there would be more such evidence coming when
its case began.

Solow's testimony ended October 7, and the next day we completed our case. We ended by reading selections from depositions of former Grace employees. Such excerpts are not as interesting to a jury as live testimony, but they are exceedingly safe. Because you are making selections from testimony that has already been given, you know exactly what you are going to get; there are no surprises. On balance, our case had gone well. We did not want, or need, to take chances at this point. There would be time enough for that when Grace's case started.

Grace's first witness was Dr. Richard Lee, an asbestos expert who testified that Monokote 3 was safe, and that Solow's own repeated air tests showed this. To counter Lee's testimony we sought to rely on the evidence that we had found during discovery that Grace had removed asbestos-containing materials from its own buildings even in the absence of positive air tests. Restivo and his colleague Lawrence Flatley argued strenuously that such evidence was irrelevant since the materials being removed were not Monokote 3, and that the evidence was highly prejudicial.

THE COURT: Certainly, it's an effort to prejudice the jury; otherwise he wouldn't bother.

MR. FLATLEY: Because they are not substantially similar circumstances.

THE COURT: Their position is that asbestos is asbestos, and if it gets into your lungs it's not a good thing—and that when you recognize the existence of asbestos, you are saying get rid of it and it doesn't matter, you know, if it's in Monokote or if it's in something else; it's the same poison.

Restivo tried (unsuccessfully) to bail his colleague out:

MR. RESTIVO: Then the issue becomes do they have evidence of W. R. Grace removing Monokote

from one of its buildings for reasons other
than renovation and the answer is no.

THE COURT: No, I don't think that's the issue. I think the
issue you have is, when you detect the po-
tential for asbestos in the air, even if it is not
in the air, are you also removing it from your
building?

As Grace's case progressed, Restivo and Flatley continued to
introduce testimony that indicated that Monokote 3 was safe. I
could tell that, unlike when Grace addressed other issues, the jurors were paying close attention. In cases where jurors are allowed
to take notes, you can tell a lot about what they find important by
when they take them; as a result, it is my practice in such cases to
have a paralegal assigned to sit in the courtroom and write down
which jurors take notes and when. However, not every judge permits note talking, and in the *Grace* case Justice Wilk decided not to
permit it; as a result, my paralegal had the more difficult and subjective task of trying to record when jurors were most attentive.

As the case neared its conclusion Grace concentrated on the
question of the safety of Monokote 3. We had the burden of proof,
so if the jury decided it could not figure out whether or not
Monokote 3 was safe, we would lose. The most important witness
for Grace on this issue was Dr. Morton Corn. Dr. Corn had served
in the Public Health Service, as a professor at Johns Hopkins University, as director of the Division of Environmental Health Engineering in Johns Hopkins's Graduate School of Public Health, as
assistant secretary of labor with responsibility for OSHA in the
Ford administration, as a delegate to the World Health Organization, and as chairman of the American Conference of Government
Industrial Hygienists. He had been retained as an asbestos consultant by the U.S. Atomic Energy Commission, the Library of Congress, the Department of Energy, the Department of State, OSHA,
and the United States Bureau of Mines. It was quite a list. Here, at

last, was a Grace witness whose qualifications matched, indeed exceeded, those of our experts. In addition, Corn's impressive résumé was matched by a confident demeanor and presentation.

His testimony on direct was powerful support for Grace's case. Two of the jurors who had seemed by body language, and by the timing of their interest in the evidence, to be most favorable to Solow glanced uncomfortably in our direction as the testimony progressed. Perhaps most impressive was Corn's statement that he had personally tested Monokote 3 to determine whether it released asbestos fibers into the air and concluded that it did not. I knew that he was a professional witness for asbestos companies, that his science was flawed and overstated, and that the studies and reports on which he relied were contradicted by other studies and reports. And yet, as I listened to him, even with all the knowledge I had, I had to admit that he was persuasive. Not for the first time I reflected on the difficulty posed for a juror who is asked to sort out conflicting opinions by well-credentialed, dueling experts.

If he had not been subject to cross-examination, Dr. Corn would have been a killer witness. However, he was, and I had prepared a surprise for the good professor.

I began with a subject that was not a surprise—the fact that Dr. Corn was a regular paid witness for asbestos manufacturers, dependent on the money they paid him for the lifestyle he and his wife enjoyed. I brought out that he had personally been paid more than half a million dollars for what he called "asbestos litigation fees." I also brought out that asbestos manufacturers had aided him in other ways, including through grants to his university that, as he finally admitted, were ultimately paid to his wife. In each case Corn made the examination longer and more painful than it had to be. For example, with respect to his own payment he initially claimed not to be able to remember this amount. When it was finally dragged out of him, the jurors were even more focused on it than they would have been had he simply answered the question immediately. In addition, it was likely that jurors would not believe that

he had initially forgotten an amount that large, which further un-
dermined his credibility.

I took Corn through EPA reports that were at odds with his
conclusions, making him repeatedly tell the jury that he disagreed
with the EPA. The reports were already in evidence, and in a sense
I was merely repeating what the jurors had been told before.
However, I wanted to remind them of the EPA statements helpful
to us and to make clear that the opinions of Grace's expert (who
during his direct had tried to make a point of how mainstream his
views were) conflicted with EPA reports. I also confronted Corn
with written recommendations he had given IBM and the Aus-
tralian Embassy recommending removal of asbestos-containing
materials even in the absence of detectable airborne fibers—
reinforcing the evidence from Grace's own files that clean air tests
do not mean that insulation should not be removed.

Our best evidence was a videotape that I did not believe Corn
knew we had. During discovery, Grace had produced a large number of tapes dealing with asbestos studies they had done. Since the
tapes did not show the results of these studies, but only showed
people as they conducted their research, the tapes were largely irrelevant. Because of the large number of tapes and their apparent
irrelevance, I suspected that either Grace's lawyers would not have
reviewed them at all, or that the review would have been done by
a paralegal or junior lawyer who would not have noticed anything
significant.

We *had* reviewed the tapes, however, and we had noticed
something. One of the tapes showed Dr. Corn performing the
tests that he said showed that asbestos fibers would not be released
into the air by someone walking on dust that contained asbestos.
This test was significant for our case because of the evidence that
Monokote 3 flaked and crumbled, resulting in dust containing asbestos. What was important about the tape was what Dr. Corn
was shown doing and wearing while he conducted the tests.

As I played the video for the jury with Dr. Corn sitting increasingly uncomfortably in the witness stand, the jurors saw a man, who

Dr. Corn admitted as I froze the tape was him, dressed in a moon suit walking with obvious care and a secure oxygen supply. The message was clear: when Dr. Corn's own safety was at issue, he treated this stuff as extremely dangerous. The effect on the jurors was palpable. Some shook their heads, others looked hard at the witness. The two who we believed (correctly, based on post-trial statements) were favorable to us, and who had seemed disconcerted by Corn's direct testimony, now glanced at our table and smiled.

Embarrassed and uncomfortable with his loss of credibility, as the cross continued Corn provided substantive concessions that he might not otherwise have made. For example, he testified, "Cementitious I define as cement-like." This was a devastating definition for Grace which had repeatedly represented that Monokote 3 was "cementitious." The jury could see for themselves, both in the photographs we had introduced and from the double-wrapped transparent bags of Monokote 3 collected from the Solow building, that Monokote 3 was soft, flaky, and easily crumbled. It was certainly not "cement-like." Dr. Corn also admitted, contrary to Grace's contentions and to the thrust of his own direct testimony, that the asbestos in Monokote 3 was "friable" (which had previously been defined for the jury as "releasing fibers").

Corn finally escaped from the stand Friday afternoon, October 22, one month after we had completed picking a jury. Although there remained two days of testimony the following week (into which we squeezed seven witnesses), the evidence upon which the jury would decide the case was in, and both sides knew it.

We presented our closing arguments October 28 and 29, with Grace's counsel going first. When it was my turn, I began by covering all the evidence that showed that the asbestos in Monokote 3 was friable and dangerous, and that Grace knew it at the time it sold Monokote 3 for installation in the Solow building. I then turned to Grace's alternative argument that, if its product was in fact unsafe, Solow had knowingly assumed that risk when he approved the purchase of Monokote 3. After my cross-examination of Dr. Corn had undercut Grace's contention that its product was safe, Grace had tried to resurrect its argument that Solow knew about any danger in 1972. I argued in response:

> Now, there's a sense in which this is one of the most outrageous arguments that Grace makes. It is a very good blame-the-victim argument.
>
> It says, Mr. Solow, shame on you for believing us, because throughout the process Grace told Mr. Solow and Mr. Patti exactly what they told you; hey, Monokote is safe, perfectly safe. Sure, it had a trace of asbestos, but it is locked in, it can never be released.
>
> And in 1969 and 1970, before the EPA had come out, before OSHA had come out, before the published studies had come out, before Grace's files had been revealed, Mr. Solow and Mr. Patti believed Grace.
>
> And so what Grace comes in here and says to you is that because they believed us, shame on them, it's their fault.

I went on to remind the jurors that what Grace told Solow about the safety of Monokote 3 in the 1970s was "what Grace's lawyers were telling you" during the trial. I noted that Grace's own witnesses had admitted that the company encouraged Michael Patti, Sheldon Solow, and others to rely on Grace as to whether Monokote 3 was safe, just as Grace's lawyers had asked the jury to rely on them and their witnesses during the trial.

> And so, when you think about Grace's argument that blames the victim, think about what it really is. It's an argument that says Mr. Solow was wrong to trust us when we said to him what we're saying to you, the jury, now.
>
> Because they are saying to you exactly what they said to Mr. Solow. They are saying it's locked in, it can't be released, it's like reinforced concrete, it's perfectly safe.

They are saying all the same things to you that they said to Mr. Solow, and yet they are saying Mr. Solow was negligent, Mr. Solow was at fault for believing them.

And you have a lot of things Mr. Solow didn't have. You have the EPA's report, you have OSHA's report, you have the documents from their own files, you have the expert testimony that you've heard from both sides.

So you've got a lot more available to you because of this trial and because of our discovery process that allows us to do what Mr. Solow and Mr. Patti couldn't do—go into Grace's files and find the truth.

Following closing arguments, Judge Wilk instructed the jury on the legal principles that it was to use in deciding the case. The instructions were completed by noon on October 29, and the jury retired to begin deliberations. Each side put on the record their objections to the judge's instructions, then walked two blocks to Chinatown for lunch. When we returned, we found that the jury had already sent in a note requesting that certain evidence be brought to the jury room. What they asked for was interesting.

The first piece of evidence requested was "Double bag specimen of Monokote 3." This was encouraging because the specimen showed how soft and apparently friable Monokote 3 was. Also encouraging was the fact that the jury asked for a large chart we had used in plaintiff's closing arguments that detailed the evidence supporting our case. However, the third piece of evidence requested was "Contract with handwritten addendum using MK3 until MK4 was approved." Were jurors, we wondered, interpreting that contract as evidence that Solow was aware of the dangers of Monokote 3 when it was initially installed? The deliberations continued all afternoon on October 29 until the jury recessed for the weekend.

On October 30 Mary and I drove to Connecticut to watch

Mary Regency play soccer. On the way, Mary asked how long I thought the jury would be out.

"If they come back Monday, we're probably in trouble," I told her. "It will probably take a couple of days to reach and decide all the questions they have to decide for a plaintiffs' verdict." (A very quick verdict is almost always against the side with the burden of proof.) I went on to speculate that we could hope for a favorable verdict Tuesday or Wednesday, or maybe Thursday. No verdict by Thursday would suggest that the jury was sharply divided.

The week of November 1 there were several additional requests for particular documents or to have the testimony of particular witnesses read. Some of the evidence seemed to favor us, some seemed to favor Grace, and some we could not figure out why they wanted it (or even what we had been thinking when we introduced it). As the deliberations dragged on, our lunches in Chinatown increased in length.

The amount of time juries devote to their deliberations varies widely, and five days of deliberation was not out of line for a five-week jury trial. However, when the jury left on Thursday evening without reaching a verdict, both sides began to wonder whether the jury would hang (not be able to agree on a verdict) and we would have to try the case all over again.

Shortly after ten Friday morning we were chatting informally with Justice Wilk about the relative merits of jury trials compared to bench trials when the bailiff announced that the jury had reached a decision. There had been a number of exciting moments during the trial, but few moments are more electrifying than when jurors file into the courtroom to deliver their verdict in an important case.

The judgment we received ($23 million including interest) was not everything we asked for, but it was the largest ever against Grace on a single asbestos claim. As I left the courtroom to fly to Washington, I reminded the team of the need to get the formal judgment entered as soon as possible. Once this was done, Grace would have to put up a bond for its amount—ensuring that after all the appeals were completed there would be money to pay the judgment.*

In November 1999 W. R. Grace was still a profitable and successful company, and its lawyers tried to get us to agree that a bond was not necessary. I politely declined. Grace faced considerable other asbestos litigation, and I did not want to assume its financial position would be the same some years later when its appeals were decided. Moreover, the record in our trial would now be available to other plaintiffs, and our result might embolden them to escalate their demands. If it turned out that there was ultimately more to be paid than Grace had, I did not want to have Sheldon lose his place in line—particularly after all he had spent and gone through to get there.

It was, as it turned out, good advice. The day after April Fool's Day 2001, with the defendant's appeals of Solow's (by then bonded) $23 million judgment still under way, W. R. Grace went bankrupt.

---

*If a bond is not posted, a plaintiff who wins a judgment at trial can attach a defendant's assets and collect the amount of the judgment immediately, without waiting for the appellate process to be completed.

9

The Auction House Scandal

For more than two centuries, Christie's and Sotheby's have dominated the business of auctioning fine art, rare books, and expensive antiques. Sotheby's was founded in the 1740s by Samuel Baker, a London book dealer; Christie's was founded two decades later in the same city by James Christie, a friend and patron of Thomas Chippendale and Thomas Gainsborough. Ever since, whether you were Catherine the Great building a collection of paintings, Napoleon's heirs selling his hoard of rare books, an Arab sheik on a shopping spree, a museum expanding or paring its collection, or a corporate baron seeking culture to go with newfound wealth, the road has usually led to Sotheby's or Christie's or both. As time went on, the two houses opened offices in other countries, expanded their wares, and discreetly moved into the computer age. But the business was much the same in the 1980s as it had been two hundred years before, with a heavy reliance on relationships, image, and a genteel rivalry that the companies were careful not to let degenerate into excessive discounting.

For more than 150 years the houses avoided competition through a gentleman's agreement whereby Sotheby's auctioned books and manuscripts and Christie's sold paintings and jewels. When in the 1900s the two began to compete, they did so with restraint. They were an effective duopoly, and each recognized there was little gain and much potential pain if either began to discount like common merchants.

Both competition and attempts to avoid it are rooted in self-interest. Individual competitors have an incentive to increase their business at the expense of rivals through lower prices or other unmatched incentives, and in an industry with many companies, no single firm can safely fail to compete because it will lose business to those who do. However, if companies can agree that they will all charge the same high price, they all win, while the consumer loses. This is why price-fixing has been a federal criminal offense for more than a hundred years—and was outlawed in a variety of ways for centuries before that.

Where there is only one company in a market, price-fixing is unnecessary because there is no one to undercut the monopolist. That is why a monopoly is so highly prized by companies and so distrusted by consumers. Where there are two principal competitors (a duopoly) or even a few principal competitors (an oligopoly), it is also often possible for suppliers to have the benefits of high prices without actually having to meet and agree. That is partly because each company recognizes that if it reduces prices, its rival will follow suit; partly because it is relatively easy to keep track of what the other is doing; and partly because the likelihood of common interests and outlooks is greater, the fewer the companies involved. Moreover, if required, a wink or a frown or a few well-chosen words over lunch or at a sports match can often be counted on to get things back on track without too much danger of the oligopolists' getting caught.

Increasing the number of companies that must be spoken to in order to avoid outbreaks of competition, or to reduce competition if it breaks out, multiplies the chances of detection exponentially. Where two companies dominate a market, the likelihood that competition can be avoided without a formal price-fixing agreement is greatest. When you add, in the case of Sotheby's and Christie's, a couple of centuries of working together in a culture that prizes cooperation and stability more than cutthroat competition, you have a business that, as long as the status quo is not shaken up, should be able to prosper without the necessity of price-fixing agreements.

In the early 1990s, however, four events combined to shake up the cozy auction house business. First, both houses were suffering financially from a worldwide recession that reduced demand for their high-end services as well as the prices at which items were sold at the auctions that did take place. Since the companies were paid a percentage of the sale (or "hammer") price of items sold, the companies' earnings declined sharply. Second, with many of their costs being relatively fixed, both houses were chasing with increasing intensity the handful of collections that were sure to generate active bids—Jackie Onassis's estate, Barbra Streisand's art and collectibles, the Duke and Duchess of Windsor's personal effects, an important Renoir or Van Gogh. Third, Sotheby's had traditionally maintained an edge in sales and profits over its younger rival. Now, through increasingly creative courting of big-ticket sellers, Christie's was threatening to equal or even surpass its rival. Fourth (and at least as important as anything else), both Sotheby's and Christie's were now being run by people with more to prove and less of a common culture to fall back on than their predecessors had.

In 1983 Sotheby's had been purchased by self-made real estate and shopping mall multimillionaire Alfred Taubman. By all accounts Taubman loved Sotheby's and the social cachet it brought him. Initially the auction house continued to be run by staff Taubman had inherited and their natural successors. However, in 1993 he made a decision that would alter the company's future and his own, replacing his old-school chief executive, Michael Ainslie, with Diana Dwyer Brooks.

"DeDe" Brooks, as she was known to friend and critic alike, was decidedly not old school in manner, although she served as a member of the Yale Corporation and on a variety of other prestigious boards. The product of a well-to-do family whose fortunes had declined, she had an appetite for accomplishment—and the intelligence, drive, and presence to carry it off. Her take-no-prisoners approach upset some customers and employees, but she could also exhibit genuine charm. Whatever her other strengths or weaknesses, Brooks's personality meant that she could not, would not, tolerate seeing Sotheby's slip behind Christie's on her watch.

Christie's too changed hands in 1993 when Christopher Davidge became its chief executive officer. Having spent his entire career of almost thirty years at Christie's, Davidge was in one sense the consummate insider. Indeed, his grandfather and both his parents had worked for the company. However, Davidge lacked the social pedigree of his predecessors, and the fact that his mother had been employed as a secretary at the firm and that he himself had started as a printer's assistant seemed to those who knew him to be more a matter of embarrassment than pride.

Whether out of loyalty to his family's long-term employer, a desire to prove himself, or simply the drive to do the job he had prepared for over more than a quarter century, Davidge embarked on a campaign to surpass Sotheby's that was at odds with the genteel combination of cooperation and rivalry that had characterized his predecessors' tenure.

Whatever the causes, from 1993 to 1995 Sotheby's and Christie's engaged in unusually intense competition (reduced commissions, financial guarantees, elaborate catalogs and events, donations to sellers' favorite charities) to induce sellers to consign their goods for sale. That competition, however, was sharply reduced in the spring of 1995. In March, Christie's announced that it would charge sellers a nonnegotiable sliding scale commission. A month later Sotheby's made the same announcement. In the months that followed many other incentives offered sellers began to disappear as well.

At the time it was not clear that there was anything wrong, or at least anything illegal. Christie's was certainly free to change its commission practices, and it would have made sense for Sotheby's, even without an agreement, to follow. Now both companies made more money; had Sotheby's not matched, Christie's would almost certainly have reverted to its prior practices—with the result that both companies would have made less.

It turned out of course that there was something very wrong, indeed criminal, in what had taken place. For whatever reason, Brooks and Davidge were unwilling even to test a unilateral increase in commissions without an explicit agreement from the other side that the other would follow suit and not try to take advantage of the increase by stealing its customers. In a series of secret meetings beginning in early 1993, the two agreed to fix the prices they charged sellers and to reduce or eliminate financial guarantees, contributions to sellers' charities, and other incentives.

The agreement to fix sellers' commissions was relatively easy to monitor; each could tell if the other was "cheating." The advantage of a policeable agreement is that each party tends to abide by it because they know that if they do not their departures will be apparent and will result in retaliation. By comparison it was much more difficult to detect cheating in offering other incentives. As a result, the two houses adhered closely to the agreement to fix sellers' commissions, but Christie's in particular departed from the other agreements when it thought that its lapses might go undetected. I later read with a mixture of sadness and amusement in DeDe Brooks's papers the outrage this trustee of Yale and the Deerfield Academy felt when she discovered that her partner in crime had occasionally cheated on their illegal agreement.

In 1997 the U.S. Department of Justice began investigating how Sotheby's and Christie's set their sellers' commissions. For two years the investigation proceeded slowly. Brooks and Davidge repeatedly and passionatcly denied any collusion, and although document subpoenas were issued, many of the papers were outside the United States and difficult to obtain. Moreover, the key agreements were oral. The testimony of a senior employee of one of the two companies was critical, but such cooperation, with its career-ending implications, was unlikely under normal circumstances.

In late 1999 the conspiracy of silence began to unravel. First, Christie's former general counsel, Patricia Hambrecht, was forced to resign following charges that she made untrue statements in sworn affidavits submitted in connection with a dispute over the valuation of the estate of photographer Robert Mapplethorpe. In the wake of her resignation Hambrecht provided Christie's lawyers with evidence that Davidge and Brooks had met and discussed prices.

More evidence soon followed, including the revelation from Christie's chairman, Lord Hindlip, that in December 1997 (shortly after the Justice Department investigation had gotten under way) Davidge had approached Hindlip requesting a written commitment that Christie's would pay Davidge the balance to be earned under his contract should he be fired or forced to resign because of antitrust charges. Davidge's request was both an implicit admission that there was more to be concerned with than was apparent on the surface and a veiled threat that without Christie's guarantee he might reveal embarrassing secrets. Lord Hindlip agreed to Davidge's request but did not reveal either the request, or the granting of it, until two years later.

As the evidence mounted, Christie's lawyers faced a dilemma. On the one hand, little of what they were beginning to discover was, as yet, known by the Department of Justice—and there was some chance that the prosecutors would end their investigation without ever learning what Christie's lawyers now knew. The lawyers had no legal or ethical obligation to reveal what they had discovered; on the contrary, they were bound to keep it confidential unless released to reveal it by their client. On the other hand, they knew that their client's position was perilous. Price-fixing is a felony that carries heavy criminal fines for companies and jail sentences for individuals.

Christie's lawyers wanted to apply for amnesty under the same Justice Department program that Rhone-Poulenc had taken advantage of a year earlier in the *Vitamins* case. But to qualify, Christie's had to demonstrate that it was revealing everything it knew, a demonstration that could not be made without the cooperation of Christopher Davidge.

As the lawyers returned to Davidge with each new revelation

he began to feel increasingly isolated—fearing for his job, his fortune, and even his freedom. He turned to William J. ("Joe") Linklater of Baker and McKenzie, one of the most highly respected criminal attorneys in the United States. It may have been the best decision he ever made. Linklater, who has a reputation for keeping clients with serious problems out of jail, quickly sized up the danger his client faced and what to do about it.

Davidge, a London resident, was warned to stay out of the U.S. until the matter was resolved. (Because price-fixing is a civil, not a criminal, violation in the United Kingdom, extradition of its citizens to the United States in connection with such charges is ordinarily not possible.)

Linklater also began to negotiate a severance package for Davidge that would provide him with financial security if, as appeared increasingly likely, his career was coming to an end. Knowing as much as it now did about Davidge's conduct, Christie's might have been reluctant to send him on his way a rich man. However, despite his problems, Davidge was not without leverage. He and Linklater let it be known that Davidge had a personal file of critical documents in his London apartment outside the reach of U.S. prosecutors unless and until he decided to produce them. Linklater also made clear that Davidge could always seek amnesty for himself, leaving Christie's (and other company executives, including perhaps Lord Hindlip) to face criminal charges.

A deal was struck in December 1999. Davidge would produce his files to Christie's lawyers and cooperate in any amnesty bid Christie's made. In return the auction house would pay him 2 million pounds with the promise of 3 million more. The agreement at Christie's insistence contained a representation by Davidge that he had not breached his duty to Christie's during his tenure and a provision relieving the company of its obligation to pay the last 3 million pounds if it turned out that Davidge had violated the law and brought Christie's into "disrepute." It was a provision that the company may have thought it could point to later to refute charges that it was knowingly paying off a felon; in fact, given the state of

Christie's knowledge at the time, the statement merely underscored what it was doing.

Almost immediately Davidge's personal file was turned over to
Christie's lawyers, Skadden Arps. The documents were even more
incriminating than Davidge had hinted, and the Skadden Arps
lawyers immediately called the Justice Department's lead prosecutor, John Greene, to negotiate an amnesty. During his initial meeting with Christie's lawyers, Greene, an experienced prosecutor,
succeeded reasonably well in masking his glee. Afterward, however,
neither he nor his staff could restrain themselves. After a two-year
investigation that had made little progress, here was the mother
lode. Moreover, as Greene knew, once Christie's had amnesty the
company had every incentive to help the prosecutors go after its
competitor tooth and nail.

On January 29, 2000, the *Financial Times* reported Christie's
cooperation with the Justice Department, setting off two races.
One was for Brooks, Sotheby's itself, and any other participants in
the conspiracy to try to do their own deals. Only the first conspirator in the door gets amnesty (although Christie's was able to negotiate amnesty for itself and its present employees, including
Davidge). Subsequent deals would involve guilty pleas and probably jail time. Nevertheless, in such matters the rule is the earlier the
deal, the better it will be. Sotheby's and Brooks therefore had to reverse course rapidly. Brooks in particular was exposed. She was the
principal remaining conspirator, and jail seemed inevitable—an as-
tonishing fall from grace for one of the most visible and admired
women executives of the 1990s.

Also potentially exposed was Alfred Taubman, Sotheby's
seventy-five-year-old chairman. He was not at the meetings in
which Brooks and Davidge agreed to fix prices, and the documents did not say that he had ordered or approved what had been
done. However, there was some evidence from which Taubman's
knowledge of the conspiracy might be inferred, and his wealth and
position made him a fat target. He and his lawyers discussed the
possibility of a plea. Given his age and limited involvement, he

could likely have received a fine, probation, and no jail time in return for an early plea and cooperation in making the case against Sotheby's and Brooks.

Taubman, however, was convinced that he had done nothing wrong. His reputation was that of a tough but exceedingly ethical businessman. That could be viewed as evidence that he would not have been a party to price-fixing. It could also be viewed as a reason why, whether or not involved, he would have been loath to admit it.

Apart from his own guilt or innocence Taubman may have been reluctant to turn on the company to which he was so devoted (and of which he was still a large stockholder) or on the woman whom he viewed more as a daughter than as a protégé. Whatever the reason, it was a mistake. Christie's and Davidge had already made Sotheby's conviction inevitable; additional testimony by Taubman would not do incremental damage. And the main consequence of his reluctance to inform on his protégé was to give Brooks an opportunity to cut a deal based on an offer to testify that Taubman himself played a key role in the conspiracy. Years before Sheldon Solow, who collected art as well as buildings, had told me (in connection with our efforts to recover what he had paid for a counterfeit Calder purchased through Sotheby's) that Brooks was tougher and less scrupulous than her mentor and that Taubman made a mistake deferring so much to her. It was a view that before the case was over Taubman would come to share.

The second race started by Christie's admission of price-fixing was the class action stampede that regularly follows such announcements. In the weeks following January 29, 2000, numerous firms filed suits on behalf of customers of Sotheby's and Christie's. The cases, all of which were filed in federal court in New York City, were assigned to Judge Lewis Kaplan. Himself a trial lawyer before being appointed to the bench, Kaplan has a well-deserved reputation as an intelligent and creative jurist. He also has a reputation for being very tough on unprepared lawyers and for moving his cases unusually rapidly. Lawyers who appeared before him colloquially referred to Judge Kaplan's "rocket docket" with a mixture of respect and foreboding.

In February 2000 Kimberly Schultz, a young lawyer in my firm's New Hampshire office, brought the press reports of Christie's admission of price-fixing to the attention of Richard Drubel, the senior lawyer in that office. Less than a year after I had formed my new firm in May 1997, I had recruited Richard, one of the leading trial lawyers in the country specializing in representing plaintiffs, to join me.

Richard immediately recognized the potential for an auction house class action, but the case was not the kind our firm ordinarily brought. Although we were one of the few national law firms that regularly represented both plaintiffs and defendants in class actions, we limited such cases to a few a year because of other demands on our resources and our desire only to take on cases in which we had confidence and where we thought we could make a difference. We were generally reluctant to file essentially me-too lawsuits following government guilty pleas.

In addition, I had publicly taken the position that in cases that were commenced only after admissions of criminal violations, fee awards should be a smaller percentage than the typical 25 to 30 percent of a recovery since such cases did not require either the risk or effort of cases like the *Vitamins* antitrust litigation. Whatever the merits of my position, the last thing most plaintiffs' lawyers wanted was a lead counsel who could be expected to recommend to the court a fee lower than the norm. This meant that it would be unlikely that we would be included in a negotiated leadership structure, and I was ambivalent about spending time and resources fighting our way into the case.

On the other hand, the case was certainly interesting, and one aspect of it particularly intrigued both Richard and myself. Christie's had admitted, and the Justice Department would pursue Sotheby's for, price-fixing of sellers' commissions only. However, in addition to their 1995 increase of sellers' commissions the companies had earlier increased the commissions they charged buyers. In November

1992 Sotheby's had announced that effective January 1, 1993, it would increase buyers' fees from 10 percent to 15 percent of the first $50,000 of the purchase price. Shortly thereafter, Christie's followed suit. These increases were particularly significant because buyers' commissions represent much more revenue for the auction houses than sellers' fees.

The government's charges, and defendants' pleas and admissions, would not help a claim that the companies had illegally fixed buyer commissions. Indeed a court and jury might well conclude that if the Department of Justice had investigated and charged defendants with sellers' commission price-fixing only, that was the extent of the wrongdoing. Another problem with a possible claim concerning buyers' fees was that during the two-to three-year period immediately following the 1992–93 buyers' commission increase, Christie's and Sotheby's had competed fiercely on sellers' commissions and other perks and services—a level of competition that was more, not less, intense than that which had historically characterized the companies' relationship, and a fact arguably inconsistent with collusion. On the other hand, there were examples in other industries where companies had conspired on certain prices, terms, or conditions but continued to compete on others. And we questioned whether Sotheby's would have risked alienating buyers by unilaterally increasing buyers' commissions without any assurance that Christie's would follow.

The buyers' commission issue was the kind of claim where our firm, with its extensive experience in litigating complex antitrust issues, could offer significant added value. It also made the case more challenging and more likely to justify a large fee were we successful. After a number of discussions, Richard and I decided to file a case teamed with Richard's prior firm Susman Godfrey.*

During February 2000 the plaintiffs' counsel in the various actions met to negotiate a proposed leadership structure. A ma-

---

*Like our firm, Susman Godfrey regularly took cases to trial, and its chairman, Steve Susman, was an outstanding trial lawyer whom I had known for more than twenty years.

jority proposed five lead counsel that did not include either our firm or Susman Godfrey. That recommendation was submitted to the court, and we submitted our competing proposal in which we asked that our two firms, together with a third firm to be selected by the court, be named lead counsel. Another plaintiffs' lawyer who was not included in either of these proposals, and who submitted his own plan to the court, was Fred Furth. Fred is a legendary trial lawyer who has led successful plaintiff's cases for four decades. He is also a confirmed risk-taker who still flies his own planes (including a Citation X and a seaplane that he lands in the most remarkable places) and who twenty years ago founded what is now Chalk Hill Vineyards in California.

Following a hearing, Judge Kaplan on February 23 designated six law firms as interim lead counsel while the court considered the matter further. The six included the five firms proposed by a majority of plaintiff's counsel plus Fred Furth. Kaplan authorized the six firms to file an amended consolidated complaint, to commence discovery, and in general to prepare the case for settlement or trial. Our offer to work with the interim lead counsel, though supported by Furth, was politely declined.

On March 15, 2000, interim lead counsel filed an amended complaint and during March and April conducted informal discovery and commenced preliminary settlement discussions with the defendants. At this time neither Richard nor I saw much point in continuing to try to play a significant role. We both thought it likely that the interim lead counsel would ultimately be designated as permanent. They had already made clear that they did not want our help, and with Furth participating they arguably did not need it.

On April 20, however, Judge Kaplan dropped the other shoe, setting up a procedure for selection of permanent lead counsel. The order required all firms who wished to be considered to state what amount (which became known as the "X factor") they would agree to have paid to the class before they would receive any fee or expense reimbursement; it also provided that the counsel selected would receive 25 percent of any recovery above its proposed X factor. The order was strikingly sensible. For claims like those in the auction house case, where the defendant's liability (at least for sellers' commission overcharges) was a virtual slam-dunk, it made sense to exclude some significant amount of recovery from any fee application. Also, by setting in advance the percentage of any additional recovery that would be paid for fees and expenses, the court eliminated any incentive to engage in make-work or artificial delay.

The day after Judge Kaplan's order Richard Drubel called me to discuss whether we should submit a proposal. We quickly agreed that we should. The buyers' commission issues were challenging, and the potential fees to be earned were large. And there would be some satisfaction in replacing the interim lead counsel who had declined our help. In addition, I had spoken publicly for two decades about the need to improve the way lead counsel was selected in class action cases; here was a well-respected judge going out on a limb to do just that, and I thought we should support him.

That left the question of what figure to propose. Although Kaplan had ruled that a firm's qualifications would be considered as well as the amount of its bid, with many qualified firms competing it was likely that the highest offer would win. This was an attractive case, and we were too competitive to want to participate in what people had already begun referring to as an auction without coming out on top. On the other hand, the higher our bid, the lower our fee; if the total recovery did not exceed our bid, we would earn nothing and would have to pay our own expenses.

The next day, Saturday, April 22, I flew to Washington to discuss remedy issues in the *Microsoft* case. On the flights there and back I considered three questions. What were the overcharges that resulted from the auction houses' fixing sellers' commissions? What were the chances of establishing that Sotheby's and Christie's also fixed buyers' commissions? And if such liability were established, what was the amount of the overcharge?

There was much to do and only two weeks before our bid had to be submitted. Because we could not compel anyone to talk to us or produce documents, we were limited to public data and old-fashioned detective work. Analyses of the fragments of evidence available from public records and interviews of auction house customers and others who were willing to talk to our investigator led us to estimate that the sellers' overcharge was approximately $75 to $100 million over the period of the alleged conspiracy, and that the increased fees resulting from the higher buyers' commissions was approximately $400 million.

We made little progress regarding whether the buyers' commission increases were the result of collusion. While we turned up some hints of meetings between Sotheby's and Christie's employees at or before the increase in buyers' commissions, there was no real evidence of collusion until 1995, more than two years later—and buyers' commissions had not changed after January 1993. Although the buyers' commissions' liability issue was challenging, the calculation of the overcharge seemed at the time relatively straightforward. If one assumed that the January 1, 1993, increase was collusive, all that was necessary was to multiply the amount of the increase (5 percent) by the purchases subject to it (the first $50,000 of all purchases).

It would, of course, have been helpful to have more information, and in fact we asked the interim lead counsel to share the materials that they had received from defendants. They refused, citing a confidentiality agreement they had signed with the defendants that conveniently limited access to themselves alone. However, life is not always perfect, or perfectly fair, and we were not going to be blocked from participating in the bidding by the refusal of lead counsel to cooperate. If anything, it may have led us to be slightly more aggressive.

Although the antitrust laws provide for treble damages, most price-fixing class actions settle for some amount less than the actual overcharge. We figured many counsel would make offers based on the relatively safe sellers' overcharge, which we had estimated at $75 to $100 million. We also believed, however, that at least some counsel would bid significantly more. A higher bid could be justified on the basis of an expectation of some recovery based on alleged buyers' overcharges, an expectation of greater than single damages for the sellers' claim, or both. We assumed for planning purposes that some firm would bid in the $300 million range.

We believed it was reasonable to make an offer based on the assumption that we would recover the amount of the alleged overcharge for buyers and sellers combined, without tripling. Such a settlement would offer defendants the opportunity to resolve the case for one-third of what they might lose at trial. Accordingly if the total overcharges were approximately $475 to $500 million, a bid of $400 million was a reasonable bid. The case of course might turn out to be worth less; it also might turn out to be worth more. As long as the $475 to $500 million was a realistic midpoint in a realistic range, it was the basis for a sensible bid. The court order provided that successful lead counsel would receive 25 percent of the excess over its bid. If we bid $400 million and recovered $475 million, our fee would be $18.75 million—a very substantial return in view of our estimate that our total investment to prepare and try the case would be in the range of $6 to $8 million.

One of the advantages our firm had was that because of its financial success we did not have to be risk-averse. We could easily afford to make the required investment of both attorney resources and out-of-pocket expenses, and even if we were to recover nothing, our firm could readily absorb the loss. By 2000 our contingency fee cases in general and class actions in particular had been sufficiently successful so that even if a few turned out to be unprofitable, they were more than averaged out by those that turned out well. In addition, by the time we submitted our final bid in May 2000, we had grown to approximately a hundred lawyers, much larger than the average size of the interim lead counsel firms. This meant that we had a larger base over which to spread the risk of any unsuccessful litigation.

Although the buyers' commission claim was uncertain, and although other than the vitamins settlement that we had negotiated less than a year earlier we were not aware of any antitrust class action that had settled for the full amount of the overcharge (that is, single damages), we believed the risk was a reasonable one. We were not the usual plaintiffs' class action law firm. We believed that the defendants would ultimately recognize that we were ready, willing, and able to try the case; when that recognition came, they would have no realistic alternative but to settle on terms that took into account what they risked losing at trial.

We now had two numbers: the $300 million that represented what we thought would probably be the high bid of competing counsel, and the $400 million that represented what we considered a conservative estimate of the value of the case. We ultimately decided to go with the higher figure. We believed a recovery of $475 to $500 million was likely, and we did not want to take the chance of losing the case because one or more of the twenty competing firms was more aggressive than we expected. We also thought it was in our long-term interest to help make this method of selecting lead counsel a success.

Another factor that influenced us was that Judge Kaplan had already set a trial date less than a year away. This meant both that we would not have to pay for a multiyear battle and that we could expect any financial return to be relatively quick.

A day before our bid was submitted, I increased it from $400 to $410 million, proving to my wife that she is wise in generally prohibiting me from going to auctions. (Ever since I purchased a 1939 Chevrolet, among other items, at an auction benefit for our children's elementary school, Mary has been understandably nervous whenever I have an auction paddle in my hand.) While the $10 million increase would wipe out our entire fee if we obtained only a $410 recovery, it would only reduce it by approximately 10 percent if we obtained the recovery I thought was more likely— and the $10 million increase was insurance against another bidder at $400 million.

Before the court acted on the bids submitted, Judge Kaplan had to resolve two complaints about his procedure. First, lead counsel objected to having an auction at all, arguing for a less competitive method of selection. Second, a number of other bidders objected that lead counsel had an unfair advantage because of their unique access to the defendants' data. In response to these complaints the court held a hearing on May 12, 2000.

I, of course, argued that the court's proposed procedure for selecting lead counsel was appropriate. Indeed I gently chided the interim lead counsel, who were advocating the need to have competition among auction houses, for being so disinclined to accept a little competition in their own line of work. With respect to access to data, I noted that we ourselves had requested such access and that more information is always better than less. I added, however, that the publicly available information was sufficient to allow people to participate in the auction, and that to the extent that interim lead counsel had some advantage it came from the fact that they had been involved in litigating the case up to this point and the advantage was not necessarily unfair.

Following the hearing the court affirmed its selection procedures but ruled that all firms would have a second chance to bid after access to certain key documents that until then had been seen only by interim lead counsel. When we received our copy of the documents, we had the first troubling intimation that our estimates of the overcharge may have been too high: our sellers' overcharge estimate was substantially higher than the estimate prepared by the economics experts retained by the interim lead counsel based upon information furnished by the auction houses. The defendants of course had an incentive to try to convince counsel that the overcharge was less rather than more. However, the information that they had provided was from the official records of the company, and we believed that the numbers themselves were accurate. We seriously considered reducing our bid. However, our investigation was already providing us with additional evidence to support a buyers' commission claim. If that claim were strong, a recovery in the $450 to $500 million range was still reasonable. Ultimately we changed our bid only modestly, reducing it from

$410 million to $405 million based on Mary's argument that 405 beat 400 as well as 410 beat 400.

On May 26, 2000, I was at the University of Redlands receiving an honorary doctorate when I received a message on my cell phone from Richard Drubel that we had been selected as lead counsel. It turned out that our predictions of other firms' bids were reasonably accurate. The six interim lead counsel law firms, which the court required to bid separately and without consulting each other, all bid within the $75 to $150 million range. Most other key players did so as well. Milberg Weiss, one of the larger firms specializing in class actions that was not included among the interim lead counsel, also bid $75 million—a figure that would come back to haunt it when, having lost out in the selection process, it later tried to object to the settlement we reached as inadequate. A few firms bid much more, but our bid was the highest.

Two days later we began a detailed review of papers previously produced by defendants and commenced additional discovery. We also expanded our efforts to interview former auction house employees and customers. Access to travel and expense records from Christie's and Sotheby's enabled us to prepare a computerized database showing where people were on any given day and when personnel from the two companies were together.

While we had the resources to prepare and try the case ourselves, there were two firms that I thought we should invite to participate as lead counsel. Since we had filed our original case jointly with Steve Susman, I felt we should offer him an opportunity to continue with us. Judge Kaplan's order had required each of us to bid independently, but now that we had won we were free to share our position with other firms. However, when Richard Drubel called Steve to invite him to the party and told him the amount of our bid, Steve (who, we later discovered, had bid $85 million) declined with his usual bluntness: "David Boies must be on some kind of *pro bono* kamikaze mission. Count me out."

The second firm we invited to join us was Kaplan Fox, one of the six interim lead counsel. Bob Kaplan and his partner Greg Arenson were excellent lawyers with whom I had worked before, and Kaplan Fox had done much of the work in developing the case prior to our selection. However, when we told them the amount of our bid, the firm (whose number had been $80 million) also declined, saying it was simply too risky.

I told Mary the good news that we had made the offers I thought we were obliged to make and that we now had the case to ourselves. In reply she gave me the smile that I had long ago learned meant "You're crazy, but I love you."

Initially our work uncovered many additional details of a sellers' commission conspiracy but only limited hard evidence to support the claim of a buyers' fee conspiracy. Several weeks into our investigation, Robert Silver and Phil Korologos, using computers to match diaries and expense records, identified key times when personnel from both auction houses met together just prior to Sotheby's announcement of its buyers' commission increase. We now had motive and opportunity, and that might be enough. However, what we really needed to know was what had happened during those meetings. Just when we began to doubt that we ever would, I received separate calls from Scott Muller, for Al Taubman, and Shepard ("Shep") Goldfein, for Christie's, suggesting that we meet and discuss a possible settlement.

In June 2000 Jonathan Schiller and I had agreed to represent the Internet file-sharing service Napster in attempting to reverse decisions against it in cases brought by the music industry for copyright violations. We were in Los Angeles when Muller and Goldfein called, so Richard Drubel and Phil Korologos began preliminary settlement discussions in my absence. When I returned, my first meeting was with Muller at his offices. I had worked closely with Scott in the *Vitamins* antitrust litigation the previous year, and he was a seasoned litigator and negotiator; he was also someone who could be counted on to evaluate his clients' position objectively. Based on our prior experience, I also believed I could trust what he told me.

Our initial meeting did not result in any progress. To begin with, it was clear that Taubman genuinely believed he was innocent—a belief later tested when he chose to go to trial rather than settle the criminal charges against him. We also learned that the potential settlement that had been discussed between defendants and interim lead counsel before our selection was in the range of $50 to $80 million. When I explained that even the higher end of that range was not close to what it would now take to settle the case, Scott told me that a settlement was not in the cards, at least at that time.

I said we thought of the class as having essentially three deep pockets—Christie's, Sotheby's, and Taubman. Scott emphatically rejected the idea, saying that any settlement had to be approached as having two sources of funds—the Sotheby's and Christie's camps—and we should not try to separate Taubman out because he would end up contributing a good part of whatever Sotheby's had to pay. I replied that we might accept $100 million from Taubman personally, but that was quickly rejected.

Our next discussion was with Shep Goldfein of Skadden Arps. Goldfein said that Christie's wanted to put this matter behind them if it was possible to do so on a reasonable basis. The issue of course was what a reasonable basis might be. Again we were told that we were seeking damages several times greater than what defendants had been led to believe by interim lead counsel would be required to settle the case. More troubling, we now discovered that the numbers we had been using to estimate buyers' commissions were significantly overstated and that a realistic estimate was approximately $300 million for Sotheby's and Christie's combined. We had earlier learned that the sellers' commission overcharge based on our analysis was approximately $65 to $75 million, and the defendants had a realistic argument that the overcharge was much lower.

To get a settlement in the range we wanted, we would have to convince the defendants both that our damage estimate for the sellers' overcharge was realistic and that we had a significant chance of prevailing on the buyers' commission overcharge claim. Given the reduced estimates with which we were now confronted, a recovery of $400 to $500 million would require recovery of the full buyers' overcharge—a challenging prospect given the uncertainty of that claim.

Assuming that any contribution by Taubman would be part of Sotheby's payment, to achieve the settlement we wanted, the defendants would each have to be prepared to pay an average of $200 to $250 million. This was several times the total profits the companies had earned during the alleged conspiracy period. Although a firm's profits are not necessarily a cap on antitrust damages, we recognized that it would be a hard sell. We left our initial meeting with Christie's lawyers convinced that to make progress we had to come up with a creative offer they couldn't refuse.

After our meeting with the Christie's lawyers, Richard, Phil, and I sat down to try to structure a settlement offer that would induce Christie's to pay the class a substantial amount of money and, equally important, provide us with the evidence we were missing to establish a buyers' commission conspiracy.

The goal in most multi-defendant price-fixing lawsuits is, as we did in the *Vitamins* case, to settle early with one or more defendants who will cooperate in making the case against the others. That strategy was complicated here by the fact that, if we settled with Christie's, we would have only one or two defendants left (depending on whether Taubman and Sotheby's were counted as one pocket or two). That meant that we could not settle too cheaply. On the other hand, one advantage we had was that if we settled with one of the two auction houses, the other would be at a severe disadvantage: not only would the price of settlement go up, but many customers and key employees might shy away from an auction house whose financial stability was threatened by litigation and a possibly massive damage award. This meant that each defendant had the same incentive to be the first to settle with us as Christie's had had to be the one to get Justice Department amnesty.

There were several reasons why Christie's was the most logical candidate for the first settlement. They had already indicated a desire to settle, and because they had amnesty, they could give civil testimony without worrying about the effect it would have on their criminal case. Sotheby's Brooks was still proclaiming her innocence; Christie's Davidge was ready to testify if the settlement price was right. The Skadden lawyers had told us at our first meeting that the documents alone would not prove a buyers' commission conspiracy but that, in the event of a settlement, present and former Christie's personnel could provide the testimony we needed. In addition, because Christie's was based outside the U.S., most of its assets were more difficult to reach than those of Sotheby's and Taubman.

The question was, what offer would make sense for both the class and Christie's? Richard suggested we consider a settlement in which the company would pay a certain amount of money with the understanding that it would share in the proceeds received from defendants who settled later—often referred to as a "Mary Carter" settlement after the name of the case in which it was first approved. Such a deal might induce Christie's to settle for more than it otherwise might because of the prospect of making some of it back later—and gave it a financial interest in cooperating against its former codefendants.

When we initially broached a Mary Carter with the Skadden lawyers they were interested but concerned that if we later settled with Sotheby's for less, they would look bad and their client would be unhappy. Our initial response was that if the testimony Christie's was promising was as good as advertised, they should have no such concern. Christie's countered that if we would accept their number (approximately $70 million), they would be comfortable; however, since we were seeking $160 million from them alone some greater assurance was necessary.

Phil Korologos suggested that we consider combining a Mary Carter agreement with a most favored nations (or "MFN") clause. Under such a clause, if we were to settle with Sotheby's for less than with Christie's, we would have to pay back to Christie's the amount of the difference. Ordinarily an MFN clause carries the risk of precluding an otherwise desirable later settlement because of the negative effect it will have on previous ones. In this case, however, that risk seemed small. What we were seeking, though large to Christie's and large by comparison to what had been demanded by prior counsel, was substantially less than half of what we expected the total recovery to be. In addition, Christie's was promising oral testimony that would significantly strengthen our case. Finally, if Sotheby's were defined as including Taubman, we believed there was little chance that a combined Sotheby's/Taubman settlement would be less than what we were asking from their rival.

We decided to make the following offer: Christie's would pay $160 million; however, it would receive both an MFN clause and forty cents out of every dollar collected from Sotheby's/Taubman over $140 million. Christie's would promise to cooperate, and after an agreement in principle was reached, it would give us a proffer, or summary, of the testimony it would provide; if we did not believe the testimony was sufficiently helpful, we could call off the settlement.

This was, we believed, a good deal for the class. It provided testimony on the buyers' conspiracy and recovered $160 million for the class even if nothing further were achieved. Of course in that case we would get no fee; but our first obligation was to the class, and this settlement by itself would be about double what prior plaintiffs' counsel had sought from all defendants.

We also thought that this was an offer Christie's could not refuse. It would put the case behind it, and subject its ancient rival to both litigation and marketplace pressure. It would also allow Christie's to earn back up to $60 million from amounts later collected from Sotheby's and Taubman. (Our proposal provided that MFN rebates could not take Christie's liability below $100 million.)

Over a ten-day period we negotiated with the Skadden lawyers at their offices, at our offices, on the telephone, and even at my home over the weekend. We finally agreed on all the significant economic terms except one—who was to pay the approximately $1 million cost of class notice giving class members (here 130,000) the opportunity to "opt-out." We were anxious to get this issue resolved because until it was, we could not see and evaluate the company's proffer. We also could not understand why Christie's, having agreed to a $160 million settlement, was refusing to pay $1 million of costs that in most such settlements the defendant agrees to pay. Perhaps the company thought that $160 million was simply enough.

While we were arguing about this with Christie's, I received a call from Ira Millstein, the senior partner of Weil, Gotshal & Manges, representing Sotheby's. He too wanted to explore settlement. I explained that I was in the midst of discussions with Christie's and was not ready to sit down with Sotheby's until those negotiations were resolved.

Ira immediately understood the danger his client faced. He had hoped to outflank Christie's but was now on the verge of being outflanked himself. He asked me to meet with him and just listen. I told him that I thought Christie's was the right first party with which to settle, but again he said, just meet and listen. I have known Ira for thirty-five years. He is recognized as the dean of the defense bar in New York City, and he is a hard man to say no to. Moreover, he was right—there was no harm and some possible benefit in listening. At a minimum, if Christie's knew we were talking to Sotheby's they might get off the dime over the disputed $1 million.

When I met with Ira and his partner Richard Davis, they spent five minutes telling me that they had been assured by DeDe Brooks that she had not participated in either a buyers' or a sellers' commission conspiracy. After I noted that that was one of the reasons I believed Christie's was the best candidate for the first settlement, they quickly shifted gears.

"Tell us what you think Christie's can give you that we can't," they said.

"Of course I haven't seen their proffer yet," I replied.

"Then tell us what you hope to get," Davis pressed.

I spent several minutes laying out what I wanted. We were meeting in Ira's conference room adjacent to his office. When I finished, he and Davis went into Ira's office to talk. About fifteen minutes later they returned.

"We need to discuss this among ourselves and with our client," Ira said. "Can we meet tomorrow?"

As we left, I noted to Ira that I had not managed just to listen. "Of course not," he replied with a smile.

When we met the next day, I came with Bob Silver. Both Richard and Phil were unavailable, and I thought this might be a time when Bob's intellect would be important. From the outset it was clear that Ira and Rich meant business. They explained the disaster they believed would befall Sotheby's if we settled with Christie's first. Customers and key employees, we were told, would desert Sotheby's, questioning its ability to compete, and perhaps survive, in the face of long litigation and an exposure of $500 million to $1 billion. Crippling one of the two major auction houses would not be in our clients' long-term interest, they argued.

Ira and Rich had also brought with them a stack of key documents—copies of which, they said, Christie's also had. They walked us through them and showed how they provided the proof we were seeking. On the surface this was a risky strategy. Here were Sotheby's lawyers pointing out damning evidence against their client. On the other hand, it was an effective rebuttal to their rival's argument that we should settle with Christie's first in order to get the benefit of testimony that would give us something the documents did not. Moreover, Ira and Rich were not giving me anything I would not get soon in any event. Their interest was in stopping me from making a Christie's deal because I did not know what document discovery would provide. At the end of the meeting we agreed that Bob would meet with them later in the week.

When Richard, Phil, and I reviewed the results of the two meetings, we agreed that we needed to reconsider our offer to Christie's. At a minimum we needed to inform Skadden that based on the documents we had reviewed we now doubted that Christie's would be able to give us testimony of sufficient added value to justify the offer on the table.

Phil called Shep Goldfein with the news. Shep threatened to call off negotiations if we continued to pursue talks with Sotheby's in parallel. It was a bluff I felt we had to call despite the dangers. We did not have any indication of what kind of deal, if any, we could strike with Sotheby's, and we risked ending up with no deal at all. However, I believed Ira was serious; I had told him that we needed to get either $500 million from both companies or $200 to $250 million from Sotheby's with no strings attached (no Mary Carter, no MFN), and while he had not agreed, he had not said no.

In addition, with the documents we now knew about, it was hard to justify a favorable deal for Christie's based on the previously expected value of its testimony. As we pressed Christie's for more details, it also became apparent that the testimony it was offering was weighted toward giving us help we did not need with respect to the sellers' conspiracy rather than the help we needed concerning the buyers' increases.

Within a week of my first meeting with Ira, I concluded that the settlement on which we had worked so hard was no longer in the interests of the class. The negotiations that followed over the next three weeks reminded me once again that if litigation is like bridge, the settlement of litigation is like poker.

Richard, Phil, and I met to assess whether our target recovery number should be modified given what we had learned since our selection as lead counsel. We now knew that the overcharges were approximately 25 percent less than we had originally estimated. If we reduced our original target of $475 to $500 million by 25 percent we would be down to less than $375 million. We joked that maybe we should have bid $300 million after all. On the other hand, the claim for buyers' commission overcharges was now a bit stronger. In addition to being able to prove that Sotheby's and Christie's met several times just before the Sotheby's price increase in late 1992, we now had documentary evidence that each company appeared aware of the other's intentions before they were publicly announced. The defendants could argue that their internal discussions of the other's expected actions were simply speculation that turned out to be accurate. However, in the context of the entire case the evidence was incriminating.

Moreover, we had developed a refinement to our buyers' case. While I was discussing the gaps in our buyers' claim with Mary at dinner, she had asked: "Do you really think Ira and Shep can convince a jury that their clients agreed to fix only sellers' commissions?" I pointed out there had been no increase in buyers' commissions after the date of the admitted sellers' commission price-fixing.

"There weren't any decreases either, were there?" she replied. It was an obvious fact, but one whose significance I had not appreciated. Even if the original increases in buyers' commissions were lawful, an agreement to keep commissions at that new level would be illegal. The key would be an economics analysis showing that in the absence of collusion buyers' fees would have fallen from their 1993 levels. The economists we consulted concurred that a good case could be made; since the other avenues of competition were shut by the agreements concerning sellers' fees, one would expect competition to develop in any area not precluded by agreement. As Mary, who had been general counsel of the U.S. Civil Aeronautics Board in the late 1970s, noted, when airlines had been prevented by CAB regulations from competing on price, they competed vigorously with elaborate service.*

In the end, whether out of analysis or inertia or both, we decided to stick with our $500 million target. I called Ira and Shep with the same message. "We are prepared to settle with both of you for $500 million or with either of you for $250 million. If we do settle with one of you for $250 million, the price to the other goes up." The responses were not encouraging.

_____

*Our damages from an agreement to maintain, as opposed to originally set, buyers' commission levels would run from 1995 rather than 1993. Also, the amount of damages would not be the entire overcharge but only the difference between actual fees and the level to which fees would have fallen in the absence of collusion. However, it was a valuable fallback position if we lost our original buyers' claim.

Christie's in particular was adamant. How could I now be asking for $250 million with no Mary Carter or MFN provisions when two weeks earlier I had been willing to settle for $160 million with both a Mary Carter and an MFN provision? There were two answers, only one of which really mattered. We now knew that the promised cooperation that had led us to make the earlier proposal was neither as valuable nor as necessary as we had been led to believe. More importantly, as I told Shep, "that was then, this is now. The fact that you almost got your client a great settlement should not prevent your client from taking a good settlement when that is the best available." Sotheby's was less adamant about the unreasonableness of a $250 million settlement; they simply said they did not have the money.

We next turned to how to make Sotheby's an offer it would accept. We rejected a Mary Carter provision because Ira had been clear that there was no significant helpful testimony Sotheby's could provide, and in the absence of such assistance it did not make sense to share any proceeds we later received. We were prepared to give an MFN clause if necessary to assure Sotheby's that we would not settle with Christie's for less, but that did not help Sotheby's afford $250 million now. The solution we came up with was based on a deal I had done with Ira Millstein and Rich Davis ten years earlier.

When Tom Barr and I represented the FDIC in lawsuits against Michael Milken and Drexel Burnham Lambert, Ira and Rich had represented Drexel. As in the Sotheby's situation, Drexel wanted to settle but did not have the money we were demanding. Ultimately we reached a deal where Drexel paid a nine-figure amount and assigned to the FDIC the company's own claims against Milken. Those proved to be stronger than the FDIC's direct claims, and we ultimately recovered more than $1 billion for our client.

"Pay us $100 million, which is the amount you say you can afford," I told Ira. "Assign the class your claims against Taubman for breach of fiduciary duty for getting you into this mess. We will keep the first $130 million and share any additional recovery fifty-fifty."

The offer put Sotheby's and its board in a difficult position, as it was intended to do. Even though he had been forced to resign as chairman, Taubman was still the company's largest shareholder and had selected most of the members of the board for their position. They would not want to leave him exposed. On the other hand the board had an opportunity to get Sotheby's out of the case relatively cheaply, and the directors themselves would be exposed to shareholder suits if they did not act in the best interests of the company.

Taubman of course was informed of the proposal by people at Sotheby's, and I soon got a call from Scott Muller. He tried to convince me that our proposal to Sotheby's was not in the class's interest because we would not be successful in any claim against Taubman—which would have meant that we had let Sotheby's off the hook for "only" $100 million. I explained that I was comfortable with the offer since Taubman had dual exposure. If we could prove that he had participated in the price-fixing he was personally liable for the entire damages; even if he had not participated, he might be liable to Sotheby's for breach of fiduciary duty, including a failure to supervise Brooks.

Taubman had a dilemma. His defense to the antitrust charges was that Brooks was in charge and he did not know what she was doing. However, that defense could be used as evidence of his failure to do his job. I told Scott, "Get Taubman to come up with $115 million. I think I can squeeze another $115 million out of Sotheby's. The class will get $230 million. Both Taubman and Sotheby's will be off the hook, and we can turn our attention to Christie's." Taubman, however, was not yet ready for such a deal.

Ira and Rich Davis took our proposal to the Sotheby's board which, after extensive discussions, turned it down. Ira told me that the board wanted to bring Taubman into the deal by negotiation and that he would get back to us. At this point I called Shep Goldfein.

"We may or may not be close to a deal with Sotheby's," I said. "But I wanted you to know where things stood. We are talking in the range of $230 million with an MFN but no Mary Carter provision. Is your client interested?" Shep said he was doubtful but would get back to me. I told him that if we could get a deal done now, we would accept either $465 million to settle the entire case or $230 million from either Sotheby's or Christie's. I cautioned that we would not go lower, that this offer would be available only until the end of the week, and that if either company agreed to pay $230 million the offer would be off the table for the other.

We did not hear back from either Shep or Ira that week. Early the following week I called both of them separately. We were now, I said, at the point where we had to decide whether this case was going to be settled or tried. We had considered our options, including the results of our continuing investigation, and I had news I knew they would not like. Our number was now $512 million for a global resolution or $256 million for either company. I suggested that they confer among themselves and get back to me.

In a sense suggesting that the two defendants get together was counterintuitive—it was tantamount to suggesting that they avoid bidding against themselves to see who could be the first to settle, that they collude against me the way their clients had colluded against my clients. But there were advantages to getting the defendants in a single room. The best result for the class would be to settle the entire case quickly. And each might be prepared to settle for more than they otherwise might have if they knew the other was settling also. In any event, if it did not work, I could always go back to trying to play each off against the other.

In my conversation with Ira Millstein I reminded him of the bind the Sotheby's board was in and told him that my offer to settle with Sotheby's for a reduced amount with no release for Taubman and assignment to the class of Sotheby's claims against Taubman was still open for discussion—although at somewhat higher numbers. It was clear to me that Sotheby's was looking to Taubman to make a substantial contribution, and if he did not, the company might settle along the lines I was proposing. Both Ira and I believed that if Taubman believed Sotheby's was prepared to go without him, he would come along. The question was how to convince him that his handpicked board was prepared to abandon him. Both Ira and I agreed to do what we could to convince Scott Muller.

One factor that both Ira and I had going for us was our credibility with each other and with the attorneys for Christie's and Taubman. When I told Shep and Ira that my last, best offer was $512 million, they believed me. They may not have liked it; they may not have believed it was reasonable; but they knew I meant it and would stick to it. Credibility takes a long time to establish, and you can lose it quickly. In settlement negotiations credibility prevents your opponent's miscalculating your resolve. Ira knew that if he told Scott that the board was prepared to abandon its chairman, Taubman then would have no choice but to participate. But before Ira could say it, he had to be certain that the Sotheby's board was prepared to do it.

Mary and I were at the U.S. Open tennis tournament in early September when I got a message that Ira was trying to reach me. When I returned his call, he said he thought it would be useful for us to meet. I said that I didn't think that was necessary; either they were prepared to accept the offer or not. I had told him and Shep that this was my bottom line, and there was no point in meeting if all they were going to do was try to negotiate the numbers. "Just come and listen," Ira said. "You don't have to say anything, just come and listen. There can't be any harm in that." When I reminded him I had heard that before, he just laughed. In the end, of course, I went.

We met again in Ira's personal conference room at the GM Building in Manhattan, me with Bob Silver, Ira with Rich Davis. Shep Goldfein was also there. Shep and Ira began with a history of how I had been unfairly playing each off against the other, how I was asking five to ten times what they could have settled the case for before I was involved, how my own demands kept escalating, how I was asking several times the total earnings of the companies since 1993, how I would be a hero if I settled for $465 million but that I risked everything if I insisted on going to trial.

"The class gets $512 million," I said when they finished, "or we go to trial. You both know I am not going to draw a line in the sand and back away from it."

In fact they did know that even if I had wanted to settle for a little less than $512 million, the loss of credibility in future negotiations would be too costly. They tried to settle for $500 million even, but their hearts weren't in it. I kept repeating 512.

We all knew that it was 512 or a trial, and it was becoming increasingly clear that there was not going to be a trial. I explained I was due at a dinner. They said they needed to consult with their clients. We agreed that Bob Silver would stay to draft an agreement in principle if their clients gave their approval. Later that evening Ira and Shep reported that they were authorized to proceed, and by two in the morning an agreement had been typed and initialed. A copy was slipped under my door at the Waldorf-Astoria, where Mary and I spent the night.

When the amount of the settlement was reported, class members and commentators were unanimous in their surprise and praise for a settlement far larger than anyone expected. Much of the praise deservedly was directed toward Judge Kaplan, whose innovative approach had resulted in a total cost to the class of about 5 percent of the total recovery instead of the usual 25 to 30 percent. Although our fee was less than one-sixth of what it might have been, no one, least of all us, felt sorry for Boies, Schiller & Flexner. We were due to receive more than $26 million for our work—approximately five times what our standard billing would have been for the time we invested.

When we met at Sparks Steak House to celebrate with our wives, it was just short of four months from the day I had received Richard's call in Redlands telling me that we had been selected as lead counsel. It seemed an exceptional result in an extraordinarily short period of time.

Class action settlements must be approved by the court, in this case Judge Kaplan, to determine that the settlement is a fair one for class members. In the usual case, a client decides whether or not to settle. In a class action the clients (that is, class members) generally have no role or voice in settlement negotiations that are conducted by class counsel, so it is important that the court's review protect their interests. Before we could schedule a hearing on the merits of our settlement, we had to resolve how much, if any, of the settlement should be allocated based on purchases outside the U.S. and how broad the release of defendants should be. Based in large part on the arguments of two firms (Milberg Weiss and Cohen Milstein) who had sued separately on behalf of people who had bought and sold art outside the United States, it was ultimately agreed that our settlement would be allocated based on U.S. purchases and sales only, and that class members would be free to sue separately for their purchases abroad.*

When we did have a hearing on our settlement there was widespread support for it from members of the class, and even attorneys whom we had displaced. Fred Furth told Judge Kaplan, "Never in a thousand years could I have predicted such a large recovery. Mr. Boies has to be the Tiger Woods of the legal profession." Such praise was particularly gracious coming from Furth. A few of the displaced firms, including Milberg Weiss, objected to the settlement, but Judge Kaplan dismissed such objections as little more than sour grapes and a final attempt to earn a fee. On March 14, 2001, approximately a year after our initial complaint had been filed, the judge approved our settlement.

The defendants had reserved the right to appeal the settlement over the scope of their release. However, they agreed that since their only issue was the breadth of the release, the class (and, not insignificantly, our firm) would be paid without waiting for the appeal to be resolved. It turned out, however, that theirs was not

---

*We had originally planned to release all claims of people who received money pursuant to our settlement. The defendants had argued sensibly that they did not want to pay half a billion dollars only to have the same plaintiffs sue based on the same price-fixing, only this time for fees paid abroad. However, Milberg Weiss, having lost Judge Kaplan's auction, had filed a suit based on foreign transactions and argued loudly that any attempt by us to settle such claims invaded its territory.

the only appeal. A day before the thirty-day period in which to appeal expired Milberg Weiss (joined by Cohen Milstein) appealed on the ground that the settlement was not adequate. The chances for an appeal from approval of any class action settlement is small because of the substantial discretion given a trial judge in such matters. Here the appeal seemed outright frivolous.

Milberg Weiss argued that we should have gotten even more for the class than we did and that we should have negotiated something for class members' foreign claims. The first argument was impossible to reconcile with the fact that we had recovered several times what Milberg Weiss (and Cohen Milstein) had estimated the value of the case to be. The second argument was inconsistent with the position that Milberg Weiss had itself successfully urged Judge Kaplan to take—that class members' foreign claims were not within the purview of our case. We were not worried that the Milberg Weiss appeal would succeed. However, it could take a year or more to be decided. During that time the settlement proceeds could not be distributed.

I called Mel Weiss of Milberg Weiss to ask what was going on and to try to convince him to drop his appeal. Mel is one of the two or three most successful plaintiffs' lawyers in the country; I had worked with him on a number of major cases; and he was a good friend. Mel was not personally responsible for his firm's auction house work, but he was the head of the firm and the person at Milberg Weiss in whom I had the most confidence. Unfortunately, although he expressed sympathy for our situation, he told me he did not feel he should overrule his younger partner who he said was in charge of the case.

In subsequent conversations with Mel's partner it became clear that Milberg Weiss's appeal could be resolved if we agreed to allocate a portion of the $512 million to the plaintiffs in Milberg Weiss's case. However, this solution would be taking money out of the pockets of the plaintiffs we had an obligation to represent. One disadvantage of Milberg's appeal was to delay when the class was paid, but the settlement money had already been deposited in an escrow account and was at least earning interest. The greater disadvantage of the appeal was for my firm since most of our fee would be held up until the appeal was resolved—and, unlike the class, we received a fixed fee that did not earn interest while we waited. Bob Silver, Richard Drubel, Phil Korologos, and I were anxious to complete this case and to get paid. Nonetheless, we all agreed that we could not bargain away some of our clients' money as a payoff to drop the appeal.

Mary and I had a three-week trip to Russia and Scandinavia planned for the end of June and the first half of July 2002. We spent most of our time in Russia, where neither of us had been before. We were scheduled to return to the United States at 8:45 a.m. on Wednesday, July 17. Shortly before we left in June, we were advised that the appeal of Judge Kaplan's order had finally been scheduled for argument—the morning of July 17. I briefly considered whether to try to race from the airport to the courthouse on the morning of the seventeenth but decided that even if the argument were set at the end of the court's morning calendar too many things would have to go right for me to make it. Instead we cut our trip short and returned the evening of July 16.

The court was not impressed with the defendants' appeal, and even less so with Milberg Weiss's. Two weeks later, far faster than the usual time between argument and decision, the court issued a unanimous opinion affirming Judge Kaplan's decision in all respects. The court dismissed Milberg Weiss's argument as "bordering on the frivolous." The class, and we, were paid.

In the criminal case Alfred Taubman went to trial and, largely based on the testimony of his former protégé, was convicted. He went to jail still protesting his innocence. Sotheby's and Christie's put the scandal behind them and went back to business as usual under the leadership of executives who could be trusted not to collude, but not to compete too aggressively either. Brooks and Davidge, whose forays first into competition and then into collusion had ended so disastrously, retired with their fortunes, if not their reputations, intact. Neither spent a night in jail.

10

Bush v. Gore:
Too Close to Call

M Y FIRST IMPRESSION OF TALLAHASSEE WAS THAT IT was colder than I had expected. It was forty degrees and just before midnight on Monday, November 13, 2000, when I stepped off the plane from New York to begin a thirty-day adventure in law, politics, and history. On the flight I had reviewed court decisions interpreting Florida election law that my son Jonathan had hurriedly assembled earlier that evening. As I walked to the waiting car, I was thinking about those decisions and their application to the 2000 presidential election recount controversy, while at the same time wondering why I had not brought a sweater. I was soon to learn that Tallahassee and northern Florida shared neither the climate nor the politics of the southern Florida communities that had always previously come to mind when I thought of the sunshine state.

Around five that afternoon I had just completed an all-day meeting at my firm's Manhattan offices when my assistant Linda Carlsen handed me a long list of messages; one was from my friend and former law-school classmate Walter Dellinger. When I reached Walter, he began by describing the Gore campaign's efforts to obtain ballot recounts in key Florida counties. I was of course familiar with the bizarre back and forth of the Florida vote count. Vice President Gore had defeated Texas governor George

Bush in the national popular vote for president, but in the all-important contest for Electoral College ballots, the election was still up for grabs six days after the polls closed.

Gore needed only five of Florida's twenty-five Electoral College votes to be elected president. However, because the state, like all but two others, awards all its electoral votes to the candidate who wins a majority of the state's popular vote, whoever won Florida, no matter how thin the margin, would be president. On election night, November 7, the networks had first declared that Gore had won Florida (which would have elected him president), then that the state was too close to call, then that Bush was the winner (which would have elected him president), then for the second time that Florida was too close to call.

Only twice in history had a candidate lost the popular vote but been elected president with a majority of the Electoral College—the last time more than a century ago. In a third election, in 1824, no candidate received a majority of the Electoral College and the House of Representatives selected John Quincy Adams, who had fewer popular votes, over his opponent, Andrew Jackson.

Two days after the polls closed the unofficial but widely reported count showed Bush leading Gore by 375 votes. The Gore-Lieberman campaign requested a manual recount in four key counties. Initially the Bush–Cheney people also requested a manual recount in one county (Volusia) but quickly changed tactics and argued that no such recounts should be permitted.

Walter explained that the Gore campaign's legal team in Florida was led by Warren Christopher, that Florida lawyer Dexter Douglass was in charge of litigating for Gore in the Florida state trial courts, and that professor Laurence Tribe of Harvard would handle any litigation in federal court. Dexter was an outstanding trial lawyer with an unparalleled knowledge of Florida law, politics, and judicial personalities. Tribe was one of the top federal appellate advocates in the country. The Gore team also included Mitchell Berger (a well-known Florida trial lawyer and election law expert) and Ron Klain (former Gore chief of staff, former chief counsel of the Senate Judiciary Committee, and present partner in O'Melveny & Myers).

"Sounds like you're well represented," I said.

"We are," Walter replied. "However, assuming the Republicans continue to try to block a manual recount, this case is almost certainly going to be decided in the Florida Supreme Court. And there's a feeling that neither Dexter nor Tribe is the best person to present our case there. Can you come down for a couple of days, give us your thoughts on strategy, and be prepared to argue in the Florida Supreme Court if everyone agrees that makes sense?"

"What does Chris think about this?" I asked.

"I've spoken to both Chris and Ron Klain," Walter replied. "They agree we could use your help."

I told Walter that I was not sure how much I would add, that I needed to talk to Mary before making any commitment, but that I would like to do what I could to help. Although I had not been active in the campaign and had met Vice President Gore only once more than a decade earlier, during the campaign I had been impressed with his intelligence and judgment. I was also concerned about what a Bush victory would mean for domestic issues including equal rights, the environment, judicial appointments, and the economy.

Moreover if I had not become a lawyer, I would have been an American history teacher like my father. Although I could not have predicted what lay ahead, it was already clear that this was going to be the most important presidential election controversy since the Hayes–Tilden contest of 1876. In that election Democratic candidate Samuel Tilden (like Gore) had won the popular vote and needed only one of twenty-two disputed electoral votes to win the presidency. However, a special commission, including three members of the U.S. Supreme Court, voting strictly on party lines, gave all twenty-two votes to Republican Rutherford B. Hayes. Hayes was elected, the country was outraged, the Supreme Court was tarnished, and the army had to bring four artillery companies to Washington, D.C., to keep order. The Republicans bought peace by agreeing to Democratic demands to remove federal troops from the South—prematurely ending Reconstruction and setting the stage for decades of statutory discrimination and Ku Klux Klan terror.

In the aftermath Congress had passed laws that guaranteed that the states would conclusively control which candidate was awarded their electoral votes so long as the decision was made by a certain date (December 12 for the 2000 election), and the procedures used were not changed after Election Day. Congress also vested in itself the power to decide any disputes if competing slates of electors claimed to have been selected by a particular state. The purpose was to ensure both that the constitutionally mandated right of states to select their electors was not overridden in Washington and that if a decision among competing state claims had to be made at the national level, it would be made by the most representative branch of government—one whose members were themselves elected and could be voted out of office if the electorate disagreed with what they did. In the 124 years since the Hayes–Tilden debacle, no election had been close enough to test the reforms of 1876. The opportunity to participate in that test, or at least have a front-row seat, was not easy to pass up.

This was not the first time the possibility of my going to Florida had been raised. The previous Saturday, four days after the election, I was in my backyard with Sheldon Solow planting a copper beech tree that he had given me when I received a call from Barbara Miller. She had played a key role in managing the Gore–Lieberman campaign in Broward, one of the Florida counties at issue.

"We need you down here," Barbara had told me. "The Republicans are outmaneuvering us and are much better organized. We need someone like you who's willing and able to fight as hard for our side as the Republicans are fighting for theirs." The following day Mary and I drove to our daughter Mary's school, where we spent Sunday afternoon judging a student moot court competition. On the way back, we listened to the news on the radio. Much of it had to do with Florida. Mary could tell I was reflecting on Barbara's call.

"Don't even think about it," she laughed. "What do you think you can do? George Bush's brother is governor of the state. Republicans control the state election machinery."

The prospect of losing does not usually deter me. The best case is one where you are on the right side and you can win; the second best case is one where you are on the right side and you can't win. Although Mary sometimes chides me as "the patron saint of lost causes," in her heart she agrees. She also acknowledges that a number of my cases that were initially described as unwinnable had ended up winners. Still, this time we both knew she had a point. Her final comment clinched it.

"This is Warren Christopher's case," she said. "Chris doesn't need you showing up to give unsolicited advice or to send mixed messages. There are already more than enough volunteers in Florida. You've always said that in every case it's important to be clear who's in charge. Chris is in charge. He wouldn't horn in on you if you were in his place." She was right. Chris was a fine lawyer and a good friend. If he needed my help, he would ask; if he didn't, I should stay out of his way.

But things had changed since yesterday. Warren Christopher was now asking for my help, and with the team that was already in place my contribution should not, I thought, take too much of my time. When I phoned Mary to tell her of Walter's call, she was not convinced. To her the idea that I would go down for a couple of days, make my contribution, and come home was an illusion.

"Every client you have ever been involved with ends up wanting you full-time," she reminded me. She also remained doubtful that I would be able to change the result, and was reluctant to see me take on another controversial case. At the same time, she could tell that this was something that I now wanted to do. She paused for me to say something. After about fifteen seconds of silence, she continued, "On the other hand, if anyone can make a difference, you can. Just promise me that you'll be careful and come home as soon as you can." The good thing and the bad thing was that since we were on the phone, I couldn't see her eyes.

Ellen Brockman had been with me at my meeting on November 13 and when I returned Dellinger's call. A good friend, she had worked with me for a quarter century on all my major cases. She had another concern.

"You're going to make powerful enemies. This isn't like taking on Microsoft and Bill Gates. They went after you while the case was going on, but now they are back to business. And they didn't own newspapers and write columns. Do you want to have the *Wall Street Journal*, the *New York Post*, and right-wing columnists on your back? These people carry a grudge. They won't drop it just because the case ends."

"And how many times," she continued, "have you told me that the more publicity you get, the more you become a target? Even the press that is neutral or supports you now will find any possible mistake or problem to be news. Do you really want to have everything you do for the rest of your career examined under a microscope to see if someone can figure out something you might have done, could have done, should have done different?"

As usual Ellen had a point. However, I thought she was exaggerating both the attention I would get and its consequences. In any event, after more than three decades as a trial lawyer, I had a thick skin.

My next call was to my son Jonathan at the firm's Armonk office asking him to pull together cases and statutes relating to Florida election law as well as any materials he could find on the Internet about the status of the recount. JB said he would bring it all to me at the White Plains airport, which is ten minutes from our offices. I told him he had three hours, since I needed to meet with Sheldon Solow and Calvin Klein before I left.

I was at the plane shortly before 9:15 p.m. JB was there with two large binders. Mary was waiting with a suitcase containing half a dozen shirts and changes of underwear. "Just in case you can't get back until the weekend," she said with a straight face.

As I boarded she added, "Try to keep a low profile." I promised that I would.

During the flight I read that the Gore campaign had decided the previous Thursday to ask for a manual recount of four counties; that the Bush campaign's efforts to enjoin the recounts had been rejected by the federal court in Miami; that Florida Secretary of State Katherine Harris had issued an opinion that manual recounts were improper; that two of the counties (Volusia and Palm Beach) had decided to recount, one (Broward) had decided not to, and the fourth (Miami-Dade) had not yet decided; that Harris had stated that she intended to certify the results of the election the next day (November 14) without waiting for the results of any recounts; and that the Gore campaign had gone to state court earlier in the day to ask it to order Harris to delay certification until the recounts were completed.*

Two things were clear from the Florida cases and statutes JB had collected. First, manual recounts were a normal part of Florida election procedures in close elections (as, I was later to learn, they were in at least thirty-three other states). Second, the settled standard used in recounting ballots was whether either the county canvassing board, which was responsible for supervising the vote count, or a court could determine "the intent of the voter." The Florida courts had consistently held for at least eighty years that as long as a voter's intent could be discerned, a ballot had to be counted regardless of whether the voter had properly followed instructions for marking it.

In 1998 the Florida Supreme Court had confirmed the "intent of the voter" standard in a case involving a race for sheriff of Volusia county (ironically, one of the four counties involved in the

---

*Under Florida law one of the responsibilities of the secretary of state is to certify the winner of elections. Although the office of secretary of state was an elected position, traditionally the secretary had acted with reasonable fairness in making election decisions. On the other hand, in no prior case was a secretary of state confronted with the extraordinary pressures that Katherine Harris faced to come to the aid of her party.

Bush v. Gore dispute). Volusia uses optical character recognition (OCR) ballots rather than the more primitive punchcard ballots employed in Broward, Miami-Dade, and Palm Beach Counties. OCR ballots are like standardized tests. Voters are told to darken a circle with a number two pencil to indicate which candidate they support. In the sheriff race, most people had done as they were told, but several hundred, more than enough to change the result of the sheriff's election, had not. Some used their own pens or pencils, of varying colors. Others placed an "x" or check mark next to a candidate's name or wrote the name of the candidate on the ballot. None of these ballots conformed to the instructions given voters; none was able to be counted when the ballots were read by machines. All, the court ruled, should be included in the final tally because "the intent of the voter" was clear.

The issue of when the ballots should be counted was more complicated. Florida election laws set up a two-stage procedure for challenging vote counts: the first, for reasons I never understood, was called the "protest" phase; the second the "contest" phase. In a protest, which precedes the secretary of state's certification of a winner, a candidate can, if the results in a county were close enough, ask the county canvassing board to recount its ballots. In the "contest" phase, which follows certification, a court can be asked to review the decisions of the canvassing boards and, if the court's recount differs sufficiently from the results initially certified, declare a new winner.

Florida law contemplated that a winner ordinarily would be certified one week after the election (for the 2000 election, on November 14). One section of the law suggested that the secretary of state had no discretion over when she certified, saying that the secretary "shall" ignore returns received after the initial week. Another later-enacted section suggested that the secretary did have discretion; it provided that the secretary "may" ignore returns filed after the initial week. Florida statutes gave losing candidates two days to request a manual recount, and it would be virtually impossible for a canvassing board in a large county to decide to conduct a recount, and then complete it, all within five days. It seemed unlikely that the Florida legislature would have established a recount procedure with a deadline that made it impossible to complete that procedure. For this reason, and because of the clearly expressed legislative purpose over many decades that all votes be counted consistent with the intent of the voter, a rule requiring a case-by-case decision made the most sense.

However, it was easy to see the contrary argument, and clear that the Florida courts were going to have to resolve this legal ambiguity. Such a court case might not have been necessary had Katherine Harris, as officeholders often do, interpreted applicable statutes in a way that expanded rather than limited her discretion. But even five days after the election it was apparent that Ms. Harris (who had served as one of the chairpersons of George Bush's campaign in Florida during the election and who maintained a close relationship with the state's governor, Jeb Bush) was determined to support the Bush campaign in every way she could. In the thirty days following Election Day she made more than fifteen decisions regarding deadlines, the interpretation of election laws, acceptance or rejection of vote counts, and related issues. Every decision adopted the position taken by the Bush-Cheney campaign.

Based on the materials I read on the plane, it seemed to me that it was likely that the Florida courts would require Harris to delay certifying a winner until the recounts provided for by Florida law were completed. On the other hand, even losing that argument did not seem fatal to Gore's recount request. Regardless of what happened at the pre-certification protest stage, a candidate had a right to have the votes recounted at the contest stage if, as was certainly the case here, the results of the election might be affected. Similarly, winning the argument would not necessarily guarantee Gore a right to have all votes counted at the protest stage. Even under the Democrats' argument Secretary Harris would have discretion over when to certify a winner, and I suspected she would exercise any discretion she was given to frustrate the Gore campaign's efforts.

The car that was waiting for me at the Tallahassee airport took me directly to Mitchell Berger's law firm, Berger, Davis & Singerman. Although it was after midnight when I got there, the offices were filled. People were on the phones planning the recount in Palm Beach County, discussing issues concerning the Volusia County recount, and preparing arguments for why the Broward County and Miami–Dade canvassing boards should also begin recounts. Other people were working on papers to be filed with the Florida appellate courts.* Still others were working on issues relating to the Palm Beach "butterfly" ballot; reports of interference with African American voters in northern Florida; concerns about improprieties in connection with absentee ballots; reports of newly discovered, uncounted ballots in Volusia and elsewhere; and as yet unexplained anomalies like a precinct in which the Socialist Workers Party candidate was initially credited with 9,888 votes (the final, corrected total was 8). After *Bush v. Gore* was decided by the U.S. Supreme Court and George W. Bush was inaugurated as the forty-third president of the United States, several commentators would write that Bush's workers were more emotionally committed than Gore's or that Governor Bush inspired more loyalty than the Vice President. I saw no evidence of that during the early morning hours of November 14, or over the next thirty days.

On my arrival I was taken to meet Ron Klain. "Welcome to Guatemala," he greeted me cheerfully. Although Dexter Douglass had gone home to catch a few hours' sleep, we were almost immediately joined by Mitchell Berger, John Newton, and other members of the trial team. Everyone was guardedly optimistic that Judge Lewis would not permit Katherine Harris to certify Bush the winner Tuesday afternoon.

"He's more careful than creative," one of the team told me. "But he is fair. And it simply would not be fair to certify a winner before the votes were counted."

---

*Judge Terry Lewis, who during the day had heard Dexter Douglass's arguments why Secretary Harris should not immediately certify a winner, had said he would decide the case Tuesday morning. Whichever side lost was certain to appeal.

Klain and Berger briefed me on developing issues around the state and on the legal questions before Lewis. During the briefing I glanced through our draft appeal brief. I noted that all the key cases were those JB had pulled for me a few hours earlier. Florida election law was considerably less complicated than I had initially supposed.

The second stage of an election dispute, the contest stage, was where the courts would play a key role. Under Florida law, while a protest recount request was addressed to local canvassing boards, a contest recount application was addressed to the courts. One strategy would be to bypass the protest phase entirely and go directly to an election contest. Such an approach would speed up the ultimate resolution of the dispute, since whoever lost the protest recount would presumably file a contest. It would also bypass Katherine Harris. One of the points that concerned me about our case before Judge Lewis was that the best we could hope for was to have him rule that the November 14 deadline for certification was not absolute and that the secretary of state had discretion. It was already clear that Harris would act as a Bush partisan, and arguing for the discretion of someone you knew was against you struck me as dangerous. However, when I raised the possible advantage of moving directly to an election contest, Ron Klain and others had patiently explained that I was ignoring "the political realities."

"It's not only the Republicans and the *Wall Street Journal* who are demanding Gore concede," Ron pointed out. "The *New York Times*, the *Washington Post*, and even some Democrats in Congress are expressing impatience. If the secretary of state certifies Bush the winner, it's over." Tacked to the wall was a copy of a front-page article from the *New York Times*. Underscored in red was the passage: "By next weekend, a group of scholars and senior politicians interviewed this weekend agreed, the presidential race of 2000 must be resolved, without recourse to the courts."

"You may be right," I had replied. "You probably are. But my sense in talking to a very unscientific sample of people over the last several days is that politicians and the media are a lot more concerned about having this over with immediately, and a lot more likely to see this as a "crisis," than the average voter. The people, or at least the half that voted for Gore, may be more understanding and patient than we may fear."

I thought then, as I did from time to time over the next thirty days, of Adlai Stevenson's promise "to talk sense to the American people." Stevenson had been clobbered twice at the polls trying to do so, but I was inclined to attribute that mostly to the fact that he was running against a popular war hero who also happened to be an intelligent and likable leader (and to the fact that many voters did believe it was time for a change after twenty uninterrupted years of Democrats in the White House).

Shortly before three a.m. Tuesday I left Berger's offices and walked the two blocks to the Governor's Inn, where a room had been reserved for me. As I was leaving Klain took me aside to share with me the pessimism of the campaign's leadership. "Daley is convinced that we have little if any chance of turning this around," he told me. He also noted that Daley's view was that if Gore failed to gain a lead prior to certification, he should concede rather than file an election contest.

"Christopher is also concerned that if Gore is perceived as fighting on too long, it will damage the country, the party, and Gore's future prospects," Klain added.

Over the next few weeks I would come to respect Klain as a brilliant lawyer with an unusual capacity for objectivity. Campaign Chairman William Daley was a tough, savvy professional with the best political judgment on Gore's team (and someone who recognized the potential danger that a pro-Bush majority on the U.S. Supreme Court posed earlier than most). No one was better than Christopher at analyzing a complicated problem with both legal and political implications, or more committed to giving his client, the Vice President, an objective appraisal of the situation. And at the time, as I read the press reports and statements by people in Gore's own party, their views made sense to me. Nevertheless, one of the two significant decisions I would second-guess with 20/20 hindsight was my accepting the critical importance of Secretary Harris's certification, and therefore devoting the time we did to the protest phase.

When I arrived at the Governor's Inn I left a wake-up call for 7:30 a.m. and went immediately to sleep. Four hours later I was in the shower thinking of Barbara Miller. If we were going to put Gore in the lead, Broward County was critical. It was one of two counties (the other being Palm Beach) that, based on voting patterns, had the most uncounted votes for Gore—and it was the only one of the counties where the canvassing board had voted against a recount. If that decision were not reversed, the rest of the protest efforts would be irrelevant.* Barbara was a committed Gore supporter, and someone who had the knowledge and contacts in Broward County that Dexter Douglass had in Tallahassee. When I got her on the phone I told her that I had arrived in Tallahassee the night before and was shocked to discover that Broward of all places was the one county refusing to begin a manual recount.

"If this were a sheriffs' race, the recount would already be underway," I pointed out. "The most important elected office in the world is at stake. What do we have to do to turn this around?"

"We're already working on that," she assured me. "You have to understand that everyone is concerned about going forward in the face of the secretary of state's opinion that manual recounts are improper."

The vote not to conduct a recount in Broward had been two to one. In favor was Suzanne Gunzburger, a bright, articulate Democrat who consistently championed the cause of counting all the votes based on voter intent. Jane Carroll, a Republican and the county's supervisor of elections, opposed the recount based on Secretary Harris's opinion that manual recounts were

---

*Moreover, as I understood Florida law, the local canvassing board had the discretion to decide whether or not to conduct a manual recount. A court might, if there were time, provide guidance as to the standard to apply in making that decision; but ultimately whether to recount or not at the protest stage was a canvassing board, not a judicial, decision.

improper. The deciding vote was cast by County Judge Robert Lee, who said he would have been inclined to order a recount but was reluctant to act contrary to Harris's opinion without good authority.

"The secretary of state cannot make new law," I replied. "In three hours last night Jonathan came up with three Florida Supreme Court cases that approved manual recounts. And the Republicans themselves requested a manual recount in Volusia until they figured out that since they were ahead all they needed to do was find a way to declare the game over. Would it be helpful if we got you some legal precedent to use with the canvassing board?"

Barbara knew Lee well and believed that while he would give considerable deference to the secretary of state's opinion, if he were presented with case authorities he would read them and make up his own mind. I arranged to have materials faxed to Barbara's home, and she agreed to get them to Judge Lee and the other two board members.

By 8:30 a.m. I was back at Mitchell Berger's offices. Dexter Douglass was already there when I arrived. Like many trial lawyers, he cultivated a down-home image that, for an unsuspecting opponent, might obscure his sharp mind and instinct for the jugular until it was too late. Unfortunately for Dexter, at this point in his life he was too successful for anyone to underestimate him. A long-time confidant and advisor to Florida's Democratic governors, he knew well (and had had some role in selecting) many of the state's judges. He had about as many friends among Republicans as Democrats, including Katherine Harris, whose chief of staff used to work for him. (Douglass's friendship with Harris did not keep him from giving her unshirted hell in court, or she him outside it.) All in all Dexter seemed the perfect person to take on the mixed legal and political questions presented by the Gore campaign's recount requests.

Although everyone was optimistic that Judge Lewis would order Harris not to certify Bush the winner that afternoon, we spent the two hours before we were due in court revising our draft appeal papers just in case. To win the battles you fight, it is necessary to prepare for many battles that you end up not fighting.

Shortly before 10:30 a.m., the time Judge Lewis had said he would announce a decision, Dexter and his team walked to the courthouse. It was decided that I would go with Douglass and that Christopher and Daley would wait at the Berger offices, monitoring what was happening on television. Because everything that occurred in court was broadcast live, together with commentary, people watching from the two campaigns' offices knew as much (and sometimes more) about what was going on in court as the lawyers who were there. When we arrived at court, we discovered that Judge Lewis had postponed his decision until noon.

As we waited, Dexter generally confirmed what I had been told the previous night. "Lewis has a reputation for balanced, middle-of-the road decisions," he told me. "And it is important to him to be thought of that way."

Shortly before one p.m. the court clerk distributed copies of Judge Lewis's opinion. It held that the secretary of state had discretion to delay certification until recounts were completed, and that Secretary Harris's announced decision to ignore all late-filed returns unless the lateness was caused by an "Act of God" was improper. "To determine ahead of time that returns *will* be ignored unless caused by some Act of God is not the exercise of discretion," Judge Lewis wrote. "It is the abdication of discretion." The court went on to hold that "the exercise of discretion, by its nature, contemplates a decision based upon a weighing and consideration of all attendant facts and circumstances." (Lewis also criticized Harris for her rush to certify the election before the absentee ballots had been counted.) It was, on the surface, exactly what Dexter and his team had argued.

However, Lewis's opinion also noted that if the secretary of state made an effort to weigh all the facts and circumstances, he did not have the authority to second-guess whatever decision she made. Since I was already convinced that Harris would do whatever advanced the Bush campaign, Lewis's decision underscored the danger that lurked in our protest arguments. The judge's opinion meant that Harris had to get the form right, use the right words, and follow the right procedures, but that if she did, her decision would be final, at least as far as Lewis was concerned. I had little doubt that whatever words or procedures Harris used, the result would be the same.

We returned to Berger's offices to analyze the decision and decide how to proceed. Christopher and Daley led the discussion, as they did the subsequent telephone conference with the Vice-President, Senator Lieberman, and others in Washington. Everyone recognized the dangers posed by Lewis's opinion, but no one could suggest how to avoid them. Everyone remained convinced that the controversy had to be resolved in days, not weeks. The press was already calling with questions, including whether Gore would concede if Harris, exercising the discretion the court said she had, eventually called an end to the recounts and certified Bush the winner.

It was agreed that Christopher should make himself available to the media that afternoon. He suggested I go with him, and Daley and Gore agreed. And so it was, less than eighteen hours after I left White Plains, promising Mary I would keep as low a profile as possible, that I stepped up to a bank of microphones and television cameras at the Florida State Capitol to begin my attempt to explain to the American people why under Florida law and good public policy it was important that the votes be counted before a winner was declared. As the professor's wife says in Tom Stoppard's play *Jumpers,* "It's not the voting that's democracy, it's the counting."

When it was over, Christopher, Daley, Klain, and I had another telephone conference with the Vice-President and Senator Lieberman. Both were pleased with the way the press conference had gone. I said that the most difficult question I had been asked, and the one I was not sure how to answer, was how long the process of counting all the votes would take. I was convinced that the answer need not be by November 18 or 19, as the *New York Times* and others had earlier urged. On the other hand, the answer "as long as it takes to get it right" seemed inconsistent with what I understood to be the campaign's position.

"Right now I can avoid answering by saying that the recount could be completed in a few days if the Republicans would simply stop their efforts to obstruct and delay it," I told my new clients. "However, at some point you have to tell me if you believe we must promise an end to this process."

Everyone agreed that we needed to be prepared to assure the press, the public, and key members of the candidates' own party that there was an end in sight beyond which Gore and Lieberman would not continue their challenge. No one, however, had an answer as to what that date was. Someone suggested another week, which would have been November 21, then Thanksgiving (November 23), then the Monday after Thanksgiving (November 27). Eventually I was asked how long I thought it would take to complete the recounts.

"Four or five days after the Republicans end, or are ordered to end, their efforts to prevent them," I replied. "The problem of course," I went on, "is that none of us knows when that will be."

As a first step the Gore campaign still had to convince the local canvassing boards to conduct the recounts, and on that front the day brought two pieces of good news and two of bad. The first positive news was that Volusia had completed its manual recount with a net change of twenty-seven votes in Gore's favor, reducing Bush's lead to 300. This was significant because Volusia was a Republican county where the Bush campaign had itself initially requested a manual recount. Broward, Miami-Dade, and Palm Beach were much larger, and heavily Democratic. If the pattern continued, it would put Gore in the lead even after taking into account the absentee ballots that had yet to be counted and that were expected to add to Bush's margin.

The second piece of good news was that the Broward County canvassing board, relying on the Florida Supreme Court cases it had been given and an opinion by the state's Attorney General

Bob Butterworth that manual recounts were permitted, had reconsidered its earlier decision and decided to begin a recount.*

Tuesday's bad news consisted of the decision of the Miami-Dade board, relying on Secretary Harris's opinion, not to conduct a manual recount, and the decision of the Palm Beach board to suspend its recount until the courts had reviewed Harris's opinion. Given the several hundred net Bush votes expected from the as-yet-uncounted absentee ballots, Gore could not gain enough votes from Volusia and Broward alone to overcome Bush's lead.

To find out what was happening in Miami, I called Steve Zack. Steve, who had fled Castro's Cuba with his family when he was eleven, was now part of the Miami establishment. The first Cuban-American to be elected president of the Florida Bar, he was a successful trial lawyer active in both business (he was chairman of a local bank) and politics. Although like Dexter Douglass an active Democrat, Zack (like Douglass) was liked and respected by Republicans as well.

Steve explained that the Miami-Dade board had voted two to one against a recount. A predictable vote for a recount was Lawrence D. King, a Democrat. A predictable vote against was Myriam Lehr, who although nominally a Democrat relied on Armando Gutierrez for support. (Gutierrez, a leader of the Cuban community in Miami and the spokesman for Elian Gonzalez's Miami relatives, had been enraged at Clinton and Gore for what he saw as the administration's betrayal of Elian and the Cuban exile community; on Election Day he traveled through Little Havana with a sign reading "Remember Elian—Vote for Bush.") The deciding vote had been cast by the Miami-Dade supervisor of elections, David Leahy. Unlike other counties in Florida, Miami-Dade's supervisor of elections serves at

---

*Attorney General Butterworth, a Democrat, had been a co-chairman of the Gore-Lieberman campaign in Florida. While the Gore camp considered his opinion better reasoned than Secretary Harris's, the dueling opinions of partisan officials underscored the need for local canvassing boards and the courts to look at the applicable Florida statutes and cases themselves.

the pleasure of the mayor—at the time Alex Penelas. Although a Democrat, Penelas was dependent on Cuban-American support and would not want to offend Gutierrez and other pro-Bush Cuban-American leaders by appearing to help Gore.

Leahy was by nature cautious, Steve explained. "He won't want to act until he knows where Penelas is."* Reflecting the cautious and conflicted climate in Miami-Dade, its canvassing board did not even meet to consider Gore's recount requests until November 14, the day that Harris had earlier said was the deadline. By contrast, Volusia County had by that time completed its recount, and Broward and Palm Beach had each met, decided, met again, and reversed their earlier decisions.

The decision of Palm Beach to suspend its recount was even more unexpected and troubling than the Miami-Dade news. Palm Beach (along with Broward) was one of the two counties from which Gore expected to gain the most votes; a recount there was critical to Gore's hopes. Palm Beach, like Miami-Dade and Broward, had one predictable vote for a recount (County Commissioner Carol Roberts) and one predictable vote against (County Judge Charles Burton). The deciding vote to begin recounts and then to suspend them was cast by the county's long-time supervisor of elections, Theresa LePore. Shell-shocked by the furor over her "butterfly ballot" experiment, LePore was mainly concerned with avoiding further controversy. Although this was an impossible objective under the circumstances, Burton convinced her that her best chance was to ask the Florida Supreme Court for guidance and to do nothing until that guidance was received. Any other decision, he argued, would subject her to additional criticism for ignoring the secretary of state's opinion.

Burton was aided in his efforts by Kerey Carpenter, Katherine

---

*After the case was over, it was reported that Leahy kept a sign in his office: "My Decision Is Final: The Answer Is Maybe". Jeffrey Toobin, *Too Close to Call* (New York: Random House, 2001), p. 148.

Harris's aide who had been sent to Palm Beach to block the recount. Introducing herself correctly but incompletely as being from the state's Division of Elections, Carpenter privately advised Burton and publicly and privately lobbied LePore. On Tuesday, with LePore unwilling to go forward without the authorization of the Florida Supreme Court, the Gore campaign's only option in Palm Beach was to try to accelerate the Supreme Court's decision while preventing Secretary Harris from certifying a winner in the meantime.

At around eight that evening, Harris took the step I had been expecting: she began to make a record of exercising her "discretion," instructing the three counties where recount requests were pending (Volusia having already finished) to provide "a written statement of the facts and circumstances" that they believed justified a delay in certification. She gave the counties until two the following afternoon to comply.

Ron Klain was outraged. "This *is* Guatemala. If this were happening anywhere else in the world, the United States and the United Nations would be trying to send in observers and considering sanctions."

Bill Daley was realistic. "What did you expect?"

The consensus was that Harris would declare a winner on Saturday, the day the counting of the absentee ballots was to be completed. Bringing down the curtain before then was impossible to justify, and it was clear that there was no danger to Bush in waiting, since the vote counting could not be completed before the following Monday or Tuesday.

Dexter Douglass, Mitchell Berger, and John Newton were already planning their return to Judge Lewis's courtroom. "This is a setup," Berger said to no one in particular. "By Wednesday night," he sarcastically predicted (correctly, as it turned out), "she will have carefully considered all the facts and circumstances and concluded that the vote counting should end. We need to be prepared to be back before Lewis on Thursday." Douglass and Newton agreed.

"Harris knows the counties won't have had a fair chance to

complete their recounts." Douglass said. "And Terry Lewis will know she knows. He's a fair judge. This is an evasion of his decision yesterday. He won't let her get away with it." Everyone was particularly outraged that Harris seemed determined to declare the counting over at a time when two counties, relying on her opinion not to start counting until the Florida Supreme Court had had a chance to rule, had not even begun.

Tuesday evening and Wednesday morning Daley, the lawyers, and (by telephone) Gore and Lieberman discussed our next steps. Everyone agreed that we needed to wait to make a final decision until we saw what Harris actually did, and the candidates continued to have some hope that she would act more responsibly than all the lawyers feared; it was hard for anyone not in Florida to accept the extent to which Harris had abandoned any effort to act neutrally. In order to be ready for the worst, everyone agreed that we should prepare for another appearance before Judge Lewis.

We also continued to discuss the two questions that had concerned me Tuesday afternoon, and which had been raised again when I spoke to individual members of the press later that day and evening. (Following the Tuesday afternoon press conference it had been decided that I would play a larger role in explaining legal issues to the press, and the campaign's press staff had begun to schedule periodic interviews.) Everyone agreed that we should duck the question of how long Gore was prepared to continue to try to reverse Bush's slim lead until we saw some additional cards. However, Gore himself was increasingly convinced that something should be said to counter the Republicans' argument that there was something unfair about the Democrats' limiting their recount requests to four counties.

The people who had been involved in making the initial decision about where recounts would be requested pointed out that the Republicans were free to request a recount in any county they chose and had in fact requested one in Volusia; that there was no procedure under Florida law for requesting a single statewide recount; and that sixty-seven separate requests in each of Florida's

sixty-seven counties would subject the Gore-Lieberman campaign to charges of overreaching.* It was also noted that, up to
that point at least, the issue of whether the Gore campaign should
have asked for a statewide recount did not appear to have gotten
much traction.

Michael Whouley, Gore's chief political field operative in
Florida and the person who had the best sense of what results
recounts would or would not yield, also expressed doubt as to
whether a recount beyond the four counties selected would provide any net additional votes for Gore. I was told that Daley had
originally wanted to limit the recounts to Volusia and Palm Beach
and that it had been Whouley who had convinced Daley to add
Broward and Miami-Dade. Without Whouley's support any proposal for a wider recount would have been tough sledding. Finally,
any request for a manual recount had to have been made within
forty-eight hours of the election (by Thursday, November 9). It
was now too late to ask for a statewide recount at the protest stage,
even had we wanted to.

Nevertheless I remained concerned that the issue could undercut our ability to hold the moral high ground, a concern that was
heightened the next morning when I talked to Mary. "Why did
they ask to recount only four counties?" she asked. I tried to explain that under Florida law they probably were not entitled to a
statewide recount at the protest stage, but Mary was not convinced. "They still could have asked."

I trusted Mary's political instincts and if she, far removed from
Florida, was already focused on this issue, I was convinced that it
was likely to become more important than people then thought.

Later that day I found that the Vice President himself had con-

---

*The campaign had good reasons to believe there were uncounted votes in the four
counties selected, but casting a sixty-seven county net would be criticized as a fishing expedition. Moreover, it was proving difficult enough to convince three of the four counties
where a request had been made to conduct a recount without taking on that burden sixty-
three more times.

cluded that it was time to do something, and he had an idea for possibly solving two problems at once. He would propose to Bush that both campaigns agree to a statewide recount and to abide by the result without further challenges or litigation. The chances of Bush's accepting were slim, but making the proposal both undercut any potential claim that the Democrats were trying to limit recounts to selected counties and promised the public an end to the process. Gore made his proposal in a speech on national television Wednesday night. The Republicans predictably declined. However, the idea was generally well received. (The *New York Times*, which a few days before had been urging a quick end to the process, called it "a sensible way out of the legal and electoral quagmire.") While the suggestion did not prevent subsequent questions about why a statewide recount had not been requested initially, it provided an answer to those who wanted to listen.

At 9:15 p.m. Wednesday Katherine Harris also made a statement—underscoring, to the extent any further emphasis was necessary, why the Republicans believed they did not need to entertain any compromise proposals. Tuesday evening she had filed papers with the Florida Supreme Court asking that it stop the recounts. On Wednesday, without waiting for argument, the court denied the application. Now Harris took matters into her own hands. She announced that she would "finally certify the presidential election in Florida on Saturday."*

As we watched her performance on the television sets in the Berger offices, it was clear that we needed to be back before Judge Lewis Thursday morning. What was not so clear was what we should do when we got there. Lewis had previously ruled that the Secretary of State had discretion to decide when to declare the counting over. She had now purported to exercise it.

---

*She said that "for the past six hours" she and her staff had carefully reviewed the requests for extensions of time filed by the county canvassing boards who had not completed their work and that "I've decided it is my duty under Florida law to exercise my discretion in denying these requested amendments."

Courts regularly review public officials' exercise of their statutory discretion, but such judicial review is deferential. It is not enough that the judge would have made a different decision. An abuse of discretion will be found only when a court concludes that it is clear that the public official has acted not only wrongly, but unreasonably.

Dexter and I believed that the best way to prove this point was to subpoena Harris as a witness and cross-examine her about her motivations and the bases for her decision. We both agreed that he would make the oral argument and put on any friendly witnesses we might call; I would cross-examine Harris.

I could easily envision how I would proceed. Describe all of your contacts with representatives of the Bush campaign during and after the election campaign. Describe each of your discussions with George and Jeb Bush after the election. Describe every conversation you had with anyone about your decisions to cut off the vote-counting Tuesday, November 14 to tell local canvassing boards not to conduct manual recounts, to ask the Florida Supreme Court to stop the manual recounts. What was your legal or factual support, if any, for each of those decisions? What precedent were you aware of that was contrary to your decisions? (If she acknowledged she was aware of manual recount precedents, she would have to admit she ignored them; if she denied knowledge of such precedents, all of which were matters of public record, she would have to admit her ignorance and lack of due diligence.)

Did you believe it was possible for recounts to be completed in the time allowed? If so, did you believe that the canvassing board members who said they needed more time, some of whom were Democrats and some Republican, were lying? What was the basis for your belief that the recounts could be completed in the time you allowed? What prejudice would occur if the canvassing boards were given time to do their recounts now that the Florida Supreme Court has denied your request to prevent those recounts—particularly since the earliest that Florida needs to report its electors is December 12?

It could have been a great cross-examination, but it was not to be.

In addition to examining Harris personally, we proposed to subpoena her documents and e-mails. We already had evidence of a number of indiscreet e-mails she had sent. While under the law internal messages between Harris and her staff might be protected from subpoena, refusing to produce them would put Harris in a difficult position as she would have to argue that the courts must trust her discretion without seeing what she wrote about her reasons. More importantly, Harris's e-mails to persons outside her office (Bush campaign personnel, political supporters, friends) were clearly not protected, and we knew that she had written a number of them over the last week. Some—such as her detailed descriptions of why she thought of herself as a biblical figure—were merely background color. Others revealed the partisanship and prejudgment that we contended were inconsistent with the exercise of statutory discretion.

Dexter and I recommended that we serve subpoenas immediately, and there is no doubt that in a normal case we would have done just that. But this was not a normal case. The campaign leadership was understandably concerned with the political implications of subpoenaing Secretary Harris and her records. It would, we agreed, be provocative and confrontational. It did, we agreed, fit the cliché of "hardball" litigation. Whether it was too provocative, too confrontational, too hardball was the question. The campaign leadership thought it was and that it would damage Gore politically.

I had still been there only forty-eight hours, and I was to some extent still feeling my way. Moreover, we did not need evidence for what was probably our best argument—that it was necessarily an abuse of discretion for Harris to prevent the boards from conducting recounts, then use the delay she caused to refuse to consider the recounts' results. In retrospect, however, this was my second mistake—I should have pushed the issue harder. Lawyers must be prepared to tell a client what needs to be done even (indeed, particularly) where the client does not want to do it; and to give that advice in the strongest possible terms, even if the client is offended. Lawyers who do not are not serving their clients well.

I knew I had made a mistake Thursday afternoon when, after our arguments, Lewis complained, "I haven't received any evidence of any facts." Dexter did the best he could, telling the court, "It's like you're driving along and the policeman says, 'Stop,' and you stop. A whole bunch of cars come up behind you. And then he comes over and says, 'I'm writing you a ticket for blocking traffic.'" However, when at the conclusion of the hearing Lewis asked again whether we had any evidence, I believed I knew his decision.

My hopes were lifted somewhat later that afternoon when the Florida Supreme Court responded to Palm Beach County's petition for a decision on whether it was bound by Secretary Harris's opinion that it should not recount votes. At 4:30 p.m. the court held, "There is no legal impediment to the recounts continuing." As if for emphasis, the court continued: "Thus, Petitioners are authorized to proceed with the manual recount." With the Florida Supreme Court now clearly on record that Harris's instructions were improper, I hoped that Lewis would agree that it was inherently unreasonable for her to take advantage of the delay she had caused as the excuse for refusing to include the results of the recounts.

Judge Lewis had said he would issue a decision Friday morning. Promptly at ten a.m. the court administrator handed it out. The one-page opinion was a clear victory for the Republicans. "It appears," Lewis held, "that the Secretary has exercised her reasoned judgment to determine what relevant factors and criteria should be considered, applied them to the facts and circumstances pertinent to the individual counties involved and made her decision." The opinion, particularly in light of the Florida Supreme Court's decision the previous afternoon, was a disappointment.

The judge did not explain what "relevant factors and criteria" he thought Harris had considered or what "the facts and circumstances pertinent to the individual counties involved" were. Lewis's conclusion that the Secretary's decision represented a "reasoned judgment" lacked any indication of how or why Lewis so concluded. Judges do not always provide reasons for their judgments, certainly not to the satisfaction of losing lawyers. However, Lewis could have been a little more explicit. At the same time I could appreciate Lewis's dilemma. Neither side had provided any evidence on which to base findings. Since the Democrats were challenging the Secretary of State's decision, the Democrats bore the burden of proof; all other things being equal, in the absence of evidence from either side the Republicans should win.

The most serious flaw that I saw in Judge Lewis's opinion was his failure to address how Harris could reasonably have decided to ignore "late" recounts when she was responsible for the "lateness." The Supreme Court had made clear (twice, once in connection with Broward County and once with Palm Beach) that Harris's instructions concerning manual recounts were wrong. It might have been possible to craft an argument as to why her deadline was nevertheless reasonable, but neither Harris nor Lewis had done so.

Immediately following the release of the opinion we reconvened at Mitchell Berger's offices. On my way back, a number of reporters walked with me discussing informally what the next steps might be. Along the way I stopped to get an ice cream cone, and as I ate I had a chance to listen more than I spoke. It was clear that nobody expected Gore to abandon the fight; everybody thought that we would appeal. The question that the better reporters were asking was whether we would try to get the Supreme Court to issue a stay order preventing Harris from certifying a winner on Saturday and, if we did, what were our chances. As we discussed those same questions back at the office, Bush's reported lead increased from 300 to 930 votes as the absentee ballots were counted.

One possibility was not to appeal Lewis's second order at all, let Harris certify Bush the winner, then immediately file an election contest. Lewis's opinion had, in fact, explicitly noted that after certification any candidate could commence an election contest on the same basis that we were seeking a protest recount; and in an election contest, which was a judicial proceeding, Harris would not have the power to stop a recount or decide when any deadline would be.

She also would not have any discretion to which the court might defer. I was convinced that the press did not expect Saturday to be the end of the matter and that whatever the views may have been a few days earlier, the pressure on Gore to avoid a continuing controversy had abated considerably. While the notion of a post-certification election contest had been anathema to the campaign leadership when the original protests were filed, there now seemed to be a developing consensus that if Harris certified on Saturday, an election contest should be filed.

Despite this view, there was also a consensus that we should appeal Lewis's decision. Avoiding a certification of Bush's winning Florida was still first choice, and all the lawyers believed that we had a good shot at overturning Lewis on appeal. In addition, the question of what "standard" to use in determining voter intent was already an issue. In Palm Beach Judge Burton, who had recently been appointed to the circuit court by Jeb Bush and who appeared particularly responsive to Harris's people, had succeeded in getting the Palm Beach board to vote two to one to change the way ballots were reviewed. Initially the board had simply looked at each ballot to determine whether the intent of the voter was clear; if it was, the vote was counted. In some cases that intent was unanimously determined (including by Burton) based on indentations made by voters who had not punched through the card.

However, after consulting with one of Harris's representatives, Burton had convinced LePore to join him in requiring that the card had to be punched through sufficiently to allow light to shine through, an approach that soon became known as the "sunshine standard."* The effect of this change was dramatic. The board had

---

*Voters were instructed "to be sure your voting selections are clearly and cleanly punched and there are no chips left hanging on the back of the card." Burton and the Republicans argued from this that any voters whose ballots were not punched through had not followed the law and their votes should not be counted.

finished just half a precinct before Burton changed the ground rules. That half a precinct had resulted in a net gain to Gore-Lieberman of 50 votes. After the change in standard, the board reconsidered that half precinct under the "sunshine standard"; Gore's gain dropped to 6. Forty-four Palm Beach voters who registered, came to the polls, and cast a ballot (actually many more, since the fifty-vote shift netted new ballots for Bush against new ballots for Gore) were judged not to have voted for president.

We believed that, if we could get the Florida Supreme Court to address the issue, it would confirm that where the intent of the voter was apparent the vote had to be counted whether or not the voter had succeeded in punching through the ballot card.

There are good policy arguments that can be made both for and against such a rule. It vindicates the important public policy that in a democracy people have the right both to vote and to have that vote counted. On the other hand, ascertaining intent is inherently subjective, particularly in close cases. A machine count is not as accurate in ascertaining voter intent as a manual count, both because of machine errors and voter errors; that is why most states, including Texas pursuant to a statute signed by then Governor George W. Bush, provide for manual recounts in close elections. However, the advantage of machines is that they are indisputably neutral; there are not Republican machines or Democratic machines. People, or at least many of them, are Republicans and Democrats—and when making subjective decisions may be influenced by their political interests. A state might well decide that, for all their imperfections, machine counts should be the last word to avoid either the fact or appearance of partiality, just as a state might decide that the person in charge of elections should not be an elected political official. Florida, like most states, long ago made a contrary decision, that machine counts would not be the last word. The issue in 2000 was not what rule Florida should have; it had a rule. The issue was whether that settled rule would be applied in the closest and most important election in the state's history.

Ideally the court would explicitly reject the sunshine standard.

However, whatever standard it provided, we (and the boards and lower courts) would know what the authoritative rule was. We did not want to have a recount conducted under one standard or standards only to have the Supreme Court later decide that a different standard should have been used. The question of what standard to use had not been an issue before Judge Lewis, so technically the supreme court would not have to address it when it reviewed his decisions. However, an appeal from Lewis's order gave us an opportunity to seek such guidance, and gave the Supreme Court the opportunity to provide it if it so wished.

We decided that we should appeal but that we would not ask the supreme court to stop Harris's Saturday certification before hearing argument. One factor in our decision was the political concern that Harris's certification would carry more weight with the press, public, and politicians if the Supreme Court had implicitly approved its going forward by denying our request to enjoin it.* Lawyers know that denial of the unusual remedy of an interim injunction does not suggest that a court will deny the underlying appeal on the merits. However, there was understandable concern that such a nuance could get easily lost as reporters raced to report the latest judicial development. "Florida Supreme Court OKs Certification of Bush as Winner in Florida" was a headline the campaign wanted to avoid.

There would be, of course, no damage to the Republicans if Harris's certification were postponed a few days until after the Supreme Court had had an opportunity to consider our appeal. That was an argument in favor of staying certification until the appeal was decided. On the other hand, it also could be argued that the Democrats would not suffer any great harm if the certification went forward, since the court could always vacate the certification.

We also noted that our written submissions to the Florida

---

*Another factor was that we bore a heavier burden in seeking to enjoin Harris's certification before a hearing than we did in seeking to reverse Lewis's decision after a hearing. We did not want to force the court to start out by making a decision against us.

Supreme Court already made clear the bases for our view that certification of a winner without including the results of manual recounts was contrary to Florida law, and that Harris intended to go forward on Saturday unless the court stopped her. If the Supreme Court believed it was appropriate to stay the certification until the appeal was argued, it could either schedule the argument to precede the planned certification or issue a stay on its own motion. We did not consider either possibility very likely.

We also began preparing for an election contest to be filed immediately after Harris's expected certification. There was some concern that filing an election contest before the Monday argument in the Supreme Court might make the court believe it could affirm Lewis and sort everything out in the election contest appeal. I concluded that risk was worth taking because we did not want to waste valuable time waiting for a contest to begin and because I believed the supreme court would vacate the certification in any event. I did not believe the same court that had twice that week ruled that manual recounts should take place would now rule that the results of those manual recounts could be ignored.* In the end everyone agreed to pursue the appeal and the contest simultaneously.

Nevertheless, the concern with the political fall-out from a certification of Bush as the winner was palpable. Daley pointed

---

*On Tuesday afternoon Judge Lewis had barred the Secretary of State's planned certification of the election later that afternoon. On Tuesday night Secretary Harris had responded to Lewis's decision by asking the counties to justify why they had not yet finished their recounts (which they could have done only by ignoring her prior instructions to stop) and simultaneously asked the Florida Supreme Court to block the recounts in Broward, which was by then ignoring her directions. On Wednesday afternoon the Supreme Court denied Harris's request to block Broward's recount, and on Wednesday evening Harris had declared her intention of certifying the election on Saturday without waiting for that recount to be completed. Thursday early afternoon we had had our hearing before Judge Lewis; Thursday late afternoon the Florida Supreme Court overruled Harris's opinion on the propriety of manual recounts and directed Palm Beach County to complete its recount. Thursday evening Harris reaffirmed her intention to certify the winner in Florida on Saturday anyway.

out privately what Secretary Jim Baker was arguing publicly on behalf of the Republicans: no presidential candidate since 1876 had challenged a state's certification of the winner of its electoral votes. Assuming the certification proceeded as scheduled, after Sunday we would be in uncharted waters. However, I saw the possibility of the result that I most preferred but that ordinarily was not available under Florida law—simultaneous protest and contest proceedings. Ordinarily a contest cannot start until the protest phase is completed because a contest must follow certification and the protest phase precedes certification. A Saturday certification would permit us to start the contest immediately, without spending valuable time waiting for the protest recounts to be completed. At the same time, the fact that our appeal of the certification was in process mitigated the political concerns that had prevented the Gore campaign from accepting certification the prior Tuesday and moving immediately to an election contest.

As it turned out, we did not get very far preparing our election contest papers that Friday. At about four p.m. the Supreme Court issued an order scheduling argument of our appeal for the following Monday. The order went on, "In order to maintain the status quo, the Court, on its own motion, enjoins the Secretary of State . . . from certifying the results of the November 7, 2000, Presidential election, until further order of the Court."

The order was immediately perceived, and reported, as a dramatic victory for Gore. We expressed satisfaction. Secretary Harris, silent in public, expressed shock and rage to her chief of staff and others. Jim Baker, who earlier that day, following Judge Lewis's order, had been expressing his commitment to "the rule of law" and his respect for the Florida courts, held a hasty press conference to denounce the Florida judiciary.

It began to look as if Gore would overtake Bush before Harris could certify a winner. Broward's recount was well under way; Palm Beach had started to count its votes the previous day; and Steve Zack had told me at noon, even before the latest order, that he believed the Miami–Dade canvassing board would finally begin counting that day or the next based on the Court's Thursday order.* The three people least convinced that Gore was going to prevail were Barry Richards, Michael Whouley, and me.

Barry Richards, Bush's lead lawyer in Florida, was an experienced trial lawyer who shared my reluctance to grieve or celebrate while a case was still going on; both of us had seen too many turns in too many cases to have any confidence that we could predict how this one would end up. Moreover, as we discussed over a drink at the sports bar in Andrew's Capital Grill across from the Governor's Inn, this was an easy interim injunction for the court to grant. There was no prejudice to anyone in maintaining the status quo over the weekend. The canvassing boards that were counting could continue doing so. Whether those votes would be included in the certified results could be determined on Monday. We both agreed that the stay order was a straw in the wind indicating that the court, at the very least, took our claims seriously, but it was not more than that. Before the order I had believed the court would reverse Judge Lewis; I now became more confident, but still not certain. Before the stay order Barry had believed that the court would affirm Lewis; he still held that belief, but with somewhat less confidence. Each of us knew that the fight was far from over.

Michael Whouley's problem was different. Looking at statistics and voting patterns, he was not sure that even if Broward, Miami-Dade, and Palm Beach had time to complete their counts, Gore would win. If the county canvassing boards approached their task the way Broward and Miami-Dade did, and the way Palm Beach did at the beginning, counting ballots where the intent of the voter could be ascertained, everyone was confident that the three counties would garner more than the 930 net votes Gore needed to win.

---

*Although Miami-Dade had technically not been a party to Palm Beach County's case in which the Supreme Court had ruled that there was no impediment to continuing recounts, Steve believed that Miami-Dade would have a hard time distinguishing its situation from that in Palm Beach.

However, if the sunshine standard adopted in Palm Beach were used, predicting the outcome was more difficult. The recount in Broward ultimately yielded 567 net votes for Gore. Whouley predicted that a broad "intent of the voter" standard would yield another 600 to 800 votes in Palm Beach, more than enough to put Gore over the top even without Miami-Dade. (After the case was over, a *Palm Beach Post* count of the county's ballots using the intent of the voter standard showed a 784 net vote gain for Gore.) On the other hand, using the so-called sunshine standard, Palm Beach was on track to come up with only 150 to 250 net votes for Gore. And if the same standard were used in Broward, the net gain there for Gore would probably be reduced by half or more. Gore could still win under a sunshine standard, depending on what happened in Miami-Dade and whether the recounts came in at the higher end of Whouley's estimates, but Whouley was dubious. Too much had to happen right.

There was one more complication that I mentioned to Mary when we spoke on Friday night. The Supreme Court's order staying Secretary Harris's certification prevented us from beginning our election contest Saturday. "Does that matter?" she asked.

"I hope not," I replied. "We should have enough time to accomplish both a protest recount and, if necessary, a contest sequentially. But it would have been good to have been able to proceed on both paths simultaneously." As it turned out, we did have enough time, but I did not realize how close it would be.

In the context of the Florida election controversy, Saturday and Sunday were relatively relaxed. Except for a few press interviews and the Florida/Florida State football game Saturday night, I was free to work on our briefs to the Supreme Court and prepare for my oral argument. Even during the press interviews, and in discussions during and after the game, I was testing and refining my argument—trying to find the best way of explaining the Florida cases and statutes so that I was both clear and accurate. It is easy to be clear and simple if you sacrifice accuracy, or accurate if you sacrifice clarity and simplicity. A trial lawyer's success depends on his or her ability to be clear, simple, *and* accurate at the same time. A lack of simplicity and clarity prevents a lawyer from communicating effectively. A lack of accuracy will destroy a lawyer's most important asset, credibility. In a short case a lawyer sometimes may manage, if so inclined, to rely on misstatements of law or fact without the other side, or the court, catching on in time. In a long case, or a case as intense and public as the Florida election litigation, everything will come out; accuracy is not only good ethics, but critical to credibility.

The price of becoming immersed in a case is that a lawyer soon has very few people left who know enough to debate the case's key issues, or who are interested in doing so.* In most cases that comes down to the lawyers on the other side, if they are good—which is one reason lawyers tend to socialize, often more than clients like, with the lawyers on the other side. In a case like the Florida election litigation (or like *Microsoft*, or *Westmoreland v. CBS*) many reporters' interest in, and knowledge of, the case matches the lawyers' own. And many reporters, like many lawyers, enjoy talking and drinking late into the night, about the only time one can do so during a difficult case.

Late Saturday night at Andrew's Capital Grill & Bar, reporters and one of Bush's lawyers regaled me with Katherine Harris's de-

---

*The detailed knowledge that is essential to a lawyer's preparation comes with a danger. The danger is that the lawyer will forget how a fact or argument appears to someone who has not accumulated the lawyer's specialized knowledge. To regain that insight lawyers sometimes practice their arguments before scientifically assembled panels of people chosen to match, as closely as possible, the characteristics of the jurors and/or judges who are expected to hear a case. A quarter century earlier, when I was trying a case in Los Angeles for IBM, I had teamed up with a young professor of sociology at U.S.C. to experiment with a panel who actually attended the real trial, listening to the evidence (and only the evidence) that the real jury heard. Every night the professor would debrief the members of the panel as to what they understood and what they did not understand, what arguments and evidence they believed and what they did not believe, what questions they had, what facts would make them more likely to support one side or the other. The experiment successfully provided important insights. The young sociology professor, Don Vinson, went on to become the best-known and most successful jury consultant in the country.

scription of a dream in which she rode into the Florida State football stadium on a horse, carrying the FSU flag in one hand and the certification of Bush as the winner in Florida in the other, with the entire stadium cheering and calling her name. I can't say that that particular piece of information was useful, but it did provide some lighthearted amusement.

More practical was the testing and challenging that I got from reporters, both in formal interviews and socially. These were tough, smart, hardworking people whose mission in life sometimes seemed to be to find a hole in our facts, an inconsistency in our arguments, or simply something they knew that we did not. It was fun to be with them; other than the other lawyers and our clients, no one knew as much, or cared as much, about what I was doing as they did. And I knew that if my arguments could survive their challenges they could probably survive most of what I would face in court.

As I prepared for Monday's argument, I became increasingly confident. Usually the closer I get to a hearing, the more I understand the other side's point of view. This time the more I read and thought, the more I was convinced there was no reasonable basis under Florida law to bar the manual recounts or ignore their results. The only problem that I saw was that the law left the issue of whether to conduct a recount up to local canvassing boards. As long as the boards chose to count (and all three boards were counting as of Sunday), we were in good shape. However, each of the three had already changed its mind at least once. I knew that the Republicans were working hard to convince all three to change their minds again, and given what I was learning about Florida politics I knew they had a shot at succeeding. Since I could not find any prior case where the court had reversed the decision of a local board and itself ordered a protest stage recount, I was concerned that if one or more of the boards stopped counting, we would be without an effective remedy. I did not yet appreciate, however, the lengths to which the Bush campaign would go to convince a board to stop.

One other issue demanded attention over the weekend. Beginning Saturday morning the Bush campaign had begun a major press offensive complaining about the disqualification of absentee ballots from military personnel. During the initial counting of these ballots earlier that week, Republican and Democratic observers had successfully challenged a number of ballots that did not meet the requirements of Florida law. A memo from the Gore campaign to Democratic observers advised them to concentrate on ballots from military personnel which could be expected to favor Bush. A memo from the Bush campaign to Republican observers advised them to concentrate on ballots from civilians, which particularly in South Florida counties could be expected to favor Gore.

Ballots were disqualified, among other reasons, because they lacked evidence (such as a postmark or official dating) that they had been submitted on or before Election Day; because the voter was not a resident of the county; because the handwriting was not legible; or because military personnel had used a federal write-in ballot without (as the law required) first requesting an absentee ballot from their state. The local canvassing boards had decided which ballots to disqualify, and the tallies reported to the secretary of state reflected those decisions. There was no evidence that the boards used different criteria than they had in past elections; in fact both Republican and Democratic board members told reporters Saturday and Sunday that they had done what they had always done. Nevertheless Gore, Daley, and Christopher were all concerned with the potential PR damage that the campaign's challenges to military absentee ballots might entail.

We did not have to decide what to do about absentee ballots that weekend, and we didn't. What we did have to do was to get ready for Monday's Florida Supreme Court argument. And that we did. When I went to bed late Sunday night, I had been in Tallahassee just under six days. It seemed longer.

11

Bush v. Gore:
Winning in Florida

Prior to Monday, November 20, the Florida Supreme Court had decided the parties' appeals based on their written submissions. This would be the first time we appeared in person. The argument was scheduled for two p.m., and that morning we reviewed again how we should respond to the two questions I had raised six days earlier—should we ask for a statewide recount, and how much time should we request to finish the counting? As to the first, we quickly agreed I would, if asked, respond that we continued to be prepared to accept a statewide recount, but that we did not seek one over Bush's objections.*

The question of how much time to ask for was more complicated. The candidates and the campaign leadership continued to believe that some definite point of closure was necessary politically. I believed that the court would also want a schedule for completing the recount. The position of Florida's Attorney Gen-

---

*We had not previously asked the courts for that relief and we did not want to do so for the first time on appeal; a statewide recount would increase both the time and burden of completing the task; and we proposed one not because we believed it would gain significant votes but because we wanted to eliminate any legitimate claim by Bush that the four-county recount was unfair.

eral, Bob Butterworth, was that as a legal matter the final certification of a winner in Florida had to be completed by December 12. The electors were not set to meet until December 18. However, following the 1876 contest, Congress had provided, in what became known as the "safe harbor" provision, that if a state had determined its electors by a particular date (December 12 for the 2000 election) pursuant to procedures in effect on Election Day, that determination would be final. There were political as well as legal reasons for there to be a final resolution by December 12; the Democrats could not afford to have the presidency decided by the Republican-controlled House of Representatives. Everyone agreed that December 12 was the outside date, but should we suggest an earlier cutoff? December 12 was more than three weeks away, and there was concern that suggesting that the controversy would continue that long would invite the same calls for Gore to concede that had plagued the campaign when I first arrived.

Ultimately we decided that, if asked, we would say that we believed there should be a final resolution (protest and contest) no later than December 12, but that we also believed it should not take that long. If asked how much time we thought was needed for the protest phase we would try to avoid giving a cutoff date since it was the protest recount that the political experts believed was most likely to turn the election; if pressed we would ask for a week. At the time that seemed more than long enough to complete the recounts, all of which were then under way.

I had an early lunch and was in the courtroom an hour and a half before the argument was scheduled to commence. Immediately before an important argument or cross-examination, I try to take time to organize my thoughts. It is not always possible, but on November 20 I had all the time in the world. It was a good thing too, because once the argument started the questions came fast and furiously.

Paul Hancock, counsel for the state attorney general, argued first, followed by me, then by counsel for the Bush campaign and for Secretary Harris. Predictably, the court (led by Chief Justice Charles Wells) wanted to know when this was all going to end. Hancock said his understanding was December 12, and the court did not press him further. When my turn came, Wells asked whether I agreed with this date, and I said I did.

The justices had read the briefs carefully and asked each side probing questions. They focused on the need for finality, but they also, as I had hoped, focused on the long line of Florida cases that emphasized the importance of counting every vote according to the voter's intent. My argument came down to three basic points. Florida law had historically provided manual recounts in close elections with the intent of the voter given precedence. Florida law was consistent in this respect with that of most other states, including Texas. It was wrong and unfair for Secretary Harris to abandon settled Florida procedure in an attempt to gain a partisan advantage for her candidate. (Bush's attorney, Michael Carvin, had a particularly difficult time explaining why manual recounts were good in Governor Bush's state of Texas but bad in Florida.)

As we walked back to Berger's offices that afternoon, I believed the argument had gone well. When we arrived, we learned that a state judge in Miami had denied yet another attempt by the Bush campaign to stop the recount there. We appeared to be on the right track. My enthusiasm was tempered only by the increasingly cool Tallahassee weather and the fact that the standard used by Judge Burton in Palm Beach County was resulting in fewer net additional votes for Gore than we had expected.

The following morning both the weather and the news from Palm Beach turned colder still. With below-freezing temperatures Tallahassee was now colder than New York, and Judge Burton was refusing to count an increasing number of ballots. When my assistant Pat Dennis had flown down from New York to help me deal with other cases that I could not put off, he had brought me a sweater to deal with the cold. I had not, however, discovered how to deal with Judge Burton. Even if the results of the ongoing recounts were included in the final tally, the race was going to be very close.

We spent most of Tuesday analyzing legal and factual issues relating to Seminole County, which had gone for Bush by a reported margin of 75,677 to 59,174. Bush's 16,503 vote margin included a net gain of 4,700 votes from absentee ballots, and I learned there was a good argument for excluding such ballots. Under Florida law, to vote absentee a voter must sign and send in an application. The application must include, among other things, the voter's identification number—a requirement that enables the state to be sure that the voter is registered and that no one will vote twice. In Seminole the Republicans had mailed preprinted absentee applications to registered Republicans. All the voter had to do was sign and send it in, which several thousand did. There was only one problem. The preprinted applications omitted by mistake the potential voters' identification number. No one noticed, and the Republicans ended up with thousands of invalid applications on file.

The omission was first spotted by county election officials, who informed the county's supervisor of elections. At that point the supervisor, a Republican, reported the omission to Republican campaign workers. That step alone subjected the supervisor to some criticism since she was supposed to act neutrally. On the other hand, the action was probably better than one alternative (doing nothing, and probably misleading some Florida residents into believing until it was too late to correct the problem that they would receive an absentee ballot) and more efficient than the other alternative (notifying each individual applicant). If the supervisor's initial action had stopped there, Seminole would not have been in the spotlight. However, she next turned the ballot applications, and her offices, over to Republican Party workers, who came in and amended the filed applications by adding the missing identification numbers.

It was probably improper for the supervisor to allow Republican Party workers access to her offices and the ballot applications without giving Democratic representatives the opportunity to be present. It was certainly improper to permit the applications to be altered after they had been submitted.

The Democrats' argument was simple. The applications were not prepared as Florida law required. Therefore the supervisor of elections should not have issued absentee ballots. Therefore the ballots she did issue should not be counted—which would once and for all put Florida in the Gore-Lieberman column. There was no conceivable way for Bush to recover from losing 4,700 votes regardless of what happened in Broward, Palm Beach, or Miami-Dade.

The problem was that the voters were all registered and entitled to vote if they had followed the proper procedure. Although intrigued by the potential of Seminole County to resolve the Florida election controversy, from the beginning Gore, Lieberman, Daley, and Christopher were all doubtful. How, they wanted to know, could we argue that Florida should "count all the votes," respect "the intent of the voter," and ignore technical failures of voters to follow instructions in South Florida, while at the same time acting to block these absentee ballots, which equally reflected the intent of the voter, in northern Florida?

As we discussed the issue over the next eight days, I said that the question was backward. The issue was not whether the Democrats could be inconsistent, but whether the Republicans could be. We did not have to win both in Seminole and in South Florida to prevail; if we won either, Gore would win Florida. It was the Republicans who had to convince the courts that the intent of the voter controlled in Republican Seminole County but not in Democratic Palm Beach County, that the courts should overlook "technical" (and perhaps more serious) violations north of Orlando, but not south (and west) of Palm Beach.

I wanted to go to court and say: count all the votes and respect the intent of the voters, even if the voters may not have technically complied with each instruction; but if you decide to require strict compliance and uniformity, you must be consistent.*

At shortly after ten Tuesday evening the Florida Supreme Court issued a unanimous decision reversing Judge Lewis and holding that Secretary Harris's decision was "unreasonable, unnecessary, and violates long-standing Florida law." Bush had gone to separate Florida state courts in Broward, Palm Beach, and Miami-Dade counties to stop the recounts. At his campaign's request Harris had earlier tried going directly to the Florida Supreme Court for the same relief. In each case Bush's efforts had been rejected. Now the Supreme Court had made it final. The ruling meant that Governor Bush would not be certified as President-elect Bush, at least for the time being. Even more important, it was now clear that manual recounts were proper under Florida law and that the intent of the voter controlled. This meant that at neither the protest nor the contest phase would Bush be able to argue that manual recounts were somehow prohibited. As it had turned out, Bill Daley and Warren Christopher had been right: we had not needed to subpoena Katherine Harris. (That did not, however, change my belief that I had made a mistake in not pushing them harder to do so.)

There was only one point I looked for in the forty-one-page opinion that was missing. In our briefs we had asked the court to define what criteria canvassing boards should use in determining the intent of the voter. We wanted such a definition because we believed that the standard provided by the court would be more expansive than the "sunshine standard" employed by Judge Burton in Palm Beach; we also wanted such a definition to defuse the Republicans' argument that potentially different interpretations of intent rendered the process unfair.

---

*There was a sense in which the deliberate favoring of the Republicans in Seminole County was more disqualifying than the inadvertent failure to punch through a ballot, particularly in light of evidence that the punch-card machines were at least partly at fault. That was a more complicated argument, however, and one that I did not have to make.

Nevertheless an "intent of the voter" standard that left determinations up to local election officials (at the protest stage) and to a district court (at the contest phase) provided much of the clarity and uniformity that we sought, and the approach of the Florida court was certainly consistent with that of most other states. There was also a good argument that trying to define the specific criteria to be used to determine the intent of the voter was both inconsistent with past Florida practice and not possible to do with particularity. Even states like Texas that specified certain criteria for counting ballots did so *in addition to,* not instead of, a general intent standard—providing that a ballot should be counted either if certain specific criteria were met *or* if election officials concluded they could ascertain the intent of the voter in some other way. It was understandable that the court did not provide greater specificity, although it was equally understandable for us to ask for it.

The court gave the three canvassing boards until the afternoon of Sunday, November 26, to complete counting. No one could figure out how it picked that date. Someone suggested that the justices were adding back the days lost by Harris's directing the boards not to recount, but the arithmetic did not work. We assumed that the court wanted to provide a reasonable period for the boards to complete their work while also providing enough time for an election contest, but that did not account for making the cutoff Sunday afternoon as opposed to Monday morning.

Around midnight on Tuesday Jim Baker gave a press briefing. Only about one hundred hours had elapsed since his briefing following Judge Lewis's decision in favor of Katherine Harris, but much had changed, including Baker. His earlier praise for the Florida courts was replaced by criticism even harsher than his language Friday evening. His earlier respect for the rule of law was replaced by support for the Florida legislature's naming the state's electors directly to nullify the vote of the state's citizens.

The Constitution gives the legislatures of every state the right to decide how that state's electors will be chosen. Every state, including Florida, has decided that its electors should be determined by a vote of the people of that state. Two weeks earlier it would have been unthinkable that a state legislature would attempt to deprive its voters of the right to vote for president. For a state legislature to attempt to do so *after* an election had already been held was more than controversial—it was unconstitutional.

The Constitution provides that Election Day shall be determined by Congress and "shall be the same through out the United States."* Congress had set November 7 as Election Day. The Florida legislature had no power to choose electors on a subsequent date. Tradition, respect for the will of the people, and good sense might counsel against a modern state legislature's attempting to arrogate to itself the power to choose the state's presidential electors, but as long as the legislature voted itself that power on or before Election Day and exercised that power on that date, such actions would be constitutional. Once November 7 had come and gone, the Florida state legislature was without power to change its mind. That former Secretary of State Jim Baker, a well-respected lawyer, would make such a suggestion (and that certain vocal Republican members of the state legislature would take steps to respond) showed how determined the GOP was to take any action necessary to prevent the results of the recounts from deciding the election. Baker also announced that the Bush campaign would appeal the Florida Supreme Court's decision to the United States Supreme Court.

I watched Baker's press conference on television at Andrew's Capital Grill & Bar and then walked across the street to the capitol to speak to the press myself. When I talked to Mary sometime after two in the morning, I told her my work was done, and that I would fly back to New York in the afternoon. "Larry Tribe will handle

---

*It was this provision that deprived the Democrats of any effective remedy for Palm Beach County's infamous "butterfly ballot," which alone confused enough voters to cost Gore the election. In most elections a revote could have remedied the situation. However, the Florida courts held (correctly) that a revote here was barred by the constitutional requirement that Florida's electors be elected the same day as the electors of every other state.

any appeal to the U.S. Supreme Court," I told her. "And monitoring the recount at the local canvassing boards is up to Ron Klain, Michael Whouley, and Mitch Berger."

"How confident are you that Gore is going to win?"

"I think he will, but it's going to be very close," I told her. "I don't think anyone can tell you for sure how the recount will come out."

"It would be ironic if after all this it turned out that Bush actually won the popular vote in Florida," Mary mused.

I responded that I hoped Gore would win but that even if Bush won at least everyone would know he had done so legitimately. "That's important," I told her. "It's important now, and it's important as a precedent for the future. If this had ended up that whoever controlled the election machinery could win by changing the rules as to how votes could be counted, it would have been a poor lesson in democracy."

Something in the way I said that I hoped Gore would win the recount caught Mary's attention. "It sounds as if you've developed more than a professional interest in the outcome," she teased.

"I like Gore," I admitted. "He's smart, honest, and he works hard. He's tough without being cynical. I like the way he has handled this fight. I can see why Clinton picked him. I think he would be a good president."

"That's the longest, and probably most favorable, political endorsement I've heard from you since we were in Washington," she said gently. "You always were a sweet drunk." I insisted gamely that my views were unaffected by my time at the sports bar. And in fact I did feel the same way the following morning as I packed to leave.

Klain and Berger had asked me to stop by Ft. Lauderdale on my way back to New York. The Broward canvassing board had scheduled a meeting there to consider Republican claims that ballots should not be counted based on an assessment of voter intent unless the voter had followed instructions and punched the ballot completely through. Although Ft. Lauderdale, 400 miles south of Tallahassee, was not technically on my way home, I was happy to go there both because of the importance of the issue and because I had planned to stop by there anyway to bring my daughter Caryl back home with me for Thanksgiving. (Caryl lived and practiced law in Ft. Lauderdale.)

On November 19, the previous Sunday, all three Broward board members, including Republican Jane Carroll, had agreed that the intent of the voter standard should be used. That approach was also supported by Republican Ed Dion, the chief lawyer for Broward. However, thereafter Carroll had resigned from the board citing family commitments, and Judge Lee, its chairman, had appointed County Judge Robert Rosenberg as a replacement. Both Bush's and Gore's lawyers believed that Rosenberg was likely to follow the lead of the Bush campaign, and could be expected to make a major effort to convince Judge Lee to adopt a more restrictive standard. If Rosenberg and the Republicans succeeded, Gore's chances of overtaking Bush would be reduced considerably.

Although I enjoyed my brief presentation to the Broward board, it turned out, as Barbara Miller had predicted, that Judge Lee had read the Florida statutes and Supreme Court cases himself and made up his mind that the intent of the voter standard applied. Judge Lee and the other canvassing board members listened attentively and asked a few questions, but neither we nor the Bush lawyers offered anything new.*

As I left the county building where the board was meeting, I noticed that the demonstrations that I had passed on my way in had grown in size. When I had arrived, the only demonstrators I had

---

*Ron Klain and I had discovered on Tuesday that an Illinois elections official, after talking to Republicans, had said that he had been mistaken in an affidavit that he had signed, and that Gore's lawyers had given to the Broward board, describing procedures followed in a particular Illinois recount. To retain our credibility with the board, and to prevent the Republicans from making this an issue, we immediately obtained a second affidavit from the Illinois man that included his current recollection. The affidavit was not a critical part of our argument, but we all thought that if the Republicans tried to make an issue of the alleged error in the first affidavit, I would be there to put the matter to rest. In fact the board had little interest in either affidavit.

seen were Bush supporters. Although a Gore contingent had now appeared, the Republican demonstrators were still larger in number and more aggressive in tone than their Democratic counterparts. The board had called in police officers to maintain control, and everything was orderly despite the noise. Nevertheless, on our way to New York, I mentioned to Caryl that there seemed to have been something ugly about the crowd, and I wondered whether Baker's rhetoric and the Broward crowd's attitude foreshadowed worse things to come. Unbeknownst to me at the time, the controversy had already become uglier than I would have predicted, both in Florida and at home.

While Caryl and I were still in the air, I received a message from Mary to phone Al Gore as soon as I landed. When I called, the Vice President described what had happened in Miami; as he did so, I listened to the same report over a television set in the airport lobby. Republican demonstrators had stormed the offices where the Miami-Dade board was conducting its recount and staged a sit-in until the board abandoned its work. Although there were the same scattered obscenities and threats that I had experienced in Broward, and reports of minor violence, it was hard for me to believe that the Miami-Dade board would cave in to such pressure—but they had.

"Why didn't they just call the police?" I asked. Gore told me that although the Miami supervisor of elections, David Leahy, had admitted that the crowd was a factor, the board was attempting to justify its decision on the ground that there was not sufficient time to complete its work by Sunday afternoon.

That was absurd. The Miami board had limited its recount to the county's 10,800 undervotes (ballots where the machine had read no vote for any presidential candidate). They would already have finished the job had they started when Palm Beach (let alone Broward or Volusia) had; they could still easily finish in one long day, judging by the pace at which the Broward, Volusia, and Palm Beach recounts had proceeded. They had four and a half days left, three and a half if they considered Thanksgiving a religious holiday.

If I had not been receiving real-time confirmation over CNN, I would have thought Gore was mistaken. As it was, I still harbored the hope that the election officials of Miami-Dade would reconsider. They did not, of course, and this victory for mob rule was my second-biggest disappointment in the 2000 election controversy.

Gore had not finished. "I appreciate all you have done and the burden that it has placed on you and your family," he told me, "but I need you back in Florida." He explained that our request to the lower state courts for an order requiring the Miami-Dade board to resume the recount had been denied and that he hoped the Florida Supreme Court would hear our appeal before the Sunday cutoff.

I said that I would return to Florida the next day, but that we should be prepared for a refusal of the Supreme Court to overrule the local board. The court had repeatedly ruled that manual recounts at the protest stage were authorized; it had not, however, either in this election or any prior one, ordered a recount before certification where the canvassing board had decided not to undertake one. The court might be so offended by the disruption of the recount by demonstrators, and the dereliction of duty by the Miami board members, that it might make an exception, but I was not optimistic.

"We have to assume that the Miami decision stands. Based on the way the Broward and Palm Beach recounts are going, we also have to assume that you will pick up several hundred votes but probably fall just short of overtaking Bush. We are about at the time where you have to decide whether you are prepared to file an election contest after Harris certifies Bush the winner."

In the discussion that followed it seemed that whatever ambivalence Al Gore had had about extending the election controversy by contesting the Florida vote after certification was gone. He knew he had won the popular vote nationally. Over the previous two weeks I had seen him become increasingly convinced that a fair count of the Florida ballots would show him winning there as well. As the attacks on him, and on the Florida courts, by Baker and others became increasingly harsh, he had become more determined than ever to see the matter through.

The demonstrators' disruption in Miami was the last straw. He was still concerned with the potential cost to the country of prolonged uncertainty, but that concern had faded as Democratic Party and public support for completion of the recount rose. In any event, he told me, whatever harm another two or three weeks of uncertainty might cause was much less than the harm that would result from allowing the final result to be determined by mob rule.

Soon after I got home Wednesday, I started to explain that I was going to have to go back to Florida. "I spoke to Al Gore when I landed in White Plains," I began.

"I know," Mary interrupted. "He called here looking for you. He explained what happened in Miami. When do you have to go back?"

"By tomorrow afternoon. Earlier if there is an expedited hearing in the Florida Supreme Court. We've asked them to intervene. If they don't, Bush will almost certainly be certified the winner, and we will have to file an election contest or give up."

"He can't give up," she said. "Not now. This can't be the way it ends."

It was, I thought, not only my attitude that had changed. Mary has a temper; she can be quick to take offense but equally quick to forgive. Occasionally, however, something will cause in her a cold, dark, unforgiving rage—usually when she feels her family is threatened. Mary had that look now, and I was puzzled. To be sure, the events in Miami were disturbing, perhaps even outrageous, but as Bill Daley said several times when the moral outrage of one staffer or another seemed about to boil over, "People get screwed every day." Mary had not been a Gore partisan during the campaign. Even had she been, his being cheated by a combination of overzealous demonstrators and weak county officials was not something that would cause the anger that I saw now.

It was only after dinner, when our son Alex had gone to his room, that she supplied the missing piece to the puzzle. I had worried earlier in the day that the election dispute was taking an ugly turn. I discovered that night that it had turned ugly for my family several days earlier.

From the moment I assumed a public role in Florida, our home had been plagued by crank calls, some laced with obscenities, some with vague threats. They were offensive but not intimidating. When Mary suggested that Alex not answer the phone at night, he responded in the tone teenagers reserve for explaining points that are entirely clear to them, if not to their apparently dense parents. "Mom, my friends call me on this line." After a moment he continued, in a more neutral tone, "Anyway, I am not going to let these people change my life." Mary had not told me about the calls, but I was not surprised to learn of them. They (and, more recently, similar e-mails) are a normal aspect of high-profile, controversial litigation.

However, the previous Friday afternoon a threat directed at Alex had been called to his school in Bedford, New York. He had been on the school's playing fields at the time, and the head of the school had dispatched several teachers to find him. One of them quickly found Alex and asked him to go immediately to the administrator's office. On his way a second teacher, then a third, gave him the same message. As any fifteen-year-old might, by the time he got to the principal's office he was wondering what he had done. When he was safely in the office, the school called Mary and explained the situation. Mary of course rushed to collect him.

She also immediately arranged Guardsmark guards for the house and thereafter personally drove Alex to and from school. It was agreed that he would stay in the building from the time Mary dropped him off until she personally picked him up. Fortunately for this plan, the football season was over.

Law enforcement officials and friends who had experienced similar threats told us that such calls rarely resulted in any action and that the purpose was to scare and upset. Mary and I accepted this advice, but it was impossible not to worry. (Later Alex got a second threat, and someone called the New York Bar Association to say that he was going to kill me. The association notified the Florida state police and for a couple of weeks a uniformed officer accompanied me in Tallahassee.) As predicted, nothing came of any of the threats. Nevertheless even today I would not want to be the caller if Mary discovered his identity.

The Florida Supreme Court did not schedule an expedited hearing on our appeal, and I had time for Thanksgiving dinner with my family before returning to Florida late Thursday afternoon. When I arrived in Tallahassee, I discovered that the Supreme Court had denied our Miami-Dade appeal without a hearing. I was disappointed, but the court would have had to break new ground to decide in our favor, and I understood why, in this most contentious of elections, it would try to stick to well-settled rules.*

Before returning to Florida I had called Steve Zack and asked him to come to Tallahassee to work on the contest. Steve agreed, and soon he was working with Dexter and the others on the arguments and evidence we would submit to whichever Leon County trial judge was assigned our contest.

On Friday and Saturday, November 24 and 25, I reviewed the possible claims we might assert and concluded that we should ask the court both to count the Miami-Dade undervotes that the canvassing board had not reached when it decided to stop and to review certain Palm Beach ballots that the canvassing board was, by a divided vote, rejecting because they had not been punched through completely.

A third contest claim related to the northern Florida county of Nassau. Under Florida law, because of the closeness of the election,

---

*As we worked on our election contest the next day, the candidates and the campaign leadership expressed concern that the court's summary denial of our appeal indicated that it had been intimidated by Jim Baker's attacks and the subsequent threats from the Republican-controlled state legislature to take punitive action against the court. I agreed that the partisan political nature of the controversy, of which the attacks by Baker and the Florida legislature were a part, might lead the court not to extend existing law when it could avoid it. However, I believed that it would not shirk from applying existing law, and settled legal precedents gave us a right to a court-supervised manual recount as part of an election contest.

all counties were obligated to conduct a machine recount (referred to as the "automatic" or "mandatory" recount) and to submit the results to the secretary of state. Nassau undertook the mandatory recount, and Gore gained 51 net votes. However, the Republican-dominated Nassau canvassing board had refused to submit the results, arguing that since the recount resulted in fewer total votes than the original count, there must have been something wrong. Where a mandatory recount was required, Florida law seemed to be clear that those results, not the original count, were the official tally; that had been the approach of every other county in the state. Moreover, it will almost always be the case that one count or the other will have more votes. Since both counts were made by the same machines, there was no obvious reason to believe that the largest count would always be the most correct one. Fifty-one votes might not seem to be a lot, but it could end up the difference between winning and losing.

In addition to the ballots we sought to have counted, there were two groups of counted ballots I wanted to exclude. Over Thanksgiving and the days immediately before and after, the Republicans had succeeded in convincing canvassing boards in several counties to count certain military absentee ballots that the boards had excluded when they had submitted their vote tallies. Although no one had filed a timely protest in any of these counties asking for a recount of absentee ballots, and although each of the excluded ballots violated Florida law in some way (for example, because it was filed too late, was faxed from a domestic location, lacked a date or postmark, or was not properly signed), the Republicans had convinced certain local canvassing boards to reverse themselves and count 680 previously excluded military ballots—enough to add 123 net votes to Bush's total. Both sides independently came to refer to these ballots as "Thanksgiving stuffing." Ron Klain, the contest team, and I all believed there were good grounds for the court to overrule their belated inclusion.

I also continued to believe that including a Seminole claim made sense. If we won that claim, Gore won Florida. If we lost, we should win our manual recount claim. It was clear that Seminole County Democrats were going to pursue the issue themselves even if the Gore-Lieberman campaign did not; but the claim would be treated much more seriously if we brought it, and only by bringing it ourselves could we make the Bush-Cheney campaign (and a court) confront the inconsistency between their Seminole argument and their Palm Beach, Broward, and Miami-Dade argument.

On Sunday, November 26, we discussed our options with the candidates, the campaign leadership, and their political advisers. No decision was made, and we agreed to reconvene early Monday morning. At five p.m. that same Sunday, Harris, as expected, officially certified Bush the winner of Florida's electoral votes. Before she did so, one more subplot had to be played out. The Florida Supreme Court had given the canvassing boards until Sunday (or until Monday, November 27, if the secretary of state's office was not open on Sunday) to complete their recounts. Ordinarily of course the office was closed on Sundays. Unsurprisingly, Harris specially opened her office that day so as to reduce by sixteen hours the amount of time available to complete the recounts. The decision was irrelevant to Miami-Dade (which had stopped counting) and to Broward (which had finished). However, it was relevant to Palm Beach. As Broward had showed, Palm Beach could easily have finished its recount on time had it proceeded with equal diligence. But Judge Burton and the Palm Beach board were moving at a pace that seemed designed to ensure they would not be done in time. To make matters worse, Judge Burton decided (unlike Broward) to take Thanksgiving Day off.

Sunday afternoon Judge Burton formally asked Secretary Harris for a few hours' grace to complete the recount. Predictably, she refused. Palm Beach faxed in the interim results of its recount by five p.m., and ninety minutes later sent in the balance. Secretary Harris refused to include the results of the recount (and the consequent votes for Gore) that were ninety minutes late, and even refused to include the partial results that were received on time (a total of 215 net votes for Gore). She also refused to include the results of

Miami-Dade's recount prior to its premature termination (a total of 157 net votes for Gore). This left Bush ahead by 537 votes.

On Sunday evening Ron Klain and I calculated that by adding Palm Beach's completed recount (215 net votes), Miami-Dade's partial recount (157 net votes), and Nassau's mandatory machine recount (51 net votes) and subtracting the "Thanksgiving stuffing" absentee ballots (123 net votes), Gore would gain 546 votes—nine more than Bush's lead.

At our conference call Monday morning there was initially some support for limiting our contest to these four claims, all of which could be presented as legal arguments that would not require a trial or factual findings. This would have the virtue of speeding the resolution of the contest and could easily be explained politically as a series of narrowly focused issues rather than a broad attack on the certified vote count. I opposed such an approach for two reasons.

"First," I explained, "the nine-vote margin is too small even if we win everything and the Republicans do nothing. We could lose on some of the Thanksgiving stuffing ballots; if the court disagrees with us on 10 out of 121 contested ballots, Bush wins by one vote. It's a bad idea to assume that you will win more than 90 percent of anything in a court case. And we have to assume that the Republicans may file some kind of claim; it wouldn't have to be very broad to net them 10 votes. We could also lose Nassau County; although Nassau was required to report the results of the mandatory recount, that's why it's called "mandatory", the Supreme Court has a history of deferring to local canvassing board decisions as to how votes should be counted."

In addition to my tactical concerns, Al Gore had a policy concern about limiting our claims. It was wrong as a matter of principle, he believed, to permit the precedent of Miami-Dade's vote counting being terminated by a threatening crowd to stand uncorrected.

It turned out there was another reason why we had to make additional claims—the campaign was unwilling to challenge the

"Thanksgiving Stuffing" military ballots. This meant our choice was to give up, which no one was prepared to do, or to add claims.

We quickly agreed to ask to have Miami-Dade's recount completed. We also agreed, after some additional discussion, to ask the court to review the disputed Palm Beach ballots—more than 2,000 uncounted ballots where the intent of the voter could be seen from the pattern of indentations but where the ballots had not been completely punched through. That left Seminole County. I believed we should include that claim, and I again explained why. The question in both Palm Beach and Miami on the one hand, and Seminole on the other, was basically the same: should the intent of the voter, and the desire to count every vote where that intent could be ascertained, be given precedence over a failure to follow instructions? I thought it should, but I wasn't the Florida Supreme Court.

"I am," I said, "prepared to believe that I could lose our Palm Beach and Miami arguments. However, I am not prepared to believe that I could lose those arguments *and* at the same time in the same court lose Seminole County. If there is a rule of strict compliance, it cannot apply only in South Florida, Democratic counties."

Someone said in response that that was a "lawyer's argument."

"Of course it's a lawyer's argument," I replied. "That's the kind of argument you make in court. The question is, is it a good lawyer's argument or a bad one? I think it's a good one."

It may be an oversimplification, but not by much, to say that all the lawyers and political staff in Florida thought we should make a Seminole County claim and everyone in Washington believed we should not. There were three basic reasons for the reluctance to bring the claim. First, there was concern about the possible political fallout of another effort to exclude absentee ballots. Standing alone, I do not believe this would have stopped us. Second, there was concern that such a claim would be inconsistent with our "count every vote" arguments. Again, without more this would not, in my opinion, have been enough; we could easily have made the point that it was right to count every vote and we wanted to count every vote, but if votes were going to be excluded, the rules had to be applied consistently.

Third, and the only reason that ultimately mattered, Al Gore did not believe it was right to disenfranchise several thousand voters who intended to vote because of an innocent mistake. After the fact, some people would criticize him for not being more ruthless, for not being prepared to match the no-holds-barred approach of the Bush campaign; they would suggest that he did not want the presidency enough or that he somehow lacked the commitment to do what was necessary to win it. From my viewpoint he certainly wanted the presidency and was prepared to make the sacrifices and tough decisions necessary to pursue it. He was not, however, prepared to sacrifice principle to win; there were simply certain means that the end of winning the presidency did not, in his mind, justify.

I could make contrary arguments. There was nothing unprincipled about arguing for uniform compliance with whatever rule the Florida courts ultimately adopted; if Bush won Florida by improperly excluding votes in Palm Beach and Miami, *everyone* who voted for Gore was effectively disenfranchised; it was important not merely to Gore himself but also to his principles and goals (and, if one believed in those principles and goals, to the country) that Gore and not Bush be elected president. But it was clear that Al had made up his mind. There would be no Seminole County claim by the Gore-Lieberman campaign.

Around ten-thirty Monday morning Dexter walked over to court to file our contest. When a complaint is filed, a trial judge is assigned to the case, and that assignment will often determine the outcome. Even law schools have given up pretending the contrary. Individual states, and sometimes individual courts in the same state, differ in how they assign judges. Most courts purport to do so randomly through use of a wheel or other lottery-type device.

One way to avoid a random assignment is to designate a lawsuit as a "related case" to a prior suit. (A related case is one that arises from the same set of facts and legal issues as the prior suit.)

In such a situation the complaint will be automatically assigned to whichever judge heard the prior proceeding. We discussed whether we should designate our case as "related" to our prior litigation before Judge Lewis. Although his decisions had, on balance, supported Bush during the certification litigation, we believed that Lewis was a fair judge and (perhaps even more important in a case with time constraints that was almost certainly headed for the Florida Supreme Court anyway) he was an expeditious judge.

Dexter, however, believed that either of the other judges likely to be assigned, Judge L. Ralph "Bubba" Smith and Judge Nikki Clark, were at least as good, and that by letting the case be assigned by the clerk, we avoided any charge of judge-shopping. There was a fourth judge in Leon County, N. Sanders Sauls, who theoretically could be assigned. Sauls, Dexter told us, "certainly voted for Bush" and, unlike the other Leon County judges, would not put aside his political preferences in deciding a case. He was also slow. Sauls would be a disaster if we drew him, but Dexter believed that was unlikely.

Two years earlier Sauls had been severely reprimanded by the Florida Supreme Court in a patronage scandal, with the court criticizing him in language that would have caused many judges to resign. Sauls had stayed on; but it was inconceivable to Dexter that the county's chief judge would permit Sauls's name to be included in the lottery to be assigned the biggest case in Leon County history.

Two minutes after Dexter filed our complaint he was informed it had been assigned to Judge Sauls. As soon as he returned to our offices, we examined our options. We quickly decided to ask Sauls to transfer our suit to one of the judges who already had an election case. There was some optimism that he would grant such a motion, but we had to decide what to do if he denied it. We could either proceed before Sauls and, if Dexter was right, almost certainly lose, or we could move to recuse him.

We had a reasonable ground for recusal. John Newton, who was a key member of the legal team and whose name was on many of our papers, had recently served as the campaign manager for Sauls's opponent in a harsh reelection contest. Sauls had won, but bitter feelings persisted. It would have made a respectable, but not overwhelming, recusal motion. I was not enthusiastic about having Sauls as our judge, but I was opposed to a motion to get rid of him. The burden to recuse should be high, and I was not convinced that we met it. We were also concerned with the appearance, both to the public and to the Florida Supreme Court, of judge-shopping.

Moreover, everyone who knew him agreed that if Sauls denied our motion to transfer he would almost certainly deny a motion to recuse. If we appealed, we would waste valuable time. Our goal was to get this matter decided by December 12 so that we did not lose the safe harbor protection against an attempt by a Republican-controlled House of Representatives (or a Republican-controlled state legislature) to take matters outside the judicial system. A motion to recuse would hinder that goal. We decided to make a motion to transfer, and if we lost (as we promptly did) to play the hand we had been dealt.

In an effort to find out more about Sauls, Steve Zack and I had dinner at the Silver Slipper with a lawyer who was a drinking buddy of the judge. The Silver Slipper was a restaurant located in a shopping mall a short drive from the capitol. It had the best food, if your tastes ran to red meat, and the best wine list in Tallahassee. It also had booths with curtains. Stories differed as to whether the curtained booths were designed to protect influence peddlers dining with state legislators, or politicians and lobbyists spending time with women not their wives, or both. Whatever their origin, the booths provided us a discreet venue in which to seek discreet insights.

Although Sauls's friend predictably had a warmer view of Sauls than did Dexter, he essentially confirmed what Dexter had said. Sauls was "self-important" (Dexter had said "arrogant"), "relaxed" (Dexter had said "lazy"), and "conservative, with the social attitudes that most people in this part of the country used to have and quite a few still do" (Dexter had said "redneck"). We also discovered that Sauls had said a number of uncomplimentary things about Gore and Lieberman.

We already knew that trying our case before Judge Sauls would be an uphill battle; further confirmation might make interesting dinner conversation, but it did little to help us plan our case. We did, however, learn one useful fact. Sauls, we were told, had expressed to friends a mixture of envy and pique over the fuss, as he saw it, that the press was making over Terry Lewis. This, I thought, might be the reason why, contrary to what Dexter had expected, he had wanted to keep the suit. Still smarting from the Supreme Court's rebuke two years earlier, Sauls might see this case as a means of redeeming his reputation. If so, we could expect him to be influenced by what would, and what would not, garner him the favorable reviews he sought. This fit our limited experience with Sauls. Before he had held his first hearing in the case, he had issued a press release, complete with references to people whom he hoped the press would contact. His wife also made herself available for interviews.

Even if Sauls were concerned with garnering favorable publicity, this fact did not suggest a way to convince him on the merits of our contest. The people whose opinion he most valued would applaud a decision in favor of Bush, and the media could be expected to be favorable so long as he was colorful and appeared to be fair. The media would not take him to task merely for deciding the case against Gore.

What the press might criticize would be undue delay in deciding the case, permitting the Republicans to run out the clock. When it had become clear that Sauls would be our trial judge, I had told Al and my team only half-jokingly that my strategy for dealing with him was "to lose quickly." Everyone knew that, time permitting, this case would be decided by the Florida Supreme Court; Sauls was a way station on our trip to final resolution. Moreover, while the trial court is usually a very important way station because it makes findings of fact that appellate courts must accept unless there is no significant support for them, in this case because the fundamental dispute was over questions of law and appellate courts give no deference to a trial court's views as to what the law is, Sauls's decision would be much less significant.

But before the Florida Supreme Court could decide the case, it had to get it; and that meant Sauls had to complete his work quickly. In order to run out the clock, Sauls did not have to live up to the view of him as lazy or to engage in unusual delay; business as usual for even a good judge would run us out of time. For us to get to the Supreme Court on time, Sauls would have to be unusually expeditious. To make his desire for favorable publicity work for us, we had to find a way to make him believe that speed was a means to that end.

We started by making a series of motions to expedite. A motion to shorten Bush's time to answer. A motion for an expedited hearing. A motion for the court to decide matters of law immediately without waiting for an evidentiary hearing to resolve any issues of fact. A motion to bar certain right-wing organizations from intervening (and, when that lost, a motion to limit their role). A motion to limit and expedite the extensive discovery that the Bush camp said it needed. We of course wanted to win these motions, but, even if we did not, they put pressure on Sauls to move the case along. A judge who is concentrating on being fair does not worry about whether he or she consistently decides issues in favor of one side if that is what the law and facts dictate. However, one who is concentrating on appearing fair often tries to split his decisions. In such a situation it is often true that the more you ask for, the more you get.*

---

*Most of us are interested in what people think of us. This can have both a good and bad influence on judicial decisions. On the one hand, it is certainly better to have a judge who is determined not to abuse the enormous power that our society vests in judges, and concern for reputation can play a positive role in restraining such abuses. At the same time, the federal district court and court of appeals judges in the South who had the burden of enforcing the Supreme Court's rulings outlawing segregation in the late 1950s and 1960s succeeded in direct relationship to their willingness and ability to ignore what their neighbors, colleagues, and the local bar thought of them. For a judge seeking public approval, especially one who might be less likely than most to separate his personal feelings from his judicial actions, the desire for favorable publicity, and to avoid another media slap in the face, could significantly shape what he did. Being fair and balanced is not always the same as appearing so.

Despite his courtroom manner, Sauls was warm and friendly to me in his chambers and in hallway conversations. Early in those conversations I tried to make clear that no one could criticize him if he felt it was right to put points on the scoreboard for Bush; all we asked was that he not hold the ball until time ran out. I wanted him to understand, without my saying it too explicitly, that if he was going to decide against us, he could balance it by doing so quickly. If he decided for Bush, the Republicans were certain to laud him as a great jurist; if he did so expeditiously, we could be counted on to praise his expedition.

We also tried to interest the press in the Republicans' strategy of winning by delay and on the question of whether Judge Sauls would aid and abet that strategy. The more Sauls believed that the press was focused on his possible role in running out the clock, the less likely he would do so. Although he did not give us everything we wanted in terms of timing, on balance he gave us what we needed. Bush's time to answer was reduced from ten to three days. Discovery was limited and expedited. The trial was scheduled to begin Saturday, December 2—less than a week after our contest was filed.

On Tuesday, November 28, I went to court to request that Sauls begin an immediate review of the uncounted Miami–Dade ballots and the Palm Beach ballots that had been excluded over our objections. "Here, the witnesses are primarily the ballots," I argued. "The issue is whether particular ballots do or do not express the voter's intent."

Sauls split the difference. Over Barry Richards's vigorous objections the judge ordered the Miami–Dade and Palm Beach ballots brought to the clerk's office in Tallahassee, but he declined to say when, if ever, he would review them. Once the disputed ballots arrived, I was convinced it would be difficult for any court in an election contest to refuse to look at them, and if he did, that refusal could never be justified to the Florida Supreme Court. Bush's lawyers felt the same way, and they pulled out all the stops to convince the court not to bring the ballots to Tallahassee.

One of the arguments they made was interesting. The right

standard, they said, for the court to use was whether or not the local canvassing boards had "abused their discretion" in counting votes. The reason this was interesting was that discretion entails a broad range of decision making that is acceptable; decisions outside the range may be viewed as an abuse of discretion, but any reasonable decision is acceptable. By definition, if local canvassing boards had such discretion, different boards could make different judgments. This was inconsistent with one of the arguments Bush's lawyers were making in federal court.

A second interesting aspect of the Republicans' argument was that it made it virtually impossible for them to undo the 567 net votes Gore had gained in Broward County's manual recount, and made it very difficult to exclude the 215 from Palm Beach or the 157 from Miami-Dade. This alone brought Bush's margin down to 165. Nobody knew how many net Gore votes were to be found in the Miami-Dade precincts that had not been recounted when the board there terminated its recount, but 165 was easily within what was possible. (Of course many more than 165 votes would have resulted if Palm Beach had used a broad intent of the voter standard instead of Judge Burton's sunshine standard.)

When we reviewed where things stood Tuesday evening, there were both good and bad aspects to the thirty hours since we had filed our contest. On the positive side, the contested ballots were on their way to Tallahassee; Sauls had said that the contest hearing would be held on Saturday; and Bush's lawyers had taken some potentially helpful positions. On the negative side, we had drawn Sanders Sauls; he had refused to transfer the case; and he had refused to rule on when, if ever, he would review the ballots.*

---

*Tuesday night we decided to ask the Florida Supreme Court to order Sauls to begin reviewing the contested ballots. This was a long shot; the Florida court, like the U.S. Supreme Court, rarely intervenes until a case is completed. It was, nevertheless, a shot worth taking. If the court did act, it would speed up a final resolution by several days. Even if it did not, we would avoid a later argument that we waited too late to seek relief. I did not want the court next week to say that it was too close to December 12 (or December 18, when the Electoral College would meet and elect a president) to start counting ballots and that we

Wednesday, Thursday, and Friday we worked on the evidence, witnesses, and arguments we would present beginning Saturday. Foreseeing a danger that the hearing could drag over several days, I seriously considered calling no witnesses to expedite a decision. The primary fact witnesses *were* the ballots; the remaining issues were primarily questions of law. Nevertheless, we ultimately decided to call two: Kimball Brace, an election consultant, and Nicholas Hengartner, who taught statistics at Yale. There were two factual propositions that I wanted to establish for purposes of the appellate record. First, punch-card ballot machines fail to record the votes of a number of people who intended to vote. Second, different Florida counties used different types of voting machines, and those using punch-card machines had a statistically significant larger number of ballots for which the machines read no vote (the so-called undervotes) than the counties using optical character recognition (OCR) and other voting machines.

Neither proposition was essential to our main argument, which was that Florida law gave candidates in close elections a right to a manual recount and that there was no basis for changing the rules in mid-election. The propositions did address issues that would be relevant if a court determined to decide whether manual recounts were or were not a good idea. We of course argued that this was not the proper role for a court, particularly after the votes have been cast. Still, it is generally a good idea to have a record that permits you to win even if the court does not

---

should have come to the court for relief earlier. Baker and the Republican legislators were already turning up the heat on the court to discourage it from playing any further role in interpreting the state's election law. This was not going to be a pleasant task for the Florida Supreme Court, and I did not want to give it any easy out.

On Wednesday we filed our application, which the court promptly denied. I had now been to the court three times in less than three weeks and was one for three. Baseball players get elected to the Hall of Fame based on a .333 batting average; lawyers are expected to do better. Nevertheless everyone on both sides knew there was one decision of the Florida Supreme Court that would be decisive—the resolution of the appeal from Judge Sauls's election contest proceeding.

agree with your primary argument. In any event a court might be more comfortable with the legislature's decision to provide for manual recounts if the reasons for them were clear. Taken together the two propositions demonstrated that without manual recounts, voters in punch-card counties would have less chance of having their ballots counted than voters in OCR counties.

Neither witness was particularly strong, but they were the best the contest team could get, and get prepared, in the time available. Kimball Brace was an experienced witness in election cases but did not have detailed knowledge of the mechanics of punch-card machines. Professor Hengartner was a brilliant statistician but not experienced as a witness. Also, he had submitted an affidavit earlier in the election litigation that contained a mistake; the error did not relate to what he would testify about, but it could be used to attack his credibility.

After opening statements, we entered into evidence the ballots from Palm Beach and Miami-Dade. We also introduced the statewide statistics showing the votes and the undervotes by county, and evidence showing which counties used which type of machines. We could have stopped there. Neither of our two witnesses advanced our case greatly.

Brace had a simple proposition that he presented well: punch-card machines do not accurately record all votes. That was all we needed. However, we made the mistake of having him try to explain several of the reasons this might be so—which chewed up valuable time (particularly since Bush's lawyer on cross-examination took even more time to question him in detail about every reason), gave Bush's lawyers an opportunity to expose his lack of technical knowledge, and distracted from our central argument.

Professor Hengartner made the point that the undervotes in punch-card counties were significantly higher than those in counties with other voting machines. This reinforced Brace's testimony that punch-card machines were not recording all the votes and showed that without manual recounts residents of punch-card counties would have less of a chance of having their votes recorded than residents of OCR counties. However, those points were already made from the county-by-county vote tallies we had introduced, and he was clearly uncomfortable on cross, particularly when confronted with the error in his earlier affidavit. It was a mistake that it had been our responsibility to catch, and I regretted his embarrassment.

Things got better when the Bush team began to put on witnesses. Bush lawyer Fred Bartlit began with Judge Charles Burton from Palm Beach. Fred did an effective job of presenting Burton's view that Palm Beach had done the best it could have under trying circumstances. Burton's manner and outlook matched Judge Sauls's, and it was clear that Sauls was favorably impressed, volunteering that he considered Burton "a great American." The problem for Burton was inherent in what had happened in Palm Beach. The thrust of Bush's argument was that punch-card machines accurately counted the votes. On my cross-examination, however, Burton had no choice but to admit that he had found several hundred ballots (resulting in 215 net votes for Gore) where it was clear that the voters intended to vote (and clear for whom) but the machine failed to record them.

Bush next called Laurentius Marais, a professional witness on statistical issues. His basic testimony was unremarkable: that you could not tell statistically whether undervotes in Palm Beach would have favored Gore or Bush. In fact, our central point was that the only way to tell was to review the ballots. My cross of Marais was short, and should have been shorter. I tried to point out that the witness had an unusual approach to statistical analysis—previously testifying, for example, that well-accepted studies linking lead paint with injuries in children were not reliable. However, Sauls was not interested, and it was not worth the time it took.

Bush's next witness was John Ahmann. At the time of his testimony Ahmann was a rancher in California, but he had earlier designed punch-card machines and held several patents relating to machine design. He was called to testify that punch-card machines were reliable, and on direct examination his relaxed, confident manner and his obvious knowledge made him an effective witness. Steve Zack, who had the responsibility of cross-examining him, had been trying to find out everything he could about the witness. Among the areas Steve asked people in his office to research were Ahmann's patent applications.

While Ahmann was on the stand, a paralegal delivered a fax from Zack's partner, Jennifer Altman, attaching an Ahmann patent application from twenty years ago. As Steve listened to Ahmann's testimony I read and highlighted the document. A few minutes later Zack confronted Ahmann with his two-decade-old admission that punch-card machines result in "potentially unreadable votes" and the fact that he had invented a new stylus (*not* adopted in Florida) designed to reduce the problem. It was devastating testimony. At the Bush counsel table, Fred Bartlit turned to his co-counsel Phil Beck with a look that said, what the hell is going on? Phil, who had done an effective job cross-examining Brace and Hengartner, could only shake his head with a rueful smile. Like every trial lawyer, I knew how Fred and Phil felt. I had been there myself.

Ahmann was clearly nonplussed by being refuted by his own patent application; and as often happens with a witness who has taken an unexpected body blow, he lost his confidence and his commitment, agreeing with question after question as Zack pressed his advantage. When Zack finally asked whether Ahmann believed you needed to review punch-card ballots manually in very close elections, Ahmann responded, "You need either reinspection or a manual recount if you have that situation, yes, you do." We now had Bush's own machine expert saying what we had argued for nearly three weeks.

As we left the courthouse close to midnight, Bush's lawyers and I joked that each of us had done better with the others' witnesses than with our own. If we had known what we would get from Bush's witnesses, I never would have called Brace, and either would not have called Hengartner or would have put him on for the limited purpose of comparing undervotes in Florida's counties. On the other hand, had we not called any witnesses, perhaps Fred would not have either.

Throughout the trial, despite a number of frustrating rulings and Sauls's obvious predisposition, we had treated him with respect and deference. Lawyers must be prepared to stand up to a judge, but they must be prepared to do so with the respect that the judge's position deserves; if they don't the public support necessary to preserve our justice system erodes. Moreover, no matter how bad a judge seems, it is sometimes possible to make the situation better, and it is always possible to make it worse. By treating Sauls with respect, we hoped he would act to deserve it. On balance, I think he did.

On Sunday the court had kept going until after eleven p.m. in order to finish, and the judge promised to render his decision first thing the following morning. While I appreciated the court's relative expedition, I had no doubt what Sauls's decision on the merits would be. Before going to bed I stopped by our offices to read the draft of our appeal to the Florida Supreme Court.

Monday afternoon Judge Sauls sent word that counsel should appear in court at four-thirty p.m. Instead of simply issuing his written opinion as Judge Lewis and others had done, he had decided to read his in open court to counsel and the cameras. It was clear from the first few minutes that Sauls's ultimate conclusion was exactly what Dexter Douglass had predicted. While Sauls was still talking, I gave the word to lawyers who were standing by to deliver our notice of appeal. Sauls's opinion tried to list every reason included in the Bush camp's papers why the contest should be denied (including reasons as to which no record had been made), but it did contain one useful fact. After the testimony of Brace and Ahmann even Judge Sauls had to concede that the "record shows voter error and/or less than total accuracy" in the voting machines' operations and that those errors had led to votes not being counted during the machine counts. Sauls concluded that that did not matter. I did not think that the Florida Supreme Court would agree, but the important point was that we now had findings of fact showing why manual recounts were needed.

At the inevitable impromptu press conference that followed, I avoided being drawn into the judge-bashing that reporters had become accustomed to hearing from Jim Baker when the Republicans lost a legal round. There were, I said, only three important facts: "We lost. They won. We're going to appeal." I explained that while we obviously disagreed with Judge Sauls's decision, it would be up to the Florida Supreme Court to tell us whether we were right or he was. I also praised Sauls for deciding the case relatively quickly. It had taken only one week and four hours to go from filing our contest to answers, discovery, evidentiary hearings, and a decision on the merits. To what extent Sauls had been motivated by a desire to appear fair and efficient, and to what extent the importance of the case caused him to act more responsibly than his reputation predicted, I did not know and really did not care. He had given us what we needed in terms of timing and perhaps a critical finding of fact as well. We had lost, not as quickly as I had hoped, but quick enough.

Monday also brought unexpected news from Washington, D.C. At Bush's request the U.S. Supreme Court had agreed to review the Florida Court's November 28 decision ordering Katherine Harris not to certify Bush the winner prior to the completion of the initial protest phase recounts. Acting with unusual haste, the U.S. Court had heard that appeal on December 1, only three days after the Florida decision and less than forty-eight hours after Bush had lodged his appeal.

The argument had not gone as well as we had expected. As the Court had emphasized in its 1892 decision of *McPherson v. Blacker,* under the Constitution a state's electors are to be chosen in a manner set by the state's legislature (and at a time set by Congress). The Florida Supreme Court's decision had discussed both the state's election statutes and the Florida Constitution. What was the justification, Laurence Tribe was asked, for relying on a state's constitution when the federal Constitution said that the state legislature alone had the power to determine the way electors were selected?

There were two good answers. The first was that in Florida (unlike many other states) the state legislature had itself enacted the constitutional provisions relied on by the Florida court. Unfortunately we had not been able to convince the Court that this meant that the Florida legislature had determined the election procedures whether the court's decision was based on statutes *or* the state's constitution. The second answer was that the Florida court's decision was based on statutes passed by the state legislature, and the discussion of the state's constitutional provisions merely confirmed the court's interpretation of what the legislature intended by those statutes. The problem with the second argument was that the Florida court had never considered the implications of the 1892 *McPherson* case (neither side had argued it), and as a result its opinion was not explicit. The argument was on Friday, December 1. The following Monday the Court acted.

In unanimous, unsigned opinion, stating that "there was considerable uncertainty as to the precise grounds" of the Florida court's decision, the justices sent the case back and asked the Florida Supreme Court to clarify whether the basis of its decision was statutes (which would be safe) or the state constitution (which might be questionable). The good news was the decision explicitly recognized that the U.S. Court should defer to the state court on issues of state law—and implicitly recognized that it was acceptable to implement manual recounts if state statutes (but, perhaps, not the state constitution) provided for them.

The Florida Supreme Court set the oral argument on our appeal from Judge Sauls's decision for Thursday morning, December 7. Minutes before the argument was set to begin, Al called on a cell phone to express his optimism, wish me well, and thank me for my efforts.

When the hearing began, it was clear immediately that the atmosphere had changed considerably from that on November 20. Chief Justice Charles Wells announced that he wanted "each counsel" to address the importance of the *McPherson* case. The subtext was, why hadn't we argued this case to the court the first time around? My answer was simple: *McPherson* did not apply. Nothing prohibits a state court from interpreting state statutes, including laws relating to the selection of electors, after they are passed; that is what they do all the time, and that was all the Florida Supreme Court was being asked to do here.

Half an hour later, when his turn came, Barry Richards on behalf of Bush agreed that the court had the power to interpret the state laws in question. Justice Wells seemed a little surprised. I sensed that he would have liked to have found a way to let this cup pass from his lips.

Wells and other members of the court also asked whether the result of an election was "in doubt" (which was the statutory standard for permitting a contest) every time a losing candidate made a claim. No, I assured them. Here you have an extremely close election, with undervotes many times the margin between the candidates, and proof from every county that examined the undervotes that a significant number represented ballots where the canvassing board could ascertain the clear intent of the voter.

When Barry Richard's turn came he gave a polished defense of Judge Sauls's decision—better reasoned than the decision itself, we joked later. He also responded patiently but firmly to the questions of Justices Anstead and Pariente, which were every bit as probing of his position as Justice Wells and Harding's questions had been of mine. There was one problem. Trying to explain why undervotes should be reviewed in one county but not in another, Richards replied that each board should be entitled to decide for itself, an argument related to his position that each county had discretion. This answer did not seem to satisfy the court, which appeared to have difficulty reconciling it with the argument that it was unfair to recount in certain counties and not others.

Barry's argument was also inconsistent with Bush's contention in federal court that not only did local canvassing boards not have discretion in counting votes, but it was a violation of the Equal

Protection Clause if counties differed at all in how they interpreted the intent of a voter.

After dinner Thursday I had drinks with some of the Bush lawyers at Andrew's Capital Grill & Bar. (Barry Richard was having dinner with his wife for their anniversary.) A television reporter spotted us, and soon a camera crew arrived to ask on camera what were talking about. After several unsuccessful attempts to get us to say something substantive, the reporter asked, "Don't you have *anything* to say?" We replied, in unison, to the camera: "Happy anniversary, Barry!"

Most of what we talked about did not relate to our case. When we did talk about it, we agreed based on the argument that this time the Florida Court's decision would not be unanimous. I thought the decision would be 5–2 or 4–3 for Gore; they thought it would be 4–3 for Bush. In an ordinary case it would not have been unusual for a bet to have resulted from such discussions. That night no one raised the possibility. Perhaps even for hardened trial lawyers the matter seemed too important. Or perhaps none of us wanted to jinx our positions; trial lawyers, after all, are known to be superstitious.

It was not only the Bush lawyers who expected us to lose. The *Tallahassee Democrat*'s "Fourth Down and Long for Gore" headline the next day reflected a widespread feeling that the game was almost over. When I spoke to Al after the argument (which he had viewed on television courtesy of Florida's "Government in the Sunshine" law permitting cameras in all courtrooms) he remained upbeat. He again thanked me for all I had done, saying he was grateful "regardless of how things turn out," but I could tell that he believed we would win. On Friday he predicted to the press that the Florida Supreme Court would reverse Judge Sauls. As the day dragged on, I sometimes thought we were the only two who believed it.

Shortly after two p.m. we received news from another front. When we had decided not to raise Seminole County issues in our contest, local Democrats filed their own case, which was assigned to Nikki Clark, a well-regarded state court judge who had been recommended for appointment to the Florida Supreme Court. Despite her qualifications Judge Clark, an African American woman, was the Republicans' "worst nightmare," in the words of a Bush lawyer one night at Clyde's and Costello's bar. Bush moved to disqualify Clark on grounds so specious that Barry Richards refused to allow his name to be put on the motion.

Judge Clark, who had refused to recuse herself, ruled for Bush and denied the election contest, holding that under Florida law a technical failure to follow procedures would not disqualify ballots where the intent of the voter could be determined. Although she found the actions of the Seminole election officials "faulty," she held that the votes counted represented "the will of the voters." I found out about Clark's decision from reporters who caught up with me as I walked back to Dexter's offices after a late lunch. One reporter who had been in Tallahassee almost from the beginning said, not unkindly, "It looks like you are down to a single arrow."

"It's not a comfortable position to be in," I agreed, "but sometimes you only need one."

A little less than an hour later I was talking to Mary on the telephone with the television on in the background. As we were talking, the image of Craig Waters, the Florida Supreme Court's unflappable spokesman, appeared on the screen in front of the Supreme Court Building. This could mean that the court had reached a decision or simply that he would advise the throng of waiting reporters that a decision would not be forthcoming that day. "Just a minute," I told Mary, as I turned up the sound. "There may be some kind of announcement."

The first words that I heard as I turned up the volume were: "The Court has authorized the following statement: By a vote of four to three, the majority of the Court has reversed the decision of the trial court."

I didn't have to tell Mary what was happening. As she was turning on the television at home, a loud cheer erupted from the crowd in Dexter's offices. I did not understand how pessimistic most people had been until I saw the surprise and relief with which the news was greeted. When we spoke to Al Gore a few minutes later, he too was happy, but also focused on our next steps. We began by explaining what the court had done. First, the 215* net additional Gore votes from Palm Beach and the 168 net additional Gore votes from Miami had to be included. Second, the Miami–Dade recount had to be completed. That was the good news. The court rejected our effort to reverse the decision by the Nassau County board to use the vote tallies from its election night count rather than the subsequent mandatory recount, and it denied our request to review Palm Beach's undervote ballots, which our observers had identified as ballots where the intent of the voter was clear but which the Palm Beach board had refused to count because they did not satisfy the sunshine standard.

With respect to the issues we had raised, the court had ruled for us on three issues and against us on two. The Court, it appeared, had accepted Barry Richard's argument that local canvassing boards had broad discretion in deciding how to count votes. In each case where a local board had counted votes, the court upheld the board's tally; it was only when a board (Miami) prematurely interrupted its count that the court reversed. If that was all the court had done, Bush's margin would have shrunk to 154 and we would have had to gain at least that many net votes from the completion of the Miami–Dade recount. That was a possible, indeed plausible, scenario. However, Michael Whouley and others were unsure whether that many additional net votes could be harvested from the unrecounted Miami–Dade undervotes—which was why we had pressed so hard for a contest phase review of the disputed Palm Beach ballots.

But the court had not limited its action to the issues we had raised. Taking the Republicans at their word that a four-county re-

---

*There was a question based on the disarray of the papers submitted by Palm Beach as to whether the number was 215 or 176; the court remanded to the trial court the decision as to the right number.

count was somehow unfair, it ordered a statewide recount of all undervotes in sixty-four counties—every county in the state other
than the three counties (Broward, Palm Beach, and Volusia) that had
completed their recounts. This would give us a much broader potential field from which to harvest votes, but Bush in the aggregate
had carried those sixty-four counties (including the uncounted Miami precincts) by substantial margins; we would be trolling for votes
in Republican waters. Although Whouley and others were cau-
tiously optimistic, no one could predict how this recount would
turn out. What we knew for sure was that we had to mobilize resources not only in Tallahassee, where Leon County and the uncounted Miami-Dade undervotes would be reviewed, but in
sixty-three other counties too. And we had to do it by the following
morning. The court had said that because "time is of the essence,
the recounts shall commence immediately." To us "immediately"
meant that night, or at the latest Saturday morning, assuming local
canvassing boards were prepared to work over the weekend.

Before that could happen, however, the Leon County trial
court, to whom the case had been remanded by the Supreme
Court, had to establish procedures and a timetable. Judge Sauls recused himself without our having to ask. His replacement was
Judge Terry Lewis, who now took on his fourth election-related
assignment in less than a month. The lawyers were directed to appear before Judge Lewis at eight p.m. that evening.

At the hearing we asked to start the recount as soon as counters
could be assembled. "The Court meant immediately when it said
immediately," I told Lewis. "Hours make a difference here." Equally
predictably, Phil Beck on behalf of Bush asked Lewis to adjourn until the following day, at which time he proposed to begin to "educate" Judge Lewis as to issues regarding the appropriate standard to
be used. In our appeal to the Supreme Court from Judge Sauls's decision we had again asked it (as we had in our earlier appeal from
Judge Lewis's order) to provide guidance concerning how boards
should determine the intent of the voter. Each time the court declined, most recently by simply restating what had been understood

to be Florida law—that a ballot should be counted if there was "a clear indication of the intent of the voter."

Lewis asked Beck what instructions, if any, the Bush side believed should be given to the judges (Lewis had already assembled a number of other judges in Leon County to work under his supervision in the recount process) and canvassing boards who would initially review the fifty to sixty thousand remaining undervotes. Beck tried to delay answering until the next day. When that failed, he told Lewis that there was no criteria other than the general "intent of the voter" standard.

Lewis pressed Beck further. Did the lawyer think a more specific standard should be set? Beck responded that Lewis could not set a specific standard now, since that would be changing the rules after Election Day.

Lewis had smoked out the Republican's strategy: if no specific standard is set, complain about the absence of a single statewide standard; if a standard is set, complain that the courts have altered the rules after Election Day, forfeiting safe harbor protection and raising the specter that the court was not merely interpreting existing statutes but impermissibly writing rules itself. In this light the reluctance of the Florida Supreme Court to provide additional specification became understandable. Had that court, I wondered, understood the possible trap that providing additional specification might entail?

At about ten p.m. Judge Lewis took a recess to confer with his fellow Leon County judges before deciding how to proceed. When he returned about ninety minutes later, it was clear that Beck had not succeeded in delaying the start of the recount. The biggest collection of undervotes, the nine thousand from Miami, were already in Tallahassee and would be reviewed by judges starting at eight a.m. Vote counting would also begin in each of the other unrecounted counties the following morning. All the counting was to be completed by two p.m. Sunday. Lewis would try to put judges in each of the recount locations. In addition, he would be available around the clock to answer questions or resolve disputes, including about how to handle individual ballots. Each side would be permitted to have observers present and to file objections with Judge Lewis over any decision with which they disagreed. All counties would be required to fax to Lewis no later than Saturday morning their plans for compliance with his and the Supreme Court's directives.

It was a fair, expeditious, and orderly plan. As we walked into the Tallahassee night (which oddly seemed to be warming as we moved later into the fall), it was clear that whatever doubts we might have about how this recount would come out, the Republicans had none. They were convinced that the recount that would start in eight hours would make Al Gore president, and there was nothing any of Bush's lawyers in Florida could do to stop it. The Republicans did make one last effort to run out the clock by suggesting to some Republican canvassing board members that they could wait until Monday to come to work. The effort was short-lived and unsuccessful. On Saturday morning canvassing board members across the state, Republicans and Democrats alike, assembled to do their duty. Some of them groused to themselves and to cameras that they felt this particular trip was not necessary, but the Florida courts had made their ruling and these citizen officials would implement it to the best of their ability. It was a great moment for democracy and civic responsibility, and a rebuttal to all the cynics who, after the controversy was over, tended to see every action or reaction in partisan terms.

As the results of the statewide recount began to roll in Saturday morning, the news was good for Gore. Except possibly in Duval, where an all-Republican canvassing board was proceeding slowly, every county was on track to meet the Sunday deadline. Indeed, the largest job, the Miami-Dade recount, would be finished Saturday night, having taken only a single day (demonstrating again the absurdity of the Miami board's excuse that it could not complete a review of the undervotes in the four and a half days then available). Not only was the recount proceeding expeditiously, but the net votes for Gore were slightly greater than we had predicted. Judge Lewis had directed the county canvassing boards to report their results directly to him and not to the press. However, each side, and the media, had representatives throughout the state and by noon it appeared that Gore was gaining votes even in counties Bush had carried; it might only be a matter of hours before the press reported unofficial tallies showing Gore in the lead.

Scheduled to fly back to White Plains at three p.m., I walked to the sports bar at Andrew's for one last unhealthy lunch with people who over the last twenty-six days had become my friends. Just before I left Dexter's office for lunch I had learned that the U.S. Court of Appeals for the Eleventh Circuit (the federal court of appeals for the southeastern United States, including Florida) had issued a decision refusing, by an en banc vote of eight to four, to stop the recount. The court was clear: "Nothing in this order should be construed to prevent, obstruct or impede the continuation of the manual recounts that are currently being conducted." The Court reasoned that, first, the votes should be counted, and then any objections to the way the votes were counted could be heard.

U.S. District Court Judge Donald M. Middlebrooks in Miami had earlier rejected Bush's attempt to use the federal courts to stop a state recount. Judge Middlebrooks had ruled: "Under the Constitution of the United States, the responsibility for selection of electors for the office of President rests primarily with the people of Florida, its elections officials and, if necessary, its courts. The procedures employed by Florida appear to be neutral and, while not yet complete, the process seems to be unfolding as it has on other occasions."

When Bush appealed that decision, even his lawyers in Florida predicted he would fail. One of Bush's lawyers told me that Bush had originally asked former United States Senator John Danforth, a one-time state attorney general and a national figure respected by both sides of the aisle, to represent him in asking the federal courts to block the recounts. Danforth declined, saying he thought the chance of Bush's convincing federal courts to intervene was "near zero."* Danforth's judgment seemed vindicated by the court of appeals' ruling.

The Bush campaign had now lost its battle to stop the recount in the Florida courts, in the federal district court in Florida, and in the federal court of appeals. I felt good about what we had accomplished. Although it was by no means certain, it was beginning to look as if Al Gore would win; even Klain and Whouley were optimistic. And whatever the final result of the recount, I believed democracy and the rule of law had already won. The ballots were being counted, and the counting would be completed within the safe harbor deadline.

---

*It was later reported that Senator Danforth tried to discourage the Bush campaign from trying to use the federal courts to interfere with Florida's recounts saying, "You could ruin Governor Bush's career. He's only fifty-four years old, and the decision to file a court case like this one would be a black mark that followed him forever. And it would destroy the reputation of everyone involved on the Bush side." Jeffrey Toobin, *Too Close to Call,* p. 49.

12

Bush v. Gore:
Losing in Washington

As I ate my hamburger and French fries at the sports bar, I thought about the irony that Bush's last chance to invalidate the Florida recount depended on the United States Supreme Court. Here was an advocate of federalism, a candidate running on opposition to federal government interference with states rights, a critic of federal judicial activism asking the U.S. Court to overrule the Supreme Court of Florida's interpretation of Florida state law to save his bid for the presidency. There was nothing necessarily improper in Bush's appeal. We too made the arguments that favored our objectives; and if the situation had been reversed, each side's arguments would probably have been different. But it *was* ironic.

I was just finishing a leisurely lunch when one of the television screens scrolled a report that the U.S. Supreme Court had, by a five-to-four vote, ordered Florida to stop its recount. My first reaction was denial. I could not accept that the Court would actually stop an ongoing vote count—particularly before we had even had a chance to argue the merits of the case. As it became clear that this was in fact exactly what had happened, I returned immediately to Dexter's offices.

When I got there, I found that the excitement and optimism

of less than two hours earlier had been replaced by shock and despair. The Court had set a schedule that had our brief due the next day and oral argument on Monday, December 11; yet it had already taken the extreme, and extremely unusual, step of stopping the vote count before either had taken place. As Justice Antonin Scalia noted in a short opinion, the Court would not have done so unless a majority had already made up their minds that Bush was likely to win his appeal.

One of the reasons the Court's order was such a jolt was that, as Justice Scalia acknowledged, such an order was only proper if the plaintiff would otherwise suffer irreparable injury between the time of the order and the argument of the case on the merits—between Saturday afternoon and Monday morning. Nothing was going to happen during that time except for the counting of votes.* What could possibly constitute irreparable injury in votes being counted by Florida's duly authorized election officials? Scalia's answer was that if the vote count of those officials (most of whom were Republicans) showed Gore as the winner, any later attempt by the Supreme Court to ignore that vote count would be unpopular and Bush's "legitimacy" would be questioned.

What Scalia was saying was that five members of the Supreme Court (himself and Justices Rehnquist, O'Connor, Kennedy, and Thomas) had decided that they wanted to be free to bar the results of the Florida recounts without the American people knowing for sure that doing so made a difference as to who would be elected president. Never before had the Court held that such information could, by itself, constitute irreparable injury. To do so in a political context was disturbing. To do so in connection with the Court's first intervention in a presidential election was shocking.

---

*The U.S. Court of Appeals had already ruled that no change in Secretary Harris's certification of Bush as the winner in Florida could be made until after the U.S. Supreme Court had ruled on the merits of Bush's appeal.

Only Scalia signed his opinion, but all five joined in blocking the vote count.*

The chances that the five-justice majority would take this unique step to protect Bush's "legitimacy" and then decide the case for Gore seemed remote. Moreover, by stopping the recount until the case was decided, the Court was making it impossible for the count to be completed by the December 12 safe harbor deadline. To decide on December 11 or 12 that recounts could proceed after all would make the Court look worse than foolish for having unnecessarily deprived Gore and the voters of Florida of the safe harbor advantage. This fact further reinforced the sense that the majority were not likely to change their minds.

I gave Ron Klain some thoughts on what our brief might include, commiserated with him and the team, and left for the airport. It was not going to be the flight home that I had contemplated a few hours earlier. But either way my work in Florida was finished; and the upcoming argument in Washington was in good hands.

From the day after Election Day, Gore's counsel in federal court had been Laurence Tribe, a long-time professor at Harvard Law School, the author of a definitive constitutional law text, and one of the country's leading federal appellate advocates for liberal causes. Up until the afternoon of December 9, Tribe had remained convinced that the U.S. Supreme Court would not intervene to save Bush's bid for the presidency since the decision ordering a statewide recount was a ruling on state election law by the state's highest court based expressly on state statutes.

The Court's opinion five days earlier seemed to support Larry's view. In addition, while three Supreme Court justices had served on the ill-fated 1876 commission, the Court itself had never be-

---

*A year later Barry Richards and I appeared together on a panel at a meeting of the American College of Trial Lawyers in Palm Beach. In the time reserved for questions, a trial lawyer in the audience asked Barry if he could justify the Supreme Court's December 9 decision to stop the recounts before briefing and argument. Barry replied that he could justify the Court's ultimate decision on the merits but not the December 9 order.

fore intervened in a presidential election and had always shown great reluctance to use its unique power to pursue a partisan political agenda.

In the initial appeal from Florida, the United States Supreme Court had taken the first, tentative step into the rolling political waters of a partisan presidential campaign. It now appeared that the Court was prepared to nullify a vote count supervised and certified by the Florida courts. I still wanted to believe that the Court would ultimately show the restraint it had for 200 years, but five justices seemed not only willing, but anxious, to play a role in interpreting Florida election law.*

On my way to the airport Ron called me to say that he had spoken to Gore and that they were thinking of asking me to do the Monday argument instead of Larry Tribe. Ron explained that they had been disappointed in Tribe's performance at the argument of the first appeal and believed that I might be more effective this time. I told Ron that I thought it was a bad idea. I did not think it made any difference who argued for Gore; the die were already cast. Replacing Larry under these circumstances was an unnecessary embarrassment.

In addition, Tribe had been working on the federal issues for a month; I had been concentrating almost exclusively on the issues before the Florida courts. I could never duplicate in the next forty-eight hours the familiarity with key and obscure federal cases that Larry had studied, taught, and written about for decades. I like my style of argument more than I like Larry's; he probably feels the

---

*It had been unusual for the Court to act at all. The U.S. Supreme Court takes only a fraction of the cases presented to it; and when it does take a case it does so usually only after considerable deliberation and after the court below has completed its work. In the earlier appeal relating to Harris's certification, the U.S. Court had taken the case while the recount was under way, had set an argument schedule that was even earlier than Bush's lawyers had requested, and had decided the case the first business day after argument. On December 9, the Court had again taken the case while the votes were being counted and before the Florida courts had had an opportunity to resolve any objections that might be made to the treatment of individual ballots.

same way in reverse. But any possible advantages I might have had in presentation were, I thought, outweighed by his greater knowledge of federal jurisdiction and constitutional law precedent. Finally, at this late date there was no realistic alternative but to have Larry and his colleague Tommy Goldstein prepare the brief. While I was sure they would write a good brief (Tommy had been an associate at Boies, Schiller & Flexner), arguing a case where you have not personally done the briefing is always complicated.

Klain listened without comment. I had come to know him reasonably well over the last thirty days, but in this instance I could not tell how much he was just a messenger and how much this is what he thought was right. He said he would pass my views on. Since it was late Saturday afternoon and the argument was Monday morning, I assumed Larry would, as planned, present our case. Nevertheless on the flight to New York my mind inevitably wandered to how I would approach the arguments were I making them.

When I arrived home, Mary told me that Al had been trying to reach me. "I think," she said, "he may want you to argue in the Supreme Court on Monday."

When I reached Gore, he got right to the point. He, Christopher, Daley, Dellinger, and Klain all believed I was the right person to make the argument. Our only chance to win was to convince one of the five majority justices to break ranks. No one held out any hope of moving the three most committed Republicans on the Court—Rehnquist, Scalia, and Thomas. It had to be either O'Connor or Kennedy, and our best chance with them was to convince them that what the Florida courts were doing was merely implementing settled state law. The chance might not be a great one, but it was the only one we had, and I was in the best position to take it. Knowledge of what had happened in Florida was more important than scholarly expertise in Constitutional law. "Anyway," Al concluded, "Walter tells me you're a quick study."

There was no point playing games, making Al or Walter or Chris convince me. They wanted me to do it, and I would.

Mary and I were just sitting down to what was ending up as a late dinner when Gore's press people called. They knew I was busy preparing for the argument, but it was important that Gore's views be represented on the Sunday morning news shows. Christopher and Daley thought I should do them. I figured that responding to questions from Tim Russert and others was equivalent to a moot court, so I said yes, if they could do it from my home. The networks agreed, and I went back to dinner and then to bed. As I drifted off to sleep, I considered briefly why I was doing this. Partly I agreed with Gore that whatever chance we had to win depended on issues of Florida state law and precedent, and I was in the best position to deal with those issues. Partly I did not want to say no to him. Partly, after twenty-six days this had become my case and, whatever the prospects, I wanted to see it through.

Sunday I did three morning shows from my library, flew to Washington with Mary, worked with Larry Tribe and Tommy Goldstein on final edits to our brief, met with Walter Dellinger to get his ideas, then went to the Mayflower Hotel to prepare for my argument with Bob Silver.

Monday morning I got up around five-thirty, went through my materials one more time, and headed over to the Supreme Court. The courtroom was packed with members of Congress, other judges, selected members of the press, and people who could get a Supreme Court justice to intervene on their behalf.

Arguing for Bush was Theodore Olson, a former Department of Justice official who was then a partner in Gibson, Dunn & Crutcher. Olson was an exceptional lawyer and the preeminent appellate advocate for conservative causes. His effectiveness was rooted in careful preparation and a thoughtful, intelligent presentation. Although we were on opposite sides of this and many issues, I liked and respected Ted, and we were friends as well as adversaries.

Bush's appeal presented three basic arguments. The first was that the Florida court had violated Article II, Section 1, Clause 2 of the U.S. Constitution, which provides that each state's electors shall be appointed "in such Manner as the Legislature thereof may direct." Bush's argument was that the Florida court had not merely interpreted existing law but had made new law.

His second argument was that the Florida court ruling failed to comply with the requirements of 3 U.S.C. § 5, which gives conclusive effect to state court determinations only if those determinations are made "pursuant to . . . laws enacted prior to" Election Day. Again Bush was arguing that the Florida court had established new rules.

Bush's third argument, which was buried on pages 40 to 45 of his 50-page brief, was that the Florida recount procedures violated the Equal Protection Clause of the Fourteenth Amendment to the U.S. Constitution. When Bush had brought his first appeal to the U.S. Supreme Court, the Court in its opinion had considered Bush's Article II argument but had declined to review the Equal Protection Issue. Bush's lawyers in Florida had privately expressed serious doubts about Bush's even making an equal protection argument, and the five justices who on December 9 had blocked the continuation of the recounts had previously opposed the use of the Equal Protection Clause to limit state action, particularly in the absence of clear proof that the challenged state action represented a pattern of official discrimination against an identified class. No such proof had even been attempted in this case: Bush's argument was that different canvassing boards had interpreted voter intent differently, not that any particular board had applied one approach to Republican and another to Democratic ballots. For all these reasons Tribe and Goldstein viewed Bush's equal protection argument as weak. I agreed.

As petitioner, Ted Olson went first. He was less than sixty seconds into his argument when Justice Kennedy asked, "Where is the federal question here?" Ted replied, "That the Florida Supreme Court was violating Article II, Section 1 of the Constitution, and it was conducting itself in violation of Section 5 of Title III of federal law." There was no mention of the equal protection issue.

Ted's answer and the argument and questions that followed seemed to confirm that this case was about Article II and 3 U.S.C. § 5. Both arguments depended on Bush's contention that the Florida Court had made new law. As expected, Rehnquist, Scalia, and Thomas appeared a lost cause, but Kennedy seemed to understand that prior Florida precedents supported what the Florida court had done—that there was not any "new law." I began to think we might just win.

Ted Olson was more than halfway through his presentation before any mention was made of Bush's equal protection argument, and it was raised not by him but by Justice Kennedy. Ted had again repeated that the bases of Bush's appeal were Article II and 3 U.S.C. § 5 when Kennedy interrupted: "Oh, and I thought your point was that the process is being conducted in violation of the Equal Protection Clause and it is standardless." Alarm bells went off immediately. Was Justice Kennedy trying to warn Olson that there was not a majority for Bush's "new law" plea and remind him that he had an equal protection argument that he was ignoring?

Ted agreed that he did have an equal protection argument, but after acknowledging that he could not come up with a uniform standard more specific than the "intent of the voter," he returned to his main theme that the Florida court's interpretation of state statutes was "so far unreasonable" that it amounted to a judicially created new law.

Joseph Klock, on behalf of Secretary Harris, came next. Klock made two basic points. First, "a ballot that is not properly punched is not a legal ballot" and it was improper to count ballots where the voter was not "following the instructions." Second, any attempt by the Florida court to provide a more specific standard than "intent of the voter" as interpreted by local canvassing boards or a court would constitute impermissible new law. Neither Klock nor any justice mentioned the Equal Protection Clause during his argument.

The unusual nature of the Court's foray into presidential election politics was underscored by the fact that neither Olson nor Klock had cited a single precedent relating to the Equal Protection Clause or any other case supporting federal jurisdiction, nor had any of the nine justices. If the Court did follow through and confirm its December 9 order blocking manual recounts, it would be the U.S., not the Florida Supreme Court, that would have made new law.

The initial questions to me as I started my presentation also dealt with Bush's "new law" contentions. With respect to the issue of the Florida court's prior order extending the protest period beyond seven days (Justice Scalia in particular kept coming back to protest issues, even though the issue before the Court was the entirely separate contest proceeding), I pointed out that the Florida Supreme Court had ruled in 1988 that the seven-day period was not a final deadline and that the Florida legislature's most recent enactment said that returns after the seven days "may" be ignored, compared to the earlier provision that they "shall" be.

With respect to the Florida court's reliance on the "intent of the voter" standard, I pointed out that this standard had come word for word from a statute passed by the Florida legislature. I also emphasized that Bush's own counsel had just acknowledged that there was no more specific standard and had asserted that if the Florida court had supplied more specific criteria, it would have violated Article II and lost the safe harbor protection of 3 U.S.C. § 5.

With respect to the argument that only ballots that were machine readable should be counted, I noted that there was no point in the statutory "intent of the voter" standard if the only ballots to be counted were those that were machine readable; and Bush's counsel had conceded in the Florida courts that it was proper to count the 215 net additional votes in Palm Beach County, where voters had not followed instructions but where the canvassing board had found it could determine the voter's intent. With respect to the "new law" contention, I noted that Florida courts had employed manual recounts and the intent of the voter standard consistently for eighty years.

I was well into my presentation when the equal protection argument was raised, again by Justice Kennedy. First he suggested there was no uniform statewide standard. When I pointed out that there was a uniform statewide standard and it was the intent of the voter, he responded that since there was no single objective standard as to how to determine the intent of the voter, it was possible that different vote-counters might reach different conclusions about the same ballot. Justice Scalia went further, asserting that "it was clear that Broward and Palm Beach Counties had applied different criteria to dimpled ballots."

I noted that the same was true whenever judges, juries, or administrative personnel applied general standards of intent. For example, there is no doubt that juries in certain Florida counties are much more likely, on the same facts, to sentence a defendant to death than juries in other counties. The Supreme Court (and, particularly, the five justices that comprised the December 9 majority) had repeatedly ruled that such differences in application did not constitute a violation of equal protection. Bush's argument, if accepted and applied generally, would massively expand the reach of the Equal Protection Clause.

An additional problem with Justice Scalia's assertion was that it was not based on the record. The Republicans had not filed a contest over the Broward vote count; indeed, the results of the Broward recount were included in the certified results Bush was defending. And the Republicans had conceded in the Florida courts that the Palm Beach vote count was proper. Moreover, both at trial and before the Florida Supreme Court, Bush had argued that the boards had discretion and that their exercise of discretion had to be accepted.

Appellate courts, and the Supreme Court most of all, are not permitted to assume, make up, or find facts that are not in the trial record; they must deal with the evidence and arguments presented. Assumptions are not substitutes for facts or evidence. Similarly, in ordinary cases the Supreme Court (and Justice Scalia most of all) strictly requires that arguments and evidence presented to the Court have been fully and fairly presented in the lower courts, and that litigants be held to their positions below. But as was perhaps already clear, this was not an ordinary case being decided by ordinary rules.

The hardest question I was asked came from Justice Souter. Assuming that the Court concluded that there were impermissible variations from county to county that had to be corrected by a statewide objective standard, what should that standard be? The question was hard for two reasons. First, setting such a standard now could support Bush's "new law" argument under Article II and 3 U.S.C. § 5. Second, the question was one of Florida law, and the Florida legislature had chosen to adopt a general standard subject to judicial review rather than specific, objective criteria. Since Florida law did not provide the basis for a specific, objective standard, and since it was Florida law that was at issue, if the U.S. Court were to change that choice, it was hard to know what rule the Court should adopt. (Ironically, after the great concern that the Supreme Court had shown in its first opinion for the constitutional provision that left the manner of selection of electors exclusively to the state legislature, it appeared that the Court was now about to quarrel with the legislature's adoption of a general "intent of the voter" standard.)

I suggested that if the Court wanted to articulate a specific objective standard, the Texas rule (which provided a number of specific bases for counting a ballot in addition to an intent of the voter standard) was a good one. I also, however, continued to argue that such an approach was not necessary, including because each side had an opportunity to object to any ballot that it believed was dealt with improperly, and the procedures being followed in Florida provided for a consistent judicial resolution of those objections. In addition, I pointed out the difficulty of avoiding some subjectivity because ballots could differ in unpredictable ways.*

Juries, governmental officials, and administrative agencies are all permitted to make different inferences from objective, physical evidence (such as fingerprints, DNA, photographs, crash results, scientific tests) and reach different conclusions on the same facts so long as the findings are within the range of reasonableness. Bush's argument was not that the decisions of the canvassing boards were unreasonable; there was no finding or evidence of that. His argument was that the decisions might vary.

If Souter's question was the hardest, a question from Justice O'Connor was the most frustrating. Late into my argument she asked, "Well, why isn't the standard the one that voters are instructed to follow, for goodness sakes? I mean, it couldn't be clearer. I mean, why don't we go to that standard?"

It was a frustrating question because both in our brief and in oral argument we had repeatedly answered this point. Part of me wanted to answer: "For goodness sakes, Justice O' Connor. Haven't you read anything we've written or heard anything we've said?" Of course, I didn't. Not only because of my respect for the Court and for Sandra O'Connor personally, but also because I recognize the role that justices' questions play in a Supreme Court argument. Nevertheless, I was frustrated and disappointed by what I saw as her ignoring inconvenient facts and precedents. What I did say was:

*For example, a ballot where there is an indentation rather than a hole for every race on the ballot (*e.g.* president, congressman, state legislature) could be treated differently from another ballot where the voter successfully punched the ballot through in every race but president. Likewise, if an unusually large number of ballots from a given precinct were indented but not punched through, a board might reasonably infer that there was some problem with the equipment. Ballots can also vary based on the extent and pattern of an indentation. It is for such reasons as these that even states like Texas with objective criteria also rely on an intent of the voter catchall.

Well, your Honor, because in Florida law, since 1917 in *Darby against State*, the Florida Supreme Court has held that where a voter's intent can be discerned, even if they don't do what they're told, the votes are supposed to be counted; and . . . in the *Beckstrom* case, that was a case that used optical ballots, voters were told, fill it in with a number two pencil. Several thousand didn't. They used everything else, but not a number two pencil. And so the machine wouldn't read it. It was voter error. The Supreme Court in 1998, well before this election, said you've got to count those votes.*

I did, however, retain my sense of humor enough so that when the *Wall Street Journal* at the end of its lead editorial the next day quoted Justice O'Connor's question without the answer, and with the suggestion that there had been no answer, my first reaction was to smile. My second reaction was that it was too bad that the U.S. Court, unlike the Florida court, barred cameras from the courtroom; the fact that the public could listen to the Florida arguments live enabled people to understand what actually happened and make up their own minds whether what the court was doing made sense. The more a court ventures into the political realm, the more important it becomes to allow the public to see firsthand how it operates.

At the end of my argument the Chief Justice and Justice Kennedy returned to the equal protection issue and the fact that different counties might count votes differently, suggesting that "the fact that there is a single judge at the end of the process" might not provide standardization of ballot treatment. I replied:

---

*I would have liked to be able to add that if strict compliance by the voter was the standard, several thousand net votes for Bush in Seminole County should have been thrown out, but we had not included that claim in our contest.

First, I think that the answer that they did it differently, different people interpreting the general standard differently, would not raise a problem even in the absence of judicial review.

Second, even if that would have raised a constitutional problem, I think judicial review provides the standardization that would solve that problem.

Third, any differences as to how this standard is interpreted have a lot less significance in terms of what votes are counted or not counted than simply the differences in machines that exist throughout the counties of Florida. There are five times as many undervotes in punch-card ballot counties than in optical ballot counties. Now, for whatever that reason is, whether it's voter error or machine problems, that statistic makes clear that there is some difference in how votes are being treated county by county. That difference is much greater than the difference in how many votes are recovered in Palm Beach or Broward or Volusia or Miami-Dade, so that the differences of interpretation of the standard, the general standard, are resulting in far fewer differences among counties than simply the differences in the machines that they have.

After the hearing Mary and I joined Al and Tipper Gore and Joe and Hadassah Lieberman at the Vice President's residence for lunch. The Supreme Court had just released the audiotape of the argument, and as we listened to the questions and answers, Al became guardedly optimistic. "You really nailed their questions. They will look terrible if they decide this for Bush on this record," he said at the end.

They might indeed look terrible, but I had three concerns. Everything about the way the Court had handled the case led me to question whether this was a case where the result could be predicted based on normal principles. In addition, any of the five justices in the December 9 majority who did not support Bush now would look foolish for stopping the vote-counting on Saturday; the justices of course had an obligation to rise above such concerns, but on a human level that might not be easy. Finally, I was concerned that the fact that the next president might well appoint replacements for two or more of the current justices who were close to retirement might not be irrelevant to their decision.

After lunch Mary and I returned to New York. Monday night and all the next day passed without a decision. Finally, after ten p.m. Tuesday, December 12, with less than two hours to go before the safe harbor deadline expired, the Court issued its opinion. The majority held that manual recounts violated the Equal Protection Clause because of the lack of a single, specific, objective statewide standard, and held (after having stopped the recounts the previous Saturday afternoon) that it was now too late to let the recount go forward under such a standard. The five justices who joined in the majority opinion were the same five who had voted to stop the recounts on Saturday. Each of the four justices who dissented from the Court's Saturday order filed bitter dissents. Justice Scalia, joined by the Chief Justice and Justice Thomas, filed a concurring opinion in which they asserted that the Florida Court's rulings also violated Article II of the Constitution and 3 U.S.C. § 5.

We had received a few minutes advance warning that an opinion would be released, and when it was I was already on a conference call with Al Gore and Joe Lieberman. We struggled together to read and understand the decision, while reporters on camera were going through the same exercise. Although the number of dissenting and concurring opinions caused the press some confusion, the judgment was clear—it was over.

The majority opinion conceded that punch-card machines produced "an unfortunate number of ballots" where voters tried to vote but their ballots could not be counted by machines; but it held that there was now no remedy for this "unfortunate" forfeiture of the right of citizens to have their vote counted. The majority opinion tried to limit the applicability of its Equal Protection Clause ruling to this case alone ("Our consideration is limited to the present circumstances").

Justices Stevens, Ginsburg, and Breyer joined in a dissenting opinion:

> When questions arise about the meaning of state laws, including election laws, it is our settled practice to accept the opinions of the highest courts of the States as providing the final answers. On rare occasions, however, either federal statutes or the Federal Constitution may require federal judicial intervention in state elections. This is not such an occasion. The federal questions that ultimately emerged in this case are not substantial.

The dissent went on to observe:

> Nor are petitioners correct in asserting that the failure of the Florida Supreme Court to specify in detail the precise manner in which the "intent of the voter," Fla. Stat. §101.5614(5) (Supp.2001), is to be determined rises to the level of a constitutional violation.

The dissent noted that the majority of all states approached the issue of determining the intent of the voter the way Florida did and pointed out that:

> . . . we have never before called into question the substantive standard by which a State determines that a vote has been legally cast. And there is no reason to think that the guidance provided to the fact-finders, specifically the various canvassing boards, by the "intent of the voter" standard is any less sufficient—or will lead to results any less uniform—than, for example, the "beyond a reasonable doubt" standard employed every day by ordinary citizens in courtrooms across this country.

The dissenters also emphasized the fact (ignored by the majority opinion despite its emphasis in our briefs and oral argument) that "a single impartial magistrate will ultimately adjudicate all objections arising from the recount process." The dissenters concluded:

> Although we may never know with complete certainty the identity of the winner of this year's presidential election, the identity of the loser is perfectly clear. It is the Nation's confidence in the judge as an impartial guardian of the rule of law.

Justice Souter filed his own dissenting opinion. He began: "The court should not have reviewed either *Bush v. Palm Beach County Canvassing Bd.*, or this case, and should not have stopped Florida's attempt to recount all undervote ballots." He went on to describe the majority opinion as "another erroneous decision." He noted that if the majority had not stopped the recount, the entire issue might well have already been satisfactorily resolved.

Justice Ginsburg, who had joined in Justice Stevens's dissent, filed an additional dissent in which she carefully analyzed how the cases cited in the majority's opinion failed to support their conclusions. She gently noted the inconsistency between the majority's opinion and the traditional advocacy of federalism and deference to state courts by the five justices who constituted that majority: "Were the other members of this Court as mindful as they generally are of our system of dual sovereignty, they would affirm the judgment of the Florida Supreme Court." The justice went on to observe that the petitioners had "not presented a substantial equal protection claim" and that, even had they done so, there was no justification for the majority's not permitting the recount to proceed now.

Justice Breyer, who had also joined in Justice Stevens's dissent, filed a separate opinion as well. "The Court was wrong," he began, "to take this case. It was wrong to grant a stay." The justice noted "the absence of *any* record evidence that the recount could not have been completed in the time allowed by the Florida Supreme Court" (emphasis in original). He also noted:

> . . . in a system that allows counties to use different types of voting systems, voters already arrive at the polls with an unequal chance that their votes will be counted. I do not see how the fact that this results from counties' selection of different voting machines rather than a court order makes the outcome any more fair.

The dissents also attacked the "new law" arguments of the three-justice concurring opinion as wholly lacking in factual or precedential support.

Ron Klain and a few others were not prepared to accept what we all viewed as an unjust outcome. Ron believed that the opinion left it open for the Florida Supreme Court to set an objective statewide standard; order the recount of all sixty thousand under-votes using that standard; and complete everything by December 18, the day the electors were scheduled to meet. The resulting certification would not have the benefit of the safe harbor provision, but perhaps Congress would conclude it had to accept the state's popular vote as certified by the state's highest court, particularly after having been counted under a single statewide standard. Ron wanted to prepare papers to be filed with the Florida Supreme Court the following morning.

No one wanted to dismiss this possibility out of hand; we all wanted to find some glimmer of hope. However, even a quick reading of the majority opinion made it clear that five justices were telling us in the clearest possible terms that it was over. Even if I agreed that this was "a judicial coup," it was still over.

"It may have been wrong to shoot us," I said softly, "but we're still dead."

In the end Al said he wanted to sleep on it and that he would make a decision first thing in the morning. Ron went to work with the team that remained in Tallahassee, preparing papers to file in the morning if that was the decision. I stayed up in New York, reviewing and commenting on faxed draft arguments as they were produced. It was more ritual than work. I was convinced these papers should not, and would not, be filed; but like someone trying to revive a friend who has drowned even after it is clear there is no hope, it did not yet seem right to stop.

Wednesday morning Al made the decision he and I both knew had to be made, and that evening he publicly conceded. It was a gracious speech in which he tried to unite the nation behind the man who would be president for the next four years. Afterward as Mary and I reflected on the exciting, rewarding, frustrating, satisfying, disappointing thirty days since Walter Dellinger had called to ask me to come to Florida, I thought about what was wrong with the five-justice majority opinion in *Bush v. Gore*.

As the dissents emphasized, the majority abandoned virtually every rule the Court ordinarily follows in deciding cases. It did so by:

- disregarding a state supreme court's interpretation of state law;
- prohibiting Florida from recounting ballots prior to a decision on the merits;
- intervening before the Florida process had been completed and a record fully developed;
- deciding issues that had not been fully and fairly litigated in the court from which the appeal was taken;
- allowing an appellant not only to raise on appeal arguments not made below but to rely on arguments contrary to positions taken below;
- ignoring normal requirements for record evidence and findings to support factual determinations;
- ignoring admissions and concessions in the court below;

- assuming that the procedures established in Florida to assure uniformity, including judicial supervision and a review of disputed interpretations by a single judge, would not work (without waiting to see whether they in fact worked).

Yet, that was not all, nor even the most important thing, that was wrong. The rule of law means, first, that what a court (or other decision-maker) will do must be reasonably predictable, and second, that what a court does must be independent of the identity of the parties. The majority opinion flunked both tests.

A court's predictability comes in part through adherence to precedent. This means that a decision should be derived from the principles of past decisions. It also means that the court must be willing to decide future cases according to the principles it uses to decide today's case. Justice Scalia has been a particularly vocal advocate of principled decisionmaking and has been an outspoken critic of justices he believes are unwilling to articulate, and abide by, consistent principles. "When," he has said, "in writing for the majority of the court, I adopt a general rule and say 'This is the basis of our decision,' I not only constrain lower courts, I constrain myself as well. If the next case should have such different facts that my political or policy preferences regarding the outcome are quite the opposite, I will be unable to indulge those preferences; I have committed myself to the governing principle."

The majority's equal protection decision was contrary to principles used to construe the Equal Protection Clause in prior cases, particularly in opinions in which Chief Justice Rehnquist and Justices Scalia and Thomas joined. Moreover, all five Justices in the majority explicitly recognized that they would be unwilling to apply the principles of *Bush v. Gore* to other cases; this was a decision for this case only, the majority declared.

Principled decisionmaking also requires that a decision should be internally consistent. The undisputed fact was that the different types of voting machines used in different counties had a much greater effect on whether a vote would be recorded than any difference in the interpretation of what represented the intent of the voter. If it was, as the majority ruled, a violation of equal protection to give voters in one county a greater chance to have their ballots counted than is given to voters in another county, it was a violation of equal protection for Florida to have different voting machines in different counties. The majority opinion never dealt with this inconsistency; like so much that did not fit, it was simply ignored.*

The majority opinion also ignored the fact that the procedure established in Florida provided each side an opportunity to object to any ballot that it thought was improperly counted (or not counted) and provided that all unresolved disputes would be decided by a single judge. This procedure went to the heart of the majority opinion's conclusion that the Florida process would inevitably result in unacceptably large differences in how ballots were treated from county to county. If Bush failed to file a contest, or failed to object to the way certain ballots were counted on December 9, there was no case to decide; if Bush did file a contest, or make an objection, Florida had established a procedure to resolve the issue. The majority's opinion depended on the assumption that the treatment of ballots during the recount would vary greatly from county to county. It was hard to reconcile that assumption with the procedures established by Judge Lewis. The majority simply ignored those procedures. But facts are stubborn things, and ignoring them does not make them go away. The failure of the majority to deal with anything at odds with its assumptions further undercut any claim to principled decisionmaking.

Finally, if there has been one guiding principle of the jurisprudence of Justices Rehnquist, Scalia, and Thomas (and to a lesser

---

*A ruling that different voting machines, with their different abilities to count votes, violated the Equal Protection Clause would have thrown out Florida's electoral votes—which would have left Gore leading in the Electoral College as well as the popular vote.

extent O'Connor and Kennedy) it has been the overriding importance of federalism and states' rights. The need to defer to state courts has been used to justify case after case limiting the protection that federal law, including the Equal Protection and Due Process Clauses, was earlier thought to provide. We are not deciding, and are not supposed to decide, what the best rule might be, the justices have argued; we must defer to the state courts in the name of federalism. The justices have argued, among other things, that federalism requires deference to a state's decisions regarding everything from outlawing homosexual behavior and abortion to how prisoners are treated and whether guns should be permitted in the vicinity of public schools. If federalism means anything, it must mean that the states have the right to make decisions the U.S. Supreme Court would not make if it were sitting as a state court. In *Bush v. Gore*, the majority was unwilling to defer to the Florida court unless that court ruled the way the majority wanted it to rule.

The majority opinion also flunked the requirement that decisionmaking be independent of the identity of the parties. Even conservative constitutional scholars have conceded that they doubt the result would have been the same if the case had been *Gore v. Bush*—with Gore leading in the vote count and trying to get the Supreme Court to stop manual recounts requested by the Republicans and ordered by a state supreme court.

In our democracy we give the most final decisionmaking authority to our least democratic institution. In search of a nonpartisan way to make certain important decisions, we have given unique power to nine individuals who are appointed for life and are not subject to political sanction or recall. Justices may, and sometimes do, come to the Court from partisan political backgrounds, but we as a nation hope and expect that partisanship ends with their appointment. During the more than two hundred years of our republic, that hope and expectation has been fulfilled to a surprising extent. In particular the Court has avoided using the unique power it has been given to influence elections for the president that will appoint their successors.

We believe that whether or not we agree with a decision of the Court, that decision reflects the Justices' best principled judgment as to how that case, and every case, should be decided under the law—that the Justices are not seeking a particular result in a particular case for political reasons. The worst decisions of the Supreme Court have been decisions like *Dred Scott*, *Plessy v. Ferguson*, and the Japanese internment cases where the Court abandoned principled decisionmaking to reach a result that the Court believed society required.* It may be even worse to render an unprincipled decision not to comply with a perception of what society will accept, but to place a judicial thumb on the political scale.

After December 12, 2000, some conservative commentators, unable to defend the stated basis of the majority's decision, defended the result on the ground that the majority believed what they were doing was necessary for the good of the country to avoid a national "crisis." The five Justices (all of whom have dedicated their lives to public service) certainly made the decision they did because they concluded it was in the best interests of the country. The problem with the commentators' explanation is that judges, unlike legislators, are limited in the extent to which they can pursue what they personally conclude is in the country's interest. Elected legislators can, and are supposed to, enact whatever laws they believe serve the public interest; voters choose legislators who they believe will act in a way consistent with what the voters want, and they can replace legislators who don't. That is the way a representative democracy works. If no candidate received a major-

---

*In *Dred Scott* the Supreme Court in 1857 decided that slaves were property and that slaves who escaped to the North could not become citizens because they remained the property of "their owners." In *Plessy* the Court in 1896 upheld the right of states to segregate citizens based on race and to require black and white children to go to different schools. In *Korematsu v. U.S.* the Court in 1944 upheld the right of the government during World War II to force all citizens of Japanese ancestry into concentration camps without any evidence of disloyalty or any evidence of misconduct.

ity of electoral votes and the contest had to be decided by Congress, each member of Congress would be free to vote for the candidate he or she personally favored.

The Court, by contrast, is neither elected nor subject to recall. Its legitimacy, and our willingness to accept its pronouncements, is based on the faith that it will interpret the country's laws (including its Constitution) based on consistent legal principles. The interpretation of our laws, and particularly our Constitution, will necessarily be influenced by Justices' personal conclusions as to what principles best serve our society. However, we trust that that influence will be constrained by the requirement that each interpretation be grounded in principles that are generally applicable—principles derived from past opinions, and principles that the judges are prepared to apply in the future. Legislators are not required to be consistent; judges are.

Accordingly, when a judge decides a case inconsistently with his or her prior opinions, when an opinion ignores undisputed facts inconsistent with its result, when a judge decides a case based on principles he or she is not prepared to apply to future cases, or decides a case to achieve a particular result rather than to confirm or extend generally applicable rules of law, the judge impairs the trust that is the source of the Court's power. The judge also forces legislators increasingly to politicize the process of judicial selection; if judges act as political agents, their successors will inevitably be required to pass political tests at the time of their selection.

It is also obvious but worth emphasizing that both Article II and 3 U.S.C. § 5 provided an institution to resolve any perceived "crisis"—that institution is the United States Congress, a political body whose members *are* responsible to the voters. It is also obvious but worth emphasizing that even if the justices perceived a crisis that they (and, for some reason, not the Congress) needed to resolve, that perception could not justify the particular decision they made. If the majority had stuck with their prior (and likely future) principles and decided the case for Al Gore, that too would have resolved any perceived crisis. As the four dissenting justices point out, it was wrong for the Court to intervene and, if the Court decided to intervene, it was wrong to decide the case the way the majority did.

In the aftermath of the Florida election litigation and the wide-spread criticism of the Court's decision I was interviewed by several reporters from foreign countries. They all had a common question. "This is very hard," a Russian reporter put it, "to explain to people in my country. They do not understand why the people of your country appear to have accepted the Supreme Court's selection of your president. Why are not people demonstrating in the streets, marching on Washington? Where is your Yeltsin?"

There are many partial answers to that question. The fact that the election was so close is relevant, although it is precisely in close cases that the integrity of the process matters. Another factor may be that the reaction to what occurred is being reflected not in street demonstrations but in greater scrutiny of judicial nominees to reduce the likelihood of a similar decision in the future. However, I believe that the primary answer to the Russian reporter's question is the faith that the American people have in the stability of our democracy. Unlike the vast majority of the rest of the world, we are confident that not only will there be another regularly scheduled election but that its results will not be unduly influenced by who won the last. Three times before in our history a man has been elected president with fewer popular votes than his opponent; none of them was reelected. If George W. Bush is an exception, it will be because the American people, in a democratic election, make that decision.

Even our faith in the Supreme Court remains strong, and the strength of that faith is critical to the important role it has played over the last half century in protecting human and civil rights. The same court that gave us *Dred Scott*, *Plessy*, and *Korematsu* also gave us *Brown v. Bd. of Education*, *Miranda*, and *Roe v. Wade*. The Court's reputation, and our faith in it, will survive an occasional lapse.

Mary and I talked late into the night of December 13 about matters light and heavy, and the following morning I slept in. Around eleven I met with my partner Jonathan Schiller to be briefed on the status of the Calvin Klein litigation and other matters that required my attention.

Afterword

THIS BOOK HAS BEEN ABOUT SELECTED CASES DURING the four years from 1997, when I left Cravath, through 2000 and *Bush v. Gore*. Any one of the cases I discuss could have been the subject of a separate book, and there is much that is left unsaid. I have tried to select the key facts, events, and issues that made each important to me—and to focus on lessons that might be learned from them. I have also tried to give a sense of the personal and professional aspects of working on several major lawsuits simultaneously.

There have been cases I have had to exclude even though they were significant to me, simply on the grounds that the book would have been impossibly long to have included them all. Of all the cases that fell between 1997 and 2000 that I have left out, the most interesting may have been the defense of Banque Indosuez against charges by a consortium of currency traders that the bank had misled them into making unprofitable purchases and sales.

We knew the jury's verdict would be conclusive. The trial judge, Beatrice Shainswit, had refused to grant the defendant summary judgment, finding that the plaintiffs had established sufficient evidence of fraud to justify a jury trial—a finding upheld by the appellate court. This meant that if a jury found in favor of the plaintiffs, the bank would have no realistic chance to reverse it on appeal.

The plaintiffs were seeking $100 million in damages, but more important than the money was the bank's reputation and the precedent that would be established for the extent of a bank's duties to such customers. Much of our evidence went to demonstrating that the bank had been accurate in the information it furnished. Another important component of our defense was explaining the gamble that the plaintiffs had knowingly taken and making the jury understand that the traders had not complained when they made money; it was only when they lost that they became unhappy with the bank's advice.

The turning point may have come when one of the three leaders of the consortium, a man in his 50s, unexpectedly broke down and began to cry during my cross-examination. Some of the jurors said afterward that they were offended that someone, who still had much more money than they had, was crying over what they viewed as gambling losses. Other jurors thought it was fake, an attempt to gain sympathy—which confirmed for them that the plaintiffs were not to be trusted. Either way, it demonstrated the importance of luck (I had not been trying to make the witness break down) and the danger to a witness of over-dramatization.

During the four years since 2000 there has been no let-up in interesting cases. I defended NASCAR in a lawsuit in Texas by Johnnie Cochran claiming that NASCAR had monopolized the market for auto races; I represented Philip Morris in a case brought in North Carolina by RJR, Lorillard, and Brown & Williamson (represented by Cravath) claiming that Philip Morris violated the Sherman Act by agreeing with retailers to limit advertising and display of cigarettes; I defended Viacom in New York against claims by Spike Lee that the company's cable channel Spike TV was a misappropriation of his name; I represented Court TV in an (as yet unsuccessful) effort to declare unconstitutional the New York State statute forbidding judges from allowing television cameras in their courtrooms; and I worked with my partners Jonathan Schiller and Alan Vickery in suing Cablevision to require the cable operator to broadcast Yankee games.

I also watched from the sidelines with mixed emotions as the European Union investigated Microsoft, ultimately regulating the company's business practices and imposing the largest antitrust fine in history. On the one hand, some of the regulations were similar to remedies we had proposed in the Justice Department lawsuit before the Bush administration took over. However, other regulations seemed more intended to hobble Microsoft and advantage its competitors than to create a level playing field for vigorous competition. One of the ironies is that Microsoft may have been too successful in its negotiations with the Bush Justice Department. During our investigation and trial, the European Union had been inclined to ratify and adopt whatever remedy we achieved. However, after the department failed to correct even conduct which the court of appeals found unlawful the EU concluded something more had to be done; and when it acted, it went further than we, or Judge Jackson, would have.

Among my most interesting work during the last four years were cases for Calvin Klein, Napster, Adelphia, Tyco, and Lloyd's of London.

In 2001 I represented Calvin Klein in litigation against his primary licensee (Warnaco). Most of the clothes (and other products) that Calvin Klein designs are actually manufactured and sold by separate companies ("licensees") who pay a fee to do so. It is critical to the long-term reputation and value of his trademarks that such products are of the highest quality. As a result, Calvin Klein spends considerable time and money policing the performance of his licensees.

In the spring of 2000 Calvin called me to ask us to investigate his suspicions that Warnaco was not abiding by its obligations. The case was critical to both Calvin (who wanted to protect his trademarks) and to Warnaco (whose short-term profitability depended on its current business practices). The case also raised important legal questions concerning the relative rights of trademark owners and their licensees.

Our discovery reached to mills and other operations in Asia and Mexico as well as the U.S. Ultimately, we were able to prove that the defendant had attached the Calvin Klein name to products that he had not designed, altered his designs without authorization, used inferior fabrics, and sold through unauthorized distribution channels. E-mails, hard work, and luck played important parts, with the discovery, shortly before trial was scheduled to begin, of e-mails on the hard drives of fabric suppliers which described the alterations and the use of substandard fabrics.

A few months after its illegal conduct was curtailed, Warnaco filed for bankruptcy.

In 2001 I also represented Napster, the Internet file sharing service, against charges that it was illegally contributing to copyright infringement. Napster had been sued in 1999 by all the major music distributors and a number of artists. After a series of losses, the company called my partner Jonathan Schiller. My initial reaction was that the plaintiffs were right and that Napster's conduct was improper. However, Jonathan's children and mine argued that this was an important case for us to take, and after an initial investigation, we agreed.

In particular, we concluded that the case raised important questions both of intellectual property law and of the freedom to use the Internet to share music and other information that could lawfully be shared conventionally. If Internet sharing was to be more restricted than other sharing, we argued, such restrictions should be imposed by Congress and not by the courts.

Copyright infringement is a violation of law. "Contributory infringement," on the other hand, is a judge-made rule that holds persons liable for selling products or services whose purpose is to facilitate copyright infringement by others. In 1980 Sony was sued for contributory infringement for its sale of Betamax VCRs which were widely used to copy movies illegally. The Ninth Circuit

Court of Appeals held that Sony was liable, but the U.S. Supreme Court reversed, holding that because VCRs had other uses it was improper to impose liability on Sony even if their primary use was improper copying.

Napster had four main defenses. First, it had legitimate uses (including the authorized distribution of the music of thousands of artists who saw Napster as a way of increasing their audience and popularity, and the sharing of other music which was not copyrighted or whose copyright had expired). The primary initial use was clearly to share copyrighted music; however, under the *Betamax* case that was arguably not enough.

Second, the Digital Millennium Copyright Act (the "DMCA") appeared to offer Internet services such as Napster a safe harbor from liability—although there were technological questions as to whether Napster qualified.

Third, Napster could not be liable for contributory infringement unless its users were engaged in actual infringement. In 1982 Congress had passed the Audio Home Recording Act ("AHRA") which authorized the non-commercial copying of music by consumers. Under the AHRA a consumer who purchased a tape or disk could make as many copies as he or she wanted and give them to friends, or pass them out on a street corner, so long as the consumer asked nothing in return. Since Napster's users were engaged in non-commercial sharing, if the same rules applicable to conventional sharing of copyrighted music were applied to the Internet there was no copyright violation; and if there were no infringement by users there could be no contributory infringement by Napster.

Fourth, Napster had offered music distributors hundreds of millions of dollars for a license to permit its users to share the distributor's copyrighted music lawfully; all had refused. Napster believed that the music companies' refusal represented a joint effort to eliminate a competitor and alternative distribution channel. If so, this would violate the antitrust laws and constitute "copyright abuse"— which in turn would render their copyrights unenforceable.

On July 26, 2000, the district court Judge Marilyn Patel entered a preliminary injunction which effectively required Napster to be shut down. We immediately appealed and asked the Ninth Circuit Court of Appeals to stay the trial court's injunction until our appeal could be heard. On July 28, 2000, a three-judge panel granted our application. This made us optimistic that the preliminary injunction would be reversed because the stay would not have been issued in the absence of serious doubts concerning the order's propriety. In addition, the appeals panel included Judge Alex Kozinski—a particularly technologically savvy judge who we believed was likely to understand both the law and the technology and not fall into the trial court's trap of seeing widespread sharing of copyrighted material and concluding there must be a violation there somewhere.

Unfortunately, neither Kozinski nor any of the other judges who stayed Patel's order was on the panel that decided the case on the merits. The panel that did hear the case reversed the district court's injunction as too broad but upheld the plaintiff's entitlement to some injunction. The court ruled that consumers could use VCRs, CD players and other devices for the non-commercial copying of music, but not computers;* that we had not yet developed proof of our "misuse" defense; and that Napster could be liable for contributory infringement even if it had other legitimate uses.

We were especially disappointed by the court's refusal to rule one way or the other on our DMCA defense saying a fuller record was required. Since the plaintiffs had the burden of proof, one might think that would mean Napster should win. However, the court found the "balance of hardships" tipped in favor of the music companies because if copying went on during the trial there might not be an adequate remedy if the plaintiffs ultimately won. The court dismissed as "speculative" the damage to Napster if it were shut down.

We believed that the Ninth Circuit's conclusion, like its ear-

---

*This position had support in the text and legislative history of the AHRA, but was contrary to other legislative history and to some language in a recent Ninth Circuit Court of Appeals opinion.

lier *Betamax* decision, might eventually be reversed by the U.S. Supreme Court. However, that Court generally does not accept appeals before a case is finally over. In the meantime, the largest shareholder of Napster sold control of the company to Bertelsman, one of the leading music suppliers, which abandoned the litigation and put Napster into bankruptcy. The litigation was abandoned shortly after the district court permitted significant discovery of facts relating to the music companies' possible antitrust violations and copyright abuse.

The music industry has gone on to sue other Internet services and even consumers. Thus far no defendant has had both the resources and determination to see the litigation all the way through.

In April 2002 Christopher and I began representing Adelphia and Tyco. In each case we were approached by members of the company's board of directors who had become concerned with indications that their top management might be enriching themselves at the expense of the company and its shareholders.

We began immediate investigations and within 30 days had uncovered sufficient wrongdoing to require the replacement of the companies' chief executives. Throughout 2002 and 2003 we cooperated with prosecutors and the SEC in bringing criminal charges against Adelphia and Tyco's former officers; and we sued those executives on behalf of the companies to recover civil damages for the harm they had caused their shareholders.

Even though the conduct of Adelphia and Tyco's former executives was less egregious than the conduct of officers at Enron, WorldCom, and other examples of corporate crime, with the support of the board we moved faster and more aggressively to remove the wrongdoers, and to pursue them criminally and civilly, than other companies had done. Each of our two clients was also fortunate to secure the services of talented new management teams who moved proactively to restore employee, customer, and investor confidence; to repair the damage prior executives had done; and to support our cooperation with the government and our civil actions against prior executives.

The result was that both companies were restored to profitability, and lender and shareholder losses were a fraction of the losses of those who lent to, and invested in, Enron, WorldCom, and similar victims of corporate malfeasance. Tyco's shareholders in particular saw their stock recover to levels above what it sold at before the executives' crimes were revealed.

In February 2004, I began a three-month trial arising out of the September 11, 2001, attack on the World Trade Center. More people were killed on September 11 than at Pearl Harbor or any other battle with foreign forces on American soil in the history of the country. Secondarily, the tragedy generated one of the largest insurance controversies ever.

Less than two months before the attack the owner of the WTC, the Port Authority of New York and New Jersey, had leased the twin towers to Silverstein Properties for ninety-nine years. Silverstein became responsible for insuring the WTC and obtained property damage insurance commitments for $3.5 billion "per occurrence". The insurance coverage was substantially less than the replacement cost of the property because neither Silverstein nor the Port Authority contemplated the possibility of its entire destruction.

Within hours of planes crashing into each of the twin towers it was clear that the unthinkable had in fact occurred. The property was a total loss and it would take at least twice the $3.5 billion in insurance to rebuild. Even before the towers collapsed, the focus of Silverstein's people turned to insurance. At trial Silverstein's insurance broker testified how as he watched the second plane strike the second tower he turned to his fellow worker and

> I expressed my just complete shock and horror at what was clearly happening. I remember saying to him, "Oh, my God, America is under attack." And I said to him, "Is the [insurance] placement all tidied away?" And he turned to me and said, "Yes, it's all done, it's all bound, it's bound on the Travelers form, and really that's it."

Because there were two planes, each hitting a separate tower, there was an argument that each step in the attack was a separate "occurrence". Since the policy limits were written on a "per occurrence" basis, this contention if successful would mean that the insurers as a group would be liable for $7 billion.

To press its argument Silverstein Properties turned to a team led by Herbert Wachtel. At 73, Herb had been a New York legend for decades, and he had three important facts in his favor. First, this would be tried by a jury of New Yorkers, and Herb could be expected to exploit the chance that their sympathies would favor getting the money to rebuild the World Trade Center rather than protecting insurance companies, most of which were foreign enterprises.

Second, there were two planes, two towers, and two collapses—which Herb would argue inevitably should lead to a conclusion of two occurrences. There was, of course, one bin Laden, one Al Qaeda, one terrorist plan, one insurance program, and one World Trade Center. But the closer the case, the greater the chance that sympathies might play a role.

Third, some confusion was introduced by the fact that formal insurance policies had not yet been issued when the attack occurred. Coverage was evidenced by "binders" or "slips" which were on their face incomplete; the terms of coverage would have to be inferred from what was said and exchanged in the course of negotiating these slips and binders. Again, confusion would tend to favor the party with the more sympathetic case.

Lloyd's of London was one of the two largest insurers of the WTC with total exposure (including two London insurance companies jointly represented with Lloyd's) of either $720 million or $1.44 billion depending on whether the attack was one occurrence or two. In late 2001 Lloyd's asked me to defend them, and a little more than two years later after extensive discovery around the world, the first trial (involving what insurance terms governed the coverage of Lloyd's and a dozen other insurers) began before

Chief Judge Michael Mukasey of the U.S. District Court for the Southern District of New York.

The trial was hard fought, and the jury deliberated for two tense weeks, but we ultimately won. Shortly thereafter, Mary and I flew to Florida for a brief vacation. The night we arrived we had dinner at New York Prime restaurant in Boca Raton, my favorite restaurant in Florida and one of the two best steak houses in the country.

During dinner we reflected on the seven years since I left Cravath and on our plans for the summer.

We had a family bike trip in France planned for June, a cross-country vacation scheduled for July, and a return trip to Africa in August. The firm was now 180 lawyers, with offices in Armonk, Albany, and New York City; Washington, D.C.; Hanover, New Hampshire; Oakland, California; and Orlando, Ft. Lauderdale, and Miami, Florida. Lawyer for lawyer no firm was better. At this point most of the firm's work was generated and done by my partners, and while neither I nor the firm was ready for me to retire, I was no longer critical to the firm's continued success.

Midway through dinner I received a call from my office concerning a documentary, *Fahrenheit 911,* written and directed by Michael Moore. The documentary had been financed by a subsidiary of The Walt Disney Company (which is also the publisher of this book), but because of the politically sensitive content of the film Disney did not want its affiliate to distribute the picture. The executives in charge of the Disney subsidiary responsible for the documentary wanted to buy the film from Disney and distribute it themselves, but Disney was balking. Would we, I was asked, represent the executives in negotiations and, if necessary, arbitration or litigation with Disney to achieve their goal.

I agreed we would, and asked to have a copy of the documentary and relevant files sent to me in Florida. When I returned to the table I assured a dubious Mary (correctly, as it turned out) that we would still leave on schedule for Provence.

Index

Acknowledgments

This book, like most things in life, is the result of the ideas and efforts of many people.

The suggestion that I write a book about my cases was first raised in November 2000 by Norman Brokaw, chairman of the William Morris Agency, and Bill Cosby who together called Mary while I was in Florida. It was an idea that I did not immediately embrace. Two months later Bob and Harvey Weinstein and Tina Brown took me to lunch and independently made the same proposal. Gradually they and Norman persuaded me that the story of my leaving Cravath and the cases that followed had the potential for a book worth my writing and Miramax publishing.

Over the next three years I wrote as time permitted. Mary has pictures of me on bike trips and African safaris, in our backyard and library at home, on airplanes and sailboats, in the office and on beaches, and even in casinos writing in the blue loose-leaf notebook I dedicated to the effort. Throughout the process she, my children, grandchildren, friends, and extended family provided the support and good-humored patience that they have shown for the demands of my work over the years. Without that patience and support neither that work nor this book would have been possible.

I am also grateful to the Miramax team, particularly my editor Richard Cohen, Miramax Books' president and editor-in-chief Jonathan Burnham, and director of production Kristin Powers. All were essential to making this book a reality and each provided wise guidance, patient answers, and repeated deadline extensions. Richard is a gifted editor skilled at knowing what needs to be done, explaining why, and showing how. His gentle persistence in improving the focus, and reducing the unnecessary detail, of the narrative is especially appreciated.

The burden of typing, fact checking, and obtaining necessary approvals fell on my administrative team which, in addition to Linda Carlsen, consisted of Donna Drumm, Jackie Parke, Gina Riccio, Greg Shaw, and Ricardo Singleton. Their "normal" tasks of managing my schedule, dealing with the more than a hundred calls a day that I cannot return personally, reading and summarizing correspondence and other materials, responding to inquiries, researching matters large and small, and generally doing everything I should do but can't or don't require night and weekend work as a matter of course. Although this book made their nights longer and their weekends shorter, they maintained their sense of humor and, even more important, their care and precision. Somehow Donna also found time to be admitted to the New York Bar and Gina found time to have a baby.

Before there could be this book, there were the cases about which I have written. And before there could be those cases, there had to be the people who made them possible. Even more than writing a book, litigation is a team sport; and I have been privileged to have been part of many great teams.

In the *IBM* litigation, in addition to the leadership of Tom Barr and Nicolas Katzenbach, the success in which I shared was particularly the result of the contributions of David Barrett, Douglas Broadwater, Paul Dodyk, Stuart Gold, Jack Hupper, Robert Mullins, Ronald Rolfe, Joseph Sahid, Paul Saunders, Frederick A.O. Schwarz Jr., and Robert Silver.

In *Westmoreland v. CBS*, I'm particularly grateful to Robert Baron, Ellen Brockman, Michael Doyen, William Duker, Catherine Flickinger, Randy Mastro, Mike Peyton, Robert Silver, and George Vradenburg.

In the *Texaco-Pennzoil* litigation, and in the battle with my friend Carl Icahn over control of Texaco that followed, I'm particularly grateful to Frank Barron, Ellen Brockman, William Duker, Nicholas Gravante, Linda Robinson, Robert Silver, and Dominic Suprenant.

In *Republic of the Philippines v. Westinghouse*, I am particularly grateful to Terry Adamson, Brooks Burdette, Richard Clary, Sandra Goldstein, William Isaacson, Robert Joffe, Jonathan Schiller, Randy Speck, Dominic Suprenant, and Alan Vickery.

In *New York Yankees v. Major League Baseball*, in addition to Jonathan Schiller, I am particularly grateful to Jonathan Boies, Ellen Brockman, William Isaacson, Robert Silver, David Sussman, and Lonn Trost.

In the *Habie* litigation, I'm particularly grateful to Rosanne Baxter, Caryl and Jonathan Boies, Ellen Brockman, Phil Korologos, Ted Leopold, Greg Lewen, James and Charles Miller, Edward Normand, Steve Rash, Robert Silver, and Steve Zack.

In *United States v. Microsoft*, the case could not have been won without Joel Klein, Chris Crook, and Phil Malone. I am also particularly grateful to Jeff Blattner, Mike Brille, John Cove, Rebecca Dick, Jeremy Feinstein, Karma Giulianelli, Steve Holtzman, Douglas Melamed, Steve Neuwirth, Mark Popofsky, Sandy Roth, Daniel Rubenfeld, Robert Silver, Gina Talamona, Pauline Wan, and Michael Wilson.

In the *Vitamins* price-fixing litigation, key members of the team from Boies, Schiller & Flexner, in addition to Jonathan Schiller and William Isaacson, included Caryl and Jonathan Boies, Mike Brille, Ellen Brockman, Tanya Chutkin, Carl Nichols, Robert Silver, Betsy Turner, and Melissa Willett. Key members of the team from other firms were too numerous to try to mention, but I have to acknowledge the contributions of Mary and David Boies III, without whom the case would not have gotten started; our co-lead counsel Michael Hausfeld, Tom Southwick, Steve Susman, and Ann Yahner; and Steering Committee members Martin Chitwood and Michael Straus.

In *Shandling v. Grey*, I am particularly grateful to Jonathan Schiller, William Isaacson, Mike Brille, Ellen Brockman, Peter Haviland, Steven Miller, and Todd Thomas.

In *Solow v. W.R. Grace*, I am particularly grateful to Jonathan Boies, Ellen Brockman, Diana Clarke, Andrew Hayes, and Sherab Posel.

In the *Sotheby's* and *Christie's* litigation, I am particularly grateful for the leadership of Richard Drubel and Phil Korologos, and the many contributions of Jonathan Boies, Eric Brenner, Kimberly Schultz, Katherine Eskovitz, Alfred Levitt, and Robert Silver.

In *Bush v. Gore,* I am particularly grateful for the leadership of Warren Christopher and Ronald Klain, and the many contributions of Mitchell Berger, Kendall Coffey, Dexter Douglass, Karen Gievers, Thomas Goldstein, Eric Kleinfeld,

490   ACKNOWLEDGMENTS

D.C. Newton II, Andrew J. Pincus, Teresa Wynn Roseborough, Robert Silver, Lawrence Tribe, Lyn Utrecht, and Steve Zack.

In the *Banque Indosuez* litigation, I am particularly grateful to David Barrett, Jonathan Boies, Ellen Brockman, William Duker, Nicholas Gravante, Harlan Levy, and Edward Normand.

In *Calvin Klein v. Warnaco*, I am particularly grateful for the leadership of Jonathan Schiller, and the many contributions of David Barrett, David Boyd, Nicholas Gravante, Andrew Hayes, and Jonathan Sherman.

In *Tyco*, I am particularly grateful for the leadership of William Lytton, Gardner Courson, Paul Verkuil, Ann Galvani, David Shapiro, and Frank Barron, and the many contributions of Jonathan Boies, Ellen Brockman, Ann Hinds, Marilyn Kunstler, and John Tober.

In *Adelphia*, I am particularly grateful for the leadership of Christopher Boies and Phil Korologos, and the many contributions of Eric Brenner, George Carpinello, Barbara Clay, Robert Leung, and Steve Zack.

In *Napster*, I am particularly grateful for the leadership of Jonathan Schiller and Robert Silver, and the many contributions of Mike Brille, Jonathan Boies, John Cove, Gary Francione, Steve Holtzman, Samuel Kaplan, and Edward Normand.

In *RJR et al. v. Philip Morris*, I am particularly grateful for the leadership of Robert Silver, and the many contributions of Mike Brille, Katherine Eskovitz, Ann Galvani, Seth Goldberg, Samuel Kaplan, Damian Marshall, Noah Messing, Steve Neuwirth, Carl Nichols, Alanna Rutherford, Stuart Singer, Phil Spector, Todd Thomas, and Melissa Willett.

In the *NASCAR* antitrust litigation, I am particularly grateful for the leadership of Alan Vickery, and the many contributions of David Feuerstein, Marianne Fogerty, Helen Maher, Philippe Selendy, Katie Sholly, Stuart Singer, Gregg Slemp, and Sarah Stern.

In the *World Trade Center* insurance litigation against Lloyds of London, I am particularly grateful for the leadership of Edward Normand and Kenneth Erickson, and the many contributions of Jonathan Boies, Steve Dimirsky, Sean Eskovitz, Ryan Higgins, Alanna Rutherford, and Robert Skinner.

There are many, many others who contributed to the cases that are discussed in this book. There are also many, many others who contributed to the many cases in which I participated that are not discussed. I am grateful to you all.

It is also obvious, but worth acknowledging, that Boies, Schiller & Flexner, and the cases since, would not have been possible without the courage, confidence, and commitment of people who in 1997 and the following years left secure positions with, or offers from, established firms to join a new and uncertain venture. We have come a long way since May of 1997 when Robert Silver, Jonathan Boies, Diana Clarke, Jodie Egelhoff, Ellen Brockman, and I moved into an Armonk loft; since July of 1997 when Andy Hayes left the Kennedy School and Michael Peyton left Cravath to join us; since September 1997 when Jonathan Schiller, William Isaacson, and Mary McEwan left Kaye Scholer and we formed Boies & Schiller.

In the following months and years, more than 175 exceptional lawyers and more than 225 exceptional non-lawyers have joined us. This book is their story as well as mine.

Courting Justice

FROM *NY Yankees v. Major League Baseball*
TO *Bush v. Gore 1997–2000*

DAVID BOIES

miramax books

NEW YORK

ISBN 1-4013-5984-1

First Paperback Edition
10   9   8   7   6   5   4   3   2   1